Russia Resurrected

Russia Resurrected

Its Power and Purpose in a New Global Order

KATHRYN E. STONER

OXFORD
UNIVERSITY PRESS

OXFORD
UNIVERSITY PRESS

Oxford University Press is a department of the University of Oxford. It furthers
the University's objective of excellence in research, scholarship, and education
by publishing worldwide. Oxford is a registered trade mark of Oxford University
Press in the UK and certain other countries.

Published in the United States of America by Oxford University Press
198 Madison Avenue, New York, NY 10016, United States of America.

© Oxford University Press 2021

Library of Congress Cataloging-in-Publication Data
Names: Stoner, Kathryn, 1965– author.
Title: Russia resurrected : its power and purpose in a new global order /
Kathryn Stoner, Stanford University.
Description: New York : Oxford University Press, 2021. |
Includes bibliographical references and index.
Identifiers: LCCN 2020040284 (print) | LCCN 2020040285 (ebook) |
ISBN 9780190860714 (hardback) | ISBN 9780190860738 (epub) |
ISBN 9780190054571
Subjects: LCSH: Russia (Federation)—Foreign relations—21st century. |
Russia (Federation)—Politics and government—1991– |
Russia (Federation)—Economic conditions—1991– |
Putin, Vladimir Vladimirovich, 1952—Influence. | Russia (Federation)—Forecasting. |
International relations—Forecasting.
Classification: LCC DK510.764 .S76 2021 (print) | LCC DK510.764 (ebook) |
DDC 327.47—dc23
LC record available at https://lccn.loc.gov/2020040284
LC ebook record available at https://lccn.loc.gov/2020040285

DOI: 10.1093/oso/9780190860714.001.0001

1 3 5 7 9 8 6 4 2

Printed by Sheridan Books, Inc., United States of America

For my parents,
Joan Boyd and Norman Stoner,
with gratitude for inspiring a love of learning in me
"In just 30 years, we have undergone changes that took centuries
in other countries."
—*Vladimir Putin, March 1, 2018, Presidential Address to the Federal Assembly*

CONTENTS

SECTION IV: THE PURPOSES BEHIND RUSSIAN
POWER PROJECTION ABROAD

ACKNOWLEDGMENTS

This book began on a bus in Novgorod Oblast (province) in Russia in September 2013. I was at a conference and as part of the program, our hosts took us to a monastery as part of a cultural break from our meetings. I had the pleasure of sitting next to a Russian colleague on the bus, a younger specialist in Russian foreign policy. We chatted amicably about the conference and the surrounding countryside, and eventually the conversation turned to the emerging hostility between our two countries. "What," I asked him, "is the point of Putin's foreign policy these days?" His reply both surprised and amused me: "Oh, that's easy!" he said "To beat you."

I was amused because he evidently didn't know that I am actually Canadian by birth, although I do hold dual citizenship with the United States. As an international power, Russia surely outpaced Canada at the time. But his reply also surprised me because in the United States, Russia was not seen as a "peer power" at the time, and it struck me that policy makers back in Washington would not have considered Russia a particularly capable global challenger in 2013.

I returned to the United States a few days later intent on seeing exactly where and how Russia could "beat us" in international politics. As my research progressed, and as I attended seminars at Stanford University, my home base, and conferences in Washington, DC, I came to realize that American political and military leaders I spoke with mostly dismissed Russia as either a regional power or, as one prominent member of the intelligence community said, "like North Korea; that is, Russia's at the 'little table' but it wants to be at the 'big table' with us and Europe and China. Problem is, it's just not there." My research, however, was beginning to demonstrate already that this sort of assessment of Russian capabilities was outdated. It would also prove calamitous as subsequent events demonstrated – not least of which was Russian interference in the 2016 US presidential elections. But beyond that, since Vladimir Putin's return to the presidency in 2012, Russia appeared to outfox the West at every turn.

I wondered how and why, and this study of Russia's resurrection as a global power is the result. The sober assessment it provides aims to convince the reader that under Putin's autocratic regime, Russian capabilities are beginning to approach its global aspirations.

This study could not have been completed without the opportunities that I have gained from my position as a Senior Fellow and Deputy Director at the Freeman Spogli Institute for International Studies (FSI) at Stanford University. The intellectual environment in our seminars, and the brain trust in our building, Encina Hall, proved invaluable to bringing this project to completion. I am particularly indebted to Ambassador Michael McFaul, the Institute's Director, for his patience in listening to me talk about this book for several years, providing me with the time to actually write it, and his insightful comments on the draft manuscript. Thanks also to my other Stanford colleagues Chip Blacker, David Holloway, Stephen Krasner and Larry Diamond for attending and commenting upon various presentations that I gave on the book here at Stanford. I owe a great deal of gratitude too to my colleague Francis Fukuyama for helping me to think more deeply about the concept of power, as well as to John Dunlop, and Anna Grzymala-Busse for their careful reads of the manuscript, occasional corrections and vital suggestions for improvement. Condoleeza Rice and Sheri Berman (at Barnard College) read the prospectus for this book and I am grateful for their enthusiasm for the project and encouragement. Secretary Rice also generously shared some of her insights into the younger Vladimir Putin and her experiences as Secretary of State with a few other members of his foreign policy apparatus. Rose Gottemoeller, former deputy secretary general of NATO generously reviewed chapters 3 and 6. Colleagues in Russia like Dmitri Trenin, Andrei Kortunov, and Fyodor Lukyanov (among others) were extremely patient in explaining the Russian perspective on global politics.

Back at Stanford, Tiffany Zhu provided outstanding research assistance in the final stages of research and Alice Underwood provided fantastic editing and thoughtful suggestions as well as good cheer as the project finally came to conclusion. My students in POLISCI 213C "Understanding Russia" in the winter quarter of 2020 were among the initial readers of the manuscript and their feedback made for a more comprehensible book to be sure.

Finally, on the home front, my deepest thanks to my wonderful husband, Paul Oyer, who was a constant source of encouragement and irrepressible humor. Thank you as well to our children (David Oyer, Lucy Oyer, Adam Weiss and Abby Weiss) for their patience as I wrote this book. They learned far more about Russia than they probably ever wanted to know! The COVID-19 pandemic brought Abby and Lucy even closer to this project at the bitter end as they were forced to come home to shelter in place. I owe them a special thanks for their provision of coffee (both hot and iced) from our favorite place to keep me tapping away at the keyboard happily.

Finally, I am particularly grateful to David McBride, possibly the most patient editor in the world, for sticking with me for the years it took to bring this project to fruition! Holly Mitchell saw it through production efficiently and with good cheer.

While all of these kind people helped me with various aspects of this project, any errors and omissions are mine alone.

Stanford California,
October, 2020.

FIGURES

TABLES

NOTE ON TRANSLITERATIONS AND SOURCES

Throughout this book, I use the Library of Congress transliteration system from Cyrillic to Latin scripts. In some cases, where there is a familiar spelling for a word, however, I employ the more familiar spelling (thus, Yeltsin rather than El'tsin, for example).

I have tried to use the most recent available sources and data for what follows. Still, at the time of writing, there was variation in this regard for some of the economic and demographic data. As a result, the reader will find one or two cases where the most recent data available was 2015 as opposed to 2019 or 2020. In all cases, links to where data sources can be found are provided, so that a reader may go to look for updates.

SECTION I

RUSSIA AND THE DIMENSIONS
OF STATE POWER

Is Russia Resurrected?

Assessing State Power and Its Domestic Determinants

> "Russia was never so strong as it wants to be, and never so weak as it is thought to be."
>
> —Vladimir Putin, May 2002[1]

If after the collapse of the Soviet Union, Russia was widely dismissed by the international community as nothing more than a regional power whose global influence had died with communism, then its flexing of its international muscle slightly more than a mere twenty-five years later has shown that reports of Russia's death were greatly exaggerated. From the sudden seizure of the Crimean Peninsula from Ukraine in 2014 and the rapid military deployment in Syria in 2015 to cyber interventions in Western democracies, most notably interference in the US election in 2016, under Vladimir Putin's long rule, Russia has reasserted itself, taking many professional and casual observers by surprise.

A common argument among many analysts has been that Russia has a weak hand in international politics, but plays it well. This book argues instead that Russia's cards may not be as weak as we in the West have thought. The realist approach to power sees a world organized by interests, in which states are capable of exercising influence according to their material capacities alone. Viewed through this lens, a simple tally of Russia's importance in the global economy, its human capital, and the size of its military would hardly convince an observer of its disproportionate power over other countries' decisions in international politics. After all, just over twenty-five years after the collapse of the Soviet Union, Russia had a 3.17% share of global gross domestic product (GDP), compared to 15.49% for the United States, 17.76% for China, and 7.23% for India, according to the International Monetary Fund (IMF).[2] With an estimated 144.48 million people (excluding the annexed Ukrainian territory of Crimea), Russia's population size was less than half that of the United States (321.4 million), only a tenth of China's (1.39 billion) and India's (1.35 billion), and with flat to negative growth prospects.[3] Russia also spent about a tenth (at $61.4 billion) of what the United States (at $611 billion) spent on its military, and about a quarter of what China spent (at $250 billion).[4]

Yet the focus on these sorts of metrics of power has led scholars and policymakers alike to discount Russia's actual ability to influence international politics in the twenty-first century. Undeniably, contemporary Russia does not compare in realist terms to the power resources of the United States or China. Nonetheless, Russia has developed an outsized ability to exercise considerable influence abroad. I argue that under Vladimir Putin's long rule, Russia has developed and deployed both traditional and novel means of influence abroad, and on a variety of dimensions. Putin's Russia demonstrates that a state does not have to be a great power that is at parity in all realms with the United States, Europe, or China—but it can be *good enough* to dramatically alter the balance of power in a new global order.

How and why has this happened? Is contemporary Russia strong or weak? What does Russia's evident resurrection as a global power tell us about the actual determinants of state power in the international politics of the twenty-first century? These are the questions at the foundation of this book. I offer two major corrections to the ways in which analysts and policymakers understand Russia's role in the world today. First, I present a multidimensional understanding of Russian power resources that goes beyond the traditional means of power—things that can be counted, like comparative population and military size, and the amount of money in the economy of a country. Second, I link the willingness and ability of the contemporary Russian leadership to use its power resources abroad to the nature of the domestic political regime that has evolved under Vladimir Putin's long rule.

In important ways, Russia is distinct from the former Soviet Union and from other globally powerful states today. Under Putin's leadership, Russia has re-established itself on the global stage as a great disrupter rather than as a traditional great power, with a much higher tolerance for risk than its international competitors or its Soviet predecessor. Under Putin's leadership, contemporary Russia has proved willing to assert itself against its regional neighbors, but has also moved far outside of its traditional sphere of geographic influence abroad, while on paper lacking many of the traditional means of power of its competitors—particularly the United States and China.

In a metaphor that aptly characterizes how Putin's Russia has managed to resurrect itself in international power projection, David Baldwin emphasizes the importance of understanding the game being played, rather than just judging a player's ability to win based on the face value of the cards she holds:

> Discussions of the capabilities of states that fail to designate or imply a framework of assumptions about who is trying (or might try) to get whom to do what are comparable to discussions of what constitutes a good hand in cards without specifying which game is to be played . . . a good hand at bridge is a bad one at poker.[5]

Perhaps, then, a misunderstanding of Russia's purposes and motivations abroad (the game Russian policymakers are playing) has led to an underestimation of its ability to project power and the resources it has amassed to do so. Policymakers in the West have declared in public and in private that Russia is not an equal as a global power, so there is no need to bow to its complaints about containment or the expansion of the North Atlantic Treaty Organization (NATO). Undoubtedly, it is partly in response to this belittling perspective from rivals that Russia under Vladimir Putin has sought to reassert itself as deserving of global respect. History demonstrates that Russia also has undeniable geostrategic interests in its immediate neighborhood that any Russian leader might want to protect. It is important to consider, however, whether a Russian president other than Vladimir Putin would have made the same foreign policy choices. That is, is Putin pursuing *Russia's* global strategy as any leader of a fallen "great power" would do, or is he more narrowly pursuing the interests of his own, increasingly autocratic regime?

In what follows, I argue that grand strategy under Putin has been a choice and not the natural destiny of Russia's role in international politics as antagonist to the West. Russia has not been historically, nor is it inevitably, an enemy of Europe or the United States. Rather, the new global rivalry is a strategic choice for Putin's regime to "make Russia great again"—most importantly in the eyes of the Russian people. Even though Russia today is an autocracy, the regime still fears the potential instability that comes from the Russian street more than it fears NATO.

A "Normal" Country?: The Extent of Russia's Revival

On December 25, 1991, the red hammer-and-sickle flag of the Soviet Union was taken down over the Kremlin, and the Russian tricolor flag was raised triumphantly. This moment marked the definitive end to a vast communist empire that stretched from Europe's borders in the west to Japan's in the far east, and from the Arctic Ocean in the north to Afghanistan in the south. Its demise brought about the simultaneous end to the Cold War between East and West

that defined post–World War II international relations, and marked the conclusion of an ideological and existential struggle between superpowers played out
through proxies in the Middle East, South and Central America, Eastern Europe,
Asia, and Africa. This established a unipolar global order, with the United States
the unrivaled and dominant force in international relations. It would soon, of
course, face a new rival in the fast-growing autocracy of China that would contest American economic predominance in particular. Russia, the fragile and
bankrupt Soviet successor state, was not in any position to contest the Cold War
settlement or challenge what seemed to be the establishment of a new bipolar
global order.

The Soviet legacy by 1992 had left Russia with a difficult starting point from
which to launch a recovery. In many respects, the collapse of the Soviet system
was long in coming over decades of decline in productivity and legitimacy in
the 1970s and 1980s, yet largely unanticipated when it finally arrived in 1991.[6]
Western analysts provided evaluations of the Soviet Union in the 1980s that
characterized it as ideologically bankrupt, and with its economy in stagnation.
Few, however, predicted its relatively peaceful demise and the rapid establishment of Russia as its successor state in international affairs, although a pale comparison to the superpower that was—at least in the immediate aftermath of the
collapse.[7] In 1990 and 1991, Russia was the recipient of international loans from
lenders of last resort like the IMF and World Bank. Food aid was distributed
on the streets of Moscow. As communism slipped away and the new Russian
Federation emerged, the economy was already on its knees. Six years of uneven
reforms by Mikhail Gorbachev, the last General Secretary of the Communist
Party of the Soviet Union, had worsened the already bad situation wrought by the
inefficiencies and wastefulness of the planning system of the preceding seventy
years. Russia faced a growing budget deficit of (conservatively estimated) 20%
of GDP, the threat of hyperinflation, economic growth that was at best stalled
and at worst negative, shortages throughout the economy, virtually nothing in
foreign currency reserves, and growing international loan commitments.[8]

Faced with this dismal situation, Russia's first elected president, Boris Yeltsin,
assigned a team of young neoliberal reformers, led by acting prime minister
Yegor Gaidar, to draft and implement an ambitious reform program in January
1992. The reforms attempted to free prices from Soviet-era price lists, open
the economy to a rush of imports, and rapidly privatize state enterprises. The
idea was to shake the economy loose of the trappings of the communist system.
Yeltsin's team of liberal economists created a stock market and real estate markets
and launched a massive program of privatization of small, medium, and large
enterprises between 1992 and 1997, such that a reported 70% of GDP came
from the private sector between 1997 and 2004.[9] They opened the economy
to foreign trade to ameliorate some of the shortages in the Russian economy,

but the reforms and the hangover effects of seventy-four years of communist economics also produced many negative and largely unanticipated economic outcomes. From 1992 to 1998, Russia ran roughly 9% annual budget deficits, resulting in an eventual default on international loan obligations and currency collapse by 1998.

Even with these economic woes, the years immediately preceding and following the demise of the Soviet Union were years of significant change in Russia. For all the instability during his tenure as president, Yeltsin also carried out enormous social and political changes that effectively killed off any possibility of the return of communism. In transforming the Soviet planned economy into a rough and ready form of market capitalism, he created stakeholders in a new order based on private ownership and supply and demand. Elections for all levels of government were held with regularity, although not always free and fully fair in the 1990s, and the media was remarkably open.

The late 1980s, 1990s, and early 2000s were also years of notable cooperation between Russia, the United States, and Europe. In the early 1990s, Western countries provided billions of dollars in aid, though not substantial or timely enough to avert the economic crisis of 1998. In other areas, greater gains were made. A few years earlier, when the Soviet Union still existed, Mikhail Gorbachev signed landmark nuclear armament reduction treaties with Presidents Reagan and George H. W. Bush. Under Boris Yeltsin's presidency of the reborn Russia, US president Bill Clinton pushed for, and gained, Russia's admission into what became the G-8 nations, even when its economy clearly did not merit membership among the world's strongest. In the early years of his first administration, between 2000 and 2003, President Putin himself made friendly overtures to President George W. Bush. Putin was the first foreign leader to call Bush after the 9/11 terrorist attack in the United States; Angela Stent notes that Putin looked forward to an international coalition led by the United States and Russia to combat international terrorism.[10] But under Bush, Putin's ambitions to befriend the West were thwarted by the American war in Iraq (which Russia did not support), and by US support of the Orange Revolution in Ukraine in 2004 and Georgia's Rose Revolution in 2003, both of which ushered in new governments in these former Soviet republics far less friendly to Russian interests as Putin's regime, at least, had defined them.[11] With the unilateral US withdrawal from the Anti-Ballistic Missile (ABM) treaty in 2002 and the threat of a new US missile defense system in Europe thereafter, US-Russian relations dipped to an all-time post-1991 low by the time Bush left office in January 2009.

By that point, and after a tumultuous six years of contentious market reform, punctuated by the economic crisis of 1998, the Russian economy had radically changed. A dramatic rise in global oil and gas prices reversed Russia's economic fortunes, such that in 2003, Russia's growth shot up rapidly and remarkably such

that GDP would rise on average 7% every year until the global economic crisis
hit in the fall of 2008. Between 2003 and 2008, as the economy boomed, analysts
and observers began referring to Russia as a "normal" country, meaning that its
remaining developmental challenges, like eradication of corruption, were more
or less typical of a country at its stage of "middle income" economic development.[12] Daniel Treisman and Andrei Shleifer, writing in 2005, argued: "That
Russia is *only* a normal middle-income democracy is, of course, a disappointment to those who had hoped for or expected more. But that Russia today has
largely broken free of its past, that it is no longer 'the evil empire,' threatening
both its own people and the rest of the world, is an amazing and admirable
achievement."[13] Treisman and Shleifer were not wrong, nor were they alone in
their admiration of Russia's economic achievements by the early and mid-2000s.
In 2003, Goldman Sachs analysts coined the term "BRIC" to describe the group
of high-growth transitional economies that included Brazil, Russia, India, and
China (now BRICS, with the addition of South Africa).[14] Of this group, according to Dominic Wilson and Roopa Purushothaman, Russia was a standout.
They predicted that it would surpass the poorer of the G-6 economies (France,
Italy, and the United Kingdom—the G-7 without Canada) in per capita income
by 2050.[15]

These were sanguine, and overly optimistic, assessments of the trajectory of
Russia's development. They were based primarily on the steady, high growth of
Russia's GDP from roughly 1999 to 2008, growth in foreign and domestic investment, balanced budgets, a stable ruble, the end of huge foreign debt to lenders of
last resort like the World Bank and IMF, and the tripling of per capita incomes
of Russian workers. By the third quarter of 2008, Russia had become the world's
sixth largest economy, the peak of its growth statistics and a remarkable achievement considering the extent of the crisis that its post-Soviet leadership had
inherited when market reforms began in earnest in 1992. The Russian real estate
market had become the hottest in Europe by 2006, and Russian billionaires were
buying sports franchises abroad and expensive property in European capitals,
New York, Miami, and elsewhere. Internally, Russia was booming with an as-
tounding expansion in the number of cars on its roads, the newly constructed
highways crisscrossing the heartland, a modernizing army, rising salaries, and
increasing integration into the global economy. With Washington's support,
Russia even joined the World Trade Organization in 2012—a mere twenty
years after it had embarked upon the radical transformation of its inherited
communist-era economy.

But the resource revenue dependence of the economy proved both a blessing
and a curse. As the globally determined price of crude oil, Russia's main export,
fell, so too did its GDP tumble dramatically in the fourth quarter of 2008 at
the onset of what would be a global economic crisis. Nonetheless, although its

decline was far sharper than that of the other BRIC economies, the Russian economy recovered relatively quickly from the crisis through astute macroeconomic policy aimed at supporting the ruble using reserves from Russia's sovereign wealth funds and continued payment of pensions through its state pension fund. As the rest of the world recovered through 2009 and 2010, the price of oil gradually recovered too, further aiding Russia's rebound to lower, but respectable, growth rates of 3–5% annually until 2014, when Russia's economy would face international sanctions over its seizure of Crimea in Ukraine, and another drop in oil prices.

The period of Russia's return to economic stability and growth was also a time of fluctuating relations with the United States and the West more broadly. When Barack Obama took over from President Bush in 2009, the new US president introduced a policy of "reset" with Russia. The goal was to put US-Russian relations on a more constructive path and to encourage cooperation between the two countries in the mutual interest of both nations. During the height of the reset, President Obama and then-president of Russia Dmitri Medvedev (as of spring 2008) worked together on several projects to improve the security and prosperity of both countries.[16] In 2010, they signed and subsequently ratified the New START Treaty, which eliminated 30% of the nuclear weapons held by the United States and Russia,[17] and also kept in place a comprehensive inspections regime that allowed both countries to verify compliance. In that same year, the White House and the Kremlin worked together to pass UN Security Council Resolution 1929, the most comprehensive set of sanctions against Iran ever to be adopted. Together, the United States and Russia greatly expanded the Northern Distribution Network (NDN) of air, rail, and truck routes through Russia, the Caucasus, and Central Asia to supply American soldiers in Afghanistan and reduce US military dependency on the southern route through Pakistan. Over 50% of supplies to US forces in Afghanistan were transported via the NDN by 2011.[18]

The United States and Russia also collaborated in avoiding conflict during the "reset" era. While there was continued tension over South Ossetia and Abkhazia after the Russian-Georgian war of 2008, and Russia continued to effectively occupy those parts of Georgia, violent conflict was curtailed. When another popular uprising toppled President Bakiyev in Kyrgyzstan in 2010, dozens of people died in the initial fighting (almost as many as were shot in Maidan Square in Kyiv in 2014), and tens of thousands of ethnic Uzbeks fled southern Kyrgyz cities, fearing that the regime change might unleash an ethnic civil war.[19] In response to this crisis, the United States and Russia could have squared off, yet the White House and Kremlin worked together to help defuse this dangerous situation. Perhaps most remarkably, President Medvedev agreed to abstain on UN Security Council Resolutions 1970 and 1973, effectively authorizing the use of force against the Libyan regime of Muammar Gaddafi in the spring of 2011. No Russian leader had ever acquiesced to an external military intervention in a sovereign country (indeed, the decision was so controversial within Russian foreign policy decision-making circles that it may well have been the reason that Vladimir Putin, who strongly disagreed with Medvedev on Libya, decided that he must reassume the Russian presidency thereafter).[20]

In addition to security issues, the Obama and Medvedev governments collaborated on several projects to increase trade and investment between the United States and Russia during the "reset" years. As previously noted, the United States helped Russia obtain membership in the World Trade Organization (WTO), but trade between the United States and Russia also increased dramatically between 2009 and 2012, as did foreign direct investment.[21] A new visa regime expanded the number of Russians traveling to the United States, and vice versa. And even bigger plans were afoot prior to 2014, including the massive joint venture between Exxon-Mobil and Rosneft, one of Russia's most strategically important, majority state-owned oil companies.

During these years, NATO remained a bone of contention between Russian leaders and the United States in particular, though not to the degree that Putin, once back in the president's chair in 2012, made it out to be. In fact, aside from the addition of Croatia and Albania in 2009, two countries far from Russia, NATO did not expand in the Obama-Medvedev era. Despite pressure from George W. Bush at the 2008 NATO Bucharest summit, other NATO allies refused to allow Georgian membership. After Russia's invasion of Georgia in August 2008, the issue died within the alliance. Even under President Yushchenko, the leader of the Orange Revolution in 2004, Ukraine never pushed for NATO membership. There was simply no support within Ukrainian society at that time. After President Viktor Yanukovych was elected president of Ukraine in 2010, the idea faded completely—it was too divisive within Ukraine itself. Consequently, during the "reset" years, neither President Medvedev nor Prime Minister Putin ever objected to NATO expansion. Indeed, President Medvedev even echoed other Western leaders in waxing effusively about NATO-Russia relations when he attended the NATO summit in Lisbon in November 2010. "Incidentally," he said, "even the declaration approved at the end of our talks states that we seek to develop a strategic partnership. This is not a chance choice of words, but signals that we have succeeded in putting the difficult period in our relations behind us now."[22] Medvedev also praised the "reset," stating during his last meeting with Obama in his capacity as president in March 2012, "[W]e probably enjoyed the best level of relations between the United States and Russia during those three years than ever during the previous decades."[23]

But only two years later, with Vladimir Putin back in the Kremlin as Russia's president, both the successes of the "reset" and positive relations with NATO were consigned to the past. A final repudiation of the NATO-Russia Council appeared in the 2014 Russian Military Doctrine, which identified the expansion of NATO as the primary threat to Russia.[24] In the spring of 2015 in an interview aired as part of a documentary marking his fifteen years in public life, Putin indicated that he had even been ready to put Russian nuclear forces on alert during Russia's invasion of Crimea in the spring of 2014 since he feared NATO's response.[25] Further, Mikhail Vanin, the Russian ambassador to Denmark, threatened to target the Danish navy with nuclear weapons should Denmark join NATO's missile shield program. Perhaps this was why Russia was deemed an existential threat to the United States in the summer of 2015 by several prominent US military figures, including Marine Corps General Joseph Dunford, nominee for Chairman of the US Joint Chiefs of Staff; US Air Force General Paul Selva, nominee for Vice Chair; and the outgoing Army Chief of Staff, General Ray Odierno.[26] In the fall of 2015, General Philip Breedlove, then Supreme Commander of NATO and United States Central Command in Europe, insisted that Russia was "rewriting the Cold War settlement using force."[27]

The question of whether Russia has sufficiently recovered from the economic, social, and political devastation wrought by the collapse of the Soviet Union to rewrite the rules of international politics is often answered with attention to the man who has been at its helm for the majority of those years. Vladimir Putin is the clear author of the assertive resurrection of Russia's influence in international politics. As I argue in chapter 8, it is unlikely that another leader would have responded to the set of problems facing the country in precisely the same way. Putin's leadership, and the imperative for the autocracy over which he presides, is to maintain stability in the system of government that he has built during his two decades in power, and has had marked influence on the extent and the aggressive direction of Russia's resurgence globally.

"A Country That Can Stand Up for Itself": Resurgence under Putin

Just as few predicted complete systemic breakdown of the USSR by 1991, equally few observers could have fully anticipated the rocky road to revival that Russia has followed since. A combination of circumstances, such as global oil and gas prices, and policy decisions were responsible for these changes, but Mr. Putin's ascent to power marked a turning point. After Boris Yeltsin stepped down, Vladimir Putin, as his handpicked successor, ruled Russia during the remarkable economic growth that ensued in the 2000s. His policy decisions strove for further development of the Russian economy and society, but not toward greater democracy. Instead, Putin reinserted the primacy of state over society in Russia. By 2008, he declared to Russia's parliament: "Finally, Russia has returned to the world arena as a strong state—a country that others heed and that can stand up for itself."[28] In February 2014, Russia triumphantly reintroduced itself to the world as modern and outward-facing in hosting the very successful, elaborate Winter Olympic Games in Sochi at an estimated cost of $50 billion. Less than twenty-five years after the Soviet collapse, Russia looked to be resurrected as an economic power, and seemingly politically stable under fifteen years of leadership by Vladimir Putin.

Along with the political, economic, and social transformations that the country experienced after the collapse of the Soviet Union in 1991, there was a concomitant renewal in Russia's foreign policy presence. Despite friendly and sometimes mutually supportive economic, political, and military relations with NATO, the United States, much of Europe, and China from the collapse through the early 2000s, Russian foreign policy gradually became more assertive, a trend that intensified as Putin's system of governing evolved. Initially, Russia showed its relative strengths abroad in conventional ways. Post-Soviet Russian leaders used military force to invade two sovereign neighbors (Georgia in 2008 and Ukraine in 2014) and remained involved in two other conflicts in former Soviet states—over Transnistria in Moldova and served as a mediator in Nagorno-Karabakh, a territory that is claimed by both Armenia and Azerbaijan. But the Russian military's hasty refurbishment of an old Soviet air base in Syria in the late summer of 2015 and its intervention there was the first deployment of the Russian military outside post-Soviet borders in over twenty-five years.[29] Prior to that, the Russian military reintroduced the Soviet policy of flying missions over Norwegian and Swedish airspace, as well as over the English Channel, without pilots filing flight plans or informing the affected countries in advance. Since 2015, Russian submarines have been detected not far from US territorial waters and are thought to be patrolling deep-sea cable lines, possibly looking for vulnerabilities to disable American access to the Internet.[30]

Further, Russia's nuclear doctrine appears to now anticipate the need to use nuclear weapons in the event of conventional war with an adversary (like NATO) if the homeland is under "existential threat" (never defined), and by 2020 in the event that Russia's territorial integrity is under threat.[31] In light of the growing tensions between Russia and the United States over Ukraine and Syria, as well as the Putin administration's interference in the 2016 US election, and their commitments to modernizing their respective nuclear forces, it was unsurprising that the Bureau of Atomic Scientists moved the atomic clock to 100 seconds to midnight in 2020, the closest to nuclear destruction the world has been since the Cuban missile crisis at the height of the Cold War in 1962 (for perspective, it had been 17 minutes to midnight in 1991 when the Soviet Union collapsed).[32]

Throughout these developments, Vladimir Putin insisted that Russia was merely protecting its historical interests in its natural sphere of geopolitical interest and security. For Putin, Russia had returned to international politics to retake its natural standing as a "great power" and to challenge an unfair Cold War settlement imposed upon it by the United States. In explaining Russian actions in grabbing Crimea from Ukraine in 2014, for example, Putin asserted the essence of Russia's "new" foreign policy:

> [T]he Ukrainian crisis was not caused by the Russian Federation. It has emerged in response to the attempts of the USA and its western allies who considered themselves "winners" of the Cold War to impose their will everywhere. Promises of non-expansion of NATO to the East (given yet to the Soviet authorities) have turned out to be hollow statements. We have seen how NATO's infrastructure was moving closer and closer towards Russian borders and how Russian interests were being ignored.[33]

These comments are emblematic of the rhetoric on Russia's restored greatness that characterizes its revanchist approach to international relations.

Most notable regarding Russia's return to prominence in international politics, perhaps, was its apparent interference, through state-employed hackers and members of military intelligence units, in the US presidential election of 2016. American intelligence agencies concluded that, through cyber theft, Russian operatives were able to gain access to the Democratic National Committee (DNC) and Republican National Committee (RNC) during 2016 in order to steal confidential emails. According to the congressional testimony of then–FBI director James Comey on March 20, 2017, only the DNC emails were passed through an intermediary to WikiLeaks, which then published daily digests of emails allegedly selected to embarrass and discredit Hillary Clinton prior to the election. In this way, Russia was able to strike at the very legitimacy of American democracy. This marked an unprecedented use of cyber tactics as part of a hybrid strategy to undermine countries that Russia's leadership had decided were geopolitical competitors and sow discord, rather than pursue outright confrontation, an approach has proven a key mechanism in Russia's exercise of twenty-first-century power.

While Russia's military incursions and allegations of cyber intervention are proof of an increasingly assertive foreign policy, the story of Russia's successful "normalization" has not (yet?) come to its fairy-tale ending. The country's still undiversified economy has proven vulnerable to the unpredictability of global commodities markets, as the return to deficit budgets and decline in GDP demonstrated after the drop in global oil prices beginning in the summer of 2014. While it was reclassified by the Organisation for Economic Co-operation and Development (OECD) as an "upper middle income" country because of its rise in average GDP per capita, contemporary Russia still faces deep developmental challenges. It is neither an innovation economy like Estonia, or even India, nor is it an imitation economy like China or Taiwan. Other than gas, oil, precious metals, and weapons, it is difficult to find imported manufactured products stamped "made in Russia." Despite a highly educated population, by 2019 Russia had only one university in the world's top 100; labor productivity (as measured by output per person employed converted to US dollars at purchasing power parity) remained low, such that by 2019 a US worker was producing $71.78 of GDP per hour worked, while a Russian worker produced about $26.49 of GDP per hour worked.[34] This and the relatively higher cost of labor than in many other transitional economies has made Russia a less attractive venue for foreign investment in sectors other than resource extraction, which hurts the future competitiveness of its economy. Indeed, labor productivity was the second lowest in the countries monitored by the OECD, and less than half that of the G-7 countries' average.[35] In addition, foreign direct investment had dropped by more than two-thirds from 2013 as the country struggled with sanctions after 2014.[36] Russian GDP per capita at purchasing price parity declined to $24,061 by 2015, putting it just below that of Poland (at $26,856) and Hungary (at $26,356), and below the Baltic states of Lithuania ($28,910) and Estonia ($29,213), all of which had become members of the European Union, and none of which have benefited from previously high oil and gas prices in the early to mid-2000s, as Russia did.[37] Yet by 2019, in advance of the global Coronavirus pandemic, Russia's economy was growing modestly at 1.7%, even after almost five years of Western sanctions.[38]

While Russia's economy had improved markedly for a time, especially between 1999 and 2008, this did not translate immediately into dramatic changes in human development. Russia's male life expectancy at birth twenty-five years after the Soviet collapse was 67.1 years, which, although much improved from an all-time low in 1994 of 57.6 years, was still far below that of Poland (74), Hungary (72), and all three Baltic States.[39] In 2019 the United Nations Human Development Report index recorded overall Russian adult life expectancy from birth at 72.4 years, just below those of Bangladesh and Venezuela.[40] None of these socioeconomic characteristics would predict Russia's increasingly assertive foreign policy. What, then, explains Russia's quest for more influence in the post–Cold War global order, and how has it happened that Russia under Putin has reasserted itself as one of the world's leading powers?

Is Russia Strong or Weak?: The Multiple Dimensions of Power

Power is one of the most central concepts in politics and international relations, and much time and trouble has been taken to define and measure it. Joe Nye has famously said: "Power is like love, easier to experience than to define or measure, but no less real for that."[41] The relative power in international politics that Russia possesses is debated by specialists and nonspecialists alike. In a 2016 survey of 1,600 Russian adults over sixteen years of age by the Levada Center, a respected and still independent Russian polling service, 65% of respondents indicated "definitely yes" or "probably yes" to the question, "Do you think Russia is a great power?"[42] This implies that Russians at least have in mind some commonly accepted metrics of power. What, then, are real and reasonable measures of a country's power in practice versus potential? One of the goals of this book is to undertake a thorough analysis of the available data and meaningfully assess changes in Russian power in global affairs since the collapse of the Soviet Union at the end of 1991. With these tools and a more nuanced conceptualization of power in the foreign policy sphere, one of the central tasks of this study is to evaluate whether Russia's resurrection as a global power is real or merely imagined.

The understanding of power that I apply in this study stems from the reasonably strong scholarly consensus on a social scientific definition of power, encapsulated in Robert Dahl's deceptively simple rendering in 1957: "*A has power over B to the extent that he can get B to do something that B would not otherwise do.*"[43] This short statement packs many logical punches. First, power is a relative (or in Dahl's words "relational") concept between two or more actors. Second, power, control, coercion, and influence appear to be effectively the same thing—the exercise of any of these by actor A *causes* a change in the behavior of actor B. Third, parties to a power relationship can be individuals, groups, states, corporations, or "other human aggregates."[44]

Realist theorists like Ken Waltz, Hans Morgenthau, and eventually John Mearsheimer and Steve Walt, while generally adopting Dahl's definition, have placed emphasis on the *means* of power that a state might possess, such as population size, territory, money, and weaponry, as the most important factors in determining the distribution of power among states.[45] The logical conclusion from this approach is that if one were to tally up national wealth, population, and the size of the military in any particular state, a rough ordering of national power would emerge. "Great" powers would be at the far end of the spectrum with the highest wealth and therefore, presumably, the strongest military, while weaker powers would be poor with weak militaries.

Other scholars, however, like David Baldwin, have furthered the "relational" conceptualization of power found in Dahl and challenged the realist means-based approach to power. The relational approach has engendered two important arguments. First, power can be an *actual* or *potential* relationship. The case of North Korea demonstrates, for example, that power resources, like nuclear weapons, are not necessarily actual power so much as they are power in potential.[46] Second, Baldwin, along with Michael Barnett and Raymond Duvall, has argued that power is far more multidimensional than traditional realists would allow. This "relational" school notes that states often seem to have more power or influence in international relations than the sum of the strengths of their economies or militaries would indicate.

In trying to discern the sources of Russian power in international relations, recognizing that power is multidimensional helps us to understand why it is that Russia seems to exercise influence in international affairs that is disproportionate to the sum of its global capabilities economically or militarily. In order to explore thoroughly sources of Russian power, therefore, I employ this broader conceptualization over the narrow, realist understanding that focuses almost exclusively on traditional *means* alone. Following Dahl and Baldwin in considering power as relational and multidimensional, I understand the three central dimensions of relational state power to include:

1. *Policy Scope*: Across what issues does an actor's behavior affect other actors? A's power over B increases in relation to the number and importance of issues of B's activity that are affected by A.,
2. *Geographic Domain*: How many actors are subject to A's influence? In Baldwin's words, "how big is B? How many B's are there relative to A?" Domain recognizes that "a state may have a great deal of influence in one region of the world, while having little or no influence in other parts of the world."[47]

Related to the measure of actor A's policy scope and the geographic domain of its influence over other states, we might ask how "big" actor A is and how costly the exercise of A's power is in these areas of policy and geography. That is, if A is a dominant actor in any particular economic sector (for example, oil), and B is completely dependent on A for access to the sector, then we can say that A is a particularly weighty or important actor in this area relative to B. This entails two sub-measures: first, *weight*—how regularly or reliably can A influence B, and what is the probability that B can or will be affected by A? This can vary across policy issues and across geographic domain for any particular state. Second, *costs*—what are the stakes for A of using power in a particular policy area or geographic area? Does it cost a little or a lot for A to influence B? Is it inexpensive for

B to comply with A? If it costs a lot for B to comply with A, then A may exercise more power over B than if it were cheap for B to comply.

Finally, returning to the dimensions of relational power:

3. *Means*: Through what capabilities does A exercise power over B? Means can include economic, military, diplomatic, cultural, or "soft" power, sometimes called symbolic means or the "pull" of a state rather than the "push"; this can include, for example, culture, ideology, or membership or leadership in international organizations.

The fact that power is multidimensional indicates that it is difficult to arrive at a single metric that provides a comprehensive estimate of an actor's power. Figure 1.1 demonstrates also that different dimensions of power overlap, but they may also vary independently: an increase in one dimension of power may occur simultaneously with a decrease in another, or vice versa—in other words, the circles can change in size relative to each other. For example, a state may have a wide geographic domain of influence, but its means for actually exercising this influence might be small. We might say, for example, that China has substantial means of power, but perhaps a smaller geographical domain of influence than the United States, and a smaller policy scope where it affects other states.

Most important, a multidimensional approach allows an analyst to answer foundational questions regarding a state's capabilities: power *over what or whom*, and power *to do what*? It also recognizes that means that are considered a "power asset" in one situation may be unhelpful or even a liability in another. The United States, for example, has a commanding nuclear deterrent, but in practice, for moral and political reasons, it is not able to use it to obliterate terrorists in Afghanistan. A state may lack the relative means to exercise power in one situation but have more than enough in another. Bringing into consideration the different dimensions of power helps us to understand under what circumstances

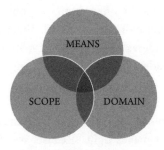

Figure 1.1. The Multiple Dimensions of State Power in International Relations

a state has the capabilities to achieve any particular policy goal in international relations.

I argue that by almost any metric, Russia today has many of the trappings of a great power, such as, for example, its expanded geographic reach inside the former Soviet states as well as far from its borders, and weighty policy influence in areas like oil and gas provision (see chapters 2 and 3); its nuclear weaponry; growing conventional military capabilities; and soft and sharp power instruments (see chapters 6 and 7). But its economy is uneven at best (explored in chapter 4), and Russia in the twenty-first century faces significant demographic challenges (explored in chapter 5) if it is to become more influential abroad. Nonetheless, if we understand "great power" to mean a country with global military, economic, and political reach, a country that influences global politics and international relations not just through hard power, but through soft and "sharp" power resources too, then Russia is certainly in the ballpark. Given the policy scope and geographic domain in which Russia's contemporary leadership is able to employ its power resources, and the agility of decision-making under a de-institutionalized and increasingly personalized political system, Russia is a formidable challenger to the stability of the postwar international system. That is, while perhaps not any longer (or not yet again?) a "great power" in the traditional realist sense, it is a "good enough" power in that *under Vladimir Putin's autocratic rule, Russia possesses the capability and his regime possesses the will* to use adroitly a variety of power resources to disrupt the prevailing international order and to define a new one.

Why Does Putin's Russia Behave as It Does?: Domestic Levers on Russian Foreign Policy

The second foundational question in this book is to try to provide an explanation for why Russia's leadership has come to exercise its state's power resources more assertively. I argue that too often domestic political variables are ignored in explaining Russia's exercise of power abroad. This has led the United States and its NATO allies to underestimate Russian capabilities, and also to misunderstand the will of its leaders to exercise power, and so, we have been caught offguard.

The predominant popular explanations of why, for example, Russian troops annexed the Crimean peninsula in 2014 stem from the realist international political analysis that "might makes right." Realists see the world in Hobbesian terms—disorganized, and as an ongoing battle between states to increase their relative standing in the global order. Power is the currency of success in such an environment, and state leaders seek to maximize the influence their country has in international politics. Ideas, regime types (democracy or not), individual leaders, and societal influences, therefore, do not matter in how states behave in the international system except to the extent that they relate to the pursuit of relative state power. Two realist arguments are often applied in explaining the purposes of Russia's evidently renewed power projection. The first sees Russia under the leadership of Vladimir Putin to be exercising power abroad in defense of historically and geographically determined national interests. By this argument, provoked by NATO expansion and combined with Western support for democratic revolutions on Russian borders in Georgia and Ukraine in particular, any regime governing Russia would eventually strike back. The Kremlin's actions in 2014, in this view, is not revanchist or aggressive, but defensive, while "the West" was on offense.

A second realist argument is that Russia has gone on international offense. Russia is disruptive because the Kremlin is trying to establish itself more firmly as a peer power to the United States, and to rising China in a new global order. This too is historically and geographically determined. Again, by this account, regime type, individual leaders, and society play little to no role in determining the purposes to which Russian power abroad is applied. Policy is not necessarily just reactive, but it is offensive in order to gain advantage against the power of the waning global hegemon—the United States—and the rising power of China. Russian cyber activities in the 2016 presidential election were intended to knock the United States off balance, to create doubt within its political system, in order to decrease American global power. Closer relations with China similarly advances Russia, by this account, to the disadvantage of the United States.

But these explanations of the purposes of Russian power overlook the importance of domestic political motivations that are as or more compelling. They assume away regime type—any Russian government, by these accounts, faced with the same international challenges would respond the same way. While acknowledging that Russia, like all countries, has national interests, one must not lose sight of the fact that there are many ways of asserting and defending them without resorting to armed force. The interactions between power resources, and the domestic political context that Russian policymakers face, play a crucial and frequently underestimated and underemphasized role in determining contemporary Russian behavior in international politics. In particular, under Vladimir Putin's regime, Russian power has been used not merely or even primarily in the service of national interests (as both strains of the arguments above would maintain), but also in the service of preserving his own corrupt regime. That is, in order to continue to govern at home, the regime that has developed under Vladimir Putin has needed to project its power abroad.

This argument proposes an important corrective to the "reactive" argument that focuses on Russia's policies as an obvious response to aggressive Western actions. Vladimir Putin and leading Russian commentators on foreign policy, as well as a few American analysts, have repeatedly blamed the West for celebrating the "defeat" of the Soviet Union in the Cold War and being poor partners to Russia. Even Mikhail Gorbachev (referring to himself in the third person) took up this theme in remarks on the occasion of the twenty-fifth anniversary of the Soviet collapse:

> They [Western leaders] did not want the Soviet Union to become a powerful democratic state. It would guarantee that neither the policy of unilateral measures, nor the policy of US domination in global affairs would work, and some American politicians saw Gorbachev as an obstacle to their plans. And then, when they made a bid for Boris Yeltsin, their goal was the same—to prevent the emergence of Russia as a powerful democratic state. Remember, when the [Soviet] Union collapsed, what was the West's reaction to this tragic event? They said, "this is a gift from God."[48]

Intriguingly, notable American scholars have also argued that Russia's aggressive foreign policy in Ukraine, for example, after 2014 was a natural reaction to Western provocation following the Cold War. John Mearsheimer insisted that "[t]he taproot of the trouble is NATO enlargement, the central element of a larger strategy to move Ukraine out of Russia's orbit and integrate it into the West."[49]

In specific contrast to this perspective of Russian foreign policy as a natural and inevitable reaction to Western provocation, I argue that it is just as much a reaction to domestic political exigencies and an attempt to meet the need to maintain popular support for an increasingly unpopular autocratic regime. Between 2003 and 2008, Putin presided over a booming economy almost completely dependent on oil and gas export revenues. At least 50% of Russia's national state budget was generated by oil and gas sales abroad. The dramatic drop in oil prices in 2014 was quickly followed by a 43% decline in the value of the ruble. In July 2015, inflation hit 15.5%. In 2015, second-quarter results from the Russian Statistical Service indicated that Russia was firmly in recession.[50] Contrary to the argument on foreign "enemies" that Putin blames for Russia's current predicament, "the West" did not put Russia in this situation. During his first eight-year tenure as Russia's president (2000–2008), Mr. Putin did little to reform the fundamentals of the economy, and took credit for the five-year economic boom (2003–2008) on the back of high global oil prices (over which he had little control at that time especially), having to face the repercussions when those prices inevitably dropped.

Despite the regime's invocation in its 2014 annexation of Crimea of the importance of the peninsula for Russia historically, and in the development of Russian Orthodoxy (Prince Vladimir is said to have been baptized in the area, thus committing the country to Christianity in the tenth century), this is a narrative meant to appeal to Russian nationalism in support of Putin's continued rule. Despite Mr. Putin's references to Eurasianism as a counterweight to the European Union, and evocations of the vision of a Russian World (*Russkii Mir*)—regions of the world with the common bond of Russian language, the Russian Orthodox Church, and Russian nationality—neither of these ideas constitutes a transformational, expansionist guiding ideology for the regime in the way that communism did for the Soviet Union. Further, while Putin has exploited a conservative, anti-Western, pan-Slavic philosophy in justifying some of his foreign policy decisions, this is not widely shared (although there has been some interest in parts of Eastern Europe to be sure) or closely linked to military activity—although it contributed to post-hoc justifications for annexing Crimea and continuing a simmering conflict in Eastern Ukraine.[51] This is not to deny that Russia may have "historical strategic interests" and goals in international politics independent from the ebbs and flows of domestic matters that any Russian leader might pursue.[52] *But private, rather than national, interests are also important drivers of contemporary Russian foreign policy decisions.* If Russian national interests were dictated largely by history and geography, then given the same resources at hand, any Russian leader might respond to changes in the international system the same way. Obviously, this has not been the case since 1991 and the collapse of the Soviet Union. As noted, through three presidents and four presidencies—Yeltsin's two terms in the 1990s, Putin's first presidency in 2000–2004, and Medvedev's in 2008–2012—Russia was perfectly capable of cooperation with Europe and the United States.

Further, economic exigencies are not determinative of Russia's ability to project its power resources beyond its border. It is true that Russia was not disruptive in international relations when its economy was at all-time lows between 1992 and 1998, but became so in 2008 in Georgia as its economy peaked. Yet it was precisely at another particularly low economic point in 2015 that the Putin leadership chose to deploy Russian forces in Syria. National economic strength and the means of power they can generate, then, do not, strictly speaking, drive Russian foreign policy, since they appear to explain both international cooperation *and* confrontation.

Often ignored in analyses of Russian power projection abroad is the degree to which society has become an important factor and the role social stability plays in ensuring the longevity and durability of even a patronal autocracy like Putin's. The primary goal of the contemporary Russian leadership is to maintain the political economy of patron-client relations that has enriched small networks of elites benefitting from access to state resources for private gain. As long as Mr. Putin remains in power, his clients and Putin himself, of course, continue to control access to the state, while privatizing the benefits that flow from using its resources. The system of governance that has blossomed under Putin's long rule in Russia is fundamentally cronyistic and corrupt. It is also especially vulnerable, since it depends on the survival of patron-client relationships, forming a hierarchy that leads all the way to the Kremlin.[53] As long as clients believe patrons in plum state jobs will provide them with preferred access to resources, like lucrative state contracts for goods and services, for example, then they will stay loyal and continue to provide kickbacks to their patrons. But should expectations of clients change regarding the access of patrons to resources to the benefit of both, then they may collectively challenge the patron, and instability would ensue throughout the system. In fact, anything that challenges the status quo, like opposition and challenges to the fundamental inequalities such a system produces—from other elites, from average citizens fed up with corruption and inequality, from independent parliaments, or from courts—must be avoided, punished, or defused.

Thus, just as the Soviet Union collapsed from within because of the failures of the state to provide for the basic needs of its citizens, rather than from an external attack by a foreign government, external powers are not the biggest threat to the regime that rules Russia today. The only *real* threat to this system comes from within Russia itself: Putin fears, above all, his own "street," and losing the loyalties of networks of Russian elites who have benefited greatly from his control of the assets of the Russian state. Russian society at large, though, must be kept pacified or, failing that, openly repressed for the regime to survive. After two great revolutions in the twentieth century—in 1917 and 1991—Putin himself in 2020 suggested that "Russia has fulfilled its plan when it comes to revolutions."[54] Mr. Putin and his clients benefit from the status quo.

In the slightly more than the quarter century that has passed since the dissolution of the Soviet Union, Russia has transitioned from a weak democracy to a hardening autocracy, one often classified with adjectives—competitive, electoral, soft, personalistic, conservative, kleptocratic, cronyistic.[55] While this too helps explain the more confrontational stance against Western democracies,[56] it is not autocracy alone that has changed the conduct of Russian foreign policy. After all, the Soviet Union was an autocracy—but one of a very different type. Perhaps one of the most surprising aspects of the exercise of Russian power abroad is how very different it is in many ways from that of the Soviet Union.

How the regime under Putin's leadership exercises power at home is also distinctive. Gone is the centralized planning system of the Soviet period, and the rigid, expansive state controls over private life that determined where Soviet citizens were educated, housed, got their food, and even whether they were able to buy a car. The much-maligned KGB is now known as Federal Security Service (FSB), and though still powerful given the place of the *siloviki* among the Putinist elite network, even it is only a pale shadow of its Soviet predecessor. Although a steadily hardening autocracy, the current regime allows some forms of free speech and tolerates the existence of a weak opposition, but within increasingly strict boundaries. But the flexibility and speed of decision-making that now characterizes contemporary Russian foreign policy is one of the biggest differences in comparison to the Soviet Union prior to 1985. The absence of institutional constraints on presidential power (Putin faces a compliant Duma, politicized and dependent courts, and appoints the senators of the Upper House) is in stark contrast to the general secretary's accountability to a Politburo that could (and did with Nikita Khrushchev, for example) overrule and overthrow him. In Putin's Russia, not dissimilar from the post-Stalinist Soviet Union, the source of regime legitimacy is based on performance more than ideology or violence alone, although a Putinist creed of anti-liberal politics emerged after 2012, as did a peppering of state-sponsored violence against opposition forces. Dissent is not without real peril in contemporary Russia. One of the troubling things about Putin's Russia is that the rules of politics and society seem to constantly change. Analysts have to stop and think of the ramifications of what they have said on television (and most critics of the Putin regime are no longer allowed on television). The media is no longer completely state-controlled, as in Soviet times, but its pro-Putin narrative is heavily scripted by the government and is an important tool to maintain public support of the regime that Vladimir Putin has built.

Generally, however, pacification of the masses is less expensive than repression as long as the economy is doing well. The economic bargain that was implicitly struck between Russian society and Putin in the early 2000s was that as long as the economy continued to grow, and real incomes effectively tripled between 2003 and 2008, then regime support was strong and its legitimacy was unquestioned despite growing social inequalities, weak rule of law, and pervasive corruption. But as economic decline and stagnation rather than growth became the most salient feature of the Russian economy after 2012, and following Putin's return to the Kremlin, the regime needed a new foundation for its legitimacy.

The popular protests that took place on the streets of Moscow following Putin's announced return as president in the fall of 2011, and parliamentary elections that December for the State Duma, which were widely viewed as rigged in favor of the ruling party, United Russia, followed by protests against Putin himself, presented a challenge to the autocracy's survival. In response, the regime became gradually more repressive by increasing fines for protesters, introducing further restrictions on civil society, and placing members of the opposition in jail or on trial. Others were poisoned and survived (Alexei Navalny in August of 2020); some were murdered (Boris Nemtsov in February 2015). The effect was to eviscerate an already weak political opposition and suppress other forms of social protest. But even after taking these drastic measures, Putin's approval ratings remained lower than they had been since he first came to power in 2000.

As I argue in this book, the assertive exercise of Russian power abroad has become a new element of the regime's legitimacy and survival. This increasingly aggressive direction in foreign policy has been a tool to demonstrate to Russians that their country under Putin is strong and influential in international relations, even in times of (temporary) economic struggle. Several examples of this strategy are worth highlighting. First, Putin effectively negotiated the removal of Syria's chemical weapons, challenging the United States' influence and resolve in removing Bashar al-Assad. Here was Russia's leader solving international problems and defusing international hot spots where "the West" had failed. This had the effect of demonstrating to citizens at home that their country was an influential geopolitical force. Second, within Russia, the regime launched an assault against foreign donors and Russian civil society organizations that accepted money from abroad. Third, and most significant, Mr. Putin intervened in Ukraine in convincing (former) President Yanukovych to forgo a trade agreement with the European Union in favor of joining the Eurasian Union, headed by Russia. The ensuing protests in Ukraine beginning in November 2013 were depicted within Russia as a fascist coup, a perspective stemming from the regime's fear that the contagion of protest might spread to Russia. The impulsive (not strategic) decision to invade Crimea at the end of February 2014, therefore, was presented in nationalist terms to the Russian people. Rather than an invasion of a sovereign Ukraine, the narrative in the Russian media was that the military incursion there was to defend the Russian diaspora in Crimea from Ukrainian nationalists and their NATO allies; the same narrative was applied in Eastern Ukraine. Increasingly, nationalist and conservative rhetoric dominated the press. Russia, by its own media's account, was a nation under siege geographically, economically, and culturally. Evidence that the tactic succeeded in bolstering public approval and shoring up regime legitimacy is the fact that Putin's approval rating shot up from 60% in February 2014, at the end of the Sochi Olympics, to 80% only a month later, following the annexation of Crimea, as indicated in Figure 1.2.[57]

The purpose of Russia's resurrection in global politics alluded to in the title of this book, therefore, is to project power in ways that maintain the current regime's fragile legitimacy at home. This argument, and the study's emphasis on the domestic political context as a crucial consideration in understanding Russian foreign policy, is an important addition to current understandings of Russian foreign policy. I do not view Russian uses of its power abroad as

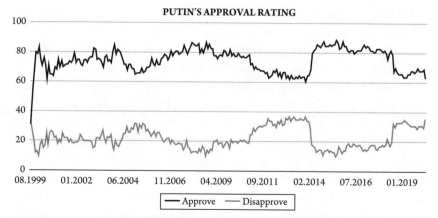

PUTIN'S APPROVAL RATING

Figure 1.2. Changes in Vladimir Putin's approval rating 1999–2020 (Question: "Do you approve of the activities of V. Putin as President (Prime Minister) of Russia?") Source: Levada Center, data accessed May 14, 2020.

only reactive to external provocations, nor do I accept that Russian foreign policy under Putin is purely the continuation of traditional interests spanning centuries. These alone, cannot explain zigzagging policy decisions over the last two decades. My emphasis, instead, is that Russia's revanchism comes from the interaction of these interests, Russia's power resources, and the contemporary domestic political environment.

The Plan of the Book

This study is distinctive from other literature on Russia's recent foreign policy in several ways; as a result, what follows should be of use to the area specialist as well as to the informed, general reader. First, it aims a spotlight on the interaction between domestic politics and foreign policy to explain Russian power and purpose in the twenty-first century. There is good work that focuses on Russian culture and history as the main explanation for Russian politics at home and behavior abroad. Andrei Tsygankov, for example, argues that how Russian leaders define national interest and identity greatly influences their conduct of international relations.[58] Undeniably, Russia's imperial and communist legacies have impressed a certain global perspective of Russian interests on its twenty-first-century leadership. As acknowledged earlier, I do not debate the idea that Russia has some international interests fixed by its geography, nor can any reasonable analyst deny that history matters. But the evidence does not support that either is determinative in understanding the arc of Russian foreign policy, since the early 2000s in particular.

Another distinguishing feature of this study is its focus on relative power, as opposed to Russia's relations with one or several other states or regions. I evaluate Russia's relative power in global politics using a multidimensional, not strictly realist, framework. I employ some international relations theory, but I make no claim to any great theoretical innovation in the field, as much as I seek to operationalize theoretical approaches put forward by others in order to examine relative power in twenty-first-century global politics. Other recent studies have focused on Russian relations with a particular country or regions, as does Angela Stent in her excellent study of US-Russian relations.[59] Nikolas Gvosdev and Christopher Marsh have also produced an expansive overview of the different regions or "vectors" of contemporary Russian foreign policy.[60] While these books are important and inherently valuable, they do not look at the issue of relative power explicitly or empirically in the way this study does, and they were written prior to Russia's more controversial foreign policy moves in Ukraine in 2014, Syria in 2015, and its interference in US election in 2016. Similarly, Bobo Lo's more recent book looks at how Russia is challenged by the post–Cold War order, but he does not provide as much consideration of how or really why Russia itself has become such a challenge to global stability.[61] Dmitri Trenin, too, has provided valuable evaluations of Russia's re-emergence in global politics in its "near abroad," and also an insightful but largely polemical argument regarding whether the West should fear Russia.[62] But none of these studies includes clear discussions or systematic evaluations of the multiple dimensions of Russian power, nor consideration explicitly of Russian internal politics.

Finally, this study empirically explores Russian power resources and the regime's decisions to use them. Other recent studies of Russia have focused principally on Putin as a master tactician who has seemingly outmaneuvered the West at almost every turn. Too often, domestic political considerations in these studies can be overlooked in favor of elite behavior alone in explaining Russian foreign policy. Indeed, there is sometimes an assumption by various analysts that Mr. Putin controls the system to such a degree that there are in fact no politics in Russia.[63] But such a perspective can place too much emphasis exclusively on Vladimir Putin and his psychology with respect to foreign policy. Necessarily, the biographical/leadership approach shines light on only one part of the elephant in understanding what kind of animal we are viewing, so to speak, whereas I seek a broader awareness of the interaction of domestic politics and foreign policy. In sum, clearly there is plenty of room for a different perspective on why Putin's Russia has come to act as it does in contemporary global politics.

From a theoretical standpoint, this book is also distinct in its emphasis on how political scientists evaluate state power in international relations. I seek to assess through what means, where, and when Russia can and does influence the behavior of other states. In doing so, I try to provide a more expansive

understanding of the tools states have at their disposal in the twenty-first century beyond airplanes, ships, tanks, troops, missiles, and money. Russia has
all of these instruments, although comparatively fewer or less of each than the
United States, the European Union (EU) 28, and China, yet it has emerged as a
threat to all three. Putin himself has been called "the most powerful man in the
world,"[64] yet as Russia's president he does not possess even remotely the traditional means of power of the American or Chinese presidents. This characteri-
zation of his and Russia's influence may well be wrong, of course, but so might
our traditional metrics of power, and so I offer others, as well as attempting to
better understand why the Putinist regime is able to translate the various resources it has into usable power abroad. Even without having "the most" of any
of the traditional means of power (which can be thought of as the 3 Ms: "men,
military, and money"), under Putin, Russia has managed, rather unexpectedly,
to be one of the most disruptive influences in contemporary international relations. It is high time, then, to rethink these frameworks in order to better understand state power and the purposes for which it is employed. As noted earlier
in this chapter, it is too often said that Russia has "played a weak hand wisely"
in international relations under Mr. Putin.[65] There is some element of truth to
this, especially if one adapts a purely realist view on the metrics of power. But if
we expand our understanding of what power is in contemporary global politics,
then Russia's hand has a few very strong cards, depending on the game that is
being played.

The remainder of this study develops these arguments as follows. Section
II goes on to assess the geographic *domain* and policy *scope* of contemporary
Russian power. In this section, chapters 2 and 3, respectively, examine these
components of Russian power in the former Soviet republics and, in chapter 3,
in other parts of the world relative to other contemporary great powers (the
United States, China, and the EU) to which Mr. Putin gamely compares Russia.
In the chapters that compose Section III, I use a variety of sources to compare
the *means* through which Russian leaders may propagate power and influence
beyond their country's borders: economic mechanisms in chapter 4, its human
capital in chapter 5 (including the physical health, education, and productive
capacity of its citizenry), hard power in chapter 6 (conventional and nuclear
weaponry), and soft power in chapter 7 (powers of attraction like the culture, its
diaspora), which, as Joseph Nye argues, can "shape the preferences of others,"[66]
and its cyber-based or "sharp" means of power.[67] In Section IV, I turn to the
question of the purposes of Russian power projection in the twenty-first century. Specifically, chapter 8 presents the argument that state and society relations within Russia play a key role in determining how Putin's patronal autocracy
uses power resources abroad. The book's final assessment of the implications of
Russia's resurrection for international relations and the current international

system makes an argument against the inevitability of a new Cold War between Russia and the West.

As this introductory chapter has shown, Russia's balance sheet of change and revival is decidedly mixed, and this fact throws into question its status as a resurrected global power. Nonetheless, as the epigraph that opens this chapter demonstrates, Russia is complex: it is neither as weak as we think, nor as strong as its leadership would like it to be viewed. It is a patronalist autocracy that has an interest in maintaining the domestic status quo, and that has driven the purpose to Russia's resurrection on the global stage and its unique hand in the international game of power.

THE GEOGRAPHIC DOMAIN
AND POLICY SCOPE
OF RUSSIAN POWER

Where Does Russia Matter?

The Geographic Domain and Policy Scope of Russian Power in the "Near Abroad"

"[T]he collapse of the Soviet Union was the greatest geopolitical catastrophe of the twentieth century."

—Vladimir Putin, 2005

As noted in chapter 1, specifying the geographic domain and policy scope of Russian power addresses the question of *power over whom and to do what?*[1] In answer to the first part—power over whom?—this chapter surveys Russia's influence in its nearest neighbors—the fourteen other former Soviet republics, while the next chapter surveys Russian power globally. In what follows, there are three important takeaways regarding the purposes (or the "to do what?" part of the question) of Russian power in the fourteen other countries that emerged from the collapse of the Soviet empire. First, the Kremlin has successfully reestablished tremendous political and economic influence over all the former Soviet republics relative to the 1990s. Second, there is, however, variation in the means with which Putin's regime has employed its influence in these new countries, although the policy scope in which it has sought to influence their leaders has been relatively consistent. Third, the pattern of variation in what means have been used is such that successor states that have liberalized politically—either joining the EU and NATO, as have the Baltic countries of Lithuania, Latvia, and Estonia, or openly aspiring to do so, as in the cases of Ukraine, Georgia, and Moldova—have faced far more aggressive use of the Kremlin's power resources. This stance has been for the purpose of trying to get them to abandon any ambitions their leaders may have to turn to the West rather than to the East for allies,[2] trade, and, most important for a political model that is not potentially disruptive, to Russian autocracy. In contrast to the manipulation of economic, social, and political environments of these six states, and the additional use of the Russian military in Ukraine, Georgia, and Moldova, the remaining eight former Soviet republics, as autocracies, however, have enabled Putin's regime to expend less effort to get their leaders to do what it wants. This is because the interests of these regimes in maintaining domestic stability are more in line with Putin's patronal autocracy. The autocracies of Central Asia, Belarus, Azerbaijan, and to a lesser extent, Armenia, have sought to maintain the status quo domestically so that their leaders can remain in office and, as in Russia, continue to privatize state assets for personal gain. None of them wants to be toppled by social instability. Moreover, Moscow seeks to retain security and economic dominance in both groups of former Soviet states, but in the more liberal-minded, Putin's regime has also worked to interfere directly in their political systems.

While this chapter is focused on Russian power projection in the geographic domain of the former Soviet republics, and chapter 3 will look farther beyond its borders, it is useful to pause and establish a few basic facts concerning Russian geography. Russia is territorially the largest country in the world in the twenty-first century. Its borders stretch from the European enclave of Kaliningrad to Vladivostok in the Russian Far East and beyond to Sakhalin Island, and to the Kurile Islands even farther eastward. The Russia Federation spans from the Arctic Circle in the north to the Caspian Sea in the south. It covers eleven time zones and borders fourteen foreign states in Asia, Central Asia, the Caucasus, and Europe: China, North Korea, Mongolia, Kazakhstan, Georgia, Azerbaijan, Ukraine, Belarus, Latvia, Lithuania, Estonia, Poland (at Kaliningrad Oblast), Norway, and Finland. The geographic area of contemporary Russia may be significantly smaller than was the Soviet expanse, but it is still outsized relative to every other country on the map today. Similarly, the policy areas—or policy scope—and Russia's "weight" or importance in many areas over which it has international influence have decreased relative to that of the Soviet Union. That said, Russian influence is still weighty, significant, and—usually, but not always—decisive in much of the former Soviet expanse.

Although geography, like genetics in humans, does not alone determine a state's developmental destiny, it does create certain opportunities and constraints. Again, a few geographical facts hint at Russia's potential (and real) power in international affairs. First, at over 17,000,000 square km, and although a pale shadow of the Russian empire in 1917 or the Soviet Union in 1989 (each about 22,000,000 square km),[3] the modern Russian Federation shares a very similar footprint with the borders of the seventeenth-century Russian empire. Despite losing territory with the Soviet collapse, Russia remains almost twice as big in terms of physical landmass as the next biggest country in the world, Canada (at almost 10,000,000 square km), and roughly 1.8 times the size of the United States (the third largest country in the world) and China (the fourth largest). Second, only China has as many external borders as contemporary

Russia—fourteen.[4] Since in this study, power is not simply conceptualized as an ordering of the amalgamation of resources of states, the fact that Russia is large and has so many borders is significant in understanding the extent and nature of over what and whom Russia has power and in what ways. When we consider the different dimensions of a country's relative power over other states, there is often a particularly significant interaction between *geographic domain* (what other states country A affects) and *policy scope* (over what issues A affects other states). The degree to which one dimension—geographic domain or policy scope—causes the other is not always clear, but geography necessarily affects the kinds of policy areas with which states might be most concerned. For example, geography and resulting natural resource endowments (or lack thereof) can influence the makeup of a state's economy to some degree—natural resource export-dependent, agricultural, etc.—and therefore the policy areas with which its government might be most concerned in dealing with other states.

Geography also determines the degree to which one state's security relative to other states is important. A country that has one big neighbor and one especially long land border, such as Canada, for example, has a more narrow set of security concerns (or few at all) than a country like China or Russia, each of which shares borders with a large number of other states. But geography alone does not determine foreign policy or the power of states in international affairs. Japan, after all, is a relatively small island nation that proved quite disruptive to international order in the twentieth century. It is the other dimensions of power and the will and capability that their leaders have to employ those power resources that determine their roles and goals in international relations.

Russia's Revival in Its Neighborhood

Vladimir Putin's lament (in the quotation that opened this chapter) for the fall of the Soviet Union as "the greatest geographic catastrophe of the twentieth century" is one of his most infamous statements, but it is also the most often misunderstood. Putin was not sorrowful over the collapse of the Soviet planned economic system, or the fall of the Communist Party, nor was he advocating the return of Marxism-Leninism. Instead, he regretted the loss of territory and resources wrought by the Soviet collapse, as well as the populations of ethnic Russians stranded outside the homeland in former republics that were now new countries.

When the Soviet Union collapsed in December 1991, fifteen sovereign states, including Russia (also officially known as the Russian Federation), were created. Successive Soviet-era constitutions created the conditions for secession by guaranteeing each republic's right to leave the Union, although when these documents were written, it was inconceivable that any state would actually exercise the "exit" option. The Union had been held together by the three main institutions of the communist system: the Party, the planned economy, and the pervasive internal security apparatus, the KGB, that perpetrated fear within the population. Each republic (except the Russian Soviet Federative Socialist Republic) had its own communist party, but these republic-level parties and their parallel governments were secondary in importance to the All-Union Communist Party of the Soviet Union (CPSU). The top-down organization of the CPSU and the highly centralized nature of economic planning meant that virtually every political and economic decision was determined in Moscow. Even trains in distant time zones such as Kazakhstan or the Russian Far East, for example, ran on Moscow time. It is important to recognize how highly centralized the Soviet Union had become by 1985, when Mikhail Gorbachev became the (last) general secretary of the CPSU, because it helps explain the degree to which many Russian leaders and citizens—even more than thirty years later—still view Russia as the hub of a greater, although now defunct, empire.

Some of the new states that emerged after the Soviet breakup were reluctant members of the international community, including all five of the Central Asian states (Kazakhstan, Uzbekistan, Kyrgyzstan, Tajikistan, and Turkmenistan), none of which had prior histories of independence from the old Russian empire. Others, like the Baltic countries of Estonia, Latvia, and Lithuania, were enthusiastic independent nation-states that had been fledgling democracies during the interwar period, free from Soviet power and Russian influence. These histories partially conditioned the purposes of Russian power in the region after the collapse of the Soviet empire.

To the consternation of President Putin, Barack Obama once referred to Russia as a "regional" power. Presumably, this assessment came from Russia's disproportionate political, economic, and security impact in relations with the countries on its borders and the low cost of using these means of power in its neighborhood, as opposed to Russia's influence beyond its immediate borders, where it appeared relatively inconsequential. Given its geographic dimensions, relative population size, gross domestic product (GDP), and historical legacy as the seat of both the Russian and Soviet empires, it is not surprising that modern Russia should have significant influence over the politics and economies of the other fourteen post-Soviet states. But Russia's contemporary leadership has sought and maintained more control over some former Soviet states than others, and their success in different countries has been highly varied. Indeed, it is safe to conclude that Russian power even in this traditional sphere of influence has fluctuated—relative to the highly centralized Soviet period, of course, but also across time and geography since the Soviet collapse.

As table 2.1 indicates, Russia is a behemoth geographically, economically, and demographically in comparison to its post-Soviet neighbors. It dwarfs its two nearest regional competitors, Ukraine and Kazakhstan, in terms of land area, GDP, and population size. Notably, however, the three Baltic republics are competitive with Russia in terms of GDP per capita, in no small part due to their memberships in the EU, which has helped them reform their economies to meet European regulations, and to address the trade imbalances with Russia that are suffered by most of the other former Soviet republics.

While Russia's geographic size is staggering, and its economy relative to those of its post-Soviet neighbors is also immense, these are not the only factors that condition the patterns of Russia's varied abilities to project its power over the

Table 2.1 **Russia in Comparison to Other Former Soviet States**

Country	GDP at PPP*	GDP Per Capita at PPP $	Population (in millions)	Land Area (sq. km)
Russia	3.196 **trillion**	26,669.22	144.48**	17.10 million**
Ukraine	521.173 billion	8,207.27	44.62	603,550
Uzbekistan	221.95 billion	6,734.85	32.96	447,400
Kazakhstan	466.86 billion	25,548.97	18.27	2.72 million
Belarus	179.098 billion	18,885.24	9.48	207,600
Azerbaijan	141.119 billion	14,197.35	9.94	86,600
Tajikistan	29.439 billion	3,234.72	9.10	141,380
Kyrgyzstan	32.375 billion	5,120.39	6.33	199,950
Turkmenistan	86.859 billion	14,845.33	5.85	488,100
Georgia	53.094 billion	14,247.61	3.73	69,700
Moldova	33.193 billion	12,266.10	2.71	33,850
Lithuania	99.147 billion	35,389.98	2.80	65,286
Armenia	37.532 billion	12,714.96	2.95	29,740
Latvia	57.889 billion	30,038.47	1.93	64,490
Estonia	46.676 billion	35,308.09	1.32	45,340

Figures are from the World Bank, 2018, the most complete and recent available at time of writing. https://data.worldbank.org/indicator/NY.GDP.MKTP.PP.KD?end=2018&locations=RU&start=1996, accessed June 30, 2020.

*GDP at purchasing power parity and GDP per capita calculated at PPP in 2017 constant international $.

**Russian population data here do not include Crimea. They are included in the data as part of Ukraine.

policies of what Russians sometimes still refer to as the "near abroad." In terms of patterns of Russian power within the fourteen other former Soviet states, a number of variables matter, such as whether politics are more open or more autocratic, or whether populations are predominantly ethnically Slavic. But common to Russia's power relationships with all fourteen are three key policy areas of particular concern: energy, trade, and the security of Russian borders. In all fourteen, a fourth policy concern is the political orientations of the other former republics and how those too might impact Putin's patronal autocracy. Thus, under Putin, Russia has sought increased political influence in the domestic politics of the other former Soviet republics—especially those that could infect Russian society with political aspirations damaging to the regime.

The Six Liberalizing States: Estonia, Latvia, Lithuania, Georgia, Ukraine, and Moldova

Politically, there is clearly a pattern to the attempts of Putin's regime to exercise influence within the republics of the former Soviet Union, and to its relative success in doing so. The six that have attempted to decrease their dependency on Russia and turn to the West for security and deeper economic and trade ties— Lithuania, Latvia, Estonia, Ukraine, Georgia, and, to a lesser degree, Moldova— are all in various stages of transitioning to a more liberal form of government at the time of writing. Russia's relationship with these six former republics has often been antagonistic and punitive, geared toward changing their political orientation to better serve Russia's interests—in particular, related to trade, energy, and security policy. In Georgia and Ukraine, Russia came into armed conflict and still occupies portions of each country at the time of writing (2020).

The Baltics

The Baltic States—Estonia, Latvia, and Lithuania—have been members of NATO and the EU since 2004. As figure 2.1 indicates, all three are regarded as democracies, although not perfect ones, to be sure. Politically and economically they are oriented decidedly westward, not toward Russia. Holding fast to memories of their independence in the decades between the two world wars,[5] the Baltic republics were the first to leave the Soviet Union following the failed putsch against Mikhail Gorbachev in 1991. Never having accepted their annexation by the Soviet Union as legitimate, and having long memories of oppression under Soviet rule, Estonians, Latvians, and Lithuanians fiercely asserted their independence from Russia and Russian cultural hegemony. Rebuffing Russian

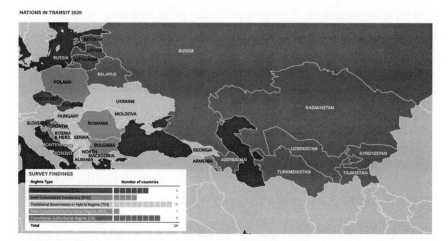

Figure 2.1. Regime Types: Russia and Its Neighborhood, Nations In Transit, 2020 Source: Freedom House, Nations in Transit, 2020, https://freedomhouse.org/explore-the-map?type=nit&year=2020, accessed July 23, 2020 (Data are from 2019).

attempts through the 1990s to bring them into the newly evolving Russian security fold, they turned instead to Europe and NATO. In Estonia and Latvia, new, freely elected governments instituted aggressive language laws in the early 1990s requiring citizens to speak the titular languages of their respective countries. For millions of ethnic Russians who had lived in those countries during the fifty or so years between annexation and independence, this became a tremendous obstacle to gaining full citizenship. Not surprisingly, these policies raised fears on the part of Russian political leaders, beginning with Boris Yeltsin, Russia's first president, that ethnic Russians were being mistreated. Concerns about the treatment of the diaspora, and the fact that all three Baltic countries were EU and NATO members, fueled further tensions with Russia as Yeltsin's successor, Vladimir Putin, tried to build the Eurasian Economic Union as an alternative trading bloc among former Soviet republics. Since 2003, successive Russian military doctrines have referred to NATO as the main threat to Russia, in no small part because its Baltic members sit directly on Russia's northwestern border.[6]

Despite Baltic realignment with the West following the Soviet collapse, Baltic integration in the Soviet Union between 1944 and 1991 created other opportunities for Russia to extend its power resources into these tiny independent countries. The Soviet legacy of creating infrastructural dependence on oil, gas, and electricity remains a key area of leverage. All three Baltic States use an electricity grid built in the Soviet period that remains tied to Belarus and Russia. Regarding oil and natural gas, Latvia and Lithuania depend almost entirely on pipelines from Russia, while Estonia is somewhat less vulnerable, importing some of these resources from elsewhere.[7] Russia used the strategy of cutting off oil and gas deliveries in the Baltics at least forty times between 2000 and 2006 alone,[8] usually in response to government policies that Moscow wanted to change. The most notorious incidents, as Agnias Grigas notes, "include the halting of oil supplies to the Latvian port operator Ventspils Nafta (VN) since 2003 and to the Lithuanian oil refinery Mažeikiu Nafta (MN) since 2006, as well as interruptions to the oil supply via rail to Estonia in May 2007."[9] Since 2000, Russia has also embarked upon a project of re-routing energy flows around the Baltics to Western European customers, which allows it to cut off gas to the Baltic States without negative effects on European customers.[10]

The legacy of the Soviet gas pipeline infrastructure means that the Baltics rely heavily on gas supplies from Russia. Lithuania has attempted to get more independent from Russia regarding gas supply, but Latvia and Estonia have made decisions more favorable to Russia, and been rewarded with lower gas prices.[11] These patterns show that Russian gas decisions do not merely follow a commercially based logic; moreover, Russian gas companies are not clearly independent commercial companies, but largely state-owned and -controlled, and therefore serve as powerful instruments for extending influence over energy-dependent neighbors. Grigas also argues that Russia has lured investors away from Lithuanian attempts to build its own nuclear plant, thus trying to ensure Lithuania's continued dependence on Russia for electricity. [12]

Under Putin, Russia's relationships with each of the Baltic States have become more threatening and antagonistic as Estonia, Latvia, and Lithuania have moved politically and economically closer to the EU and developed strong security relationships with NATO and the United States. As one analyst notes, Russia's "discourse and policies demonstrate a resolve to maintain a 'zone of privileged interest' in the Baltic region and post-communist Europe, often irrespective of the wishes of the countries concerned."[13] Yet Russian cultural hegemony in the Baltic States, compared to that in Ukraine or Belarus (discussed later in this chapter), is not strong. These states have no shared religion with Russia, so the Russian Orthodox Church cannot be used as a vehicle by which to spread the values of the "Russkii Mir," or Russian World (Estonians are Lutheran; Latvians a mix of religions including Catholic, Lutheran, and Orthodox; and Lithuanians predominantly Catholic).[14] Further, the majority populations are not ethnically Russian, nor do they speak Russian as their primary language. Indeed, their languages are not even recognizable to a Russian speaker; Estonian is in the Finno-Ugric language family and is linguistically closest to Finnish, while Lithuanian and Latvian are Baltic languages, not Slavic, with ties to the Germanic and Indo-European language families; all three use Latin script rather than Cyrillic. The vast majority of citizens in the three Baltic States speak their respective titular languages, although, depending on their age group, they may also have working knowledge of Russian.

The principal potential cultural lever available to Russian policymakers in the Baltics, then, is the set of large ethnically Russian populations, in Latvia and Estonia in particular, which the Soviet Union initially transplanted following World War II in an attempt to assimilate these new republics. After 1991, their poor integration is as much a result of Baltic-language policies as Russian efforts to maintain the populations' loyalties to their ethnic homeland. Nonetheless, the ethnic Russians in Estonia and Latvia have remained and present a potentially destabilizing political force should they choose to mobilize as a community.

Other factors contributing to Russia's influence over decision-making and agenda-setting (or constraining) include the relative size of the Russian population and economy. The population is 146.8 million (if one counts Crimea, as Russia did after 2014), in comparison to the tiny Baltic States: Estonia's population is 1.32 million, Latvia's 1.93 million, and Lithuania's 2.8 million.[15] These differences alone make the Baltic countries vulnerable to Russian influence. Less obvious, however, is the "commercialization of politics or high degree of penetration of politics by business interests, particularly in Latvia and Lithuania."[16] In the Russian system of patronal political economy, business and government are closely intertwined, however. The Kremlin is able to influence the political systems in the Baltics by financing parties, although this is difficult to document definitively given the nebulous relationships involved. Still, one major investigation by the Estonian secret police in 2011 involved the mayor of Tallinn and leader of Estonia's Center Party, Edgar Savisaar, who allegedly received 1.5 million euros to fund the party's parliamentary campaign that year from Putin's friend and appointee Vladimir Yakunin, then head of Russian Railways. More well known was the impeachment of Lithuania's president Rolandas Paksas in 2004 for his entanglements with Russian business interests. Russian influence in the Baltic economies is also exercised through networks of Baltic business elites, many of whom are former members of the Soviet nomenklatura and not necessarily of Russian descent. This is particularly true of the energy sector, especially gas distribution companies like Itera, Vikonda, and Stella Vitae, where ownership structure is closely linked to Russia's state-owned Gazprom and relationships between the companies are not transparent.[17]

Another area of the Kremlin's coercive power in the Baltics is cyber-based. Perhaps the best-known use of this disruptive capability in an area that Russia considers its area of historical geographic domain occurred in Estonia in the spring of 2007. It was set off by a controversy surrounding the Bronze Soldier memorial marking the Soviet liberation of Estonia from Nazi Germany, which many Estonians associated not with liberation, but occupation. On April 30, 2007, the Estonian government moved the statue from its historical place in central Tallinn to a less conspicuous location in the city's military cemetery. Many ethnic Russians interpreted the statue's relocation as an affront to their community and diminishment of their nationality within Estonia, and riots ensued, led by members of the large ethnic Russian diaspora (ethnic Russians constitute about 25% of the population).[18] Beyond violence and rioting, hackers, either from within Russia or Russians within Estonia, orchestrated a denial-of-service cyber-attack that shut down all Estonian government ministry websites, at least two banks, and the parliament's email server.[19] Parts of government were effectively closed, and credit cards and bank machines were inoperable for several days. EU and NATO technical specialists were never able to directly connect the attacks to the Russian government, but Russian officials accused the Estonian government of violating human rights during the clashes that followed the relocation of the Bronze Solider, and provided encouragement to the hackers. As Stephen Herzog noted, "one unnamed NATO official did not mince words: 'I won't point fingers. But these were not things done by a few individuals. This clearly bore the hallmarks of something concerted.' "[20]

Another means by which Russia has extended its influence in the Baltics has involved a concerted disinformation campaign broadcast into Russian communities, in Latvia and Estonia in particular, through Russian media. Typically, RT (Russia Today, an international cable network, whose influence abroad is covered in more detail in chapter 7) and Russia's main television channels broadcast anti-government material, intended to spread discontent within the ethnically Russian populations in each country. Often this includes historical references to the German occupation of the Baltics in World War II and the "fascistic" governments that welcomed them into the Baltics. It also propagates the Russian nationalist historical narrative that the Soviet Union liberated the Baltics through annexation.

The cost to Russia of broadcasting television into the Baltics or disrupting the Internet or infrastructure in these countries is relatively low, as long as this interference does not trigger a NATO Article 5 response ("an attack against one member is an attack against all"). Membership in NATO and in the EU does, therefore, provide important brakes on the exercise of Russian power in the Baltics, but clearly does not eliminate it. Latvia, Lithuania, and Estonia have been able to develop as democracies and liberal market economies despite their proximity to their outsized autocratic, illiberal neighbor, but the struggle to decrease Russia's influence remains, since the goal of Russian policy is to divide the Baltics from Europe and NATO.

Georgia

The former Soviet republic of Georgia in the South Caucasus is another good example of the rocky relationships Putin's regime has pursued with former Soviet states that have liberal leanings. Georgia long resisted the reassertion of Russian influence following the collapse of the Soviet Union. Georgia's leaders, like those in the Baltic States, Moldova, and Armenia, refused to participate in the March 1991 All-Union referendum on the future of the Soviet Union because they did not intend for Georgia to continue to be a member state, regardless of whether a renewed Union survived in another form. Georgian leaders issued a declaration of independence from the Soviet Union on April 9, 1991. After the Soviet Union collapsed, Georgia was consumed by political and economic instability, in part fueled by ethnic differences. Eventually, Georgian politics stabilized with the election of Eduard Shevardnadze, who had previously served as Mikhail Gorbachev's foreign minister, but Shevardnadze's government was popularly viewed as increasingly corrupt, and was overthrown in a peaceful "people's revolution" in November 2003 known as the Rose Revolution.

The Rose Revolution was significant both for changing the course of Georgian politics and for initiating Russia's fears of "color revolutions" in its neighborhood. In the Georgian case, parliamentary elections held on November 3, 2003, produced results that were widely regarded by the international community as falsified in favor of Shevardnadze and against the party of Mikhail Saakashvili, Shevardnadze's former minister of justice (2000–2001). Saakashvili had left Shevardnadze's government, complaining about pervasive corruption, and encouraged Georgians to protest the election results, which culminated in tens of thousands of private citizens taking to the streets. Georgia's Rose Revolution was the first of the "color revolutions" in the former Soviet states, and was followed by a similar popular uprising in Ukraine in 2004 and Kyrgyzstan in 2005, which stoked Russia's fears about losing influence in the region.

After Shevardnadze's resignation, Saakashvili was elected Georgia's president in January 2004 on a reformist and decidedly pro-NATO, pro-EU, and anti-Russian platform. He remained president of Georgia for two terms, until 2013. While he accomplished some impressive reforms, particularly in dramatically reducing levels of state corruption and improving efficiency, he was criticized for becoming increasingly authoritarian by the end of his term, and in 2015 the Georgian government indicted (and then convicted) him in absentia (he was in the United States and then in Ukraine) on multiple counts of abuse of power.[21]

Perhaps the most important event in Russian-Georgian relations during Saakashvili's leadership took place in August 2008, when Russia and Georgia waged a five-day war. Formally, the conflict was over the formal status of the two restive Georgian regions of South Ossetia and Abkhazia, where there had been armed conflict since their declarations of independence from Georgia in 1991 and 1992, respectively. In 1994, as part of a ceasefire agreement between the Georgian government and separatists, Russian troops were sent as peacekeepers to Abkhazia and then South Ossetia, but tensions and occasional open conflict remained in both regions. This suited the Kremlin's purposes in making Georgia, especially under Saakashvili, seem too unstable for NATO membership, and also too unstable to encourage any similar uprising in Russia itself. In 2006, South Ossetia again declared its independence from Georgia, and Russia began issuing passports to the region's residents. The ceasefire between Georgian forces and separatists broke in August 2008. Although what sparked it is contested, Russian president Medvedev claimed that he ordered forces to protect South Ossetia from advancing Georgian troops. Russia countered by moving forces across the Georgian-Russian border, claiming to act in response to Georgian aggression against what were now Russian citizens.

But, as with the Baltic States, Russia's deeper concern was not with the treatment of minorities within Georgia, but with the possibility of yet another former Soviet state joining forces with the West and, in particular, NATO. The contentious NATO Summit held in Bucharest in April 2008 fueled these tensions. Ukraine and Georgia had both requested a Membership Action Plan (MAP), and while the George W. Bush administration, in a concession to France, Germany, and other European actors, did not extend formal invitations to Ukraine and Georgia to instigate the MAP process, they did issue the declaration, "We agreed today that these countries [Georgia and Ukraine] will become members of NATO."[22] In this, they sought to reassure liberalizing Ukrainian and Georgian leaders that they should continue preparations to eventually join the alliance. From the Russian perspective, as the Russian analyst Dmitri Trenin has argued convincingly:

> Moscow saw NATO membership for any of its ex-satellites or former provinces as both a symbol of U.S. political influence and a potential platform for the U.S. military to use as a pressure instrument against Russia. Stopping NATO's eastern advance beyond the 2004 lines— that is, beyond the Baltic states—thus became its overriding foreign policy and security goal.[23]

This, in part, explains the Kremlin's increased aggression after the NATO Summit. In particular, the deployment of forces into Georgia in August 2008 marked a major change in foreign policy objectives and beliefs in the appropriate use of force to defend Russian interests. As Trenin notes, the Georgian war was the first time that Russia had sent troops into conflict on foreign soil since the Soviet withdrawal from Afghanistan in 1989. Although Russian soldiers came within a few miles of the Georgian capital, Tbilisi, they ultimately retreated, and a peace deal was brokered by French president Nicolas Sarkozy. The war officially ended on August 16, 2008, but both South Ossetia and Abkhazia were left occupied by Russian troops and, at the time of writing, are effectively no longer part of Georgia. Putin's regime recognized them as independent states on August 26,

2008, but only Nicaragua, Venezuela, Nauru, and Tuvalu joined in recognizing their independence. Nonetheless, if one of the goals of the Russian regime in the 2008 war was to gain greater influence in Georgian politics, economy, and society, then the result was mixed. Russian influence decreased, though it certainly has not disappeared, since the war in 2008, except in South Ossetia and Abkhazia, and Georgia persisted in pursuing closer ties with NATO and the EU.

The Georgian case, however, demonstrates the panoply of tools that contemporary Russia's leadership has available in attempts to influence the internal affairs of neighboring states. Given the comparative size of the Russian population, and therefore its potential as a market for Georgian products, the remaining area of leverage, beyond use of the military, is largely economic. In 2006, for instance, to oppose former Georgian president Mikhail Saakashvili and his anti-Russian and pro-Western policies, Russian leaders introduced a trade embargo on Georgia that inevitably affected the Georgian economy far more than it hurt Russian consumers, who found alternatives to Georgian products. Yet Georgia largely managed to wean itself from Russian gas supplies, and funds from fees for gas flows in transit through the country, but the Georgian economy does not depend on Russia alone for its domestic consumption needs anymore. Nonetheless, the Soviet infrastructural legacy in electricity that affects the Baltics also remains a factor in Georgia, and ample Russian business investments have re-emerged there since the lifting of the Russian embargo in 2006.

Despite the continued use of these economic levers of Kremlin influence and successive changes in governments, Georgia has retained its European aspirations and resisted Russian government attempts at closer integration. In this case of a David fighting a Goliath, David has scored a few wins, but has lost territory for the foreseeable future, and remains vulnerable to the economic power of its huge neighbor to the north.

Ukraine

Ukraine, in many ways, has followed a similar path to Georgia in its relations with Putin's Russia, although the depth, length, and costs of conflict for its people have been far greater. For many Russians, including President Vladimir Putin, Ukraine is symbolic. It is more than a neighbor; it is seen as a "little brother" in terms of both culture and language. To even "soft" Russian nationalists, Ukraine is considered to be part of greater Russia and is emblematic of Russia's historical sphere of influence. The traditional heart of the argument for this perspective is that the Crimean Peninsula of Ukraine was where Prince Vladimir, ruler of Kyivan Rus', first adopted the Orthodox religion, and had the Slavic people of his growing empire baptized in the Dnieper River in A.D. 988. Crimea, therefore, is considered the cradle of Russian Orthodoxy and, for some, sacred ground—in the way that Boston Harbor is to the American Revolution, or the site of the Bastille in France. It is a crucial part of the history of the making of the Russian nation. Indeed, Vladimir Putin himself invoked this national mythology in his March 18, 2014, speech to the Russian parliament justifying the Crimean invasion.[24] It has been put to good use in the new narrative in support of the regime's legitimacy.

The circumstances of Ukraine's possession of Crimea are also, to some Russians at least, somewhat questionable. In 1954, Nikita Khrushchev, as first secretary of the Communist Party, and himself Ukrainian, transferred jurisdiction of the Crimean Peninsula from the Russian Soviet Federative Socialist Republic to the Ukrainian Soviet Socialist Republic, both then constituent republics of the Soviet Union. At that point, it was difficult to imagine that the Soviet Union would one day break apart and that an independent Ukraine would include Crimea as a result. It is not entirely clear why this transfer occurred, given that Crimea had been part of the Russian empire since 1654, but it may have been to fully consolidate Soviet control over Western Ukraine or to consolidate Khrushchev's control over the Communist Party of the Soviet Union following the death of Joseph Stalin in 1953.[25]

The emphasis on Crimea's historically important place in Russia's national mythology also stresses cultural ties between Russia and Ukraine in general, and not with Europe explicitly. The Ukrainian language is close, though not identical, to Russian, and the Orthodox religion dominates in Ukraine as in Russia, although under a different Patriarchate. Culturally, with the possible exception of Belarus, Ukraine is the closest to Russia of all the post-Soviet states—at least, that is the Russian perspective. (In a statement that encapsulates the emotions of many Russian citizens, Vladimir Putin is purported to have remarked once to George W. Bush that "Ukraine is a made-up country."[26])

Beyond the symbolic and the cultural affinity between the Ukrainian and Russian peoples—both Eastern Slavs—Ukraine's Crimean Peninsula in the imperial and Soviet periods was the home of the Black Sea Fleet, and Sevastopol, the capital, is Russia's main warm water port. In one sense, this is becoming less important from a defense perspective, given the increased abilities of Russian submarines to operate in ports to the north and in the Far East, and the fact that Russian warplanes and missiles can be launched into the Middle East just as easily from southern Russia as from Ukraine, for example (or, as was done in 2016, from Iran with Iranian government permission). The Russian navy also has other access points into the Black Sea for its frigates and subs.

There is a deeper domestic political concern for Putin's regime regarding Ukraine, however. Through the Orange Revolution of 2004, Ukrainian citizens took to the streets and demanded transparent government and free and fair elections. Through the Supreme Court, election results were actually overturned, and a liberal opposition ruled from 2004–2010 when Yanukovych was (legitimately) elected president. And it was in 2013, when again Ukrainian citizens took to the streets to demand that Yanukovych sign an accession deal with the EU, ultimately toppling him in February 2014. The possibility of this kind of social instability and public mobilization leaking into Russia by example is an existential threat to the regime, not to mention the additional possibility of yet another former Soviet republic turning to the West rather than to Russia.

Russia under Putin has used the same kinds of tools in Ukraine as in Georgia and the Baltics in attempts to corral its leaders back into Russia's economic and security spheres: energy dependence on the Kremlin, trade, and, most notably, interference in political processes. Under Putin, Russia was a strong financial backer and supporter of former Ukrainian president Leonid Kuchma. In 2004, Kuchma termed out of the presidency and campaigned hard for Viktor Yanukovych, his prime minister, to succeed him. President Putin also campaigned personally for Yanukovych and against Yushchenko, a former minister in Kuchma's government who had left with complaints of corruption. When fraudulent election results were announced in Yanukovych's favor after the first round in November, Ukrainians took to the streets in protest, occupying Kiev's central Maidan Nezalezhnosti (Independence Square). Waving orange flags and wearing orange hats and scarves—the colors of Yushchenko's party—protesters demanded the electoral results be overturned and that a free and fair second round take place. This peaceful "Orange Revolution" succeeded in forcing a Supreme Court decision to overturn the initial results, paving the way for a second round of clean elections to take place. These were won by Yushchenko's Orange coalition on December 26, 2004. President Yushchenko's administration was decidedly pro-European and anti-Russian, with the clear goal of bringing Ukraine into the EU. The prospect of a democratic Ukraine marching toward Europe was a threat to the very existence of Putin's regime—what if Russian citizens wanted the same? The success of the people-powered Orange Revolution clearly also made Russian leaders nervous about a contagion effect from Ukraine into Russia itself.

As with Georgia and the Baltic States, Russia's leaders used Ukrainian dependence on Russian gas to try to force Ukraine back into line and more firmly under Russian influence. In the 2000s, Orange Revolution leaders wanted Russia to pay more for the transit of Russian gas across Ukraine to Western Europe, while Russia wanted to end the generous gas subsidies Ukraine received. In January 2006, after repeated attempts to reach agreement on the price of gas and transit, Russia's Gazprom stopped gas flowing to Ukraine for three days. Ukrainian negotiators and Gazprom then agreed on a higher price for gas to Ukraine, though still about a third of what Germany, for example, paid Russia. This did not end the ongoing dispute, and Ukraine gradually fell into

arrears over gas payments to Russian companies. Because the fundamental issues were unresolved, three years later, at the height of the global financial crisis
that hit both countries hard, Russia again pushed unsuccessfully for higher gas
prices. When no deal was reached, Gazprom once again cut off gas supplies to
Ukraine on January 1, 2009, in the midst of another cold winter. Initially only
Ukraine was affected, but a week later, Gazprom cut gas supplies to pipelines
that ran through Ukraine into various parts of Europe, presumably in order to
hurt Ukrainian transit revenues. As a result, not only did Ukraine lose transit
fees, but some Europeans had no gas for heating in the dead of winter. They were
suddenly made aware of their own energy vulnerabilities to Russia.

As with the Baltics, Ukraine's energy dependencies onto Russia are a clear
source of Kremlin influence over internal politics. This was even more the
case given Moscow's ability to exploit disagreements within Ukrainian politics. During the 2009 gas conflict, for instance, Putin was able to play off the
emerging schisms between the former leaders of the Orange Revolution, Prime
Minister Yulia Tymoshenko and President Viktor Yushchenko, to Russia's advantage. Putin, then prime minister, ultimately signed a deal with Tymoshenko in
Moscow on January 19, 2009.[27] The sharp disagreements between Tymoshenko
and Yushchenko, and the re-emergence as prime minister of Viktor Yanukovych,
the "villain" of the Orange Revolution, crashed the hopes for reform in Ukraine
that had been brought by the Orange Revolution in 2004.

In free and fair elections in 2010, Yanukovych was legitimately elected
president of Ukraine. Although his government was predatory and corrupt,
Yanukovych, like Tymoshenko and Yushchenko, remained committed to an EU
Association Agreement for Ukraine and resisted the Eurasian Economic Union
that Russia led with Belarus and Kazakhstan (joined eventually by Armenia and
Kyrgyzstan). As Anders Åslund notes, "this was a dangerous game: By taking this
step, Yanukovych aroused great popular hopes in Ukraine while antagonizing
Moscow."[28] Without signing the agreement, Yanukovych stood little chance
of winning re-election in March 2015; polls showed that most Ukrainians, including powerful oligarchs who controlled the heart of the Ukrainian economy,
strongly supported European association. The European market was also huge in
comparison to the Eurasian Economic Union proposed by Putin, and by moving
closer to Europe, Ukraine would be less constrained by the protectionism in
trade that Putin's regime often imposed.

But by July 2013, Moscow threatened retaliation through trade should Ukraine
open its borders to the EU. Russian officials blocked Ukrainian imports of choc-
olate, steel pipes, agricultural products, and other items, and held up most other
Ukrainian exports at the Russian border for ten days. Nonetheless, Yanukovych
reiterated his intention to sign the Association Agreement and pledged to meet all
EU conditions by the November 21, 2013, Eastern Partnership Summit.[29]

Yanukovych was clearly under great pressure from Moscow, as evidenced in the contrast in his words and actions during the month of November: on November 6, he stated, "By choosing to get closer to the European Union, we are making a pragmatic choice for . . . modernization," but by November 21, he refused to sign the agreement with the EU.[30]

As in the Orange Revolution in 2004, Ukrainian citizens once again flooded Kiev's Maidan with demands that Yanukovych sign the agreement with the EU or resign. In a movement that became known as Euro-Maidan (or the Revolution of Dignity), protesters occupied the square for months, despite counter-demonstrations and attacks by pro-government police. Russia under Putin used its still considerable financial clout to try to save Yanukovych in December 2013, buying $15 billion of Ukrainian bonds to tide over a nearly bankrupt Ukraine until the presidential elections. Russia also cut the cost of gas exports to Ukraine and eased some trade sanctions, while signing production cooperation agreements in armaments. There were also violent attempts to quell the protests, when the Ukrainian police and interior ministry troops shot protesters, killing an estimated 100 people. Despite the dangers protesters faced and Putin's attempts to bring Ukraine back into the fold, the growing opposition eventually won this second Ukrainian revolution. Claiming that he feared for his life, on February 22, 2014, after signing a European-brokered agreement with opposition representatives, Yanukovych fled Ukraine, emerging as he sought asylum in Southern Russia. He was subsequently officially removed from the presidency in a vote by parliament.[31]

Almost at the same moment, "little green men," as Ukrainians called them at the time—soldiers without insignia on their olive-colored uniforms—appeared around Sevastopol on the Crimean Peninsula. These reportedly friendly fellows evidently spoke Russian and turned out to be Russian special forces troops; that they were Russian troops was first denied, but then confirmed by Putin's government that April. Putin's Russia had quietly, and relatively peacefully, invaded Ukraine and annexed Crimea. Russian authorities held a rump referendum in occupied Crimea in an attempt to make the takeover seem legitimate, although it was obviously in breach of international and Ukrainian law. Voters had the option to either choose for the peninsula to join Russia or to restore the 1992 Crimean constitution that had asserted Crimean sovereignty. There was no third option—to remain part of Ukraine. Beyond this, the election was neither free nor fair—armed guards manned polling stations, and there were reports of low turnout, and that some voters were not even citizens of Ukraine. Nonetheless, by mid-March 2014, representatives from a rump Crimean government and Russia had signed a treaty of accession, ratified by both houses of the Russian parliament by March 21. That was that. Russia had fully absorbed Crimea as a province by 2016, complete with a Kremlin-appointed governor. A bridge over the

Kerch strait was completed in May 2018 (a rail bridge was finished a year later), connecting Crimea to the mainland and built at the cost to the Russian state of about $3.7 billion by Stroygazmontazh, owned by Vladimir Putin's friend and former Judo partner, Arkady Rotenberg. Putin himself celebrated the bridge's completion by driving a truck over it on opening day.

In the late winter and spring of 2014, fighting broke out between pro-Russian separatists in Eastern Ukraine and the Ukrainian military. Russian authorities maintained (but denied) a military presence in the Donbas region of Ukraine to aid separatists and began referring to a large swath of Ukraine as "NovoRossiia," harkening back to an imperial, nationalist term for the broader region that included the Donbas as a natural part of the Russian nation. The conflict in the Donbas region heated and cooled from 2014 onward, despite European-brokered ceasefire agreements (Minsk I and Minsk II) that failed to end the conflict or restore the eastern border of Ukraine with Russia up to the time of writing in 20120 The United Nations estimated that almost 10,000 Ukrainian civilians perished in the fighting in the Donbas region, and another 21,000 were injured in the first two years of the conflict.[32] According to a leaked report, in 2015 the Russian military evidently paid compensation to about 2,000 families whose relatives were killed in battle (although the Russian military continued to deny any official presence in Eastern Ukraine).[33]

The Russian regime's strategy of maintaining conflict in Ukraine, especially the predominantly ethnically Russian part of the country, mimics its tactics in Georgia: keep the country off balance and ungovernable, and therefore less attractive for NATO or EU membership, while claiming to be acting to protect Russian ethnic minorities. But, as with Georgia, this strategy has had mixed results. Ukraine's first post-Maidan president, Petro Poroshenko, signed the Association Agreement with the EU in May 2015 as one of his first acts in office. Ukrainian popular opinion has become more in favor of EU membership since 2014,[34] and the NATO alliance has established a stronger presence in the border areas of Russia since the seizure of Crimea. Ukrainians seem to be more united than ever about turning to the West for economic development and state security. Yet more than six years after its initial annexation of Crimea, and the initiation of armed conflict in Donbas, Ukraine remained in a war with Russia that it could not afford. The ongoing conflict in the east forestalled Ukrainian economic development despite the election of a new president (Volodymyr Zelensky) and parliament in 2019 that appeared initially to be even more committed to establishing Ukraine as a European state, independent of Russian influence. Given the asymmetry between Russian and Ukrainian capacities, and flickering American support of Ukraine (especially during Donald Trump's presidency), the end of that conflict will likely be on Russian terms, or it will remain on a low boil indefinitely, as has the conflict between Russia and Georgia over Abkhazia and South Ossetia. It is clearly in the interest of Putin's regime to maintain the status quo in Ukraine and in Georgia—ongoing instability in both would ideally stop further integration into Western economic and security structures, as well as demonstrating to the Russian people that "color revolutions" bring only uncertainty and declining living standards. Thus, the continuing occupation of Georgian and Ukrainian territory supports the regime's domestic as well as foreign policy goals.

Moldova

Since the Soviet collapse, Russian interests and actions in Moldova have evolved slowly in parallel to events in the Baltic States, Georgia, and Ukraine. Unlike those states, however, Moldova does not share a physical border with Russia, and it does not have the same cultural resonance or political and economic importance in Russian minds as does Ukraine. In addition, the other five more liberalized states of the former Soviet Union have been more decisive in moving trade and foreign policy orientation westward. Contemporary Russia's main concerns in Moldova, as in Georgia, the Baltics, and Ukraine, are the gas lines that flow through the country; the status of ethnic Russians in Moldova's region of Transdniestria; and the economic and security drift of the country toward the EU and NATO.

Behind Armenia, Moldova is the second smallest of the former Soviet republics, and it is the only one to have become a parliamentary democracy (since 2000). As early as 1989, Moldovan leaders followed the example of Latvia, Lithuania, and Estonia by passing a language law that gave preference to Romanian over Russian, thus repudiating the Molotov-Ribbentrop pact (to which Moldova also had been subject).[35] Charles King notes that by 1989, most Moldovans spoke Moldovan (really Romanian) as their mother tongue, with Russian as a second language.[36] Moldovan leaders also joined their Baltic and Georgian colleagues in not participating in the 1991 All-Union referendum on the fate of the Soviet Union, already viewing Moldova as effectively independent. The adoption of Moldovan as the state language in 1989, however, presaged the outbreak of ethnic violence in the Transdniester and Gagauz regions. Protests and strikes by ethnic Russians in Transdniester in the east, and the Turkic Gagauz minority in southern Moldova, were aimed at changing the stringent language requirements for non-Moldovan speakers and required language tests for state employees. References to Russians in speeches and newspaper articles at the time as "the oppressors," according to King, demonstrate the anti-Russian dimension of the more extreme Moldovan nationalists.[37] In September 1990, Russian separatists in the east declared the establishment of the Dnestr Moldovan Republic, following the Gagauz declaration of their own republic a few days earlier.

In Transdniester in the spring and summer of 1991, a full military conflict broke out between Moldova and Russian-speaking separatists. In an arrangement foreshadowing the conflict in Eastern Ukraine almost twenty-five years later, the separatists received supplies and equipment from the remnants of the Soviet 46th Army, which had been based in the Transdniester area since the end of World War II and had become the Russian 14th Army after 1991. In July 1992, Transdniestria, backed by Russia, signed a peace agreement with Moldova, but only after Transdniestria, with Russian assistance, had cut gas and electricity supplies to Moldova. Although conflict ended in 1992, Transdniestria's contested status remained. As late as 2016, Russia continued to support Transdniestria financially, and Russian military equipment was still stationed in the region.

For Moldova, the permanent loss of Transdniestria had serious economic effects, in that much of the country's industrial sector was located in the region prior to 1992. Transdniestria itself is weakly governed, and is reputed to be a transit area for weapons, drugs, and organized crime.[38] In 2014, Transdniestria's Supreme Soviet requested that the region be allowed to formally join the Russian Federation, in the hope that the region could be annexed in the way that Russia had effectively annexed Crimea. Although at the time of writing Transdniestria remained part of Moldova officially, by all accounts Moscow effectively controls the area.

The parallels with Ukraine are not lost on Moldovan leaders, who now want their small country to turn more resolutely toward NATO and the EU.[39] Moldova signed a partnership and cooperation agreement with the EU in 1994 and became a member of the EU's Eastern Partnership in 2009, shortly after the election of more liberal parties to the Moldovan parliament and formation of an "Alliance for European Integration." In 2013, Moldova signed EU agreements on political reform and increased trade, and in 2014, it signed a Deep and Comprehensive Free Trade Agreement (DCFTA) that formally came into force on July 1, 2016. The agreement required Moldova to bring its laws and politics more firmly in line with those of the EU, including processes to strengthen democracy and the rule of law, enhance labor mobility, and maintain open borders.[40] In return, Moldova received ongoing EU assistance for public administration reform, agriculture, and industrial development, among other areas. Moscow, however, punished Moldova for signing these agreements by imposing a ban on Moldovan wine imports beginning in 2013, justified by the claim that Moldovan wine contained plastics. This was a repeat of the tactic used against both Georgia and Moldova in 2006, when the Kremlin punished both countries for leaning too far westward politically by banning imports of agricultural products, including wine. Both Georgia and Moldova subsequently diversified wine exports to lessen their dependency on the Russian market.

In sum, the Kremlin's concerns in Moldova are a milder version of its concerns in both Ukraine and Georgia: the incursion of the EU and NATO, control over trade and energy, the treatment of Russian diasporas, and the security of Russia's borders. But liberalization of Moldova was also a clear concern, as it was in Georgia and Ukraine. Not surprisingly, then, under Putin, Russia has projected its power in similar ways in all of these countries.

The Autocratic Post-Soviet States: Belarus, Armenia, Azerbaijan, Kazakhstan, Uzbekistan, Kyrgyzstan, Tajikistan, and Turkmenistan

In the remaining eight former Soviet republics whose political systems more closely resemble Russia's autocracy, trade relations and security ties are far stronger. Putin's Russia has exercised its influence in the former Soviet border states of Azerbaijan, Belarus, and Kazakhstan to a greater degree than in the Baltic States, and spreads its influence through economic and energy networks in many of the other former Soviet states with which it does not share borders—Armenia, Uzbekistan, Tajikistan, Kyrgyzstan, and, to a lesser extent, Turkmenistan. Even though these countries have more similar political systems to Russia's patronal autocracy, however, Russian influence over them has varied. (Note that Armenia underwent a peaceful "Velvet Revolution" in 2018 that led to a more reformist regime. By 2020 it was classified by Freedom House as "partly free" in the wake of national and local free and fair elections, but still struggling to reform the patronal autocracy that dominated its economics and politics for most of the three preceding decades.)[41] Energy and trade are the policy areas in which Russian government influence is felt most in these countries, and to a much lesser extent, the well-being of ethnic Russian diasporas and border security. NATO and the EU do not represent the same challenges to Russian influence in these states (although Armenia since 2019 has made steps toward closer association with the EU) as in the liberal-leaning Baltics, Ukraine, Georgia, and Moldova, but in Central Asia, China is an emerging trade rival.

Belarus

With Ukraine, Russian leadership considers Belarus the "inner sanctum" of its historical empire.[42] Russia, Ukraine, and Belarus were the three Slavic states at the core of the Soviet Union, and were three of the original signatories to the treaty forming the Commonwealth of Independent States (CIS), an initial attempt to create a trade and security organization following the Soviet collapse.

Culturally, there is little distinction between Belarusians and Russians; the vast majority of Belarusians speak Russian, and most are Russian Orthodox under the Moscow Patriarchate. In practice, Belarus has perhaps been the most tightly integrated with Russia politically and economically. There is no firm border or passport control between the two countries.[43]

Under its long-serving president, Aleksandr Lukashenko, Belarus has actively resisted the contagion of color revolutions that took hold in Ukraine and Georgia, and even a more modest liberalization of politics, as in Moldova.[44] For Putin's Russia, Belarus is not as strategically important as neighboring Ukraine, but has mostly been a staunch ally; throughout the 1990s and much of the early 2000s, Belarus was aligned closely with Russia economically and politically. In May 1995, shortly after his election as Belarusian president, Lukashenko held a referendum to change the Belarusian constitution to make Russian the country's official language, and also advocated for greater political and economic integration with Russia. He gained greater presidential power in another referendum in 1996, which effectively placed judicial and parliamentary authority under his office. As Vitali Silitski noted, "With the 1996 referendum, the institutionalization of personalistic authoritarian rule in Belarus was completed. The referendum eliminated all meaningful political competition and evicted the opposition from the decision-making process."[45] By the end of the 1990s, the degree of oppression of any form of opposition in Lukashenko's Belarus had earned it the distinction of being known as the last dictatorship in Europe.

Economically, Russia is Belarus's largest export market, making Belarus vulnerable to the kinds of trade sanctions Putin's regime has imposed on Ukraine, Moldova, and Georgia at various points since 2000. Unlike those other states, Belarus had no similar trade deals with the EU, solidifying its reliance on Russia. Still, Belarusian integration with the Russian economy in the 1999 Russo-Belarusian Union did not amount to much for either country, although the more recent Eurasian Economic Union, including Belarus, Russia, Kazakhstan, Kyrgyzstan, and Armenia, is potentially more significant because it required members to bring tariffs and trade laws into agreement.[46] The Belarusian economy is still largely Soviet in essence, marked by large, aging factories and relatively unreformed in terms of property rights and contracts.

One reason the initial Belarusian integration with Russia amounted to little is that Lukashenko's initial goal was not only to integrate Belarus with Russia through tighter cultural and economic ties, but also to position himself to succeed Boris Yeltsin as Russia's president.[47] Lukashenko managed to negotiate significant subsidies in gas and oil from Yeltsin, but when Vladimir Putin became Russia's president in 2000, Belarusian integration with Russia became less desirable for Lukashenko. In June 2002, Putin announced that under his administration, Russia would no longer subsidize the Belarusian economy in return for closer political union, and instead proposed to absorb Belarus into Russia as seven new provinces.[48] Understandably, this initiated an anti-Russian backlash in Belarus; Lukashenko had no intention of losing his presidency, even if it was only that of Belarus rather than Russia as a whole. As Putin eventually did with Russia, Lukashenko presented Belarusian survival as predicated on his enduring leadership. In his 2006 presidential campaign, he warned that if he lost the election, "we will lose the country."[49] In another parallel with Putin in Russia, Lukashenko introduced a bulwark of political and security measures to fend off any sort of Orange-style revolution in Belarus.[50]

Some analysts, like Vitali Silitski, have argued that this was the start of an "authoritarian international": Putin was gathering other autocrats, including Lukashenko, to form a coalition against the advance of democracy, since it would hurt Russian influence in former Soviet republics. As evidence, Silitski notes the Russian influence in the 2006 Belarusian elections to discredit the opposition.[51] Also in 2006, before the presidential elections, Putin's regime froze gas prices in Belarus at a level far lower than in Ukraine or Moldova, making it possible for Lukashenko to argue that he had managed the Belarusian economy effectively. Despite this, the Kremlin has raised gas prices several times in Belarus, even when Lukashenko was closely aligned with Putin's government, as in 2007. While this proved difficult for Belarus, parallel situations in Georgia and Ukraine were more extreme: Gazprom more than doubled Ukraine's price from $50 per tcm to $130 per tcm between December 31, 2005 and January 1, 2007, and Georgia's was raised from $100 per tcm to $235 per tcm in the same period, while Belarus paid the least at $46 per tcm in 2005 and $100 per tcm in 2007.[52] Further, Russian subsidies on oil exports to Belarus were so high that Belarus could sell extra oil for revenue to make up for the increased gas prices.

Despite some obvious parallels in regime type and practices in Belarus and Russia, Belarus attempted for a time (until the popular protests against his re-election in the summer of 2020), since Putin's offer to merge Belarus into Russia, to drift away from Russian economic and political dominance,[53] though with mixed results, especially in comparison to the Baltics, Georgia, and Ukraine. In 2010, relations hit an at all-time low when Lukashenko reneged on his promise to recognize South Ossetia and Abkhazia as independent states. He also made separate attempts to engage the EU and China in trade deals,[54] and bought oil from Venezuela to make up for Russian attempts to punish Belarus by shorting the country on oil supply. Also against Moscow's wishes, Lukashenko gave sanctuary to the former president of Kyrgyzstan, Kurmanbek Bakiyev, after the latter's ouster in 2010. But, as in the Central Asian states, Belarus has played East and West off one another, as well as Russia. For example, Russia extended Belarus a $2 billion aid package after the 2009 economic crisis, but Lukashenko also managed to get a larger aid package, of $3.5 billion, from the International

Monetary Fund.[55] In response, Putin's regime did not support Lukashenko in his 2010 presidential re-election campaign, but he won anyway.

In 2012, Dmitri Trenin noted, "Moscow lost a handle on Minsk, which, rather than buckling under pressure, is exploring an array of partnership options—from China and Venezuela to the European Union and the United States."[56] Unlike Moldova, Georgia, and Ukraine, however, Belarus under Lukashenko is an unlikely future partner for the EU, since the EU accession process would require an opening of Belarusian politics in a way that would loosen Lukashenko's tight grip on the country and possibly bring about his ouster. As a result, as was the case in the late summer and autumn of 2020, Lukashenko once again turned back to Putin to help him stay in power such that Putin offered (and Lukashenko accepted) to use the Russian military should unrest in Belarus grow.[57] The European Union also placed sanctions on his regime following his crackdown on civilian protesters in early October 2020, thereby ending Lukashenko's earlier efforts to play Russia and Europe off one another to his advantage. This has returned Belarus under Lukashenko to a situation of extreme political dependence on Putin's Russia.

Armenia and Azerbaijan

Of the three former Soviet republics in the Caucasus—Armenia, Azerbaijan, and Georgia—Armenia is the most closely tied to Russia's economy. Some analysts claim that Russian involvement is so significant in Armenia's economy "that lack of sovereignty should be Armenia's number one concern."[58] This is a dramatic shift from 1991, when leaders in Armenia, with Georgia, Moldova, and the Baltics, refused to participate in the referendum on the Soviet Union's existence because these countries' leaders insisted that they were not legitimately part of the Soviet Union at the time.

The size of Russian investments in Armenia is not that great in absolute terms, but Armenia's economy is so much smaller than Russia's that Russian state and private interests garner outsized influence as a result. For example, Gazprom, through its Armenian subsidiary ArmRosGazprom, controls 80% of Armenia's energy structure, "including the majority of the Iran-Armenia gas pipeline, thus ensuring that Armenia cannot become an independent transit country" for Iranian gas.[59] Russian firms also have controlling interests in Armenian nuclear and hydroelectric power markets, and Russian companies own 70% of the Armenian airline Armavia and 70% of the Armenian Savings Bank. In addition, Russian-owned businesses reportedly invested $570 million in the Armenian national railway, have majority stakes in Armenian mining holdings, and significant holdings in the communications sector. In 2018, Armenian exports to Russia were purportedly 28% of its total exports; and imports from Russia were roughly 25% of its total exports. Heightening Armenia's economic dependence on Russia is the ongoing conflict with neighboring Azerbaijan over the Armenian enclave within Azerbaijan of Nagorno-Karabakh (explained in greater detail below). This has limited Armenian access to trade with Azerbaijan and its big ally, Turkey.[60] As with other favored (and autocratic) former Soviet states from which Russia seeks and gains cooperation, such as Belarus, Armenia has received financing from Russia at critical moments for its economy, including a $500 million loan from Russia to ease its financial crisis in 2010.[61]

The Kremlin has less influence over Azerbaijan than over Armenia, having no controlling presence in the Azeri gas industry and control over only one pipeline running through Azerbaijan's territory, the Baku-Novorossisk. That said, Putin's regime has significant leverage over Azerbaijan in supplying half of its gas, and Russia's United Energy Systems has a stake in Azerbaijan's state-controlled electricity monopoly.[62] So, in Armenia and Azerbaijan, as in the Baltics, Georgia, Ukraine, Moldova, and Belarus, Moscow's leverage is significant in no small part due to legacy infrastructure from the Soviet period.

Another significant influence is the economic importance of remittances sent home from workers from the Caucasus and Central Asia with jobs in Russia. This is a major factor in nine of the former Soviet Republics, including Armenia, Azerbaijan, and Georgia, but also Moldova and the five Central Asian states. According to the World Bank, a startling 8.46% of Armenia's GDP was made up of remittances from Armenians working in Russia in 2017, the last year for which data was available. Moldova was at 5.5%, while Georgia and Azerbaijan were less dependent, at 6.46% and 1.91%, respectively. The Central Asian republics of Kyrgyzstan and Tajikistan were particularly vulnerable, with over 24.74% and 23.78% of their GDPs, respectively, coming from remittances from migrant workers living in Russia (see table 2.2). When economies are highly dependent on remittances from a single country, they are particularly vulnerable to currency fluctuations such as those Russia endured in 2014, when the ruble lost over half its value. Economies dependent on workers abroad are also vulnerable to any changes the host country might make in immigration and labor policy.

The Eurasian Economic Union, pushed by Putin's administration since his 2012 return to the presidency, is another instrument by which the Russian government has attempted to formalize its influence over weaker Caucasian and Central Asian states. In autumn of 2013, the Kremlin successfully pressured Armenia to join the Eurasian Economic Union rather than pursuing political association and economic integration with the EU, at about the same time Putin was pressuring then Ukrainian President Yanukovych to abandon similar policies of European integration. Yanukovych's eventual decision to abandon EU accession plans for Ukraine sparked the EuroMaidan demonstrations in November

Table 2.2 Remittances from Migrant Workers to Former Soviet States, 1995–2017

Country	1995	2000	2005	2010	2014	2017	% of GDP Total Remittances 2017	% of Total Remittances from Russia 2017	% of GDP from Russian Remittances 2017
Armenia	65	87	915	1,669	2,079	1,539	13.30%	63.61%	8.46%
Azerbaijan	3	57	623	1,410	1,846	1,050	2.80%	68.10%	1.91%
Belarus	29	140	199	575	1,231	1,200	23.00%	45.42%	10.45%
Estonia	1	4	264	357	544	559	1.90%	28.98%	0.55%
Georgia	0	210	446	1,184	1,986	1,794	11.00%	58.70%	6.46%
Kazakhstan	116	122	62	226	229	355	1.30%	63.66%	0.83%
Kyrgyzstan	1	9	313	1,266	2,243	2,486	32.30%	76.59%	24.74%
Latvia	0	72	1,209	1,258	1,774	1,090	4.20%	24.31%	1.02%
Lithuania	1	50	745	1,673	2,113	1,302	2.70%	11.29%	0.30%
Moldova	1	179	915	1,351	2,084	1,640	16.90%	32.50%	5.49%
Tajikistan	0	0	467	2,306	3,384	2,220	31.30%	75.99%	23.78%
Turkmenistan	0	0	0	35	35	10	0.00%	100.00%	0.00%
Ukraine	0	33	2,408	6,535	7,354	7,895	10.80%	51.21%	5.53%
Uzbekistan	0	0	0	2,858	5,828	2,839	12.10%	100.00%	12.10%

Source: http://www.worldbank.org/en/topic/migrationremittancesdiasporaissues/brief/migration-remittances-data, accessed July 1, 2020. (Remittances in millions of dollars in reported year dollars.)

2013 that would lead to his ouster in February 2014. Armenia was in a different position at that point, but after the Velvet Revolution 2018, its new political leadership rekindled interest in closer association with the EU through the EU-Armenia Comprehensive and Enhanced Partnership Agreement (CEPA).

Given the extent of Russian ownership of the Armenian economy, Russian is still the language of business, but Russia's available influence over Armenian politics and economics is not enhanced by ethnic or cultural ties as it is in former Soviet republics like Ukraine or Belarus: Armenians are Orthodox Christians, but not Russian Orthodox.

In addition to economic leverage, the Russian military maintains significant security resources in Armenia. Since 1996, Gyumri and Erebuni have acted as staging bases, including in Russia's intervention in Syria in 2015; there, Russia has stationed several thousand troops, along with MiG 29 fighter jets, helicopter gunships, and aerial drones. Since 1994, Russia's military has provided troops to patrol the Armenian borders with Iran and Turkey, as well as supplying Armenia with weapons, including the sale of a reported $200 million in arms in 2016. Visa-free travel is another way in which the Kremlin has rewarded Armenia's leaders for their continuing loyalty to Russia.

Another lever of security influence is Armenia's membership in the Collective Security Treaty Organization (CSTO), on which basis Putin's administration made a security guarantee to defend Armenia should it be attacked by Azerbaijan over Nagorno-Karabakh, a region physically located within Azerbaijan, but populated primarily by Armenians.[63] Some analysts think, however, that this is a largely meaningless guarantee, because Russia would have to transport troops to Armenia through a likely uncooperative Georgia and its airspace, and also because the other Central Asian states who are signatories to the CSTO would not support a war against Azerbaijan (a gas customer for Kazakhstan, for example).[64] Indeed in the 2016 and 2020 flare ups between the two sides, Moscow called for a ceasefire rather than providing troops to the Armenian side. The Kremlin's primary interest in Nagorno-Karabakh is maintaining stability between Azerbaijan and Armenia in order to protect oil pipelines that run through the region, rather than actually resolving the conflict in Armenia's favor.

Moscow has looser ties to Azerbaijan than to Armenia, having little cultural influence and relatively less economic pull. Azerbaijan's population is predominantly Muslim, but largely secular in government (relative to the Central Asian states, for example). As noted earlier, although Azerbaijan's economy is enhanced by remittances from Azeri workers in Russia, it is not as dependent on these as is Armenia. Azerbaijan is also not a member of the Eurasian Economic Union, nor is it covered by the CSTO. Its abundant oil and gas reserves in the Caspian Sea have meant that it does not have the same economic dependence on Russia that Armenia has. But Azerbaijan, like Russia, is a resource-dependent economy and therefore subject to the boom-and-bust cycles of global oil and gas demand and pricing. Perhaps because its oil and gas resources give Azerbaijan a potentially independent basis for its foreign relations with Europe, Turkey, Iran, and the United States, Putin backed Azerbaijan's strongman, Ilham Aliyev, when his father and president since 1993, Heydar Aliyev, left office in ill health in 2003. Still, there are significant disputes between Azerbaijan and Russia. Beyond Russia's support for Armenia on the issue of Nagorno-Karabakh, Russia and Azerbaijan have been in a decades-long dispute over maritime claims to oil and gas in the Caspian Sea. Azerbaijan has also pursued an independent foreign policy with Europe and could be an alternative to Russian-supplied gas for the EU. China is another market for Azeri energy resources, and provides Azerbaijan with further economic alternatives to Russian influence. In sum, Azerbaijan has far more economic and political independence from Russian influence than does Armenia.

Central Asia

Russian influence in the five Central Asian states of Kazakhstan, Kyrgyzstan, Uzbekistan, Turkmenistan, and Tajikistan remains considerable—and usually, but not always, decisive. As Alex Cooley notes, other powerful actors, like China and the United States, compete with Russia in Central Asia for trade, security, and political influence.[65] But the five Central Asian states have been able to leverage this "great power" competition for greater individual gains.[66] This has meant that Russian influence declined in Central Asia in the decade immediately following the Soviet collapse, although it recovered considerably thereafter and, despite competition from China in particular in the region, remained highly influential. The purposes of the exercise of Russian power in Central Asia, however, are somewhat different from those in the six states that have democratic governments, in the case of the Baltics, or liberalizing political tendencies, as in Georgia, Ukraine, and Moldova.

As under Putin's regime, all five Central Asian states are governed through various forms of autocracy, and therefore the Kremlin's relations with them are not complicated by conflicts over political liberalization or human rights. Russian trade with and aid to these states does not come with the strings of political rights and freedoms that American or European offers of assistance might carry.[67] Moreover, the treatment of ethnic Russians—an issue of much concern to Russia's leadership in the Baltics, and the pretext for military intervention in Moldova, Georgia, and Ukraine—does not receive particular attention in Central Asia. While the large (though decreasing) Russian diaspora in Kazakhstan has pushed for greater independence and guarantees of cultural and language rights, Putin has not typically encouraged them due to the overriding need to keep Kazakhstan a stable and reliable partner in trade and security. This also meant supporting the aging president, Nursultan Nazarbayev, until his resignation in March 2019 (although he stayed on as lifetime head of Kazakhstan's security council). Stability in Kazakhstan trumped the issue of the Russian diaspora's well-being because of key issues related to border security and energy policy in Central Asia, especially due to drug trafficking through Afghanistan and Russia's increased problems related to heroin and AIDS. These legitimate concerns, as well as trade interests for Russian firms, shape much of the Kremlin's policy in Central Asia. But the fact that Kazakhstan is an autocracy that is familial in its patronalism is important for the Kremlin's policy too. It presents a positive paradigm of autocratic government that is familiar to Putin's administration, and does not present a threat to the Russian domestic status quo in its model of politics.

The Russian empire first established a foothold in Central Asia in the nineteenth century, and under a reviving economy, Putin has sought to re-establish Russia's historical influence in this area. In part, this is a result of a recognizable security objective of maintaining a buffer zone between the Russian heartland and any Islamic insurgency in southern Central Asia and Afghanistan. But security is not the regime's only interest in Central Asia. The Kremlin is also concerned with guiding and, to some degree, controlling the oil and gas riches of the region and the pipelines running through Central Asia so that the fossil fuels industry in these countries supports Russian oil and gas companies, rather than competing with them on world markets.[68]

Until 2005, Russian border guards also patrolled the frontier between Tajikistan and Afghanistan, and foreign officials have raised the possibility of reinstituting this patrol function.[69] Indeed, in preparation for the planned (but abandoned) pullout of US forces from Afghanistan in 2014, the Russian government under Putin developed stronger bilateral ties with Kyrgyzstan and Tajikistan in particular, and became increasingly responsible for their border security. According to the United Nations Office on Drugs and Crime, about one-third of Afghan-exported heroin runs through Central Asia and into Russia.[70] In the later 2000s, Russia became the largest market for Afghan opiates.[71] There was a growing Russian HIV/AIDS epidemic fueled by heroin injection and so Russian policymakers became more serious about stemming the tide of Afghan exports of the drug northward. Part of the effort to combat the influx of heroin through porous Central Asian and Russian borders has included Russian-instituted "quadrilateral summits," which also include Pakistan, Afghanistan, and Tajikistan, and are focused on counter-narcotics and anti-smuggling. In 2013, about 6% of the Russian population was classified as drug-addicted, according to Russia's Drug Control Service, and by 2019, the United Nations reported that 43% of all drug addicted people globally resided in just three countries: China, Russia, and the United States.[72] In view of the growing addiction crisis in

Russia, Stephen Blank at the US Army War College notes that there was a shift in the Russian position on drug trafficking, which formerly involved publicly expressing concern, but doing little to actually stem the tide of drugs flowing from Afghanistan. By 2012, the Russian government was getting more serious about anti-trafficking, and according to Blank, "[t]he Kremlin's [previous] re-calcitrance had been mainly rooted in concern that the US footprint in Central Asia would grow too big."[73] As the American presence in Afghanistan declined thereafter, Russian policymakers became ever more concerned with opium and heroine exports from the region into Russia. This led to deepening partnerships with governments in Uzbekistan and Tajikistan to stem the flow of narcotics into Russia by providing Russian military assistance and technical support to seize and destroy illicit drugs flowing out of Afghanistan, with notable success.[74]

Beyond the need to combat the growing drug trade, Russian policymakers were becoming increasingly nervous about Bush's "Freedom Agenda" as a democracy-promoting policy aimed at Russia's periphery, and perhaps at Russia itself. This fear was supported by the "Tulip Revolution," a color revolution–style uprising in Kyrgyzstan in 2005, that ousted reformer-turned-kleptocrat Askar Akayev and ushered in a more liberal, pro-American regime under Kurmanbek Bakiyev. Bakiyev's administration, however, soon devolved into a repressive re-gime that continually stole state assets. Bakiyev himself was ousted in 2010 with at least passive Russian support, and replaced with successively softer forms of autocracy. As illustrated in figure 2.1, Kyrgyzstan is the only one of the five Central Asian countries that is not classified as a consolidated autocracy in being classified as "partly free" rather than "not free" by 2019.[75]

Under Putin, Russian government suspicions about American intentions in Central Asia—specifically, that the United States might refuse to leave Central Asia and could use Afghanistan as a further excuse to erode its influence—led to further security manipulations.[76] In 2005, Russian officials directly interfered to bring about the American loss of the K2 airbase in Uzbekistan and attempted to effect the loss of access to the Manas airbase in Kyrgyzstan as well. Both were im-portant for the US staging of troops and supplies going into Afghanistan, espe-cially as Pakistan became a less reliable partner. The K2 base closure came on the heels of the US condemnation of then–Uzbek president Islam Karimov's May 2005 crackdown on demonstrators in the city of Andijon, Uzbekistan, where between 300 and 1,500 people were killed by government troops. Karimov refused to submit to an international commission of inquiry as proposed by the United States and EU. Although relations between them were not always warm, Putin's regime stood by Karimov's claim that he was defending Uzbekistan from extremism. By July 2005, Karimov announced that the United States should leave the K2 base. Later that year, Russia and Uzbekistan signed a "Treaty of Friendship."

Similarly, in 2009, then-president of Kyrgyzstan Kurmanbek Bakiyev used the base as an opportunity to play the United States against Russia in an attempt to get the best deal for himself and his country. Manas had become the main transit point for NATO troops and supplies after the K2 closure. In February 2009, shortly after Obama's inauguration, Bakiyev announced that the base would be closed. That same day, Moscow offered a $2 billion loan to Kyrgyzstan. It looked as though Bakiyev had effectively been paid by Russia to close the US base. The United States managed to renegotiate the base contract, and by June 2009, Bakiyev had extracted an agreement for three times the original rent for the base and reversed the decision to close it. As noted earlier, Bakiyev was ousted in 2010 with at least tacit Russian support.[77]

Putin's Russia is in competition with China for influence over Kyrgyzstan, Uzbekistan and Tajikistan in particular. Notably, following the Russian-Georgian conflict in 2008, China pointedly refused to condone the Russian regime's recognition of North Ossetia and Abkhazia as independent. This led the Central Asian members of the Shanghai Cooperation Organization (discussed in detail later in this chapter) to take a stand against Moscow by also denying recognition to these republics of Georgia. Without China acting as buffer, however, it is unlikely that the Central Asian states would have opposed Moscow in this regard.

Uzbekistan under Islam Karimov was strictly authoritarian, and the long-serving president (until his death in office in August 2016) was strongly supported by Russia's leadership, although the relationship was often fractious in the last decade. Support for Karimov was largely due to the fact that Uzbekistan, much like Kazakhstan, is a linchpin for Russian security, although, unlike Kazakhstan, there is no Russian-Uzbek border. Uzbekistan does have borders, however, with the four other Central Asian countries as well as Afghanistan, and it straddles the unstable region of the Ferghana valley. The Kremlin fears the resurgence of Islamic terrorism in Uzbekistan and Tajikistan—a threat that is possibly overplayed for the sake of maintaining authoritarian regimes there that are friendly to a Russian presence on their borders. After the ethnic riots and shootings in Andijan in 2005, Putin's regime took advantage of Western condemnation to sign a friendship treaty with Uzbekistan, and the Uzbeks formally joined the CSTO (Uzbekistan had had a "suspended membership" from 1999 until 2006, and quit again in 2012).

Tajikistan suffered from civil war between 1992 and 1997, and Russian forces have intermittently helped maintain border security since then. But the Tajiks have shown a willingness to take aid offered by the West, as well as by Russia. According to Alexander Cooley, Tajik president Rahmon has "mastered the art of appealing to different international partners."[78] Neither Tajikistan nor Kyrgyzstan has significant oil and gas reserves in comparison to their Central Asian or Caspian Sea neighbors, but Putin's regime has nonetheless intervened in what resources they do have. Gazprom has a majority interest in exploring Tajikistan's Sariqamish gas field, and also significant interests in the Kyrgyz gas companies Kygryzgas and Kyrgyzneftegas (gas and oil company). Russian firms also have significant stakes in Kyrgyz and Tajik hydroelectric sectors, which affects Uzbekistan's water supply, arguably giving Russia further leverage there.

Despite the death of its first harshly autocratic leader, Saparmurat Niyazov, Turkmenistan remains isolated even from warm relations with its Central Asian neighbors, as well as from Putin's Russia, for the most part. But given Turkmenistan's location and borders with Afghanistan and Iran, Russian leadership views the country's stability, even in harshly authoritarian conditions, as a bulwark of security against Islamic extremists in Afghanistan, the flow of illegal drugs, and Iranian incursion into the region. Most important is Russian stability. Russia's main area of engagement with Turkmenistan has been in the area of gas supply. In the 2000s, in order to keep up with European demand for gas and sustain his regime's need to maintain high economic growth, Putin negotiated a series of contracts with Turkmenistan, Kyrgyzstan, and Uzbekistan to make up for the shortfall in Russian production, and re-exported gas purchased from Central Asia to the European market. The arrangement became problematic for Putin's administration, however, when the 2008 global economic crisis hit, and gas demand (and therefore gas prices) dropped precipitously. Putin's government was left paying more for Turkmen, Kyrgyz, and Uzbek gas than it was receiving from European customers. Even with the Kremlin's available levers of influence over these governments—in particular, their dependence on remittances from migrants working in Russia—the contract prices held up.

Since the Soviet collapse, although Russia under Putin has significant economic influence and a level of security presence in Central Asia, the states have, to varying degrees, carved out some independent foreign policies to play the "great powers" around them off one another. China in particular is a significant alternative collaborator for Central Asian states, and is now the biggest trading partner for the region as a whole. In 2010, China surpassed Russia in trade volume with Kazakhstan, Kyrgyzstan, and Turkmenistan, with China at $24 billion in 2010 vs. Russia at $22 billion.[79] Russia's investment in Central Asia, however, crosses far more sectors of the economy than does China's, with involvement in energy, mining, telecom, transportation, construction, agriculture, and the military industry. Further, Russian investors are far less risk-averse than Chinese or Western ones, for example, and are willing to brave the endemic corruption that pervades most Central Asian economies—they deal with it at home too, after all.

Other economic factors are also at play. Grain dependence on Russia is one; while Central Asia relies on Kazakhstan for grain, when there is not a bumper crop there, they must import from Russia at Russian-determined prices.

Kyrgyzstan and Tajikistan are also particularly economically dependent on remittances from Russia. As noted earlier, while the flow of remittances from Kyrgyz and Tajik workers in Russia back to their homelands has smoothed over significant cracks in these economies, it makes them extremely dependent on Russian immigration and taxation laws, and changes in the Russian economy more drastically impact the Kyrgyz and Tajik economies, for better or worse, as demonstrated after the 2008 and 2014 financial crises.

Culturally, Russian influence remains significant in Central Asia, given the legacy of Russian nationalities policies and, in the case of Kazakhstan, the high proportion of the population that is still ethnically Russian. But over the last decade in particular, there have been clear attempts to "de-Russify." Uzbekistan and Turkmenistan, for example, have gotten rid of Cyrillic script in favor of Latin script. Nonetheless, the Russian language is still important in the region, and Russian TV has spread into Kazakhstan, Uzbekistan, and Tajikistan. In Kyrgyzstan most TV is in Russian, and although in Turkmenistan it is not legal for citizens to receive Russian TV, it is widely watched by satellite. Television, then, is a powerful tool for Russian interests and political hegemony in Central Asia. Despite China's growing influence, few Central Asians speak or understand Mandarin. The predominance of Russian-language media gives Russia an advantage in maintaining cultural dominance in daily life in much of Central Asia.

In sum, the autocratic states of Central Asia are both pushed and pulled toward closer relations with the Russian Federation. They have little interest in the political reform that stronger relations with Europe or the United States would require. While they still need Russian security guarantees, in the economic sphere, China is a clear trade and investment alternative, a fact all five states have been willing to leverage in dealings with Moscow. Still, there is a more comfortable dependence among Central Asian leaders on Putin's Russia than in any other region of the former Soviet Union.

Regional Economic and Security Associations

Beyond bilateral relations with each of the other individual successor states of the Soviet Union, Russia under Putin has created several regional trade, security, and political associations to counter Chinese, American, and European influence in the areas Russia's leadership considers within its historical sphere of interest. Some of these organizations have already been mentioned, but it is worth looking at each in greater depth to demonstrate the other tools the Kremlin has available in pursuing its economic, security, and political interests in the post-Soviet region.

On December 8, 1991, mere weeks before the Soviet Union collapsed, the leaders of Russia, Ukraine, and Belarus signed an agreement creating the Commonwealth of Independent States (CIS). Armenia, Kazakhstan, Kyrgyzstan, Moldova, Tajikistan, and Uzbekistan were also initial members, and Azerbaijan and Georgia joined in 1993. The agreement initially maintained open borders (including visa-free travel for citizens of member states), the ruble, and a transitional security system such that the Soviet military stationed in all three of the founding new states came under joint command. The idea was not to replicate the Soviet system, but to establish a new political and economic framework that would enable the successor states to establish themselves as independent, though still interdependent in some areas. The CIS was never particularly effective, however. The Baltics never joined, their leaders having set their sights firmly on the EU; Georgia left the organization in 2009, following the war with Russia; and Turkmenistan declared itself to have "observer status" only.[80] Moreover, the Commonwealth's purpose was never well-defined, and there was more than a tinge of Russian imperialism to the organization from its inception.

But other regional organizations worked slightly better once the CIS was discarded in 2001. Cooley argues that Putin's rise to the presidency played a role in the trajectory of these organizations, and interest in security in Central Asia also increased after the US invasion of Afghanistan in November 2001.[81] The Collective Security Treaty Organization (CSTO in English, ODKB in Russian) was established in May 2002 to focus on Russian security policy in Central Asia in particular. This group initially included Russia, Kazakhstan, Kyrgyzstan, Tajikistan, Armenia, and Belarus. Uzbekistan joined in 2006, but had rocky relations with the organization after 2009 over the Collective Rapid Reaction Force (CCRF) proposed by Russia following its war with Georgia. The CCRF would be composed primarily of 10,000 Russian troops, with another 4,000 or so Kazakh troops and a battalion from each of the other members of the CSTO. Uzbekistan, however, had concerns about integrating militaries, especially with Kazakhstan. Under Karimov, Uzbekistan ultimately quit the CSTO in 2012.

The CSTO charter was amended several times, but in 2011 it was reinterpreted such that the organization could act collectively should one member state be threatened by domestic upheaval, as occurred in Osh in Kyrgyzstan. This followed Vladimir Putin's decision not to send CSTO troops to quell the ethnic violence.[82] The main advantages for the Kremlin in terms of expending its power over CSTO member states is that the treaty framework has enabled the Russian military to establish bases throughout Central Asia. Further, following the upheaval and disagreements between Russia, Uzbekistan, and Kyrgyzstan on the US use of military bases in the region, Article 7 of the CSTO charter was amended in 2011 to require "urgent consultation and the adoption of a resolution" between member states regarding the "placement in their territories of groups of armies (forces), objects of military infrastructure of the states which are not members of the Organization."[83] This formalized Russian control over the possible establishment of permanent military bases in Central Asia by the United States or Europe, an important lever after the eventual withdrawal of US forces from Afghanistan.

The CSTO has a weak mutual security guarantee that is a pale imitation of NATO's Article 5, "an attack on one member is an attack on all." The CSTO charter indicates in Chapter 2, Article 3 that "The goals of the Organization shall be the strengthening of peace, international and regional security and stability, *protection of independence on a collective basis, territorial integrity and sovereignty of the Member States,* in achievement of which the Member States prefer political means."[84] This is far from an unequivocal guarantee of mutual aid if one member is attacked. Further, it is doubtful that any such guarantee would actually work in practice. For example, it is difficult to imagine the Muslim states of Kazakhstan and Uzbekistan actually coming to the aid of Orthodox Christian Armenia over a conflict with Azerbaijan, a fellow Muslim state.[85]

Although the CSTO has not evolved into a genuine collective security enterprise, it has enabled Putin's Russia to extend its power over Central Asian states. China could establish itself as a competitor, in part through the Shanghai Cooperation Organization in the region, and the CSTO does not preclude its Central Asian member states from deepening their individual ties with China, but as chapter 3 discusses more, Russia under Putin has sought to cooperate rather than compete with China in Central Asia.

A second regional organization led and created by Putin's regime is the Eurasian Economic Union (EEU), which was established in 2014 and superseded the Eurasian Economic Community (EurAsEC) in 2015. The EEU is intended both as a counterpart to the CSTO and as a counterweight to the EU for the former Soviet states. The predecessor organization, EurAsEC, initiated in 2000, replaced the CIS Customs Union of Russia, Belarus, and Kazakhstan, as well as the Central Asian Economic Cooperation Organization. When the initial agreement to form the Eurasian Economic Union was announced in May 2014, with Belarus, Kazakhstan, and Russia as founding members, Putin explained, "Today we are creating a powerful, attractive center of economic development, a big regional market that unites more than 170 million people."[86] Absent at the creation, however, was Ukraine and its population of 42 million people; it was this economic association that Putin, in the autumn of 2013 and winter of 2014, was pushing Yanukovych of Ukraine to join as a fourth founding member rather than signing an association agreement with the EU; EuroMaidan arose in opposition to that pressure, as explained earlier in this chapter. Moldova has also continued to avoid membership in favor of association with the EU. Armenia, however, under tremendous pressure from Russia's regime, along with Kyrgyzstan, joined the EEU in 2014, extending the market to 182 million people. Following its "Velvet Revolution" of 2018, Armenia showed renewed interest, however, in some form of association with the EU.

Historically, the Russian leadership's attempts to create trade and security associations among post-Soviet states have not been particularly successful, but the EEU has a far more expansive and ambitious institutional framework to better integrate regional economies; the Eurasian Economic Commission, for instance, is presumably fashioned after the European Economic Commission.[87] The fact that all of the five members of the Eurasian Economic Union are various forms of autocracies (with Kyrgyzstan and Armenia classified as "partly free" by Freedom House in 2019)[88] may also help also in making the Union more coherent. Members of the EEU do not have to deal with the political demands of an organization like the EU, or worry about conforming to a system of competitive, pluralistic politics or common human rights policies. The prime minister of Kazakhstan indicated that this was an attraction when the deal forming the Union was signed, saying, "We are not creating a political organization; we are forming a purely economic union. . . . It is a pragmatic means to get benefits. We don't meddle into what Russia is doing politically, and they cannot tell us what foreign policy to pursue."[89]

The EEU is not clearly economically advantageous to any country but Russia, in that it tightly binds smaller economies to Russia's larger one. Since 2012, members have also received economic aid from the Kremlin, through the EEU's predecessor EurAsEC, to ease the contagion effects of downturns in the Russian economy.[90]

For Moscow, the creation of the EEU is an obvious attempt to counterbalance the sanctions regime imposed by the EU and the United States as retribution for the Russian annexation of Crimea in 2014, not to mention Russia's own counter-sanctions on Europe. Beyond this, the creation of the EEU is part of Putin's attempt to establish Russia as a central pole in a multipolar world— with the United States, the EU, and China serving as the other key poles. But the weakness of the EEU members' economies, with the partial exception of Kazakhstan, means that the economic rivalry is not particularly sharp.

For Kazakhstan, Kyrgyzstan, Belarus, and Armenia, however, the EEU represents a form of Russian control over those states' economic policies, as well as a mechanism for drawing them into greater trade and financial economic dependence on Russia, rather than China or Europe. Membership in the EEU, for example, imposes high tariffs on member trade with non-EEU members (like China). Nonetheless, as the preceding section demonstrates, the other non-Russian members of the EEU have still been able to maintain some independence in their foreign policies, despite the Kremlin's efforts to more tightly integrate them with Russia.

Conclusion

Particularly under the latter part of Vladimir Putin's long rule, Russia has clearly become established as a regional hegemon in terms of available power resources in its "near abroad," and in its willingness to use them. Russia's population dwarfs that of its nearest neighbors, and thus its television and radio broadcasts help citizens of countries in its neighborhood see the world the Kremlin's way. Financial injections into the organizations belonging to preferred candidates, while providing damaging stories in the traditional media and through Internet platforms, also help Moscow retain significant influence over those states' domestic politics (a theme to which we will return in chapter 7). Putin's regime stemmed and reversed the receding tide of Russian influence in the 1990s in these countries by leveraging control over legacy infrastructure like gas and oil pipelines and latent supply dependency to get their leaders to adopt Russia-friendly policies. Beyond this, the Kremlin has punished those that have continued to pull away, like Ukraine, Georgia, Latvia, Lithuania, Estonia, and Moldova, with trade sanctions, cyber espionage, and, in three cases, military invasion and occupation of territory. Yet, for the most part, policymakers in these countries have managed to maintain policies that Putin's regime attempted to reverse. Ukraine, Georgia, and Moldova, however, remain particularly vulnerable to the Kremlin's interference, since, unlike the Baltic States, none are members of NATO or the EU. For this reason, among others, as chapter 3 explains in greater detail, Putin's Russia has sought to create tension within the EU.

The Russian government and state-owned (and some private) firms retain significant financial leverage over the poorer states of Central Asia, although this has not stopped their leaders from some economic and security flirtations with China in particular, and the West more intermittently. Still, Russian policy scope is sweeping and very weighty in Central Asia and the South Caucasus (with the exception of Georgia), despite some early fluctuations.

Moreover, relative to the Soviet period, the influence of Russia as the core of the empire decreased considerably in the 1990s, but rebounded as the Russian economy grew quickly after 2003, and as Putin's regime became a consolidated autocracy. The Kremlin has used carrots and sometimes heavy sticks to maintain the loyalties of post-Soviet leaders and to keep others incapable of joining the EU or NATO. Russian power in its immediate neighborhood is hugely significant and usually, though not always, decisive. Putin's regime has the ability and the will to seriously disrupt and even control politics and economics in the post-Soviet region, and proved more likely to do so where their governments have sought to liberalize or democratize their political systems. If they can be kept politically and economically unstable, then they remain less of a threat to the political status quo within Russia itself. The next chapter explores more of Russia's resurrected geographic domain and policy influence in other parts of the world.

3

Where (Else) in the World Is Russia?

"At last Russia has returned to the world arena as a strong state—a country that others heed and that can stand up for itself."
—Vladimir Putin, 2008

In 2014, President Barack Obama infamously referred to Russia as a "regional power, that is threatening some of its immediate neighbors—not out of strength, but out of weakness."[1] Chapter 2 demonstrated that Putin's Russia is the predominant power in its own neighborhood, and has both the will and the means to disrupt politics and economics in the former Soviet region. After 2012, however, with Putin firmly back in the Kremlin, the Russian government has become far more than merely the hegemon within its immediate environs. Although it does not have the geographic domain of power of the Soviet Union, it has established significant abilities to influence policy in countries far beyond Russian borders, and not all of this has come from the renewal of inherited Soviet-era relationships. This chapter argues that contemporary Russia can clearly be considered an expanding global power in reality, not just in aspiration, given the geographic reach and the policy scope and weight it has established abroad.

Three policy areas are of special importance in Russian grand strategy beyond its borders: The first is *energy*, in particular oil and gas markets; the second is *economic and trade policy* not related to energy; and the third is *national and regime security*, specifically the establishment of *a military and especially political* bulwark against the United States and Europe. These three aspects of grand strategy are not completely distinct from one another. In some countries, these three interests converge, such as in Hungary and Bulgaria, while in others, policy areas of interest are more narrowly defined by the current Russian regime. But Putin's administration is particularly concerned with its own preservation; sometimes, this corresponds with a broader national interest that any Russian leader might pursue, but at other times, the choices that Putin's patronal autocracy has made are specific to his regime alone. That is, the purpose of the Kremlin's exercise of its power resources abroad is not predicated on "national" security or great power politics alone, but also on ways to buttress the stability and durability of Putin's autocracy in particular.

Contemporary Russia's geographic domain of power overlaps to some degree with the Soviet Union's former sphere of global activity, but not perfectly. This is not only because the current geographic domain of influence is far smaller, but also, and perhaps more significant, because the Kremlin's drive for global influence in the twenty-first century lacks a strong motivating ideological component like the spread of communism, although it is marked in some parts of Eastern Europe especially, with a pan-Slavic, socially conservative, illiberal tone. This, however, is distinct from the Soviet motivation to spread a very specific form of government, social and economic system. Soviet foreign policy (or grand strategy) was motivated by geostrategic interests—especially in the late Soviet period. But it was also guided by an exigency to perpetuate Marxist-Leninist regimes in opposition to capitalism. As Angela Stent notes, "It was only when Gorbachev came to power that the USSR officially eschewed the doctrine of the inevitable clash between communism and capitalism and began to promote the idea of mutual interdependence."[2] The commitment to spreading communism globally had to be balanced with national security interests; at least until the 1970s, Party leaders accepted that the triumph of communism over capitalism was inevitable everywhere, and that accomplishing this was a sacred trust. The Soviet Union, following World War II, took quick advantage of the chaos and destruction in Europe to assist domestic communist parties in establishing communist regimes in Eastern Europe, whether by elite coups or by supporting more popularly based national revolutions. The postwar disorder provided the Soviets with the opportunity to basically usurp domestic governments and simply install puppet communist regimes too. Stalin, and Khrushchev after him, saw opportunities to support communist parties in China in 1949, and later in Korea, Vietnam, and elsewhere by military means; the Soviets promoted similar attempted revolutions in parts of the Middle East and North Africa through the 1950s and 1960s. The USSR also encouraged and supported communist revolutions and revolutionary attempts in Latin America and southern Africa with significant success, and made a similar, though failed, attempt in Afghanistan beginning in 1979.

Although there was debate regarding the importance of ideology in Soviet grand strategy during the various phases of the Cold War, it is important nonetheless to remember that Marxism-Leninism was explicitly intended as an alternative developmental model to Western liberal capitalism.[3] While the current Russian regime, under Vladimir Putin's leadership, attempts to present itself as the tip of the spear of a group of socially conservative, "illiberal" regimes opposed to American global aggression, this representation of Russia at the head of a global movement of some sort bears little resemblance to the centrality of ideology in determining Soviet foreign policy. That is, although Putin's regime has gradually adopted an ideology or philosophy of social conservatism at home, and attempted to establish itself as an alternative pole to the overly liberal, competitive, permissive West abroad, this does not carry with it an alternative form of government or economics as did Marxism-Leninism. Beyond the strategic use of its anti-gay, traditional family values perspective to appeal to leaders (and societies) in countries that *already* share similar attitudes (as, for example, in parts of the Middle East), the regime's goal in its grand strategy is not to "export" patronal autocracy and social conservatism. For this reason, among others, the purposes of extending Soviet power abroad were distinctive from Russian global grand strategy under Putin post-2012. Because of the capitalist versus communist component, *"the Cold War was . . . an unprecedented struggle for the soul of mankind."*[4] But a transformational ideology or a new developmental model for humankind is *not* what motivates the Kremlin's power projection abroad in the twenty-first century. At most, it is merely a mechanism with which Russian policy actors may try to distinguish themselves from the liberal democratic West ("soft" power, as will be discussed in greater depth in chapter 7), perhaps, but spreading such an ideology and a new model of governance and economics based on it is not the purpose of Russian grand strategy under Putin. Nonetheless, Putin's Russia has extended its web of political, economic, and strategic contacts in new and distinct ways worldwide, frequently doing so in direct opposition to American and European interests in particular, as will become evident in what follows.

Just as the current regime's purpose in projecting power abroad is not to promote a transformational ideology, under Putin, Russia's risky behavior in pursuit of establishing a renewed global presence (like the Syrian operation in 2015, or the annexation of Crimea in 2014) is in sharp contrast to the risk-averse policies of the Soviet Union, especially after Khrushchev. As historian Arne Westad notes about the late Soviet period (the 1970s through 1985), for the West, "[i]n spite of the Cold War continuing, Moscow had become a sort of 'normal' enemy—European, straight-laced, and rather predictable."[5] Russia, after twenty years under Vladimir Putin's leadership, was anything but conventional in its approach to foreign policy.

The Soviet Union built alliances and helped domestic actors establish communist regimes in the six Warsaw Pact countries—Bulgaria, Czechoslovakia, East Germany, Hungary, Poland, and Romania. Soviet allies that constructed communist systems included Afghanistan, Angola, Benin, the Congo, Cuba, Ethiopia, Guinea, Kampuchea, Laos, Mongolia, Mozambique, Nicaragua, North Korea, North Vietnam, and Yemen. Soviet allies whose regimes were not completely socialist or communist at the height of the Cold War in 1980 included Algeria, Ghana, Guinea, India, Iraq, Lebanon, Libya, Madagascar, Mali, Panama, and Syria. Yugoslavia and Albania, though not in the Warsaw Pact or Eastern Bloc, were socialist countries. Under Khrushchev and Mao in the 1960s, the Soviet Union and China had a serious falling out over communist doctrine and policy toward the United States and remained more enemies than friends until the Soviet collapse in 1991, despite both identifying as communist countries (more on this later in the chapter).[6] This "communist international" of countries was more than just a set of like-minded leaders with planned economies and politics dominated by a communist party. Rather, it was a network of economic, political, and military relationships vital to the survival of communism worldwide, and to the survival of the Soviet Union itself. This in no way resembles what contemporary Russia's leadership has sought to pursue globally.

With the fall of the Berlin Wall in 1989 and Mikhail Gorbachev's decision to do nothing to stop the collapse of communism in the Eastern Bloc, the communist international unraveled and, with it, Soviet military, economic, and political ties around the world. Members of the Soviet military and diplomatic corps returned from their stations in Eastern Europe, the Middle East, Central America, northern and southern Africa, Asia, and, of course, Afghanistan. The global footprint that post-communist Russia inherited from the Soviet Union shrank almost to within its own borders as Boris Yeltsin struggled with difficult domestic economics and politics through the 1990s. By the end of the first decade of the twenty-first century, however, under the leadership of Vladimir Putin, Russia's geographic domain of power not only expanded once again into the other fourteen former republics of the USSR, but even far beyond, accomplishing this through tools that overlapped with, but were notably distinct from, those of the Soviet Union.

This chapter provides condensed examples of Russia's renewed and resurgent global reach. Several books could be written about Russia's increased activity in various parts of the world, and the goal in what follows is *not* to provide comprehensive coverage of every instance of Russian foreign policy involvement and influence worldwide since 1991. Instead, I focus on key instances in which Russia has established a significant, usually new, degree of influence over policy decisions and policy outcomes in Europe and in the Middle East and North Africa (MENA), in parts of southern Africa, Latin America, and its partnerships in Asia—especially with China and India. To some degree, the spread of the Kremlin's geographic influence might surprise some readers who, like President Obama, have mistaken Putin's Russia for nothing more than a regional power. On the contrary, in what follows, it is clear that the regime under Vladimir Putin has established itself as a major global influencer and disrupter.[7]

Where Is Russia Influential?

Europe Old and New

Following World War II, Joseph Stalin acted quickly in Eastern Europe to establish communist regimes; but in contrast, with the conclusion of the Cold War and the collapse of the Berlin Wall in 1989, most of those very same Eastern European communist countries moved quickly to become members of NATO and the EU. Membership in the latter required that candidate member countries construct economic and political institutions to support and sustain the infrastructure of liberal democracies with open markets—the exact opposite of what communist systems had been.

Poland and Hungary led the pack of five formerly communist countries (that also included the now separated Czech and Slovak Republics, and Slovenia) in quickly adopting market institutions and neoliberal economic reform programs to conform with the EU accession process.[8] EU accession also created the required institutions of democracies, including elected parliaments, an elected executive, professional and depoliticized judiciaries, and a free press. This group of five countries officially joined the EU in 2004; Bulgaria and Romania joined in 2007, and Croatia in 2013. Croatia and Slovenia are the only former Yugoslav states to have joined the EU; between 1991 and 2001, Yugoslavia descended into a series of long and bloody civil wars, ultimately establishing six new countries: Bosnia-Herzegovina, Croatia, Macedonia, Montenegro, Serbia, and Slovenia, with the formerly Serbian republic of Kosovo as an arguable seventh. Along with other countries in Eastern Europe that have not joined the EU, the former Yugoslav republics of Bosnia-Herzegovina, Macedonia, Montenegro, and Serbia saw gradual but generalized acceptance that democracy and markets were goals worth struggling toward. The EU, in turn, acknowledged and encouraged these efforts by forming the European Neighborhood Program in 2004 to enhance EU ties with these states, and also provided funding based on progress in the reform process.

In sum, the countries of formerly communist Eastern had become Ground Zero—not for the "end of history" of the exploitation of man by man as envisioned by communists in Russia one hundred years earlier, but for the end of Marxist-Leninist forms of government themselves. Virtually all had opted instead in favor of liberal democracy (at least initially) and that very capitalist system that Marx had so maligned more than a century earlier. But the struggle over Eastern Europe turned out not to have ended in a full victory for democracy. Elections of far-right governments in Poland and Hungary in 2010, and their rollback of many of the rights and freedoms those states had embraced twenty years earlier, have eroded the resiliency of their transformations. Under Putin,

Russia has also made efforts to entice other Central European governments away from the influence of the EU and encouraged internal political dissent in others in attempts to divide European unity.

There are geostrategic reasons behind this, of course. Russia has long had an historical and security interest in Eastern Europe. The Russian Empire fought wars with Sweden, the Habsburgs, and the Ottomans over these "lands in between" Russia proper and what is now a reunited Germany in the West.[9] As the new Russia emerged from its post-Soviet reform hangover, these interests were revived, although competition with Western Europe in this region was not inevitable. Rather, there was a conscious choice under Putin not to join Europe, even when given opportunities to do so. Indeed, despite some notable disagreements between the two sides, Yeltsin ultimately (although not always happily) worked with NATO regarding the conflict in Kosovo in 1999 (indeed, Russian forces came close to direct combat with NATO troops when the latter rushed to claim the airport in Pristina in June 1999).[10] But beyond this, after Putin re-assumed the Russian presidency in 2012, the broader region that lies between Russia's western borders and Germany's east evolved into a central political battleground for political and economic influence between Russia on the one hand, and Europe and the United States on the other.

Russian foreign policy makers became increasingly exercised about NATO expansion, although Yeltsin had come to grudgingly accept it. His concern had been that the United States and Europe were hedging on the success of Russia's nascent democracy by installing a security buffer in Eastern Europe. Opponents within the Russian Ministry of Defense and Ministry of Foreign Affairs pointed in the mid-1990s to a verbal promise allegedly made to Mikhail Gorbachev by George H. W. Bush's secretary of state, James Baker, in February 1990, that the alliance would expand "not one inch eastward" once Germany had been reunited, necessarily including what had been communist East Germany into NATO.[11] Whether or not such promises were made, they were not written down, and became largely irrelevant as more liberal and democratic governments came to power in the six countries of the former Warsaw Pact. From an American and Western European perspective, these were sovereign states, the democratically elected leaders of which could make foreign policy decisions on behalf of their people independent of Russian input. Therefore, when Poland, Hungary, and the Czech Republic asked to join and then were accepted to NATO in 1999, it was their right to do so. For the West, the benefit in including them in the alliance was not a military one (these countries had tiny militaries with Soviet-era equipment), but served to consolidate the end of communism and the democratic transitions that had taken place in Eastern Europe. It was the second branch of the larger project to ensure a Europe "whole and free," of which the EU was the other integral part.

There was some negative reaction to this from Boris Yeltsin in a letter he sent to President Bill Clinton in September 1993 (when he had just "extra-legally" disbanded Russia's Congress of People's Deputies and needed the Russian military to back him in any conflict with renegade parliamentarians; this may explain why he changed his initial acceptance of Poland's joining NATO, as outlined on a trip to Warsaw a month earlier). Yeltsin reminded Clinton in the letter that Russia also wanted to join NATO.[12] Undeniably, there was little he could do to prevent NATO's further expansion eastward, but he likely did not view NATO expansion through the Visegrad countries (comprising the Czech Republic, Slovakia, Hungary, and Poland) as a direct threat to Russian security. Rather, he viewed it as lack of faith in Russian reform efforts, undermining Russian reformers who envisioned a new Russia as friendly to the West, and having that friendship reciprocated. For them, "it was difficult to understand how [US President] Clinton could champion and assist their cause with one set of policies and at the same time frustrate their agenda by pursuing another policy, the policy of NATO enlargement."[13] But Russia had been invited to join the North Atlantic Cooperation Council in 1991, and would join the Euro-Atlantic Partnership Council by 1997. On a parallel track, initially intended to replace NATO expansion, integration into European security structures was also being pursued by NATO's "Partnership for Peace" program that included Russia and virtually every other former communist country in Eastern Europe as well as Armenia, Azerbaijan, Belarus, Georgia, Moldova, Ukraine, and the five former Soviet republics of Central Asia. As noted earlier, under Yeltsin, Russia sent peacekeepers to work with NATO forces in the Balkans in the late 1990s. The 1997 NATO-Russia Founding Act formalized relations, and in 2002 the NATO-Russia Council was established as a permanent consultative forum. Russia was an ally and Europe was there to help it recover from communism and rejoin the society of free, prosperous countries.[14]

NATO expansion continued nonetheless. In 2004, the former Soviet republics of Estonia, Latvia, and Lithuania, as well as the Eastern Bloc countries of Bulgaria, Slovakia, and Slovenia, also became members of the alliance. Unconvinced by NATO reassurances, almost all wings of the Russian political and military establishment were acutely aware of the fact that, as of 2004, NATO forces sat a mere 120 km from St. Petersburg. Croatia and Albania, farther afield, joined the alliance in 2009, but no further expansion of NATO took place until 2017, with the accession of tiny Montenegro.

Over time, perceptions of the EU and NATO among Putin and other members of Russia's foreign policy and defense establishment shifted. The former came to be seen not as a trading zone of free countries, nor the latter as a security organization with which Russia could (and did) cooperate under Yeltsin, during most of Putin's first and second terms, and under Medvedev; instead, they were institutions specifically *designed to isolate and contain Russia*. By February 2007, Putin complained loudly at the Munich Conference on Security Policy about NATO expansion:

> I think it is obvious that NATO expansion does not have any relation with the modernization of the alliance itself or with ensuring security in Europe. On the contrary, it represents a serious provocation that reduces the level of mutual trust. And we have the right to ask: against whom is this expansion intended? And what happened to the assurances our western partners made after the dissolution of the Warsaw Pact? Where are those declarations today?[15]

Allowing former Soviet satellite countries into NATO and/or the EU was, from an emerging Russian perspective, taking advantage of Russia's temporary weakness in the immediate wake of the Soviet collapse. Of course, Western powers also could point to signed commitments that were later violated on the Russian side. In interfering in Ukrainian politics even prior to the invasion and seizure of Crimea in 2014 (as described in chapter 2), Putin violated the Budapest Memorandum of 1994, in which Yeltsin promised in writing that Russia would respect Ukrainian sovereignty in exchange for Ukraine's transfer of its Soviet-era nuclear weapons to Russian soil.

Still, as Stent argues, Putin felt Russia had tried to reset relations with the United States in 2001, viewing the tragedy of 9/11 as a path to establishing a clear common interest in fighting terrorism. He told George W. Bush in his condolence call that Russia, too, had its terrorism issues. Putin also apparently truly believed, as Yeltsin had, that Russia should be able to join NATO as a full member. If Russia was not the intended focus of NATO expansion eastward, as Western leaders argued, then why could Russia not become a full member and partner?[16] In July 2001, Putin said of NATO, "We do not see it as an enemy. . . . We do not see a tragedy in its existence, but we also see no need for it," and he argued that Russia should be included in a new single security and defense space in Europe.[17] In short, according to this argument, NATO merely had outlived its purpose, but it was not necessarily a threat to Russia. By 2007, however, as Putin gave his fiery address in Munich, Russia was on the road to economic recovery and eventual resurgence abroad, or so it seemed, and as the quote from Putin that begins this chapter indicated, the rest of the world, and Europe and the United States in particular, would do well to take note.

From a security perspective, Russian policy since 2012 and Putin's return to the Russian presidency became ever more focused on disrupting and ideally breaking apart the NATO alliance and dividing the EU. Since no further NATO expansion in Eastern Europe had taken place after Albania and Croatia's accession in 2009, however, it is difficult to accept the argument that this had been the cause of Russia's policy shift against NATO five years later in 2014, when it was used as a reason to invade Ukraine. (I return to why this may have happened in chapter 8, which looks at the role of Russian domestic politics in grand strategy under Mr. Putin.)

There are three general areas of European vulnerability to Russian power that echo those areas in which Russia has influenced the former Soviet republics in its "near" abroad: national security, economics, and domestic politics. Russian power resources are greater in some European countries than others. Countries closer to Russia's borders are more vulnerable in all three policy domains, but older members of NATO and the EU, and states that are farther west, have also faced significant political, economic, and military exposure to various means of Russian power. Further, other European non-NATO member countries like Finland and Sweden also complained of Russian forces targeting their coastlines and navies, such that they initiated defense cooperation with the NATO alliance in 2015. Europeans have strong defense capabilities on paper—collectively outspending Russia—but individually, no European country can rival Russia militarily (see chapter 6 on hard power for evidence). Instead, European members of NATO must rely on the power of the alliance, and at the extreme, the power of Article 5 compliance to deter Russia from openly attacking a member state.

In 2013 and 2015, the Russian military conducted exercises along the country's western borders—an estimated 38,000 troops took part in the latter year, raising European concerns regarding Russian intentions and capabilities. Russia's nuclear forces present another security vulnerability for Europeans, especially in light of the abandonment in 2019 of the Intermediate Nuclear Forces (INF) Treaty, which the American side argued Russia had already violated in creating a conventional and nuclear-capable ground-launched cruise missile (the Kalibr) as it updated its nuclear forces. Russian nuclear capabilities are discussed in far greater depth in chapter 6; however, with respect to the scope of Russia's power in Europe, it is worth noting here that Russian nuclear doctrine could be interpreted (and has been by some in the US military) as enabling a "limited nuclear strike" to de-escalate a potential conventional arms conflict (a strategy of "escalate to de-escalate") if the Russian leadership judged that the country was facing an "existential" threat. But what constitutes a threat of this magnitude is nowhere clearly defined—it appears to be a judgment call, leaving the impression that Russia has at best an ambiguous (and at worst a low) threshold for the use of nuclear weapons in Europe and elsewhere.[18]

But even prior to the abandonment of the INF Treaty, the Russian military already had shorter-range ballistic missiles that could easily reach Eastern European neighbors. As discussed in chapter 6, in 2008, the Ministry of Defense initiated significant reform and upgrades and began work to increase the deterrent capability of its conventional forces.[19] Russia has a tank advantage over NATO forces and could quickly overwhelm even the NATO Rapid Reaction forces stationed in Estonia or Poland, for example, should a Russian military incursion into a NATO member state occur. "Eventually," according to members of the US military interviewed for this project, "we could overwhelm them, but it would take a while to get there."[20] In sum, should Russia's leaders choose to pursue the kind of military incursion executed in Crimea and Eastern Ukraine in 2014 elsewhere, there would be little standing in their way. Russian policymakers would be balancing two potential scenarios: first, that NATO would not honor Article 5 commitments with regard to new members in Eastern Europe, and second, if NATO were to counterattack with conventional forces, that it would take some time to get a significant counterforce on the ground. Russia's advantage is that NATO requires complete agreement on what constitutes a security violation that would merit invoking the Article 5 commitment to act, but decision-making within the alliance is slow. Again, although postwar Europe's strength has been its unity, it can also be a weakness that Russia can exploit.

In the years since the Soviet collapse, many European states have become *economically* vulnerable to Moscow's influence, despite an imbalance in the EU's favor of traditional means of power, as noted in chapter 1. But, in this area too, Europe's relative strength in comparison to Putin's Russia is only in its unanimity,[21] and it is the erosion of European concord that the Kremlin has exploited to gain an upper hand in setting the agenda economically—and arguably, politically too, as a right-wing nationalist-based populism has been encouraged by Putin's example and crept slowly from the east toward Western European states.

Since 1991, Russian private and public businesses have established a fair amount of trade with various European countries, but in the aggregate, this remained a relatively small part of the overall EU export market—about 5.6% by 2013, the year before the West imposed sanctions on Russian businesses and individuals associated with President Putin personally and financially. At the same time, only about 1% of the EU's non-energy imports came from Russia, and these were primarily steel and chemicals, both of which were easily available on other markets.[22] The Russian economy is a primary producer of titanium, however, an element used in a range of products made in Europe, so manufacturers using titanium for cell phones, computers, eyeglasses, paints, and medical devices, among other items, would suffer should Russian firms fail to supply this ubiquitous component.

Some countries and economic sectors became far more dependent on Russian trade than others following the collapse of the USSR. Unsurprisingly, poorer European economies were more susceptible to Russian economic influence than others; in particular, Italy, Greece, Hungary, Spain, and Cyprus, where economies weakened following the 2008 global economic crisis and remained soft thereafter, became more dependent on exporting agricultural, livestock, and fish products to Russia. Analysts from RAND, using United Nations trade data, reported that products that the Russian government counter-sanctioned in 2014 accounted for significant percentages (over 10%) of all global exports in Norway, Finland, and Poland, and over 5% of global exports in Greece, Hungary, Slovenia, and Cyprus.[23] Among these countries, Poland, at least, has remained steadfast in its leaders' support of Western sanctions on Russian entities and individuals. In Italy, Greece, Hungary, Spain, and Cyprus, though, Russian government counter-sanctions and other means of influence discussed later in this chapter contributed to declining support among these countries for maintaining a united front in leveraging sanctions against Putin's Russia. Elsewhere in Europe, German automakers suffered declining sales in the Russian market after 2014 as Russian consumers pulled back from spending in the face of the declining ruble. In industries with dual civilian and defense production, sanctions meant lost contracts and sales in Europe, as with the cancellation of the sale of two French amphibious assault ships to Russia in 2014. German companies were forced to cancel multimillion-dollar construction projects planned for Russia in the face of the EU sanctions regime.[24]

Cyprus is among the more vulnerable small European economies when it comes to exposure to Russian influence. It is simultaneously the biggest source of and destination for Russian foreign capital. It is used as a tax haven for ultra-wealthy Russian businesses, so the money that runs through Cyprus often travels a circular route. Cyprus itself, however, is highly indebted, and has sought relief from the International Monetary Fund as well as the EU. It also received loans from the Russian government of about 2.5 billion euros in 2011, which was extended with easier terms in 2013 and restructured again in 2015 after the EU joined the United States in imposing sanctions on Russia. In what seemed like a quid pro quo, Cyprus soon thereafter allowed Russian ships into its ports for resupply and maintenance.[25]

Russian companies have also invested heavily in the economies of both Bulgaria and Hungary. Regarding the former, Mitchell Orenstein writes, "Russian investors are far and away the most important."[26] The latter, too, has been increasingly open to Russian investment. Viktor Orbán, Hungary's far-right prime minister, "has been open to Russian proposals and an enthusiastic partner . . . to play an important economic role in Europe. Hungary also agreed to allow Russia to finance and build two new nuclear energy reactors at an estimated cost of 12 billion euros."[27]

Of vital importance is the fact that European investment in Russia is greater than Russian investment in Europe. At least in theory, this creates a vulnerability to Russian legislative fiat should the Kremlin decide to seize European assets within Russia. In 2014, there was, allegedly at least, a threat that the government would do so with the goal of countering Western sanctions against Russian businesspeople and political actors.[28] This threat, however, was not carried out, presumably since the EU could then retaliate, which could have created a cycle of financial chaos in Europe and Russia. As is, European investments in Russia are significant. The largest investors in the Russian economy are the Netherlands, Luxembourg, and the United Kingdom—all with total stock and foreign direct investment portfolios of between $60–78 billion—followed by France, Germany, Ireland, and Sweden, with $20–32 billion; Austria and Switzerland with $10–13 billion; and Belgium, Denmark, Finland, and Italy with $5 billion in Russia. These figures mean different things for different countries; for instance, the respective sums represent a larger proportion of the Italian economy than of the German economy, which, combined with Italy's generally weaker economic condition, contributed to Russian leverage in Italy in particular. If the goal of the Russian leadership's grand strategy was to weaken a united Europe, this meant that poorer European states like Italy and Greece were good prospects for the Russian regime. Moreover, Russian investments disproportionately affect smaller economies—for example, in Montenegro, Russian investments were about 28% of GDP in 2013, but in countries like Austria, Bosnia-Herzegovina, Bulgaria, Ireland, and the Netherlands, it is about 5%.[29]

By far, however, European vulnerability to Russian power is greatest in the energy sector, as Russian suppliers are the EU's main source of oil and petroleum products. In 2013, Russia supplied a reported 35% of the crude and refined oil products used in and exported by the EU.[30] If the Russian government were to cut Europe off from those oil exports, economic disaster would ensue. That said, oil is easily available from sources other than Russia, so if Europe were to suffer a true shortage due to Russian supply disruptions, other suppliers could eventually step in. Switching oil suppliers, however, is not without costs, and disruptions in oil supply would potentially drive oil prices up globally, possibly prompting a worldwide recession. This is a very unlikely scenario, however, given the Russian economy's own extreme economic dependence on oil revenues from European sales (see chapter 4). So, while dependence on oil imports from Russia is a theoretical vulnerability for European economies, a complete cutoff of Russian oil exports to Europe, in reality, is extremely unlikely to happen.

Brief disruptions or slowdowns in oil supplies from Russia, however, can and have happened in the past, affecting eastern Europe in particular. The old Soviet Druzhba (or Friendship) pipeline is still a core conduit of Russian oil into Europe. It travels through Belarus into Poland and eventually hits eastern Germany, while other branches run across Ukraine and into Slovakia and Hungary. Between April and June 2019, a disruption of oil supply occurred because of chemical contamination from a Russian supplier, causing about 5 million tons of crude oil to be effectively trapped in the pipeline supplying various parts of Europe. Since the crisis occurred at the border of Belarus, where the pipeline divides into northern and southern branches, oil refineries in Poland, Germany, Hungary, Slovakia, and the Czech Republic were most affected. This interruption may have contributed to an increase in oil prices. Although the crisis lasted only a few months, it was a reminder of the possibility of weaponizing Europe's reliance on Russian gas and oil, should its leaders ever choose to do so. Russian policymakers have to be cautious in how they employ the tool of energy supply disruption to influence European policy, however, since doing so shows Russia to be an unreliable supplier and provides an impetus for European countries to find alternate suppliers and new sources of non-petroleum-based energy.[31]

Far more worrisome for European economies than their dependence on Russian oil is their heavier reliance on Russia as a primary supplier of natural gas. Natural gas is more difficult to transport than oil, since it requires significant infrastructure, and so finding alternate suppliers would be a greater task. In the aggregate, Russian firms supplied 20–25% of Europe's natural gas on average in any given year from 2005 to 2015.[32] Germany, Italy, and Turkey are the biggest importers of Russian natural gas by volume.[33] The first stage of Nord Stream Pipeline system, completed in 2012, directly linked Russia with Germany, bypassing former route through Poland and Belarus. And Germany, working with Gazprom, initiated construction on a second pipeline, dubbed Nord Stream II, in the same area, which will increase Russia's gas transport capacity by creating a route under the Baltic Sea. (Since 2014 and through the time of writing, sanctions on companies doing business with Russia have slowed this project's progress. After the poisoning of Russian opposition leader Alexy Navalny in August 2020, presumed to be done by agents acting on behalf of the Russian government, Germany was under tremendous international pressure to abandon the project entirely, although given that it was almost completed, this seemed unlikely at the time of writing.) But in terms of dependence, countries that receive more than 90% of their natural gas provisions from Russia include Bosnia-Herzegovina, Bulgaria, the Czech and Slovak Republics, Finland, Romania, and Serbia. Those receiving at least 50–89% include Austria, Hungary, Poland, and Slovenia; and in the 10–49% range, Croatia, France, Germany, Italy, the Netherlands, and Switzerland. Belgium, Norway, Portugal, Spain, and Sweden all receive less than 10% of their natural gas supplies from Russia.[34] The dependence of European states on Russian gas became a huge issue during Russia's gas cutoffs to Ukraine, the result of payment disputes, in 2006 and 2009. Because most European gas traveled across Ukraine at the time, some countries suffered supply disruptions, forcing them to tap into reserves. Natural gas is used in home heating and cooking and in industry, so the effects of shortages were felt widely in the largest economies of Eastern and Western Europe. Indeed, in January 2009, when Russia shut off gas to Ukraine in the middle of winter, Bulgaria was forced to cut off industrial gas provision in favor of keeping homes heated. During this episode, gas exports to sixteen members of the EU (and Moldova) were stopped in 2009 for several days. According to the Oxford Institute for Energy Studies, "The most seriously affected countries in the Balkans experienced a humanitarian emergency, with parts of the populations unable to heat their homes. Significant economic problems, but not of a humanitarian kind, were also caused in Hungary and Slovakia.[35] Still, as with oil supplies, this is a weapon that the Kremlin must wield infrequently, since these incidents have sparked interest and action in Europe to blunt the effect of further supply disruptions originating in Russia, including by diversifying gas suppliers, finding alternative fuel sources, and promoting the interconnectedness of European energy grids and pipeline networks to share resources more effectively across borders.[36]

The double-edged sword of this aspect of the Russian regime's leverage over the EU is illustrated by such projects as the eventually abandoned Nabucco pipeline (proposed by the EU and the United States) and the South Stream pipeline (planned to run between Russia through the Black Sea to Bulgaria, then through Serbia, Hungary, Slovenia, and eventually Austria). The 39,000 km Nabucco pipeline was originally proposed in 2002 to diversify Europe's gas suppliers and pipelines away from Russia, and was supported politically by the EU and the United States. Planning moved more quickly following Putin's gas war with Ukraine in 2009–2010. The EU reportedly even provided $200 million to advance the project, which was to be developed by a group of six gas companies (European and Central Asian). By 2012, however, the project was dead. From a commercial standpoint, it is possible that Nabucco simply did not make sense: the pipeline was large, and quantities of gas from Turkmenistan and Azerbaijan, where the pipeline's supply was to have originated, were relatively small.[37] Still, the dominant explanation for Nabucco's failure to break Europe's dependence on Russian gas and pipelines was lack of unity among EU members on the project; in addition, separate, bilateral negotiations were established between Russia and Germany, France, and Italy, despite public rhetoric regarding the need for EU unity.[38] Thus, the strength of Europe—the need for consensus and unity in dealing with Russia—also proved to be its weakness.

European unity, however, did manage to kill the proposed Russian alternative to Nabucco, the South Stream pipeline, launched in 2006, roughly the same time the EU was working on the Nabucco project. South Stream would have preserved Russia's access to European markets while bypassing Ukraine, with a proposed path through the Black Sea region, including Bulgaria, Croatia, Greece, Serbia, Hungary, Slovenia, and Austria. These transit countries signed intergovernmental agreements with the EU for Nabucco, but also with Russia for South Stream. This was likely in part due to pressure from the Kremlin; Mitchell Orenstein reports that "Russia bribed Bulgarian parliamentarians and

government officials to take its side in these matters."[39] But after Putin's 2014 seizure of Crimea from Ukraine, the EU forced Bulgaria into abandoning its participation in the South Stream project. This, along with some countries concerned
having signed two separate pipeline agreements, led the European Parliament
to kill the project in 2015. Russia eventually partnered with Turkey to transport its gas through a new pipeline, TurkStream. In 2018, Russia's Gazprom was
estimated to supply more than 50% of Turkey's gas imports.[40] Revenue from
extending TurkStream to Europe through Greece, Italy, and/or Bulgaria was
welcomed by these members of the EU, and would further increase their reliance on Russia to help maintain the pipeline as well as to pay transit fees. This
too, then, created leverage for Moscow in Europe.

Within individual European countries, as in countries in its more immediate
neighborhood, under Vladimir Putin, Russia has developed alliances and chains
of dependency with the goal of disrupting politics and eroding European unity.
It has used a diversity of methods to do so in what some scholars have referred
to as a "hybrid war." The concept is based on an approach to Russian "grand
strategy" articulated in 2013 by chief of the general staff, Valery Gerasimov; referred to by some Western observers as the Gerasimov Doctrine, the emphasis is
on an indirect or "non-linear" package of tools, including but not limited to military means, to interrupt the domestic politics of other countries.[41] This toolset
has included cyber technology and traditional media used to influence or confuse countries' information environment; inserting intelligence assets or "agents
of influence" into important positions;[42] financing opposition politicians;
and bribing or discrediting elected governments in Western Europe. Despite
Gerasimov's notoriety for devising this strategy, these tools are not entirely new.
These are the sorts of tactics the KGB used in Western Europe during the Cold
War, the difference being, perhaps, less in the array of tools used to exercise influence over European politics and more in the guile (and occasional sloppiness)
with which it has done so.

The intensity of these efforts is also striking, as is the willing and rather open
complicity of some European politicians. One intriguing example is the story
of Béla Kovács, a Hungarian member of the European Parliament representing
the far-right party Jobbik, an extremist bloc. Prior to returning to Hungary and
entering politics, he worked in Moscow, became very wealthy, and was evidently
recruited to the KGB. As Kovács rose in the party and donated to it, Jobbik
became increasingly pro-Russian in its foreign policy within the European
Parliament.[43] President Putin has also cultivated close relationships with key
political actors, including former Italian prime minister Silvio Berlusconi and
former German chancellor Gerhard Schroeder; the latter was installed as head of
the Nord Stream II project and, in 2017, as chairman of Rosneft, Russia's biggest
oil company.

In some cases, alliances and disinformation efforts have gone hand in hand. Prior to the French presidential elections of 2017, National Front leader Marine Le Pen traveled to Moscow to meet with Putin and expressed her support of the Russian annexation of Crimea. Although there was no obvious quid pro quo, the National Front also appeared to have received campaign support from Moscow in the form of a loan worth 9.46 million euros. Moreover, just prior to the French presidential election that year, thousands of emails of then-candidate Emanuel Macron were stolen and subsequently released; cyber security firms linked this activity to groups within the Russian GRU (military intelligence). Some documents had been edited with references to Macron's (fictitious) "Bahamian bank account," and the security firms detected that the work had been done on computers with Russian operating systems. Macron, of course, defeated Le Pen, Russia's preferred candidate, but the intent of the interference was clear. Similarly, as part of its continuous effort to thwart European unity, Russia also supported the successful Brexit referendum, possibly with financial assistance to the UK Independence Party (UKIP).[44] Hacking attacks traced to Russian intelligence have also occurred in Germany, where the Christian Democratic Party was the victim; these are discussed in greater detail in chapter 7.

Just as in the 2016 American presidential election, Russia also conducted disinformation wars in Europe, for instance, by using bots and trolls to raise the profiles of pro-Russian posts and messages and to change online conversations about Russia's intentions and policies globally. Russia's foreign-language broadcasters, the TV channel Russia Today (now known as RT) and Sputnik, also broadcast highly professional but ultimately re-processed "news" to English, Spanish, German, and French audiences in Europe. Orenstein notes that far-right politicians, like Britain's Nigel Farage, who often have difficulty getting mainstream media coverage in their home countries, have become regular commentators on RT.[45] In addition, Russian state media sources have promoted openly false stories, especially regarding immigrants from the Middle East and North Africa in Europe, to exacerbate growing tensions within specific European countries. One such story was the alleged rape of a young German woman of Russian origin identified as "Lisa" by a gang of Arab migrants in January 2016. The girl's family reported that she had disappeared for thirty hours and had been abducted and assaulted; in reality, she had been at a friend's house. Nonetheless, the story spread widely in Germany, first being reported on the Russia 1 TV channel and then picked up by RT German. From there, it appeared on Facebook and Twitter; while a video about the case on YouTube received thousands of views. There were even organized protests against the German government's alleged inaction on the case. Right-wing activists also picked up the story and promoted it further as evidence of the danger of Arab migrants. Indeed, the story was mentioned by Russian foreign minister Sergei

Lavrov, who expressed his concern about the case and German police ineptitude in a press conference on Russian-German relations in Moscow. But, as noted, the incident was entirely false.[46] Promoting the story as authentic, however, was designed to enhance distrust in migrants, the police, and German politicians, and fuel greater polarization within German society.

Perhaps more damaging to the unity of Europe is the support of illiberal politicians. Since Putin's return to the Kremlin in 2012, his administration has put great effort into cultivating their rise, especially in Hungary. Democratic decline has happened without clear Kremlin encouragement in other parts of Eastern Europe, to be sure, however. In 2018, Freedom House reported that Poland (not exactly a strong ally of Russia's historically) had the second-highest level of democratic decline in any Eastern European country since 1989. The recession of democracy in Poland, once the poster child for the triumph of liberalism and capitalism over communism, came as a result of the government's effective takeover of the independent judicial system, the politicization of the media, attacks on NGOs critical of the government, and the dominance of the Law and Justice Party in elections that were not completely free or fair. The dubious honor of first place in the category of democratic recession, however, went to Hungary under Prime Minister Viktor Orbán. Indeed, Hungary's freedom score has consistently fallen in the years since Orbán's election in 2010, such that by 2020 it was rated a "transitional or hybrid regime" and only "partly free."[47] Under Orbán, Hungary passed laws on non-governmental organizations (NGOs) that imitated restrictions in Russia introduced a few years earlier. Orbán has also imitated the Putinist use of legislative fiat and arbitrary fines to effectively shut down opposition political parties to tip the scales in favor of his own Fidesz Party. Orbán's decidedly pro-Russian bent followed a 2009 meeting with Putin; after becoming Hungary's prime minister in 2010, he emphasized economic opportunities for Hungary not just in the EU, but also to the east in Russia. While Orbán has also spoken out against EU sanctions on Russia, he must walk a fine line in this regard, since Hungary's economy is still far more dependent on the EU than on Russia. Within Eastern Europe, Orbán has become a leading proponent of illiberalism—the idea that elections are held only to legitimize the status quo dominance of one party, and that there need not be institutional independence for courts, opposition political parties, or the media. This line of thinking echoes sentiments and policy within Russia, and is presented as an alternative to the perception of the rest of Europe as placing excessive emphasis on personal rights and freedoms to the detriment of a cohesive social fabric. In an interview with the *Financial Times* in 2019, Putin referenced growing right-wing populism in Eastern Europe in declaring that "the liberal idea has become obsolete. It has come into conflict with the interests of the overwhelming majority of the population."[48]

Indeed, looking at other parts of formerly democratic or democratizing Eastern Europe, we can even speak of an autocratic or illiberal diffusion. Bulgaria is no longer classified as a consolidated democracy, with questionable elections and significant power held by oligarchs. Similarly, relative freedoms in Serbia have declined since 2015, although by 2020 it was still classified as "partly free".[49] In addition to emphasizing illiberal governance in dealing with a backsliding Serbia, Putin's Russia has actively promoted pan-Slavism in its dealings with that government. In 2019, for instance, joint military exercises were undertaken under the name "Slavic Shield," emphasizing the countries' shared cultural identity; Russia has also transported aircraft and S-400 missile defense systems to Serbia. Under Putin, Russia has further helped to fund and promote the de-democratization of Poland, although that country's right-moving leaders have remained committed to an anti-Russian foreign policy.

These drifts away from consolidated democracy in Europe are not due to Russian efforts alone; however, through the use of money, arms deals, social and traditional media, and other means, Putin's Russia has capitalized on existing cleavages in increasingly fragile democracies and further deepened those divides. Specifically, the Russian regime has promoted already budding anti-immigrant nationalism; encouraged growing Euro-skepticism; and, as in some of the countries of the former Soviet Union, used "soft" power resources to counter the pull of what is portrayed on social and conventional media. These tactics, along with Moscow's security and energy policies, have served to exacerbate already deep divisions within the Europe on a host of policy issues, while promoting the regime's interests in cutting business deals for Russian firms that are tightly linked to the Kremlin. (Whether they serve the broader Russian national interest is another question, to be addressed in chapter 8.)

The Middle East and North Africa (MENA)

While Russian involvement in the Middle East is not new, given significant historical interests in the region by both Soviet and imperial actors, Russia under Vladimir Putin has established a striking and influential presence in the Middle East and North Africa (MENA). The policy scope of Russia's renewed involvement and influence in MENA parallels the same three general themes seen in Europe: Energy, comprising oil and gas, but also nuclear power; non-energy trade, especially considering the sale of Russian weaponry is greater in the Middle East than in Europe; and finally, the buttressing of Russia's own national security and autocratic durability, specifically with the aim of countering American influence and presenting itself as an alternate pole to US influence.

Remarkably, in about a decade, Putin's Russia had established (or re-established) relationships in a broad geographical domain within the Middle East. Moreover, the Kremlin maintains trade and security relationships with states that are bitter foes of one another: Iran and Israel, Syria and Iraq, Egypt and Saudi Arabia. Turkey, formally still a member of NATO, has drawn far closer to Russia (at least at the time of writing in 2020) than to the United States or the EU, where its candidacy for membership long languished. Outside of the former Soviet Union and Europe, the Middle East is the area where the power dimensions of Russian geographical domain and policy scope are greatest. In understanding the domain and scope of Moscow's activity in the Middle East, the region can be reasonably organized into four groups. The first three groups—Syria, Iran, and Iraq; Turkey and Israel; and Egypt, Libya, Morocco, and Tunisia—form a set of their own, as states that are primary interests for Putin's regime in military and political security terms (although Russia also has some nuclear and other energy interests in Iran and Iraq). The fourth group—Saudi Arabia and the Gulf States—are in the Putin regime's sights primarily because of their role in global energy markets.

Although the Kremlin's resurgence in the Middle East in the post-communist period is significant, Russia is not exactly a newcomer. Russia's imperial regime in the nineteenth century fought with other great powers for influence in the region. Following the Second World War, the Soviet military under Stalin lingered in Iran, where it had joined with the Allies to drive the Nazis out of North Africa, though it was eventually forced to withdraw peacefully. The Soviets were among the first to formally recognize the establishment of Israel in 1948, evidently hoping that socialist Jewish settlers would adopt communism. When this proved not to pan out, Stalin briefly suspended ties with Israel in the period 1952–1953. Soviet interest in the Middle East as a buffer between the territory of the USSR and the West increased when Turkey and Greece joined NATO in 1952, and this informed much of the policy in the area.

After Stalin's death in 1953, the Soviet Union saw pan-Arab nationalism as an opportunity to undermine British and American influence in the region. When Egypt under Gamal Abdel Nasser clashed with Britain and the United States over the Suez Canal in 1956, this afforded the first opportunity for the Soviets to support a Middle Eastern state against its ideological rivals. The fight for control over the Suez Canal, with Israel, Britain, and France pitted against Egypt, marked the first time that the Soviets threatened to retaliate directly against the West on the behalf of an Arab government. Thereafter, the Middle East became a key Cold War battleground. Soviet leaders arranged to ship arms to Egypt to support Nasser starting in 1955, and the continued flow of weaponry thereafter helped to establish the Soviet Union as an important actor in the region. Indeed, Igor Delanoe claims that until the communist collapse in 1991, the Soviets sent some 80,000 military advisers and troops, and trained 55,000 Arab officers back in the USSR.[50] The Soviets viewed the nationalist revolutions against pro-Western governments in Iraq (1958 and 1962), northern Yemen (1962), Algeria (in 1962), and southern Yemen (1967) as opportunities to spread communist ideology and influence.

However, as Dmitri Trenin notes, conservative Middle Eastern monarchies, such as Saudi Arabia, Iraq (until 1958), and Turkey, were ideological foes in an anti-Soviet alliance with the West.[51] In the 1967 Six-Day War against Israel, the Soviet Union sided firmly with its Arab allies of Egypt and, by then, Syria. Despite Arab losses in the conflict, in the later 1960s, Egypt and Syria leaned further toward the Soviet Union as an arms supplier, and at about the same time, the Soviets sought to strengthen ties with new leftist governments coming to power in Iraq, Sudan, and Libya. The Soviet Union gained a stronger military foothold in Egypt in particular, establishing three ports and a permanent squadron in the Mediterranean as of 1967. As the United States armed Israel, the Soviet Union continued to arm Egypt, and Nasser actively encouraged a Soviet air and land presence for assistance in defending against Israeli incursions. But in 1972, Anwar Sadat replaced Nasser as Egyptian president. Less sanguine about a Soviet security guarantee, and evidently seeking to attack Israel unfettered by Soviet intervention and advice, Sadat expelled an estimated 20,000 military advisers and curtailed Soviet access to Egyptian airspace. Despite this, after Egypt and Syria attacked Israel in October 1973 in what became known as the Yom Kippur War, the Soviets again sided with the Arab allies, supplying dozens of ships and submarines with Soviet crews.[52] The war ended in 1973, but led to a longer peace process ending with a peace agreement signed by Egypt and Israel, brokered by the United States at Camp David in 1978. Shortly thereafter, Egypt abandoned the Soviet Union for American security guarantees and refused to pay back debts to Moscow.

After 1978, therefore, Syria was left as the Soviet Union's closest ally in the Middle East. This freed Soviet forces to move the naval vessels previously stationed in Egypt to Tartus, a port reopened by the Russian navy in 2015. Syrian president Hafez al-Assad, however, was perhaps not as useful to the Soviet Union as Soviet support was in maintaining his regime through arms sales. Libya, under an increasingly unpredictable Muammar Gaddafi, and Iraq, under Saddam Hussein, were sometime customers for Soviet weaponry, as were Algeria and Yemen.

As revolution brewed in Iran in 1979, bringing to power an Islamic theocracy that was as hostile to the Soviet Union as it was to the United States, Soviet influence there evaporated. At the same time, the resources demanded by the long war in Afghanistan (1979–1989) meant a decline in what the Soviets could provide to their allies in the Middle East. By 1991, Mikhail Gorbachev joined the

United States in condemning Saddam's seizure of Kuwait. Gorbachev's last act on behalf of the Soviet Union in the Middle East was to re-establish diplomatic relations with Israel.

In the early to mid-2000s, however, as Vladimir Putin's presidency flourished, and as the Russian economy recovered significantly from the fog of the Soviet collapse, new opportunities in the Middle East and North Africa appeared. Beginning in 2005, at the beginning of Putin's second term as Russia's president, his personal engagement with the Middle East increased notably.[53] Whereas Boris Yeltsin in the 1990s had never traveled to the Middle East, between 2005 and 2007 alone, Putin shuttled between Moscow and Egypt, Saudi Arabia, Qatar, Jordan, Iran, Turkey, the United Arab Emirates (UAE), and Israel. By Putin's re-election in 2018, Russia's policy scope in the Middle East had become relatively well defined. The intensity of Moscow's influence under Putin in different sectors of the MENA region, however, have varied according to the regime's strategic interests, not according to the ideological concerns so important to former Soviet policymakers.

In this vein, it is striking that Russia in the twenty-first century has become uniquely able to balance relations with states that are usually adversaries, such as Iran and Israel or Saudi Arabia. While the United States has chosen clear sides and is a staunch adversary to Iran but an unfailing ally of Israel, Putin's Russia has become a simultaneous partner to both—something even the Soviet Union failed to do. Some observers attribute this to a strictly transactional approach to dealing with Middle Eastern regimes. That is, successive dealings between Putin's regime and different leaders in the Middle East are not tied together with the intent of building long-term alliances based on shared philosophical beliefs or worldviews. Instead, areas of cooperation are relatively narrow and unmoored from moral judgments or requirements for further interaction. In a sense, this is an advantage not just over the United States, which has traditionally (although not always, of course, in its dealings with countries like Saudi Arabia or Iran under the Shah, for example) tied respect for human rights and liberalized politics to support for its allies, but also over the Soviet Union, since there is no concerted ideological war to wage for the allegiance of the citizens or leaders of these states. Because Putin's Russia has a transactional approach to its dealings in the Middle East (one hesitates to call them alliances), it has been unencumbered to deal with varied actors for narrow, strategic aims.[54]

Iran

Nowhere is this stance better displayed than in relations between Iran and Russia. Despite the Soviet Union's having backed Saddam during the long Iran-Iraq War of the 1980s, under Putin, Russia has managed to forge constructive trade relations with both countries. A transactional approach here means that although Putin's regime does not have a shared vision or broader strategic vision with either state, it deals with each in specific policy areas for narrow tactical benefit.[55] Significant shared strategic and economic interests have developed in relations between Iran and Putin's regime in particular, and they have cooperated in a number of key policy areas. In the area of security, Moscow and Tehran have a shared interest in fighting terrorism—at least, of a certain type. Iran (a non-Arab, Shia Islamic state) seeks to become the regional hegemon in any future realignment of the Middle East. To accomplish this, Iranian leaders must counter the influence of challenger Saudi Arabia (a Sunni Arab monarchy), backed by the United States, Iran's longtime enemy. Iran also opposes Sunni extremism in the Middle East, since it is destabilizing and anti-Shia. The Kremlin shares many of these concerns, although not all. Both the Russian and Iranian regimes are concerned with American and European influence in the region; the spread of Islamic terrorism in the Middle East (which can and has leaked into Russia); fostering stability in Central Asia, the Caucasus, and Afghanistan; and stabilizing the conflict in Syria. As former Russian minister of foreign affairs Igor Ivanov has noted, "Russia and Iran might have different opinions on the future of Syria and the Middle East as a whole; however, the sides have a clear understanding of what they do not want to see: a region in chaos torn apart by extremist groups of varying degrees of radicalism, uncontrolled and being a hotbed of terrorism and destabilization."[56]

The most significant area of clear cooperation between Iran and Russia is in Syria. Russian aviators have effectively served as an air force to Iran's ground offensive in support of the regime of Bashar al-Assad. Iran's leaders even permitted Russian strategic bombers briefly to use the Hamedan airbase in southern Iran in the summer of 2016 to stage sorties into Syria. Despite this apparently close cooperation in Syria, however, the two regimes work together on some things—including the need to reduce US influence in MENA and enhance multipolarity globally—but do not agree on everything.[57] Tehran and Moscow differ significantly, for example, regarding the future of Assad in Syria. Putin's regime does not necessarily want him out of power, since that would be further destabilizing to Syria and the region in general, with blowback possible across Russian borders on its southern flank. But should Assad have to leave for one reason or another, Russia's leadership must guide the process to ensure stability. Indeed, Putin delayed meeting Assad in person and providing a photo opportunity that might be seen as an endorsement of Assad's remaining in power. He is expendable as long as Russian leadership is involved heavily in who, if anyone, would replace him. In contrast, as Iran seeks to become the region's dominant power, it is invested heavily in Assad's Alawite (Shia) minority running Syria in perpetuity.

Russian defense policy makers also seek to maintain resurrected influence in the region by retaining access to the Soviet-era Tartus naval base as well as a military base in Latakia, and a newly established presence in the Khmeimim, Shayrat, Tiyas, and Masyaf airbases in Syria. This created a presence from which to further spread Moscow's power in the greater Middle East and North Africa. Russian policymakers also want to ensure that insurgents and Sunni militant groups like ISIS are prevented from moving their conflict closer to Russian borders or radicalizing Sunni Muslims within Russia proper—this could breed radicalism or social instability that could threaten regime stability at home.

As in its near abroad and in its relations with Europe, the issues of energy and non-energy trade are central to Russian policy scope in the MENA region. Since the Joint Comprehensive Plan of Action (JCPOA) was signed between Iran and the "P5+1" group—Russia, China, France, Germany, the United Kingdom, and the United States—in 2015, military collaboration and trade contacts between Russia and Iran increased, culminating in close military cooperation in the war in Syria from 2015, when Russia became officially involved, to the time of writing (2020). The Russian arms export administration also delivered the S-300 missile defense system that it had originally sold to Iran in 2010, but that President Medvedev had promised not to deliver on the same day that the UN Security Council Resolution 1929 against Iran had been passed.[58]

Further, the JCPOA framework provided Russia and Iran the opportunity to develop trade ties in other areas. These included assistance in building the Bushehr nuclear plant in Iran and Russian sales of materials in Iranian railway and infrastructure development. Iran primarily provided agricultural products to Russia, which became especially helpful after Russia's incursion into Ukraine and the resulting sanctions by the United States and the EU. Still, although sanctions have provided opportunities for increased trade between Iran and Russia, overall levels remain relatively small. In 2015, for example, when the JCPOA was signed, "Iran accounted for 0.2% of Russian foreign trade, whereas Russia's share in Iran's foreign trade was 1.1%." Bilateral trade was reportedly worth about $1.24 billion.[59] Significantly, in 2018, Putin's regime moved to assist Iran in marketing its oil, effectively preventing US sanctions from completely cutting off Iran's oil and gas production and exports, although Iranian production has fallen steadily nonetheless. In 2017, the Kremlin initiated a barter arrangement with Iran (originally negotiated in 2014, even before the JCPOA) such that Iran was to provide 100,000 barrels of crude oil per day to Russia in exchange for Russian goods (including food) and services provided for about $2 billion annually. This arrangement, if operational, would seriously blunt the force of American sanctions on Iran imposed in 2018.[60] The regimes in Iran and Russia have also worked to coordinate their export pipelines and crude production volumes, and established a joint Commission on Trade and Economic Cooperation.

Weapons sales play a key part in the bilateral relationship. Before the imposition of a ban on sales of major conventional weapons and weapon systems to Iran in 2010, Iran was Russia's third-largest market for military equipment (behind China and India).[61] In 2016, Russia began to export weapons to Iran again, including the S-300 missile defense system as noted earlier, as part of a $800 million deal originally signed in 2007. Between 2000 and 2018, and even during the period of 2007 through 2015, when there was technically a ban on the supply of conventional arms to Iran, Russia was far and away its biggest supplier of weaponry, outselling China in this period by almost 300% in total.[62] Putin has not been bashful about peddling weapons in the Middle East and Iran in particular; at a conference with Iran's president Hassan Rouhani in September 2019, after an attack on Saudi Arabia's major oil processing complex, purportedly by Houthi rebels in Yemen (perhaps supplied with Iranian armed drones), he even joked that "Saudi Arabia needs to make a smart decision, as Iran did by buying our S-300."[63] The next day, Putin publicly offered to sell Saudi Arabia, a long-standing US ally, Russian-made drones to protect against future attacks that may well have originated in Iran.

The vacuum left by the United States' sudden withdrawal from the JCPOA under the Trump administration, provided the Kremlin with another opportunity to leverage its presence and enhance its influence in the Middle East. Since Russia remained under sanctions from the United States as a result of its incursions into Ukraine since 2014, Russian leaders, searching for new markets, have been emboldened to spread trade and political contacts with Iran, rather than deterred from doing so.

Syria

The Russian decision under President Putin's leadership to intervene in Syria in 2015 to prop up Assad's regime is the most obvious example of Russia's resurgence in global affairs. Peter Zwack and Marie Pierre note that this move "signaled the most significant geostrategic shift in Russia's military activity since the end of the Cold War."[64] This was also the first time Russian forces were on active deployment (beyond peacekeeping missions in the former Yugoslavia) outside the territory of the former Soviet Union. After a chemical strike against civilians in 2013, provoking President Obama's threats that Assad had crossed his "red line" for deeper US military involvement, Putin led successful negotiations to remove Syria's chemical weapons. Here was Russia, back on the world stage, brokering a deal and evidently preventing a US-led attack in Syria. In September 2015, as ISIS moved further into a Syria already splintered into warring factions of the regime's opponents, the Russian military moved in to buttress Assad's forces. In doing so, the Russian leadership changed the facts on the ground and in the air, and usurped any remaining influence the United States and Europe may have had in resolving the Syrian conflict. Russian involvement also heightened the intensity of the conflict and dramatically increased the flow of millions of Syrian refugees into neighboring Lebanon, Jordan, Turkey, and eventually Europe.

The impressively rapid mobilization of forces in Syria also announced to the world—and to Russian citizens back home via daily updates on the conflict by state-controlled news services—that the Russian military was strong and battle-ready, with new weapons systems and capabilities. Indeed, Syria turned out to be a testing ground for a new cohort of young Russian officers who gained serious combat experience—contrasting, for example, with the Chinese military, which is larger than Russia's but inexperienced in prolonged conflict. The engagement also provided state-owned Russian arms exporters with an opportunity to exhibit new weapons they were eager to sell elsewhere in the Middle East and beyond. Russian mercenaries known as the Wagner Group, said to be owned by Putin associate Yevgeny Prigozhin, also emerged in Syria (and later Libya, and elsewhere). In one example of their activity, a reported 200 Russian mercenaries and Syrian government forces were killed during a fatal confrontation with US-NATO forces in eastern Syria, where US forces were supporting anti-Assad forces and defending an oil refinery, in a four-hour exchange of fire. In an interview with Russian journalists in November 2018, the US special representative for Syria, Ambassador James Jeffrey, indicated that there had been about a dozen similar incidents, "some involving exchange of fire, some not."[65] The Russian military has also deployed the S-400 air defense system in Syria, as well as the S-300 system, which, when added to its deployment of strategic bombers and land- and sea-based cruise missiles, radically altered the balance of control over Syrian airspace.

Moreover, a lack of American resolve regarding its goals and commitment in Syria added to the Russian leadership's ability to rapidly deploy its forces to the region, effectively divesting the US and NATO of any real influence in the end of the Syrian civil war. The United States was excluded from talks on civilian safe zones that took place in Astana in 2017 between Russia, Turkey, and Iran, and Russia has become the lead in negotiations with Germany, France, Turkey, and the United Nations in establishing a Syrian Constitutional Commission that might lead to an eventual end to the conflict. In this case again, the Kremlin's key policy areas of security and energy are linked, as Russian military involvement in Syria enabled it to get exclusive rights to produce Syrian oil and gas in 2017. Syria does not have much of either resource, but the real value in this arrangement was that it provided Russia with control over a transportation hub for energy exports from the Middle East.[66] The opportunity for Russia to build and control this kind of energy infrastructural web furthers its geopolitical influence, just as it has managed to do in Europe. It also provides much needed revenue to the Russian economy.

Iraq

Russia has also entered into energy and non-energy trade agreements in other parts of the Middle East, including with American allies Iraq, Turkey, and Israel. Russian oil and gas companies have operated in Iraq since at least 2003, with intensifying oil and gas development since 2015. For example, Gazprom Neft, the largely state-owned Russian oil subsidiary of Gazprom, has worked on oil deposits in Badra and two sites in Kurdistan in Iraq's north, and also developed a gas factory at the former, while Lukoil, a (private) major Russian oil company, had invested an estimated $8 billion in assisting Iraq to develop two other oil fields by the spring of 2018. [67] Rosneft, which is sate controlled and largely state owned assumed operational control of the Kirkuk-Ceyhan oil pipeline, allowing it to transport Iraqi oil from Kurdistan to Turkey. Given the troubled relations between Kurdistan and the government in Baghdad, this arrangement also inserted Rosneft into internal Iraqi politics. Indeed, Iraqi leaders may well see Russian involvement as a counterbalance to Iran and the United States. In 2015, Russia and Iraq coordinated information on terrorists and the fight against the Islamic State, even forming the Joint Information Center in Baghdad. Other important joint institutions include the newly established Russia-Iraq Working Group on Energy Cooperation and the Russia-Iraq Commission on Trade, Economic, Scientific and Technical Cooperation, headed by a Russian deputy prime minister and Iraq's minister of foreign affairs.

Perhaps most surprising, given the US-led coalition's long war in Iraq in the 2000s, Russia once again supplies a significant amount of weaponry to Iraq. During Saddam Hussein's administration, prior to his overthrow by the United States in 2003, Iraq was a major consumer of Soviet and then Russian-made weapons. According to Russian sources, between 1958 and 1990, Iraq had contracts for Soviet weapons valued at the equivalent of current-day $30.5 billion, of which it paid about two thirds or $14.261 billion in hard currency and about $8.152 billion in oil before Saddam invaded Kuwait in August 1990.[68] The USSR also trained Iraqi soldiers and weapons specialists, and Soviets also repaired equipment (for a fee) and helped develop Iraq's domestic weapons industry. After 1990, the adoption of a UN Security Council resolution prohibited further military transfers to Iraq until 2003, when sanctions were lifted. But with the United States largely out of Iraq by 2011, and with Iraq's oil industry recovering enough to produce revenue to purchase new weaponry, Russia once again became a supplier. The first new contracts, worth about $4.2 billion, were signed in 2012, after much shuttle diplomacy between political leaders in Baghdad and Moscow. This initial purchase included forty-eight anti-aircraft missile and cannon systems and forty attack helicopters. In 2013, Iraq ordered another six Russian helicopters. In 2014, with the Islamic State a serious threat in Iraq, Russia was able to quickly supply the Iraqi government with attack air-craft, artillery systems, and three flame throwers.[69]

Iraqi and Russian cooperation goes beyond weapon supplies and energy—both of which have huge potential for Russia—and also includes areas such as creating systems for enhanced water supply in Iraq and nuclear power gen-eration.[70] One Russian analyst notes that a new Iraqi-Syrian border crossing, and the need for security along the highway that would link Damascus with Baghdad, could also create lucrative construction opportunities for Russian companies.[71] Moreover, despite the fact that the United States fought a long and bloody war in Iraq to install a new, ideally democratic, America-friendly regime to replace Saddam Hussein, by 2017, Russia had become an alternate pole for Iraqi politicians, as well as a supporting actor for the Iraqi economy and national security.

Turkey

Since 2012, the relationship between Turkey (a member of NATO, but not the EU) and Russia, while not without difficulty, became closer, too. Energy and se-curity are the two central policy areas in Turkish-Russian interactions. Turkey is heavily dependent on Russian gas, and to a lesser degree on Russian oil, to meet its energy needs. Turkey has sought to leverage its location between Europe and North Africa to become more of an energy transportation hub, which has at times put it at odds with the Russian desire for supremacy in the pipeline business. But Turkey's burgeoning energy needs, and Russia's abundant supplies, as well as their shared interests in building and controlling energy pipelines, has also led to a certain geopolitical interdependence with less competition than cooperation since 2009, though with a few bumpy patches in the relationship.[72] In particular, Russia and Turkey built the Turk Stream pipeline to replace the canceled South Stream and to supplement Blue Stream, which was already present. As Dimitar Bechev noted, "Turk Stream is a commercial and geo-political coup for Russia," providing a new backdoor into Europe while bypassing Ukraine.[73] As Turkish relations with the United States and Europe have worsened, Russia has moved in as an alternative.

But Russia's relations with Turkey were not always warm. Syria has been a particular sticking point; the Turkish government, like that of the United States,

was insistent that Bashar al-Assad would have to leave power in Syria for any settlement to be made. Two months after Russia's intervention in Syria in support
of Assad in September 2015, the Turkish military shot down a Russian fighter
jet on the Syrian border. Russia quickly imposed sanctions in return, which purportedly cost upwards of $10 billion to the Turkish economy in trade revenues
alone, since Russia was a big market for Turkish agricultural products especially,
and Turkey is a popular, affordable destination for Russian tourists.[74] Turkish
president Recep Tayyip Erdoğan ultimately apologized to Putin for the downing
of the aircraft in a phone call in June 2016.

The July 2016 attempted coup against Erdoğan, and the refusal of the US
government to extradite the Islamic cleric Fethullah Gülen, who was widely
believed in Turkey to be behind the attempted overthrow, created an opening
for Putin's government to mend relations with Turkey, while also dealing a blow
to the United States and Europe. Little more than a month after the coup attempt failed, Erdoğan's government abandoned its opposition to finding a settlement to the Syrian war without Assad, which ended the chill in relations with
Russia. At the same time, Americans and Europeans expressed concern about
the increased concentration of power under Erdoğan as a result of changes
rushed through in a referendum on the Turkish constitution in the spring of
2017, and emphasized the need to protect Turkish democracy. In contrast,
Putin backed Erdoğan as he had through the coup attempt, and declared constitutional changes that would harden the Turkish leader's grip on power "exclusively an internal matter."[75] Similarly, America's arming of Kurdish groups
in northern Syria to fight the Islamic State in 2017 was viewed by Erdoğan's
government as a direct threat to Turkish security. This conflict culminated in
October 2019, when President Trump acceded to Erdoğan's request to remove
American soldiers from their position between Turkey and Kurdish forces.
Syrian and Russian forces moved in quickly to wipe the Kurds out, with Turkey
closing in on other side, while Russian soldiers moved in to former US bases on
the Syrian/Turkish border. This cemented the closer ties between Russia and
Turkey, as well as established even more firmly Russia's resurrected influence in
the Middle East.

Warmer relations with Turkey, a member of NATO, is a major plus for
Russian policymakers. With Turkey more in Russia's geographic domain of influence, Russia's ability to project power in the Middle East and North Africa
as well as in Europe was enhanced. Turkey's purchase in 2018 of the Russian
S-400 missile defense system greatly complicated its position in NATO, since
the S-400 system is intended to shoot down American-made F-35 jets. Before
the purchase from Russia went through, the United States had intended to allow
Turkey to produce parts of the F-35s, and it was to have received 100 or so of
the planes. Instead, Turkey was promptly expelled from the F-35 program.

Cooperation with Russia in maintaining the S-400 system, and training Turkish soldiers to use them, has also meant that Turkey regularly hosts Russian military technicians who may use that proximity to gain intelligence on NATO weapons systems and planning in Turkey.

Politically, Putin and Erdoğan have evolved into authoritarian populists who share a dislike of the United States and resentment toward Europe, albeit for different reasons. In the Turkish case, frustration with Europe had built up over its decades-long attempts to meet the EU's accession standards, which some in Turkey attributed to an anti-Muslim sentiment pervasive in Brussels. Turks also felt financially burdened by the influx of migrants from Syria and elsewhere in the Middle East transiting through their country en route to Europe. For these, among the other reasons already described, Russia appeared to be a good strategic alternative that could meet both Turkish security and political concerns, while enhancing ongoing economic ties.

Israel

Russia and Israel, America's strongest ally in the Middle East, have developed a particularly close relationship since the Soviet collapse in 1991. Although Israel presumably will remain a strong ally of the United States for the foreseeable future, Israeli leaders cannot ignore Russia's growing influence on its economy, society, and security. The development of a close Russian-Israeli multidimensional relationship is in stark contrast to the communist period, when the USSR was the staunch ally of Israel's Arab enemies in Egypt and Syria. Vladimir Putin's April 2005 trip to Israel was the first ever visit by a Russian leader to the Jewish state. The blossoming of the post-communist Russian-Israeli relationship was due partly to the migration of an estimated two million ethnic Jews from the former Soviet Union through the late 1980s and early 1990s. The Russian language is pervasively used across Israel; highly educated Russian émigrés have built businesses in the Jewish state, and they return frequently to Russia to invest there or sell their products. Moreover, Russian émigrés have become a force in Israeli politics over the thirty or so years since the start of huge waves of immigration. An estimated 7,000–8,000 people per year still migrate from Russia to Israel at the time of writing, and an estimated 15–16% of Israelis use Russian as their first language.[76] In a sense, the presence of this diaspora community in Israel also provides Russian policymakers some leverage over Israel's policies on Russia. For example, in 2016 the Russian government paid a symbolic sum of about $200 a month to the 100,000 or so Israeli Russians who had emigrated prior to the Soviet collapse and lost the opportunity to claim Russian citizenship and social benefits. In 2018, by presidential decree, the Russian state also began to pay each of the approximately 10,000 Soviet World War II veterans living in

Israel the small sum of $1,000 rubles (about $17) per month for life.[77] These largely symbolic gestures were presumably meant to positively incline the voting diaspora toward Russia and create leverage within Israel's politics.[78]

Since its military involvement in Syria began in 2015, Russia has again also become a crucial strategic actor in the region, directly affecting Israel's national security interests. As others have noted, Russia's thick ties with Israel "offer geostrategic leverage vis-à-vis the Arab states and Iran" as well.[79] For its part, Israel, as a leading power in the Middle East, has more than enough military might to interfere with Russia's Syrian strategy should the Israeli military bomb Iranian forces in northern Syria, as happened repeatedly in the spring of 2018. Russia's other allies in the Middle East count on it to restrain Israel from going further. In contrast to the United States or the EU, under Putin, Russia has been relatively uncritical of Israeli domestic policy on the treatment of Palestinians and extension of settlements. Increased Russian involvement in the Middle East has presented Israeli leaders, therefore, with the opportunity to diversify their regional partners beyond Europe and the United States in their attempts to advance national security.

According to Israeli diplomats, President Putin and Israel's prime minister Benjamin Netanyahu share a personal chemistry too. Between autumn 2015 and spring 2018, they met face to face no fewer than seven times: "They are each one of the other's most frequent foreign interlocutors."[80] For both, though, the regularity of contact was more strategic than based on personal affinity. The Kremlin's bilateral relations with Israel, like its relationships with Iran, Turkey, and Iraq, are broad in policy scope, but in the Israeli case, there are also domestic political and economic reasons for Putin's regime to foster closer ties. As noted, Russian involvement in Syria has necessitated closer and more frequent coordination between the Israeli and Russian militaries. Further, as with Iraq, Russian leaders share Israel's strong aversion to the spread of Islamic terrorism at home. Mark Katz argues that both countries view the other as sharing the same serious foe.[81] Indeed, in his March 2017 visit to Moscow, Prime Minister Netanyahu spoke of Russian-Israeli ties:

> One of the things that unites us is our common fight against radical Islamic terrorism. Substantial progress has been made over the last year in fighting radical Sunni Islamic terrorism led by ISIS and Al-Qaeda, and Russia has made a great contribution to this result and this progress. . . . I want to say that the threat of Shia Islamic terror is directed not only against us, but against the region and the entire world. I am sure that we seek to prevent the threat of all radical Islamic terror, no matter whether it is Shia or Sunni.[82]

The Kremlin has gotten some notable benefits from its improved relations with Israel. Israel abstained in the United Nations General Assembly vote in March 2014 to condemn Russia's annexation of Crimea, and did not join with Europe and the United States in sanctions against Russia thereafter. At the same time, Putin's regime refrained from criticizing Israeli incursions into Gaza.[83]

Egypt and Libya

The Kremlin's ties with leadership in Arab states in the Middle East have also thickened since 2012 in particular—not only because of the return of President Putin to the Kremlin from the prime minister's office, but also as a result of the uprisings throughout the Middle East that began in the spring of 2011 in Tunisia and spread to Egypt, Libya, and beyond. These uprisings presented threats and opportunities for Russia. From a security perspective, Russia had little interest in political instability in the MENA region or the radicalization of politics in the area that could, in turn, radicalize Russia's own minority Muslim populations in the North Caucasus. In his 2015 speech at the United Nations General Assembly, Vladimir Putin condemned the United States' "reckless interventionism," offering them the following rebuke:

> Just look at the situation in the Middle East and Northern Africa. . . . Of course, political and social problems have been piling up for a long time in this region, and people there wanted change. But what was the actual outcome? Instead of bringing about reforms, aggressive intervention rashly destroyed government institutions and the local way of life. Instead of democracy and progress, there is now violence, poverty, social disasters and total disregard for human rights, including even the right to life. I'm urged to ask those who created this situation: *do you at least realize now what you've done?*[84]

But at the same time, the instability caused by the Arab Spring provided Putin's regime with greater opportunities for influence in the Middle East as new governments came to power, and some states descended into civil wars.

As in Israel and Turkey, Egypt's leaders post–Arab Spring, for example, have found Putin's Russia to be a ready alternative to the United States for weaponry. The United States, which nagged over human rights abuses, came to be seen as unreliable compared to Putin's regime, which cared not a whit for internal political matters. Russian suppliers have also been able to get weapons into the region quickly, since the Russian Weapons Export Agency (Rosoboronexport) faces far fewer domestic legal hurdles than do American suppliers. After Egypt's elected president, Mohammed Morsi, was ousted by a military coup, General Sisi, his successor, signed a $3.5 billion contract to purchase Russian-made weapons. Egypt and Russia also conducted joint military exercises in 2016. As in Iran and as promised to Turkey, Russia's Atomic Energy Agency (RosAtom) constructed an Egyptian nuclear power plant. The burgeoning Russian relationships with Egypt and Turkey, until recently reliable American allies, have undermined American influence in the Middle East.[85]

Russia also re-established relations with post-Gaddafi Libya. The Soviet Union had been a weapons supplier to Gaddafi's regime, a relationship that intensified following the Egypt-Israeli rapprochement in the mid-1970s. Gaddafi signed contracts with the Soviet Union to build missile bases in Libya, requiring a sustained presence on Libyan soil by Soviet engineers and military contractors. According to one study, by 1985 there were allegedly 11,000 Russian soldiers stationed in Libya, and a continuous stream of Libyan officials going to the Soviet Union for trainings. Purportedly, Soviet soldiers may even have fought on the Libyan side in a few of its regional conflicts.[86] But by 1985, as Libya under Gaddafi became increasingly isolated internationally, and Gorbachev embarked on perestroika within the Soviet Union, relations tailed off.

In 2008, however, Putin (by then serving as Russia's prime minister under President Medvedev) rekindled the relationship by offering to cancel $4.5 billion in Libyan debt amassed in the Soviet period. This offer was contingent on Gaddafi's regime signing agreements to purchase Russian-made weapons, a contract for Russian firms to build a rail link between the Libyan cities of Sirte and Benghazi, and, finally, unfettered access for Russian ships to the port at Benghazi. This would place Russian ships in the Mediterranean, with increased access to Europe, if needed, and directly facing a US base in southern Italy. In total, the package Gaddafi accepted was worth between $5–10 billion.[87] In 2011, as NATO prepared to intervene in the conflict that would become Libya's civil war and eventually oust Gaddafi, as noted in Chapter 1, Russia under Medvedev abstained from the UN resolution that authorized the mission. Before recognizing any successor government, Russian policymakers sought reassurance that the contracts signed under Gaddafi would be honored. As a result of weapons sanctions imposed by the UN on Libya, Russia had already suffered the indefinite postponement of the rail project and full cancellation of the anti-missile systems contract.

After about 2015, as the military effort in Syria deepened, Russian government involvement in Libya gradually ramped up. The policy scope of the regime's interests in Libya is similar to that elsewhere in the Middle East, although opportunities for Kremlin influence are arguably greater than elsewhere, with the exception of Syria. Libya has large and still largely untapped oil and gas reserves in the east, an area controlled by the Russian-backed warlord General

Khalifa Haftar. Haftar opposes the Government of National Accord, although it has been recognized as legitimate and backed by the UN. Haftar has visited Russia regularly since 2016 to negotiate financial and military support. In the spring of 2016, Russia allegedly printed the equivalent of $3 billion in Libyan dinars at Haftar's request. In the fall of 2016, the Libyan ambassador to Saudi Arabia, an ally of Haftar's, turned to Moscow to request a Russian-led anti-Islamist military operation in Libya, similar to that in Syria. While Putin's regime appears to have refused this request, there is good evidence that Russian involvement in the conflict in Libya increased nonetheless thereafter, although it was far more covert than the Syrian effort.[88]

For Russia under Putin, the goal in Libya, similar to goals in other parts of the Middle East, includes selling Russian weapons systems and gaining influence over future oil and gas production and sales, as well as recouping some of the revenue lost when the Gaddafi regime collapsed, by being able to ensure a role in Libya's eventual postwar infrastructure reconstruction. Beyond economic interests, Russian policymakers are also seeking a greater presence in the Middle East beyond Syria, in part to fight political Islamism, and also to support Russia's new ally, General Sisi in Egypt, who also supports General Haftar in Libya. Beyond this, "western and military officials estimated [even by 2016] several hundred Russian soldiers [were] present in Libya," apparently aiding Haftar's militias with military support and supplying and operating drones on their behalf as they tried to retake Tripoli, the Libyan capital.[89] By the fall of 2019, Russian mercenaries from the shadowy "Wagner Group" had popped up in Libya, just as they had in Syria. Reportedly, thirty-five Wagner mercenaries were killed in Libya, fighting on Haftar's side of the civil war.[90]

Saudi Arabia and the Gulf States

Russian relations with Saudi Arabia and most of the Gulf States have also improved markedly since the early to mid-2000s under Putin. Again, as with other states in the region, Russian ties to Saudi Arabia are largely transactional and non-ideological, perhaps unsurprisingly, focused as they are on coordinating price strategies in global oil markets. Saudi Arabia had historically been a strong opponent of the Soviet Union and a traditional American ally, even funding the mujahedeen in Afghanistan in the 1980s in opposition to the Soviet invasion. But relations between post-Soviet Russia and the Kingdom improved markedly after Putin's 2007 trip to Riyadh—another "first ever" visit for a Russian leader—and grew much closer following the Arab Spring in the Middle East in 2011 and Russia's intervention in Syria in 2015. Saudi Arabia did not necessarily want to prop up Bashar al-Assad, but neither did it want to fully cede control of Syria to its regional rival, Iran. Thus, the Russian military's Syrian intervention fundamentally reshaped the geopolitics of the Middle East while at the same time serving as a platform for Putin's Russia to convey its influence far beyond its borders.

In terms of financial and energy ties, a major interest has been ongoing discussions with Saudi Arabia and other members of OPEC on oil output and production levels. These discussions began in earnest in 2016, when Russian/Saudi-led cooperation with OPEC members led to a price-fixing deal that raised prices from $30 a barrel to $80 by 2018. The deal was extended in July 2019 for another two years, giving Russia "another theater of geopolitical influence in which to exert itself, and one that is particularly important to the United States," as Jason Bordoff of Columbia University's Center on Global Energy Policy noted.[91] Combined, Russia and Saudi Arabia produce 23% of annual global oil output, so their increasingly cooperative relationship has allowed Russia under Putin to establish an especially crucial foothold on influencing global energy prices.[92] At 18% of global production total, the United States is the largest producer of oil; however, it is also the world's largest consumer of oil, at 20% of global consumption. Saudi Arabia and Russia, therefore, are the world's largest exporters and especially when working in concert can have tremendous influence over global prices and the economies to which they sell oil.

At the same time, Saudi Arabia, along with Bahrain, Kuwait, Qatar, and the United Arab Emirates, has invested in Russia through the Russian Direct Investment Fund (RDIF), which was announced following the imposition of European and American sanctions on Russia in 2014.[93] The Saudis pledged $10 million to the RDIF over a five-year period. In addition, Saudi Aramco, the state-owned oil company, hoped to purchase 30% of the Russian gas producer Novatek's liquefied natural gas project in the Arctic, estimated to be worth about $21 billion.[94] Reportedly, by 2018, Rosneft and Gazprom had also been in discussions with Aramco on joint research and development projects.

The Gulf States are also especially large customers for Russian-made weapons. In 2017, Russia and Saudi Arabia signed an agreement worth about $3.5 billion for Russia to supply the Kingdom with its S-400 missile defense system, making Saudi Arabia the second US ally (after Turkey) to purchase the system. The Russian government also signed agreements with Saudi Arabia on a host of other issues when King Salman visited Moscow in the autumn of 2017, the first such official visit by a Saudi monarch. The agreements included a memorandum of understanding that Russia would help Saudi Arabia develop its own military industry.[95]

In sum, in the uncertainty of the pos-Arab Spring Middle East, Putin's Russia has actively sought influence in a range of areas. It has gained economic opportunities in the energy sector, including oil and natural gas extraction and supply, but also control over pipelines and energy infrastructure. Russian companies with state assistance have also made trade gains in other areas across the Middle East beyond these sectors. These have included the construction of nuclear power plants and infrastructure contracts for roads, railways, and ports. Finally, Russian suppliers have stepped in to sell advanced weapons systems and more rudimentary defense materials, especially where the United States had in the past withdrawn contracts over concerns on human rights. Indeed, Russia is second only to the United States as a weapons exporter globally, and between 2014 and 2018, the Middle East became one of its biggest markets, behind Asia and Africa.[96] In pursuing all of these opportunities, Russia's leadership has steadily and effectively built a web of interdependencies across the region that has established it as the major foreign player there. Some analysts have argued that Russian policymakers on the Middle East "have pursued a strategy of creating maximum opportunities with minimal output or commitment."[97] This may have been true a few years ago, but by the end of 2019, Russian commitment and influence in the Middle East had clearly blossomed and radically expanded. The Kremlin was not only able to project significant power in the Middle East, but it also demonstrated its ability to influence the political and economic landscape in a very complicated and troubled region. At the same time, Russian policies served domestic political and economic interests in finding new markets and economic opportunities to exploit while at the same time being able to broadcast back home a narrative about Russia's revival as a great power.

Sub-Saharan Africa

Contemporary Russia's spreading global influence has moved southward from the MENA region into parts of sub-Saharan Africa, too. As in the Middle East, both the imperial and Soviet periods initially established a presence in much of Africa. The Soviet Union was a developmental model for liberation movements in some postcolonial African states. The Soviets also provided military aid to Somalia in the early 1960s, as well as military aid and training in Ethiopia at the same time. By the mid-1970s, the USSR had signed agreements with 32 of 47 African countries for technological and economic assistance, and had trade agreements with 42 African states.[98] In this period, a reported 25,000 Africans were trained at Soviet universities or technical academies as well.[99]

Struggling with its own internal problems in the 1990s as Boris Yeltsin sought to reform politics and the economy back home, however, Russia closed embassies and consular offices. The 1990s was a "lost decade" in Russia's relationships in Africa, as in many other regions with which the Soviets had had strong relations. It was not until 2005 under Vladimir Putin that Russia again increased its interactions with African Union states. Indeed, in 2006, Putin became the first Russian head of state (yet another first) to visit sub-Saharan Africa, though the region still ranked low in terms of international priorities, based on the 2008 Russian Foreign Policy Concept.[100] In 2015, however, with Russian influence in the Middle East greatly enhanced through its intervention in Syria, sub-Saharan Africa gained new importance for Russia, appearing as a priority area in a national security document emphasizing trade potential; economic, military, and technical cooperation; and opportunities for educational aid. As one study noted, "While significant consideration has been paid to the emerging role of China, India and others in Africa, the return of Russia . . . has been mostly ignored."[101] Indeed, the 2016 Russian security concept describes an intention to establish "multi-dimensional interactions with African states."[102] In what should now be a recognizable theme to the reader, Russia's interests in Africa are in natural resources extraction; the marketing and control of transportation routes; trade in arms sales; security on the continent that would require military cooperation, education, and humanitarian needs; and the providing of materials for infrastructural development, including roads and nuclear power plants.[103] Among these, arms sales have been an easy way for Russia to enter or re-establish trade relations with many African states. Somalia, an old Soviet ally, for example, needed Russian weapons in its battle with Al-Shabaab. In return, Russia has become a partner in developing oil, gas, and uranium. In Ethiopia, Russia is investing in the energy sector; similarly, Uganda, another former Soviet ally and sometime US partner, sought Russian assistance in infrastructure development and an emerging energy sector. In Kenya, the biggest East African economy, Russia has re-emerged as a key trading partner. Russia has canceled billions in former Soviet debt extended to African countries: $16 billion in 2008, $20 billion in 2012, and another $20 billion in 2019 at the Russian-African forum in Sochi. In return for what was almost certainly unrecoverable debt, Russia has gained contracts for infrastructural development across the continent.[104]

Where is the value of Russia's resurrection on the African continent? It is largely economic, especially in the wake of the sanctions imposed on some of the jewels of the Russian economy, often under the control of businesses owned directly by or tied tightly to Putin's cronies. In some cases, too, it is possibly less expensive to mine and market African natural resources, like oil and precious minerals, than in Russia itself. In addition, the continent is home to one billion consumers with emerging tech needs and interests that Russian companies are happy to try to serve as they look for new markets to replace those that were closed to them after 2014. Russia's trade and investment on the continent still seriously lag behind China's and India's. This is unsurprising, since Russia is a relative newcomer to the region, but for African countries, Putin's Russia provides an alternative to China with different strengths.[105] For instance, Russian companies have particular expertise in natural resource extraction and marketing. The Russian economy gains from collaboration with countries that export such minerals as manganese, chrome, nickel, zinc, lead, and bauxite; access to some of these was diminished by the territorial losses accompanying the collapse of the Soviet Union, while others are limited to areas that are difficult to mine east of the Urals. Some of Russia's biggest companies have projects in Africa, including some that are state-owned or very closely tied to the state like Gazprom, Lukoil, Alrosa, Renova, Rusal, RosAtom, and Norilsk Nickel, among others. Such projects exist in South Africa (helped by ties established through BRICS trade cooperation), Libya, Angola, Democratic Republic of Congo, Togo, Botswana, Nigeria, Ghana, and Namibia.[106] Big projects have focused on diamond extraction in Angola, gas pipeline construction in Nigeria, nickel mining in Botswana, oil deposit exploration in Côte d'Ivoire and Ghana, precious mineral mining in South Africa, and oil extraction in Equatorial Guinea. Other areas of cooperation include telecommunications, education, healthcare—where Russian suppliers have emerged as a cheap alternative to Western sources of vaccinations and medication—and military-technical assistance. Finally, about half of the estimated 8,000 African students in Russia in 2012 were on Russian government scholarships.[107]

In a further show of political and economic ties, President Putin played host to 43 (of 54 total) African heads of state and governments in the first ever Russia-Africa Summit in Sochi in 2019. Following the pattern in the Middle East, Putin's regime offered African leaders relief from Soviet-era debt in exchange for contracts to construct nuclear power plants, supply advanced jet fighters and missile defense systems, and obtain access to precious metal mines or oil and gas reserves and pipelines. Further demonstrating Russia's penetration in Africa, Putin claimed that 2,500 African servicemen had been trained at Ministry of Defense facilities in Russia since 2014. Russian social media training by RT and Sputnik was offered to African journalists in 2019. Overall, however, although Russian annual trade with African countries doubled to $20 billion between 2014 and 2018, it remained a fraction of the EU's $300 billion or the United States' $60 billion.[108]

But Russian influence in parts of Africa extends beyond economics alone. The Kremlin has sent election observers to endorse the fairness of elections and the legitimacy of their results in suspect cases like Zimbabwe, Democratic Republic of Congo, and Mozambique, contradicting international agencies that claimed the results were problematic. One presidential candidate in Côte d'Ivoire explained in 2019, "My experience is that the Russian authorities I meet with want business. They don't talk about ideology. They don't talk about political control." Similarly, the foreign minister of Djibouti pointed to suffering and instability in Iraq, Afghanistan, and Syria, which he blamed on American and European policy, pondering, "maybe Russia is the alternative?"[109]

Under Putin, Russia has also established more covert means of influence in Africa. Central to these tactics is the Wagner Group, a shadowy private military group that, as already mentioned in reference to mercenaries killed in Syria and Libya, is owned by Yevgeny Prigozhin—Putin's "caterer" and the purported owner of the Internet Research Group implicated in the interference in the US 2016 presidential election (discussed further in chapter 7)[110]—but that appears to have the protection and endorsement of the Kremlin. According to at least one report allegedly based on documents from employees of the Wagner Group, its constituents may have been active in thirteen African states, including the Central African Republic (CAR), Madagascar, Sudan, Zimbabwe, and South Africa.[111] In the CAR, for example, Putin's Russia with and without the help of mercenaries, is credited with helping settle a seemingly endless civil war. One political aide to the president claimed, "No one came to our aid except the Russian Federation. With the help of Russia, we will be able to secure our diamond mines."[112] Indeed, Russia seems to have made the intervention financially profitable, as Russian companies have helped mine and market CAR diamonds. A similar profit motive appeared to have been the rationale behind Russian interference in presidential elections in Mozambique, where it used social media to boost the ratings of the eventual winner. In return, another Prigozhin venture, this time a mining company was able to secure contracts in the chromium mining sector.[113] This is an excellent example of how the system of patronalism under Putin's leadership has benefited from the state's power projection abroad.

Finally, Russian operatives have used "sharp" power tools to expand influence in parts of sub-Saharan Africa in ways not dissimilar to their interventions in the 2016 US presidential election. A report by the Stanford Internet Observatory demonstrated that Russian operatives worked with local contacts in Mozambique, Sudan, Cameroon, and Libya to develop disguised Facebook pages to promote Russian policies and criticize French and US policies. One fake site in Sudan was designed to look like a real news outlet, *Sudan Daily*, but just reposted articles from Russia's state-owned Sputnik news.[114]

In sum, as in Europe and the Middle East, Russia under Vladimir Putin has sought and often gained political and economic influence in sub-Saharan Africa. It is, to be sure, still a junior player compared to China, the United States, or Europe, but the rapid growth of its interventions and the variety of instruments it has used have re-established it as an important, and often disruptive, player on the continent.

Latin America

As in other regions, Putin's Russia has sought to rebuild Soviet-era relationships and establish new partners in Latin America. Beyond Cuba, the Soviet Union was not all that active in the region during the Cold War.[115] The Soviets did provide some support to leftist regimes in Nicaragua and El Salvador, for example, but these were not fully communist regimes and did not have close trade and security ties, as did Cuba under Castro. But after the global financial crisis of 2008, clear signs of Russian engagement in Latin America emerged. These relationships continued to blossom in the decade that followed, and especially as Russian companies sought to avoid isolation in the wake of US and European sanctions after 2014. Echoing its push into the Middle East and Africa, in Latin America, Russian interests have coalesced around energy, arms sales, and infrastructure development deals. Putin's Russia capitalized on the BRICS relationships to launch its renewed presence in the Western Hemisphere. In 2014, Putin used the BRICS summit in Brazil to visit Cuba, Argentina, and Nicaragua en route. As was the case in sub-Saharan Africa, Putin forgave almost all of Cuba's Soviet-era debt of $35.2 billion in return for investment opportunities; in Nicaragua, Putin appeared to offer military support and helped supply intelligence assistance in counter-narcotics operations for the Ortega regime.[116] A few months prior to Putin's summer 2014 visit to the region, Foreign Minister Sergei Lavrov paid visits to Nicaragua, Cuba, Chile, and Peru, and in a speech noted that "Latin America is a powerful, growing and very promising region, which is turning into a pillar of the new world order."[117] In 2017, Rosneft signed agreements with Brazil for a controlling stake in drilling for oil in the Amazon Basin. Putin also requested that Ecuador, Brazil, Argentina, and Chile provide agricultural products to Russia, replacing those that would normally have come from the EU but were under counter-sanction. Increased trade with Russia also served to decrease Latin American dependence on Chinese raw material imports at precisely the time when China's economic growth slowed.

In 2000, total trade between Russia and all of Latin America was only about $3 billion; Russia's imports were largely agricultural and food products, while it supplied Latin American militaries with new tanks, helicopters, and surface-to-air missiles.[118] This changed with Russia's re-engagement with the region; such that according to one estimate, by 2013 Russian–Latin American trade had grown to as much as $24 billion. While significant, this was still about 10% of China's trade with Latin American countries, and the United States has managed to maintain top trading partner status.[119] But Russia has also established strong strategic relationships that include access to ports in Cuba, Venezuela, and Nicaragua. According to testimony to the US Senate Armed Services Committee in 2018 by the Commander of US Southern Command, Admiral Kurt Tidd, these arrangements "provide Russia with a persistent, pernicious presence, including more frequent maritime intelligence collection visible force projection in the Western Hemisphere. The sanctuary of robust relationships with these three countries provides Russia with a regional platform to target US and partner nation facilities and assets, exert negative influence over undemocratic governments, and employ strategic options."[120]

Most significant in Russia's projection of influence in Latin America is its relationship with Venezuela, the recipient of the most notable arms deals. According to the Stockholm International Peace Research Institute (SIPRI), between 2005 and 2014, Venezuela purchased two dozen fighter jets and fifty-one transport, armed assault, and combat helicopters in addition to artillery, tanks, anti-tank missiles, anti-ship missiles, air-to-air missiles, anti-missile defense systems, and infantry and assault weapons. The total sales were estimated at $12 billion. These huge Venezuelan purchases caused concern in other countries in Latin America, as well as the United States, that the region would be flooded with weaponry, some of which could find its way into the hands of armed insurgencies, the FARC in Colombia being one example.[121]

Venezuela under Nicolas Maduro has grew increasingly dependent on Putin's Russia, especially since the crash of oil prices in 2014. American sanctions on both countries also arguably drove them into one another's arms, as they have looked for new partners for their energy products. Between 2014 and 2017, Russia's leadership extended Venezuela $10 billion in financial assistance, overtaking China as "Venezuela's principal banker."[122] In 2016, as collateral for a $1.5 billion loan, Rosneft took a 49.9% stake in Venezuela's state oil company's refining subsidiary, Citgo, based in the United States. In 2017, Russia paid a $1 billion advance for crude oil produced by the Venezuelan state oil company to help Venezuela service its bond payments. In this way, Venezuela became second only to Russia itself as a source of crude oil. By the end of 2017, Rosneft was reselling about 224,000 barrels a day of Venezuela's oil, "the equivalent of 13% of Venezuela's exports,"[123] and by 2019, Rosneft was handling 66% of its oil exports.[124] In the spring of 2020, Rosneft's assets in Venezuela were transferred to an entity wholly owned by the Russian state. Despite heavy sanctions on Venezuela by the United States against the state-owned Petroleos de Venezuela (PDVSA), Putin's Russia managed to keep Venezuelan oil on international markets. Indeed, Russian support effectively saved the Maduro government from complete collapse in 2019. That spring, amid rumors of an armed American intervention, Secretary of State Mike Pompeo announced with some certainty that the embattled Venezuelan leader was preparing to flee Caracas as violent protesters demanded his ouster in favor of opposition leader Juan Guaidó. But Russia's leadership sent two military planes with Russian military "technicians" to intervene; evidently the US backed away, and Maduro remained in power.

Putin's regime also used its chair at the table in the United Nations Security Council to protect Venezuela and Nicaragua against further sanctions, as well as providing other financial avenues to lessen the impact of American and EU sanctions.[125] As with the Middle East, and to some extent parts of Africa, Russia's commercial interests in Latin America are helping to prop up governments that routinely violate human rights and that have grown increasingly hostile toward the United States. Strikingly, in February 2018, the commander of US Southern Command argued to the US Senate Foreign Services Committee that "[l]eft unchecked, Russian access and placement could eventually transition from a regional spoiler to a critical threat to the US homeland."[126]

Russia's Expanded Relations with China and India Multiply Its Global Influence

Moscow's increasing and intensifying relationships across Asia are too numerous to explore in significant depth here. Indeed, renewed Russo-Sino relations alone are worthy of a book in and of themselves. My goal here is to demonstrate that since 2012 in particular, the current Russian regime has sought to grow and diversify its trade linkages across Asia, as well as to create chains of economic and strategic dependencies and connectivity that would make it difficult for the United States or Europe to isolate Russia internationally. I begin with a brief overview of the warming in Chinese-Russian relations, arguing that economic and military cooperation has grown significantly since the early 2000s such that by 2019, Dan Coats, then director of US National Intelligence, testified to the Senate Select Committee on Intelligence that "China and Russia are more aligned than at any point since the mid-1950s."[127] Cooperation between China under President Xi Jinping and Russia under Putin went far beyond their shared 4,200 km border and poor relations with the United States (they were listed as the top two threats to US national security in the 2017 National Security Strategy) to increased energy and non-energy trade, military, and technology spheres. From the perspective of Russia's expanding global influence, warmer relations with China—the world's largest economy (at purchasing power parity)—are crucial.

Even before Russian forces appeared in Crimea and Eastern Ukraine in 2014 and the ensuing sanctions imposed on parts of the economy, Putin's Russia had begun closer economic and strategic collaboration with China under Xi. This was an axis of mutual convenience to be sure, and came at a time when relations with the United States were in sharp decline for both Russia and China, but closer relations with China also had the effect of amplifying the opportunities for Putin's Russia to project its global influence more broadly .

As in other areas, under Putin, Russian interests in China were guided by energy supply, non-energy trade, military sales and cooperation, regional security issues like North Korea, the South China Sea, and, more recently, transportation and trade routes opening in the Arctic. Given the size of the Chinese economy and population relative to Russia's, it is often argued that Russia is the weaker partner in any relations with China.[128] The asymmetry in these traditional measures of global power are obviously true, but that does not necessarily tell us much about the degree to which the relationship between contemporary Russian and Chinese leadership might affect Russian power projection in general. Russia's population is smaller, but richer per capita, than China's; its nuclear arsenal is larger; its military technology is superior; and its weighty influence in energy markets—control and ownership of vast energy resources, and energy transportation networks—all help to bring some balance to the relationship.[129] Nonetheless, there are clear areas where Putin's Russia must contend with China—for example, with respect to the latter's Belt and Road Initiative (BRI) and the possibility of pulling Russia's Central Asian partners out of its economic orbit. Perhaps to try to mitigate Russian concern in 2015, Xi agreed to coordinate with Russia on Central Asian investments with the Eurasian Economic Union. Russia and China also jointly founded the Shanghai Cooperation Organization (SCO), and despite predictions of conflict rather than comity, there is growing evidence that "their common focus does not mean they are necessarily competing against each other. . . . Rather, China and Russia share similar concerns about Eurasia's political stability and security, and similar overall objectives regarding what a future regional order should look like."[130]

Beyond stability and security in the greater Eurasian landmass, the policy areas where Russian and Chinese interests now more closely converge are in security and trade. China has purchased S-400 anti-missile defense systems from Russia, as well as Su-35 jets. According to SIPRI, about 12% of Russia's weapons sales went to China between 2013 and 2017.[131] Russian-Chinese defense cooperation goes beyond just weapons sales, however. Their militaries have conducted military joint trainings since the mid-2000s, ranging from smaller anti-terrorism exercises to the larger Vostok 2018 exercise although it featured far greater representation from Russia than from China.[132] The larger Tsentr exercise in 2019 included not only Russia and China, but also India, Pakistan, Tajikistan, Uzbekistan, Kyrgyzstan, and Kazakhstan. Tsentr involved 128,000 personnel, and included a mock invasion of a hypothetical terrorist state and a series of exercises involving special forces troops tasked with defending Russia's Arctic bases. The vast majority of the participants were in fact Russian, however, with only 1,600 soldiers from China. Officially, China and Russia have no military alliance, "but the two militaries are becoming more familiar with each other. They are taking part in joint training; making their weapons systems more compatible, and syncing their communications, logistics, tactics and military doctrines."[133] Clearly the strategic relationship between Russia and China is deepening. One could argue that there is even an "authoritarian peace" dynamic—where the two autocrats have an implicit agreement to avoid conflict with one another—in Russian-Chinese relations that did not exist prior to 2008.[134]

Cooperation on strategic matters is more extensive than is Sino-Russian economic cooperation, although by 2019, Russia had become China's largest supplier of crude oil, and bilateral trade rose from $69.6 billion in 2016 to $107.1 billion in 2018.[135] This was in part underpinned by the construction in 2011 of the Russian Eastern-Siberian Pacific Ocean (ESPO) pipeline, which provided a new pathway to supplying crude oil to China and other Asian markets. It enabled Russia to increase oil exports to China by 146 percent from 2012 to 2017. In 2016, Russia reportedly became the biggest oil supplier to China, displacing Saudi Arabia from that position.[136] In 2019, the "Power of Siberia" natural gas pipeline was completed with the capacity to export 38 billion cubic meters of liquefied natural gas to China, diversifying China's LNG sources while providing Russia with an ongoing revenue source.[137]

Arguably too, as autocrats evidently with lifetime appointments, who are close in age, and who have established their unrivaled predominance in their respective systems, there is a shared vision of the postwar global order that must be multipolar, not dominated by the United States, but that recognizes the "exceptional" roles of their two countries in the emerging international system.[138] To the extent that personal relationships between leaders matter in international politics, Xi and Putin have declared their close friendships publicly: in 2017 Putin bestowed upon Xi the Russian "Order of St. Andrew the Apostle," Russia's highest award for prominent statesmen and citizens.[139] A year later, Xi awarded Putin China's first ever "Friendship Medal," declaring on live Chinese state television in June 2018 that "President Putin is a good and old friend of the Chinese people. . . . He is my best, most intimate friend."[140] By that point, the two had met more than twenty-five times bilaterally, more than either had with any other head of state, according to Leon Aron.

All of this is in rather stark contrast to Soviet-Sino relations that progressively worsened under Stalin and Mao, culminating in a break in the 1970s. Indeed, there is no ideological component in Chinese-Russian relations in the twenty-first century; the blossoming relationship between Putin's Russia and contemporary China is pragmatic. The Russian regime needs Chinese markets and foreign investment to keep its economy growing and society stable, while China needs Russia's energy and weaponry. There are shared interests in exploring the Arctic for new energy sources, as well as in forging new, more direct trade routes through there. There are shared security interests in Central Asia. Both need new allies who might support their respective new territorial claims in the South China Sea for China and Ukraine in the case of Russia. The countries occupy two of the five permanent seats on the United Nations Security Council, and "they vote almost in unison in the United Nations."[141] China abstained from the United Nations Security Council resolution condemning Putin's seizure of Crimea in 2014, the only member (other than Russia, which vetoed it) to do so.

Moreover, as the foregoing should illustrate, Russia's rapprochement with China ultimately serves to extend Russia's global reach in international politics, the primary aspect of the relationship of interest here.

Russia and South Asia

Russia under Putin has forged new power-magnifying relations with China, the world's most populous country (at 1.42 billion people), but it has further amplified its global reach and influence by re-establishing and deepening inherited Soviet era economic and trade relationships with India, the world's second most populous country (at 1.37 billion). In contrast to relations with China, which are radically different from the fraught Chinese-Soviet relationship, contemporary Russia's warm relations with India are largely a continuation of the strong ties that had developed between India and the Soviet Union. Although Jawaharlal Nehru, India's first prime minister, was the leader of the Non-Aligned Movement, he nonetheless allowed India to accept general development aid and military assistance from the Soviets. Nehru's daughter, Prime Minister Indira Gandhi, found the Soviets easier to work with than the Americans and increased India's defense cooperation with the USSR, especially when it came to its battles with Pakistan in the 1970s. In the mid-1970s, the USSR and India expanded their economic ties and military cooperation such that the Soviets assisted India with the construction of steel plants and mining coal while supplying oil to India. In 1974 the Soviets helped with India's first nuclear test.[142]

As with states in the Middle East that have long had adversarial relationships with one another, as noted earlier in this chapter, in Asia and South Asia, Russia under Putin has proven able to balance constructive relationships with traditional rivals in the region. With respect to India, contemporary Russia has sought to continue its large volume of weapons' sales, while at the same time balancing this with expanding relations with China, India's traditional regional rival, and with Pakistan, which has long had an adversarial relationship with India. In part, Putin's Russia has sought this balance working through several regional trade and security organizations like the BRICS grouping of nations which, of course, includes Russia, but also India and China in the Asia-Pacific region and its accompanying institutions like the BRICS Development Bank; the Shanghai Cooperation Organization (SCO) described in chapter 2; the Association of South East Asian Nations (ASEAN), through which Russia has sought to develop further trade ties with growing economies in South Asia like Vietnam as well as with South Korea and Japan; and the Collective Security Treaty Organization (CSTO), which includes Armenia, Belarus, Kazakhstan,

Kyrgyzstan, Russia, Tajikistan, and the two observer states of Serbia and Afghanistan. Since the mid-2000s, the CSTO, which Russia leads, has sought closer ties and cooperation with the SCO in the areas of counterterrorism, anti-narcotics trade, arms trafficking, and transnational crime, for example. The BRICS nations have in some areas acted collectively, now holding, for example, almost 15% of votes in the membership of the International Monetary Fund, cooperating in development funding with BRICS bank, and also holding similar positions in the United Nations General Assembly.[143]

Despite this comity with regional organizations and the UN, contemporary Russia has had to seek balance in its blossoming trade and political relationships with China and with its inherited warm relations with India. The volume of trade between India and post-Soviet Russia has been much smaller than it has become with China. Indian investment in Russia has also been relatively limited, although it has been in vital areas of mutual interest like defense, pharmaceuticals, diamond, and non-fossil fuels energy sectors—as in India's agreement in 2017 to have Russian firms build twelve nuclear power plants.[144]

Contemporary Russia's relationship with India has bridged other regions and arguably helps to extend its geographic reach. For example, in 2015, Moscow, New Delhi, and Tehran signed agreements in principle to build a high-speed rail system to connect Russia, India, and Iran in a trade corridor.[145] India, despite its warm relations with the United States, like China also did not support Western resolutions in the United Nations against Russia's seizure of Crimea in 2014. Indeed, since 2014, India has not only continued its high volume of defense purchases from Russia, it has increased investment in Russia's Arctic oil interests, purchasing a $1.27 billion (15%) stake in the Vankor oilfield, for example, at a time when the West imposed sanctions on companies exploring there. Further, Rosneft and India's Essar agreed in 2015 to refine 100 million tons of oil in India over a ten-year period, and Rosneft gained a 49% stake in the shares of the refinery and a chain of more than 3,000 gas stations in India.[146]

Russia has maintained its position as India's main supplier of defense equipment—supplying as much as 56% of Indian military-technical equipment between 2015 and 2019, and that high figure was actually a decrease from 74% in the preceding four year period.[147] As with Turkey, Saudi Arabia, and elsewhere, Russia has also supplied India with S-400s. Russia is not, however, just a military supplier to India; by 2017, Putin's Russia had licensed some of its military technology for India to develop fighter jets, tanks, ammunition, and helicopters. Since 2003, Russia and India have also held annual joint military exercises. According to the Russian International Affairs Council, India even provided Afghanistan with five Russian-Indian made helicopters in 2015.[148]

Despite this close cooperation in the defense area, other areas of trade and security cooperation between India and Russia are more aspirational and prospective. Aside from notable investments in the energy sector by India in Russia, and in general economic development in the Russian Far East, the volume of trade and investment between the two is low and focused on construction, pharmaceuticals, and transport. India's Narendra Modi and Putin, however, pledged to increase trade between the two countries by three times the 2018 volume, to $30 billion by 2025, although this would only be a fraction of India's trade with the United States, which reached $US84 billion in 2018.[149] India's growing energy needs (by 2019 it had become the third largest energy importer in the world) are an important market for Russian firms, but the two countries are also seeking to partner in high technology fields like artificial intelligence, robotics, biotechnology, space technology (satellites in particular), and nanotechnology.[150]

Russia's renewed relations with India, not dissimilar from those with China, have provided avenues by which to avoid the full impact of Western sanctions on its economy since 2014, while also representing large new markets in reality, in the case of China, and in potential, in the case of India. Russia under Putin has thus far deftly managed the political and strategic tensions simmering between these Asian powerhouses to further its global reach more generally. Moreover, Putin's regime has not so much exercised its power resources against or over these two nations as much as sought to partner with them in strategic areas to make them "force multipliers" for Russia's influence beyond its borders.

Conclusion

In virtually every region of the world, the resurgent Russia has emerged with an ever-growing geographic scope aimed at increasing its political and economic influence far beyond its borders. In some countries, Russian government involvement has been merely disruptive, as it was in parts of Europe in various instances of electoral interference. In other countries, Moscow's involvement has been decisive, as in Syria, where the Russian military intervention truly changed the facts on the ground not only in Syria itself, but also for the greater Middle East. The geographic domain of Russian power has expanded dramatically in comparison to the 1990s, although it does not match that of the Soviet Union. The policy scope in which Putin's Russia exercises its influence is focused on energy, trade, and national security and the regime's own domestic political security. The involvement of the Russian military in the Syrian conflict provided the regime with the opportunity to promote the narrative at home that under Putin's leadership, Russia was again reclaiming its status as a global power or, as in the quotation that opened this chapter, "as a strong state—a country that others heed and that can stand up for itself." The question remains, however, as to whether modern Russia has the economic, social, hard, soft, and "sharp" power means by which to maintain and extend its influence across the globe. The next section of this book addresses this question by turning from a focus on the first two dimensions of power in the multidimensional framework employed in this study—geographic domain and policy scope—to an evaluation and comparative analysis of the relative means that Putin's regime has available in pressing for a new global order.

SECTION III

THE MEANS
OF RUSSIAN POWER

The Unsteady Economic Basis of Russian Power

"Our aims are absolutely clear: They are a high living standard in the country and a secure, free and comfortable life."
—Vladimir Putin, 2006

Despite this statement by Vladimir Putin in 2006 that the goal of his economic policies was to establish an ever higher standard of living for his people, the economy has often been viewed as a reliable brake on Russia's global ambitions. The late US Senator John McCain once referred to Russia as "a gas station masquerading as a country," characterizing its economy as excessively resource-dependent and therefore not particularly threatening to the United States and the postwar order. Other observers have referred to it as a "basket case," pointing to the numerous economic crises the Russian economy has faced since the Soviet collapse in 1991. Still other analysts, in characterizing what ails the Russian economy, point to the seemingly endemic corruption of Russian politicians in stealing state assets and revenues, highlighting the role of "oligarchs" who made money in the fast and loose economic rules of the 1990s and amassed great wealth at the expense of the Russian people.[1]

There is some truth in all of the foregoing, though the reality, naturally, is more complex. In turning to an evaluation of the Russian economy, this chapter refocuses the study of power to look at the economic and financial means available to its leaders in projecting its influence abroad. Can the Russian economy finance the global ambitions of Russia under President Putin? Russia's growth trajectory since the collapse of the Soviet Union has been far from linear. Its economy was far too dependent on revenues from raw materials exports, leaving state budgets vulnerable to the inevitable variations in global prices for oil, gas, and minerals. The state remained too heavily involved in the Russian economy in ways that clearly impaired the development of a thriving private sector.

Corruption at different levels of bureaucracy, including at the very top of the political system, remained a drag on growth and a deterrent to foreign investment even a quarter century after the Soviet collapse. Without a doubt, with better governance, better policy, and more diversification of production, the Russian economy could have been performing far better.

Nonetheless, given the Russian Federation's dismal starting point in 1992, it has come a very long way. The spectacular growth at the beginning of this century was an especially stark contrast to the contraction of the late 1980s and tumultuous path of the 1990s. Maintaining high growth in the early-to-late 2000s fueled Russian leaders' ambitions and capabilities as a disruptive force in global affairs. Even after the global economic crisis of 2008, the Russian economy recovered from the crash between 2009 and about 2014, when oil prices again turned downward. This second big downturn in oil export revenues compounded Russian economic challenges, occurring at the same time that Europe and the United States imposed economic sanctions following the annexation of Crimea. Nonetheless, at the end of calendar year 2019, just before the global economy was shaken by the global pandemic of the COVID-19, the Russian economy had settled into a modestly positive growth pattern of about 1–2.5% per year.[2] (The pandemic, of course, produced a sharp decline in growth of 6% by mid-2020, according to the World Bank estimates because of the high infection rate in Russia, but the global economic effect of the pandemic was similarly traumatic.[3])

While respectable, this was considerably slower than the boom period of 2003–2008, when gross domestic product (GDP) topped 7% annual growth on average and real incomes doubled or even tripled for some Russians. Clear signs of development and modernity were pervasive. The price of real estate in Moscow bubbled up to higher levels per square meter than in London at the same time. "New Russians"—those who made their money quickly, and sometimes corruptly, in the wake of the Soviet Union's demise—accumulated Ferraris, Jaguars, Bentleys, Mercedes, and BMWs. In the blink of an eye, the sad, mostly empty little stalls of the Soviet-era GUM (GosUniverMag), the shopping center that borders Red Square, turned into an upscale mall for the moneyed class, offering high-end wares the likes of Gucci, Chanel, and Fendi. Decrepit tourist lodgings in Moscow and St. Petersburg were hastily transformed into ultra-luxury hotels to house foreign consultants, investors, and businesspeople. The streets of Moscow and St. Petersburg became choked in the kind of traffic that is the curse of other bustling European cities.

Within twenty-five years from the disintegration of communism, Russia had private property, real estate and insurance markets, a floating currency, and, by 2012, through its membership in various trade organizations and the World Trade Organization, had further integrated its economy into the global system of commerce. Despite this rapid progress in establishing a new capitalist frame-work, the hastily and haphazardly built market system was not completely free; often, under Putin's patronal autocracy, politics was still paramount in deter-mining who could enter. Over seventy-four years of communism, politics came to dominate economics through a planning system designed to control every aspect of production. The system's construction was in reaction to the miserable inequities of the Russian imperial system, in which a small aristocracy headed by an autocratic Romanov tsar ruled over a largely uneducated, impoverished, and rural population. Vladimir Lenin and his Bolshevik Party comrades twisted Karl Marx's theory of a proletarian paradise to fit Russian conditions in the early twentieth century, certain that the equality of Russian workers, peasants, and aristocrats could be ensured by stripping citizens of all private ownership. Those egalitarian ambitions gave way to repression and deference to an omnipotent and omnipresent Soviet state.

In the immediate post-communist period, the state's role in the Russian economy became far smaller, but the system of patronal politics (described in greater detail in chapter 8) still largely determined who owned what. Competition, although present, was not consistently transparent in Russian markets. Rather, the distribution of property and profits was dependent on proximity to state actors at the federal level and across local governments, which controlled access to various markets. Taxation was often negotiable and non-transparent for firms, and bureaucrats at all levels treated the state as a means of extracting bribes to supplement their meager salaries. The protection of pro-perty rights was similarly uneven and corrupt. Indeed, corruption at all levels of the state was pervasive, some of it newly created by the opportunities presented in a largely lawless environment in the early 1990s, some of it carried over from Soviet past bureaucratic practice, and in the 2000s some of it newly created by Putin's patronal autocracy. The entire system is aptly described as crony capi-talism, or as a kleptocracy—a system by which those in power use, or simply appropriate, state resources for personal enrichment.[4]

None of this sounds encouraging as a basis for the projection of Russian power abroad. Russian development in the early 2000s was swift but lumpy and unevenly distributed, and the soaring growth rates of the mid-2000s proved unsustainable once global oil prices plummeted in 2008. When they declined again in 2014, the same year that sanctions against Russia were introduced, the vulnerability of the still insufficiently diversified Russian economy was further underscored. Russia's economic cycles of boom and bust demonstrated its en-during and deep developmental challenges. After slightly twenty-five years of reform, the Russian economy still produced very little that was globally export-able other than military equipment, vodka, caviar, energy products, and metals. It was neither an innovation economy with Googles, TenCents, Facebooks, and

Apples,[5] nor an emerging "imitation" economy that could more cheaply produce products designed elsewhere. There turned out to be no Putinist economic model or miracle as in China, South Korea, or Taiwan. Russia had slipped into a low-growth equilibrium.

Nonetheless, Russian policymakers became more nimble in navigating the economy through successive crises. As noted, some good policy decisions (and a little luck with rising prices in global oil markets) blunted the full force of the economic downturn that began again in 2014.[6] The Russian government invested in transportation infrastructure and social projects and, significantly, rebuilt its military before doing so. In order to smooth the cycles of volatility that can be endemic to economies heavily reliant on extractive industries like oil and gas, in 2002 astute Russian policymakers created two large national funds, the Reserve Fund and the National Wealth Fund, which could be tapped for infrastructure development and social welfare projects, but also to bail out large state-owned companies saddled by huge debt in the wake of the 2008 crisis. As a result, as 2017 drew to a close, the Russian economy was emerging from recession, even as oil prices remained far lower than ten years earlier and as economic sanctions continued to impact some gems of the Russian economy.

Indeed, a close examination of how far and how fast Russia progressed in the twenty-five years following the demise of communism demonstrates that although its economy had significant challenges in returning to the high rates of growth of the mid-2000s, the abilities of its economic policy makers improved, as did the fiscal instruments they had at their disposal. Further, even during the economic downturns between 2008 and 2014, Russian foreign policy makers continued to convey power abroad rather effectively. So, the fact that continued economic growth prospects were uncertain proved not to be a definitive constraint on Russia's re-emerging global ambitions under President Putin; indeed, they may have been a reason to expand Russia's global reach in order to ensure economic, and therefore social, stability at home.

The next section of this chapter provides an overview of the Russian economy from the years leading up to the Soviet collapse in 1991 through the end of 2017, before the section "Emerging from Crises" turns to assessing Russia's economic trajectory in comparative context. If the means of economic power is calculated in terms of gross domestic product per capita, then Russia is no challenge to the United States, China, the EU, or even some of the weaker individual economies in the BRICS configuration. Nonetheless, I argue that Russia's economic development since the collapse of the Soviet Union was not only impressive, but also should not be seen as merely a result of the windfall of oil revenues it received in the early to mid-2000s. The Russian economy returned to positive growth territory after successive shocks because of modest growth in non-extractive economic sectors, and also as a result of some good macroeconomic policy. The following section, "The Structural Features of the Contemporary Russian Economy," reviews the general structural features of the contemporary Russian economy and how these have both helped and hindered Putin's global ambitions, including policies and strategies designed to sustain the economy. The concluding section then discusses the obstacles to continued Russian economic development that hinder the regime's expanded global ambitions.

The main takeaway from this chapter is that the Russian economy has come a long way from its difficult starting point in 1992, and although it remains an unsteady basis for the projection of other dimensions of power, it has shown notable resilience in the face of successive shocks.

The Starting Point

When the Soviet Union collapsed in December 1991, Russia succeeded it as the owner of all state property on the territory of the former Russian Republic, including the ailing Soviet military and its weaponry—both conventional and nuclear. The new Russia assumed Soviet-era international financial obligations, and was further burdened with an economy designed for a failed system of central planning that tried to capture economies of scale in virtually every economic sector. This meant that it had huge state-owned factories located throughout the country, run by managers who had no experience (and often no interest) in running businesses under conditions of competition, whether domestic or international, or the iron laws of supply and demand that ruled markets. The new system had to account for decades without private property ownership or a commercial banking system; although Mikhail Gorbachev's reforms had allowed some haphazard, unregulated proliferation of entities that called themselves banks, they did not function as such.[7] The centrally planned system of production inputs and outputs that substituted for market-determined supply and demand was in chaos after seventy years of communism and six years of halting reform under Gorbachev's perestroika.

As Gorbachev assumed the office of general secretary of the Communist Party in March 1985, the Soviet economic system was in urgent need of reform. In his 1995 memoir, Gorbachev explained that as a child of Khrushchev's cultural thaw, but also a committed communist, he had come to the conclusion when he reached the pinnacle of Soviet power that "we can't go on living like this."[8] He knew systemic reform was long overdue. The Soviet economy was underperforming: despite Khrushchev's boasts in 1961 that the Soviet Union would surpass the GDP per capita of the United States within twenty years, in 1980 Soviet GDP was only about one-third of America's.[9] In the 1970s, annual growth dipped to below about 3% per year on average, but by 1985 had further declined to just 1.6%. This steady decrease was driven by declines in production outputs in previously stellar industries like coal and steel. Making matters worse, oil production was also sliding by the mid-1980s, and agricultural production was "anemic" by 1982, purportedly dipping below plan levels.[10]

There were multiple causes of the Soviet economy's weakness by the time Gorbachev assumed responsibility. Dropping rates of worker productivity were certainly part of the story. Absenteeism was a growing problem, in part driven by alcoholism that had grown so rampant that Gorbachev himself deemed it worthy of note at the 1985 Party Congress, as well as orchestrating a massive anti-alcohol campaign.[11] Time spent in long lines attempting to purchase scarce goods was another inefficiency created by a faltering planning system, and one that also helped drive absenteeism up and productivity down. With very little for Soviet consumers to buy, savings rates were artificially high, which might also have depressed worker output—why bother to work hard or often when you have many months of savings stuffed in your mattress?

Beyond this, an aging capital stock and low investment rates to modernize it also proved problematic in boosting Soviet production. Soviet firms were not required to live within their means, or to adjust production in response to demand for their products. There was no "hard budget constraint."[12] Bureaucrats in Soviet ministries found that inputs for production and Soviet satellite countries (at least until about 1990) provided guaranteed markets for low-quality consumer goods. If a manager needed more money or inputs to stay apace of the plan, money could be printed. It had little meaning or value in the system anyway. By the time of the Soviet collapse, annual inflation rates approached 100%.[13]

The Soviet Union had also been affected by some of the problems that rippled through the broader world economy, particularly in the 1980s when world oil prices began a long, lumpy decline that continued through the late 1990s. Indeed, former acting prime minister Yegor Gaidar once noted:

> The timeline of the collapse of the Soviet Union can be traced to September 13, 1985. On this date, Sheikh Ahmad Zaki Yamani, the Minister of Oil of Saudi Arabia, declared that the monarchy had decided to alter its oil policy radically. The Saudis stopped protecting oil prices, and Saudi Arabia quickly regained its share in the world market. During the next six months, oil production in Saudi Arabia increased fourfold, while oil prices collapsed by approximately the same amount in real terms.[14]

This sudden and dramatic drop in oil prices, and the resulting revenue decline for the Soviet economy, was estimated to be as high as $20 billion per year.[15] Such a huge decline in revenues meant that Gorbachev's new government had several unsavory options: the first would be to stop "bartering" trade in oil and gas to Eastern Bloc countries in exchange for agricultural products and start charging its satellite states for energy in hard currency. With political unrest in Poland at that time, however, the leadership feared that further economic hardship in Eastern Europe could foment greater disaffection. Ironically, of course, it would likely not have made a difference, given communism's quick collapse in Eastern Europe in 1989. A second bad option would have been to cut food imports proportionate to the drop in annual revenue from oil exports ($20 billion) and start rationing state-subsidized food within the USSR. This, too, was not politically feasible, given the new regime's concerns about domestic support. Just as unpalatable was a third politically impossible option: cut military spending and risk serious backlash from the powerful military-industrial complex.

Since none of these three paths proved feasible, a fourth possibility would kick the problem down the road for at least a few years: borrowing hard currency on international markets. Under Gorbachev's leadership, the USSR borrowed heavily between 1985 and 1988, amassing a huge foreign debt, while dabbling in reforms that would introduce "cooperatives" (limited private enterprises) and releasing some of the constraints of the planning system. But by 1989, the economy was in deep crisis: oil prices were still falling, the Soviet Union could not pay for the grain imports needed to feed the population, and with the collapse of the communist bloc in Eastern Europe in November of that year, barter for products from there dried up as well. The heavy borrowing to keep the economy afloat meant that the Soviet Union's total external debt at the time of its collapse was estimated to be about $117 billion, over half of which Russia assumed after 1991.[16]

However, as Gaidar, among others, also noted, it was not oil alone, or Gorbachev's inconsistent and incomplete attempts at reforming the economy, that brought about the terminal economic crisis in the Soviet Union in the late 1980s; *it was the communist system itself.* Soviet agriculture had long been problematic following collectivization in the 1930s. By 1963, grain production had basically hit its peak output, remaining at the same level until the late 1980s, even as population (and therefore, demand for grain) increased. Grain imports gradually increased through the 1970s and 1980s, and in 1984 reached a high of 46 million tons (compared to 2.2 million in 1970). The communist system had so mismanaged agriculture that "Russia had been the largest exporter of grain at the beginning of the century and by the mid-1980s, had become the world's largest importer."[17]

In manufacturing, the Soviet economy also lagged. The planning system brought relentless pressure for enterprises to fulfill ever-rising state-determined production plans. Quantity of output was prioritized over quality to ensure meeting plan targets, but this system bred greater economic inefficiencies and declining production rates. To ensure achieving increased annual plan targets, enterprise managers would often pad reports of production outputs. Timothy Colton reported that when the public prosecutor's office conducted a random accounting of enterprise production in 1985 in three industrial ministries, it found inflated production numbers in 50–85% of the factories studied.[18] Underreporting production figures was also at times problematic, as managers would hoard and resell excess output on the side. This type of behavior, often with the overt (for a fee), or at least tacit, acceptance of bureaucrats who were supposed to oversee and stop such activity, helped to fuel the growth of the black market, or shadow economy, and official corruption, further dragging down economic performance.

Due to the inherent emphasis on output volume, the quality of Soviet manufactured products was often notoriously poor. This meant that when oil export revenues declined, manufacturing could not make up the shortfall, since it was not easy to find new markets beyond those guaranteed in the Eastern Bloc. Exports had gone into steep decline even in formerly guaranteed markets in CMEA countries (Eastern Bloc plus Cuba, Mongolia, and Vietnam), dropping from $40.1 billion in 1991 to just under $16 billion.[19] Within the Soviet Union, supply channels for production were interrupted by the collapsing communist economy as well. The USSR was importing machinery in increasing proportions from the mid-1960s onward. Oil had been used to pay for these imports, and so the price drops of the 1980s compounded production problems that had existed for decades, and also meant that the USSR would fall farther behind the West technologically if it could not import new equipment.[20]

In addition, negative demographic trends in the late Soviet period also fueled economic problems. The pace of Soviet population growth dropped about 50% between 1960 and 1980, causing a shrinking work force and gradual rise in the number of pensioners in need of state support—two legacies of the Soviet system with which, under Putin, Russia continues to struggle more than three decades later (see chapter 5). Death rates for both men and women were increasing by the time Gorbachev came to power in 1985. In 1960, life expectancy for Soviet men was 67 years, but declined to 62 years by 1980 (it would hit 60.1 years for men in 1997).[21] For women, life expectancy declined from 76 to 73 years. Certainly, alcohol abuse and poor healthcare fueled these problems, but overall standards of living were rapidly declining from the 1970s onward in comparison to those in the Organisation for Economic Co-operation and Development (OECD) countries, especially in areas like housing (in chronic short supply) and education.[22]

Thus, when Russians awoke to a new year on January 1, 1992, there was little reason to rush out of bed. The Soviet Union had collapsed a week earlier, but its economy had been in terminal decline for years. Throughout the autumn of 1991, store shelves had been emptied as the state-run supply system collapsed, and Russians squirreled away necessities at home as best they could. Wages for average workers were far exceeded by state-initiated price increases under Gorbachev, reducing Russians to bartering with one another for butter, soap, and other everyday necessities.[23] The budget deficit was estimated to be 20% of GNP in 1991. Russia had inherited more than $65 billion in external debt from the Soviet Union, and faced almost completely depleted foreign currency reserves. David Lipton and Jeffrey Sachs, citing the International Monetary Fund, report that as reform began in 1992, "the foreign exchange reserves of the Russian Central Bank were only a few hundred million dollars, or enough to cover only a few hours of imports!"[24] As economist Anders Åslund noted, by the autumn of 1991, "Russia was in a rampant economic crisis with nearly complete shortages and an actual state bankruptcy."[25]

It is important to fully appreciate the radical structural differences between the Soviet command economy and the new system, given how much had to be created from scratch to transform the Russian economy into something resembling a competitive market. The central tenets of communism involved the elimination of private property, prices, private trade, and, eventually, even the need for currency altogether. The ruble was *not* convertible; prices for all goods sold throughout the country were determined not by supply and demand, but by central planners sitting in the State Planning Committee (GosPlan) in Moscow. Until the mid-1980s, reportedly 95% of production was owned by the state.[26] There was virtually no private property ownership, no private shops, no commercial banking system, no mortgage market, no insurance market, no system of personal or corporate tax, no stock or bond markets, no private domestic investment, very little foreign direct investment, and very low labor mobility; even where Soviet citizens worked and lived was determined and tightly controlled by the state. The structure of the economy was tilted heavily toward heavy industry and in support of the Soviet military. Mammoth Soviet enterprises were financed directly by the state, and their powerful directors had not been trained to live within their means. They lived by the plan.

As far as consumer products went, the retail sector was tiny in comparison to those of the United States, Japan, and other leading economies in the 1980s. For example, in 1985, the Soviet Union had 20 shops per 10,000 citizens, while the United States had 60, France had 86, and Japan had 135![27] Consumer goods were scarce and notoriously of low quality because there was no competition from imports. The service industry was small and quality suffered due to lack of competition as well. In what few stores and restaurants existed, Soviet citizens had to put up with surly, slow-moving salespeople and servers. The economy purportedly ran at 100% employment, but this meant that some people were essentially employed to do nothing. State price controls created a system of chronic shortage for literally everything, which only worsened as Gorbachev tinkered with the economy in the late 1980s. There was an extensive, and expensive, system of cradle-to-grave social support in the form of state pensions, guaranteed employment, free but low-quality health and dental care, free pre- and post-secondary education, and heavily subsidized housing and utilities. The legacy of this system would create high expectations for rapid improvements among post-Soviet Russians, and inevitable disappointment with some of the results.

Moreover, the Soviet economy came with virtually none of the institutions that exist in modern capitalist economies, and with a huge degree of state involvement. The challenge of tearing down this system and reconstituting it as a market economy with a supporting regulatory and legal environment was, needless to say, enormous. Viewed from this perspective, the progress made in Russia in a mere thirty years is impressive.

Emerging from Crises: The Russian Balance Sheet, 1992–2019

Progress, though, did not come without high costs. Russia's economic transformation has been deep, sometimes radical, and unquestionably painful for the average citizen. The short-lived attempt at "shock therapy," which began with price liberalization in January 1992, has been well documented elsewhere.[28] The high percentages of the population living at or below the official poverty level between 1992 and 2002 varied from 20% to 30%[29]. State-sector pensions and wages in the early 1990s went unpaid for months at a time as the Russian government struggled to impose a stiffer macroeconomic policy and fiscal constraints. Also well-known is the story of Russia's controversial privatization program for small and medium enterprise between 1994 and 1996, which benefited few at the expense of the many and caused major disillusion among the Russian citizenry regarding capitalism and democracy. This period also bred an oligarchical class of Russian businessmen (described in greater detail in chapter 8), a group that operated under largely unregulated economic conditions, and some of whom were linked to political decision-making through the type of shady deals that were endemic in the period. A prime example is the Yeltsin government's 1996 loans-for-shares program, which transformed a small cadre of these oligarchs who helped bail out the government into billionaires by giving them major shares in the gems of the Russian economy in return for loans to keep the government solvent.[30] The often tragic history of Russian reform efforts will not be repeated here.

Instead, this chapter's task is to evaluate the reformed economy as a means of extending Russian power across international borders.

Between 1992 and 2017, the Russian economy endured no fewer than *four* major economic crises. First, following the release of price controls in January of 1992, inflation shot up overnight by an estimated 1,000% and Soviet-era savings became practically worthless, although this situation lasted only weeks. Second, in 1998, the Russian government defaulted on its international loan commitments and its currency crashed completely, again making any savings Russian citizens may have had at the time practically worthless. Third, the global economic crisis of 2008 was notably deeper for Russia than for other countries because of the steep drop in global oil prices. Fourth was the 2014 economic crisis, which resulted from a drop in global oil prices and was compounded by sanctions imposed in response to Russia's annexation of Crimea. Although these were catastrophic events, such examples also demonstrate Russia's economic resilience. After each crisis, the economy recovered to positive growth against predictions and all odds.

That said, purely by the numbers, the maturing post-Soviet Russian economy, unsurprisingly, was not a serious challenger to the West twenty-five years after the communist collapse. Russia generally falls far behind the United States and the EU 28, for example, on traditional measures of national wealth, like real GDP, GDP per capita, and its comparative contribution to the global economy. As figure 4.1 demonstrates, Russian GDP from 1992 to 2017 lagged far behind the leaders, and even dipped below those of India and Brazil from 1994 to 2002. This is perhaps not surprising, since Russia was new to capitalism relative to this

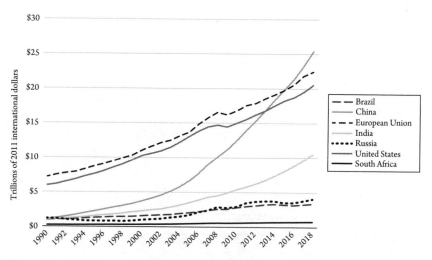

Figure 4.1. GDP of Russia vs. BRICS, EU, and the US, 1990–2019 (at Purchasing Power Parity)

set of countries, and spent the first decade following the communist collapse attempting to build the structures that could sustain a market economy.

Figure 4.2 shows that between 1992 and 2018, Russia's portion of global economic output declined, although the 1992 numbers likely show a hangover from unreliable Soviet statistics, which may overestimate production at that time. Still, Russia's development by this measure has been relatively flat over twenty-five years. By 2017, Russia represented only a fraction of global GDP— 3.15% compared to 15.59% for the United States, 17.76% for China, and 7.23% for India, according to the World Bank. In 1992, Russia and China had similar shares of global GDP (5% and 4%, respectively), but over a quarter century, Russia's global share of GDP *dropped* to about 3% while China's *soared* to 18%, beyond the EU 28 and even the United States. Russia's comparative growth trajectory in comparison to China's on this measure is clearly negative.[31]

An important qualifier is that this figure is *not* a per capita measure of national GDP. China and India, of course, have populations of over 1 billion, while Russia's hovered between roughly 142 and 145 million in this period. Perhaps, then, it should not be surprising that Russia produces a smaller share of global output than either of these two BRICS "peers." Russia's political and economic turmoil in the 1990s also explains the disparity; China's governance was relatively stable following Deng Xiaoping's introduction of sweeping economic reforms in 1989. In percentage terms, both the EU's and the United States' share of global productive output also declined significantly between 1992 and 2017, although neither to the extent of Russia's. Clearly, after twenty-five years of tumultuous political and economic change, Russia could not be considered a

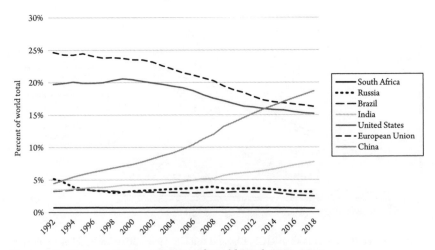

Figure 4.2. National GDP as a Percent of World Total, 1992–2018

global economic leader beside the EU, the United States, and China, the world's economic powerhouses, or even a newer transitional economy like India.

Considering other factors in comparing Russia's economies to those of the other BRICS, however, suggests a different assessment. As figure 4.3 demonstrates, Russia's gross domestic product *per capita* (and at purchasing power parity) grew markedly from about $8,000 just prior to the Soviet collapse in 1991 to a high of about $26,000 in 2014. Despite their remarkable growth trajectories in the same period, both China (at a high of about $16,000) and India (at about $7,000), *were still poor countries relative to Russia on a per capita basis.* Indeed, while these other two "emerging economies" have done remarkably well in the same short period of time, Russia, by OECD standards, has become an "upper-middle-income" country. Given the conditions of the Russian economy when it embarked on market reforms in 1992, its trajectory is in many ways impressive, and its ability to rebound after successive traumas has too often been underappreciated when evaluating the Russian economy as a means of extending its influence abroad.

Russia's rising numbers in relation to international development are also striking. Through some good fortune with respect to booming oil prices in the 2000s and good policy, Russian policymakers have weaned the economy off loans from lenders of last resort like the International Monetary Fund and World Bank. In 2018, the World Bank estimated Russia's economy as the world's sixth largest in terms of GDP at purchasing power parity (the cost of buying the same basket of goods in one country versus another). It has one of the world's lowest debt-to-GDP ratios in the countries compared here, declining from 143% in 1998 to an all-time low of 6.5% ten years later, and even with a rise to about 16% by 2017, Russia remains one of the least indebted nations in the world.[32] (For

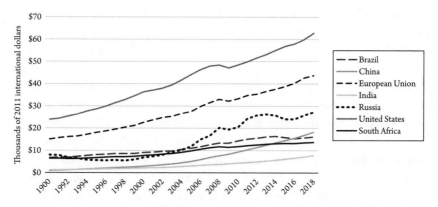

Figure 4.3. GDP per capita of BRICS, EU, and the US, 1990–2018 (at Purchasing Power Parity)

reference, among the comparative set of country cases included here, the United States had the highest national debt-to-GDP ratio of 106% at the same time.[33])

Indeed, Russia shifted from serious *global debtor* to emerging *global donor* in under thirty years. Russia's net international development assistance expanded rapidly, rising from about $100 million annually in 2007 to $1.2 billion in 2017.[34] While this remains low relative to the United States (about $49 billion in 2017), in percentage terms of gross national income (GNI), the United States gave 0.18% in development aid in 2017, compared to Russia's 0.77%. (Sweden was the highest net development assistance donor at 1.02% of GNI in the same year.[35]) Proportionately, then, Russia's rate of increase in international development assistance far exceeded its rate of economic growth.

Although Putin tended to accept credit for Russia's economic recovery, some of the groundwork for the resurrection was laid by policymakers in the 1990s, who conceived initially of the 13% personal income tax and value-added tax (VAT) that was implemented by Putin's regime in 2001. Indeed, the Russian economy had shown initial signs of growth in the early quarters of 1999, before Putin became Yeltsin's last prime minister in August of that year. Just before he unexpectedly assumed the Russian presidency in 2000, Putin published his economic aspirations for Russia in the short paper "Russia at the Turn of the Millennium."[36] It is a fascinating document in many respects, but particularly in hindsight. Putin was acutely aware of the economic challenges Russia faced at the time. He begins this remarkable essay by noting how far backward Russia fell in the 1990s and laments its former status as a global power in the imperial and Soviet eras. He recognizes Russia's dangerous historical dependence on raw materials extraction. Consistently measuring Russia in relation to China and the United States, he notes, "Labor productivity in the real sector is extremely low. While our production of raw materials and electricity is close to the world average, our productivity in other industries is much lower—for instance, at 20–24% of US indicators." Another issue is low foreign investment, which, as he states, amounted to slightly more than $11.5 billion, while China received as much as $43 billion.[37] He also pointed to the low proportion and low output of enterprises engaged in innovative production, noting, "Foreign competitors have pushed Russia especially far back in the market of high-tech civilian commodities. Russia accounts for less than 1% of such products on the world market, while the US provides 36% and Japan 30%." He recognized the dramatic fall in Russian living standards, stating, "There has been a steady decline in real incomes since the beginning of reforms. The greatest plummet was registered after the August 1998 crisis. . . . Currently, Russians' total monetary income, calculated by UN methods, adds up to less than 10% of the analogous figure for a US resident." At least in 1999, Putin blames not the flaws of Yeltsin's governments in the 1990s, as he would later, but rather the "excesses" of the

Soviet system—its distortions and excessive dependence on raw materials; its focus on heavy industry as opposed to consumer products and services; and the fact that it did not require competition among producers, thus hindering scientific and technological progress that could have boosted the Russian economy's competitiveness in world markets.

After providing an insightful, accurate, and largely dismal diagnosis of Russia's economic situation on the cusp of the millennium, Putin provided what, at the time, seemed a bold prognosis: "In order to achieve per capita GDP at the level of present-day Portugal or Spain, which are not among the world's industrialized leaders, it will take us approximately fifteen years and at least 8% annual growth of our GDP. If we are able to maintain an annual growth rate of 10% during the same fifteen years, then we will reach the current per capita GDP of Britain or France."

By some (though certainly not all) measures, and not necessarily by design, Putin's forecast in 1999 turned out to be partially correct. By 2014, Russia's GDP per capita at purchasing power parity had jumped from just below $6,000 in 1999 to almost $26,000 (see figure 4.3).

Still, Putin's projections proved overly ambitious. Not only did the average EU 28 per capita GDP at purchasing power parity outproduce Russia over those fifteen years, but so did France and the United Kingdom individually, reported by the World Bank to be just below $44,000 while Russia's hovered just below $26,000—close to Portugal's $28,742, but also not quite there.[38] The growth curve for the Russian economy, however, is much steeper in this period than that of almost any other country charted in figure 4.3.

Clearly, revenues from oil, gas, and other mineral resources were crucial components of the Russian economy (as they were of the Soviet economy before it), and key to its recovery in the early to mid-2000s, though it would be wrong to explain this away as merely a result of high oil prices. Prices were indeed at record levels in this period, and this had a dramatic effect on the state budget, enterprise revenues, and household incomes. 4 shows the close correlation between global oil prices and Russian GDP growth from 1992 to 2018. Between 1992 and 1998, the average price per barrel was $17.41, in sharp contrast to almost $50 per barrel between 2000 and 2008 and the rise to $110 per barrel in 2012.

Nonetheless, the correlation between world oil prices and Russia's GDP growth, though very close for a good part of this period, is not perfect. Russian GDP dipped when oil prices plummeted in 2013 and 2014, but not nearly as much as might be expected. This indicates that there were some successful policy efforts initiated after 2008 and in response to other shocks to the economy, including diversification and better fiscal planning to smooth over the inevitable boom-and-bust cycles of global oil prices. As a result, although

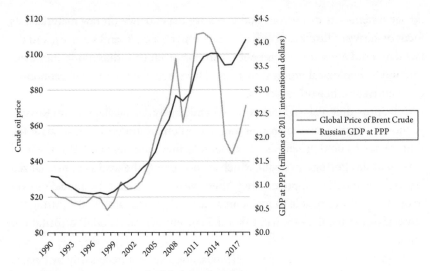

Figure 4.4. Russian GDP and Global Crude Oil Prices

the Russian economy shares some of the pathologies of a resource-cursed economy, almost thirty years after the initiation of economic reform, it was not a classically "oil-cursed" state in the way the Soviet Union had been by 1991. Economic policies pursued in the 2000s have created significant reserves, good fiscal and macroeconomic policy, and low debt-to-GDP ratios. Examining these developments in greater depth, the next section reviews the structure of the Russian economy.

The Structural Features of the Contemporary Russian Economy

When Vladimir Putin was inaugurated as Russia's second president in May 2000, he described Russians as "poor people living in a rich country."[39] He was referencing the economic devastation left in the wake of communism and the chaotic changes of the 1990s that left many Russians poorer than they had ever been. The fact that Russia has become an upper-middle-income country a few decades later demonstrates how far Russia has come. Not all of Russia's considerable growth is due to exogenous factors alone, like high oil prices; some endogenous factors, such as good macroeconomic and fiscal policies, as hinted at earlier, also helped Russia rebuild its economic resources. In 2002, the government established the National Welfare Fund and the National Reserve Fund to smooth out the boom-and-bust cycle characteristic of global oil prices. These funds proved useful in helping the economy withstand further exogenous shocks in 2014. Between 2003 and 2008, the Russian Central Bank built up considerable foreign reserves from the oil boom, Following the 2008 crisis, policymakers worked to diversify Russia's export base, helping Russia avoid Dutch disease (the growth of one sector of the economy—in this case oil—at the expense of manufacturing, for example). Also in wake of the crisis, the Russian government worked to improve its ranking on the World Bank's measures of Ease of Doing Business in an effort to increase foreign and domestic private investment, and was somewhat successful in doing so, and also in attacking measures of smaller scale corruption. None of these efforts has been executed flawlessly, but clearly they have helped Russia climb out of the deep economic holes it fell into in 1992, 2008, and 2014. We turn now to understanding the structure of the Russian economy after nearly thirty years of reform to evaluate it as a means of sustaining and extending Russian power beyond its borders.

The Evolving Structure of the Russian Economy

The Russian economy underwent a sweeping transformation, if incomplete in some areas, following the collapse of the Soviet Union. Privatization of small, medium, and many large-scale enterprises; liberalization of markets; and macroeconomic stabilization took place primarily in the 1990s, although each of these processes continued well into the 2000s. There was also, however, some reinsertion of the state into the economy in certain notable "reverse privatizations"— for example, the confiscation and transfer of ownership to the state of Mikhail Khodorkovsky's Yukos following the oligarch's arrest in 2003, which will be discussed further in chapter 8—especially in the minerals extraction sector. In the decades since the disintegration of the Soviet system, however, the Russian economy has continued to struggle with the constraints of its complicated Soviet era legacy, and this has necessarily impacted its ongoing growth prospects. As the OECD has noted, in contemporary Russia, "technological nodes of excellence" coexist alongside "a rather large, stagnant pool of firms and organizations with very low productivity and little innovation."[40]

Nonetheless, over the last thirty or so years, the Russian economy achieved dominance in a few key sectors. Most important has been its dominant global market presence in raw material resources like natural gas, ferrous and non-ferrous metals, raw aluminum, and, most important, oil, in which Russia alternates the position of leading global exporter with Saudi Arabia. Given that these were strengths in the pre-collapse Soviet economy, this is perhaps not surprising. More significant was that the Russian Federation became the world's largest grain exporter in 2016, overcoming decades of ineffective agricultural production during the Soviet period.[41]

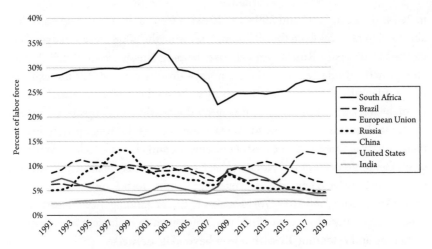

Figure 4.5. Unemployment Rates in BRICS, EU, and the US, 1991–2019

Positive change was also felt at the consumer level. As a result of the growth that began in 1999, and the oil revenue boom that arose in 2003, Russian per capita income reached 1991 levels by 2006.[42] This meant that the purchasing power of average Russians increased markedly—by over 10% year-on-year between 2003 and 2008, according to most estimates. Consumers now had the choice to buy imported products as well as new, better-quality, often cheaper Russian commodities. The high poverty rates of the 1990s (hovering around 30%) decreased dramatically (see figure 4.6); while the deep but brief recession following the global oil price collapse in 2008 saw Russian domestic productive output decline by 11% in total (from a growth rate of 9% to −2%) in the first six months of 2009, according to OECD reports, by the spring of 2010, most Russians were back to making what they had before the crisis. Although unemployment rose, it was still relatively low compared to the average in Europe, and in 2009, at 8.4%, was even lower than the US rate of 9.3% (see figure 4.5). Significantly, unemployment did not rise in direct proportion to the size of the economic contraction.[43] Similarly, the proportion of the population living at or below the official subsistence minimum dropped significantly, from 29% in 2000 to 13% in 2017 (see figure 4.6).

Despite the recovery, regaining the oil-fueled growth rates of the previous decade proved difficult. Still, astute and disciplined macroeconomic policy allowed the Russian economy to continue to grow modestly. In late 2008, Russian policymakers moved quickly to protect the ruble, using the substantial foreign reserves accumulated in the preceding boom years. This allowed the state, some private enterprises, and banks to service debt with foreign exchange without suffering long-term declines in their valuations. Further, and

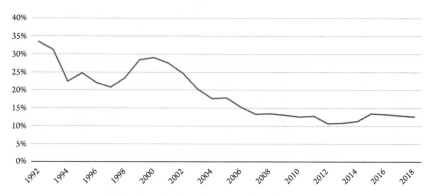

Figure 4.6. Percentage of Russians Living below Federal Subsistence Minimum, 1992–2018

rather controversially, the Russian government used the National Welfare Fund to directly assist a few particularly gigantic state-owned corporations in extractive industries, most notably Rosneft, Russia's third largest company in terms of assets.[44]

In sharp contrast to the classic model of a resource-cursed economy, then, Russian policymakers instituted cautious policies to protect the economy from the inevitable price shocks that hit global oil prices. These involved a disciplined macroeconomic policy to try to protect the economy from price fluctuations in raw materials exports, including the 2004 establishment of the Russian Stabilization Fund to store and invest the accumulated windfall of oil and gas revenues. The Stabilization Fund was split in two in 2008, creating the National Reserve Fund (which received $125 billion) and the National Welfare Fund (which initially received $32 billion). The Reserve Fund held government revenue from oil and gas exports to shore up the budget when oil prices dropped below a certain level (this peg would vary, as it turned out). The Reserve Fund was not to accumulate assets in excess of 10% of Russian annual GDP, with any surplus assets rolled over to the National Welfare Fund. The Reserve Fund was invested abroad in safer, low-yield securities and used when oil and gas revenues fell below historically established levels to prevent the government from running the high budget deficits that were so problematic in the 1990s. This has helped Russia keep budget deficits well under control, even through periods of crises (with the exception of the COVID-19 pandemic period). The National Welfare Fund (sometimes referred to as the National Wealth Fund) was invested in higher-risk and possibly higher short-term return investments, and could be used to fund projects that were in the annual budget, as well as support the pension system in particular.[45] Following the 2008 and 2014 financial crises, the Finance Ministry used the Reserve Fund to avoid huge budget deficits and bail

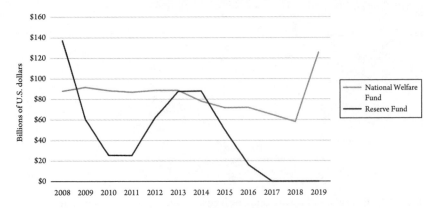

Figure 4.7. Volume of National Welfare Fund and National Reserve Fund, 2008–2019

out a few large state corporations and some banks, while the Central Bank used its substantial foreign reserves to battle inflation. By the end of 2017, however, the Reserve Fund was largely spent, with only $17 billion left of the original $125 billion. The National Welfare Fund, was still well-funded, with $65 billion in assets (see figure 4.7). The budgetary rule at the time of writing was that the National Welfare Fund had to reach a minimum of 7% of Russia's annual GDP in any given year for the government to draw from it to fund the state budget.[46] (Similar "budgetary rules" existed in the past, however, and were broken in order to stabilize the economy during crises, which could presumably happen again if the need arose as seemed likely as the COVID-19 pandemic continued through 2020.)

The Russian National Welfare Fund and the Reserve Fund existed independently of Central Bank Foreign Reserves, putting Russia's macro-economy in a comparatively better place. Figure 4.8 shows Russia's foreign reserves in billions of US dollars in 2016, compared to those of the US, EU 28, and Brazil, India, and South Africa. Russia's reserves grew during the boom years of 2003–2008; the Central Bank spent this during the crisis, then accumulated over $500 billion until this was again spent down in 2013, 2014, and 2015. By the end of 2017, however, Russian foreign reserves topped US$400 billion, exceeding the foreign reserves of the European Central Bank, the United States, Brazil, India, and South Africa. Again, considering that the Russian Central Bank started out in 1992 with only a few hundred million dollars in reserves, this was admirable.

A vast improvement in the external debt-to-GNI ratio was also in the positive column of the Russian balance sheet by 2017 (see figure 4.9). Russia began the 1990s with a debt-to-GNI ratio of about 30%, still consistent with other transitional economies. Its debt soared in the early 1990s as Boris Yeltsin's successive prime ministers struggled to reform the economy to fit market parameters,

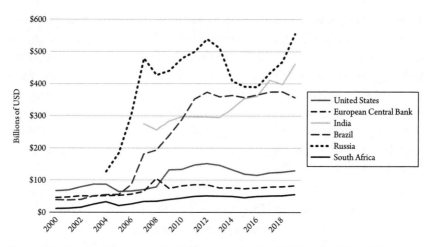

Figure 4.8. Foreign Reserves in Brazil, Russia, India, South Africa, the US, and European Central Bank, 2000–2019

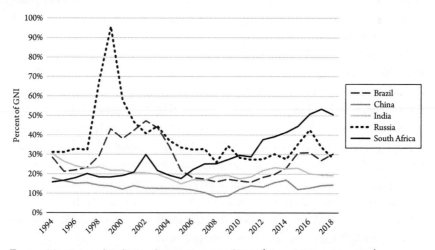

Figure 4.9. External Debt Stocks as a Percent of GNI (Gross National Income)

reaching an all-time high of 95% before dropping precipitously after 1999 to its lowest point, 25%, in 2008. Thereafter, it has bounced as high as 42%, but ended 2017 at a more respectable level of 32%. This was still higher than those of all the other BRICS economies, save South Africa, but about where it had begun in 1992.

Beyond these broad macroeconomic measures, Russian policymakers had modest success in diversifying the economy away from extractive sectors. Between 2006 and 2008, the value added in Russian agriculture, industry, and service sectors grew more rapidly than in any other OECD country, but these economic sectors were still dwarfed by energy.[47] There was also growth in Russia's manufacturing exports between 1998 and 2008, with average annual expansion of 19.1%, versus 8.8% for the OECD overall. At the same time, high-tech exports from Russia were close to the OECD average of about 8%, again reflecting some improvement.[48] Russia mainly relied on high-tech imports, however, another legacy of the late Soviet Union. While this still allowed for significant technology transfer into the country, it meant that Russian manufacturing exports were medium- to low-tech at best, and therefore not fetching high prices on global markets.[49]

Diversification and Innovation: Two Steps Forward, One and Three-Quarter Steps Back

Even before the crash of 2008, however, Russian policymakers were acutely aware of the need to diversify and even restructure the economy. In 2009 and 2010, under the new president Dmitri Medvedev, the Russian government established a series of development goals for the ensuing decade in a plan entitled "A Concept for the Long-Term Social and Economic Development of the Russian Federation until 2020" (more familiarly known as "Russia 2020").[50] The plan's key goal was to change fundamentally the structure of the economy, diversifying toward a more high-tech base. Another goal was to enhance competition within the economy by breaking up monopolies. Among these policy initiatives was the establishment of Skolkovo, a technology center just outside Moscow, which Medvedev described as a Russian "Silicon Valley"—never mind that it would be built top-down by the Russian government, rather than develop organically through the creation of government incentives. As Medvedev acknowledged in a speech delivered from his brand-new Apple iPad (gifted to him by Steve Jobs himself during a trip to California's Silicon Valley) at Stanford University in summer 2010, "that's how things are done in Russia."[51]

The "Russia 2020" concept was developed in 2007, when economist Elvira Nabiullina, who would later become chair of the Central Bank of Russia, was appointed minister of economic development and trade. It painted three scenarios for the Russian economy over the coming decade: first, the "inertia scenario," in which dependence on exports would remain and growth would be slow or grind to a halt with declining prices; the second scenario involved diversification in exports and some innovation in raw materials extraction to enhance efficiency; while, third, the innovation scenario, saw Russia fully developing its comparative advantages in natural resource extraction and exports, but also becoming a leader in technological innovation.[52] To achieve the third scenario, the most optimistic of the three, the Russian government would have to modernize the country's manufacturing sectors and infrastructure and significantly increase domestic and foreign investment in innovation. One way to achieve both was to further integrate into the global economy by formally acceding to the WTO, which the Medvedev administration manage to do in 2012. Economic planners hoped that technology transfer into Russia through trade would quickly move economic diversification forward, as would inward foreign direct investment and Russian outward investment in companies abroad. Russian producers also had to diversify purchasers, in particular, relying less on the EU and turning toward the huge market potential for Russian goods in China. Reaching these goals would also require transforming the labor force to better match skills and needs in the economy. This would demand significant investment in higher education and research and design, especially in high tech.

Domestically, during Medvedev's presidency between 2008 and 2012, Russia invested more in human capital (discussed in detail in chapter 5) and developed an industrial policy, which increased state regulation of foreign participation and investment in forty-two "strategic" sectors of the economy, including energy, aircraft, shipbuilding, automobile manufacturing, and financial services. The policy also introduced a system of national champions, a decision that is controversial in most economies since it can have the effect of hindering competition and creating high barriers to entry in those sectors deemed to be strategically important, for foreign private investors in particular.[53] Indeed, the policy may have had exactly this effect, as indicated in figure 4.10, since foreign direct investment (FDI) as a percentage of Russian GDP never fully regained the record level it had attained before the introduction of this policy.[54] However, FDI still increased as a percentage of GDP (as GDP was also increasing), and in 2017, Russia's GDP

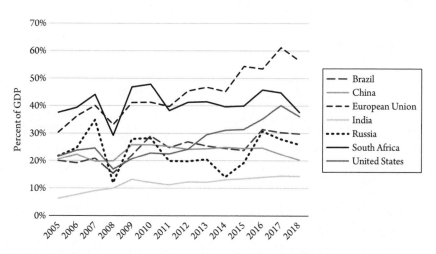

Figure 4.10. Inward Foreign Direct Investment (FDI) as a Percent of GDP in BRICS, the EU, and the US

was at its highest point in the preceding twenty-five years (see figure 4.1) and FDI regained upward momentum.[55] It is particularly notable that FDI continued to flow into the country at historically high absolute amounts even after the United States and EU initiated sanctions targeting the Russian economy in the fall of 2014. This may indicate that the sanctions were not effective in stifling foreign investment (although this was not their purpose, arguably), but undoubtedly some of this money came from Russian sources and was being repatriated, as opposed to it being a clear sign of confidence from foreign investors in Russia's economy.[56] The leading sources of Russian inward investment by 2018 were the Bahamas, Bermuda, the British Virgin Islands, France, China, Germany, Ireland, the British dependency of Jersey, and the United Kingdom.[57]

Figure 4.11 shows the pattern of Russian *outward* foreign investment—the money from private and public sources that originated in Russia and went abroad. The pattern is again intriguing, since it indicates that by the end of 2017, Russian external investment had proportionally regained its previous peak despite sanctions, and a slow but steady overall economic recovery after 2014.[58] The destinations of the outward flow of Russian FDI from the mid-2000s varied, with by far the largest share going to Central Asia and Europe. A UN report noted that Russian outward investments had as their goal

> not simply to secure the supply of raw materials to their home country, but also to expand their control over the value chains of their own natural resources, to build sustainable competitive advantages vis-à-vis other firms, and to strengthen their market positions in key developing countries. For example, Rosneft formed a joint-venture with CNPC

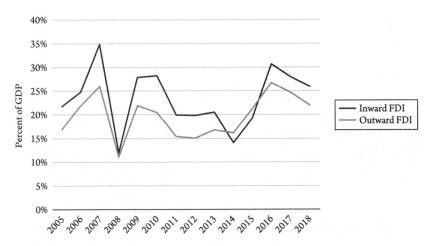

Figure 4.11. Foreign Direct Investment into and out of Russia as a Percent of GDP, 2005–2018

(China) to develop oil extraction projects in the Russian Federation and downstream operations in China.[59]

Russian FDI in sub-Saharan Africa also increased, as did China's and Brazil's, in the 2000s, with Russian mineral extractions companies and banks moving into countries such as Angola, Côte d'Ivoire, Guinea, Namibia, Nigeria, and South Africa.[60]

Economic Complexity: Beyond Oil and Energy?

After 2013, Russia achieved a degree of diversification of its exports, but undeniably had a long way to go in this regard. Figure 4.12 provides some insight into Russia's relative economic "complexity" as measured by the "knowledge intensity" of a country's exports, with higher index numbers representing greater diversity in products exported. Germany is displayed below the figure as a proxy for the EU, which leads in the index of complexity (diversification), followed by the United States and China. While Russia trails all three, its trajectory is positive, and shows that the economy's exports have grown slightly more diverse— particularly since the onset of Western sanctions, which coincided with another drop in global oil prices.

Figure 4.13, which shows the percentage of oil product exports from Russia and other transitional economies alongside the EU and the United States, also supports the pattern of diversification displayed in figure 4.12. When global prices soared between 2003 and 2008, Russia clearly increased its exports tied to oil and gas. The proportion of exports comprising oil-based products in Russia,

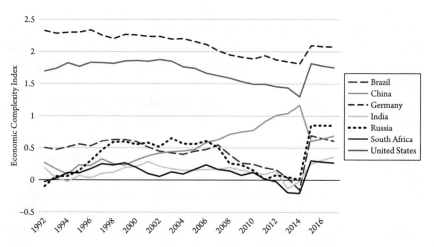

Figure 4.12. Economic Complexity of BRICS, the US, and Germany

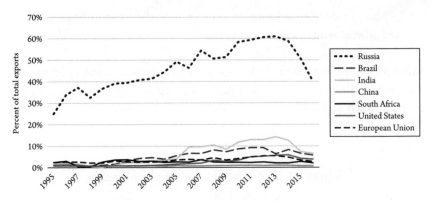

Figure 4.13. Crude Oil, Refined Oil, and Petroleum Gas Exports as a Percentage of Total Exports in BRICS, the EU, and the US, 1995–2016

compared to that figure in the other transitional countries, the United States, and the EU, is staggering. The proportional increase of Russian carbon-based energy exports over time is also notable. Predictably, this proportion contracted significantly as the global economic crisis affected the economies of its customers in 2008 and 2009, but then soared to an all-time high of almost 61% of all exports by 2013. Perhaps in response to a further drop in oil prices in 2014, but also possibly due to an increase in other exports, the proportion of oil and petroleum gas exports dropped precipitously through 2016 to 40%.

Figures 4.14a and 4.14b show the change in export structure between 2013 and 2017, further supporting the claim that the Russian government was at least modestly successful in diversifying its export structure. In 2013, as Figure 4.14a demonstrates, a staggering 70% of Russia's exports was in the area of carbon-based energy products. But just four years later, that proportion had dropped to 59%, as shown in Figure 4.14b, with growth areas in metals, machinery, and chemicals, but also agriculture. This is not just because prices of oil dropped at this point on global markets, since Russian GDP stayed relatively flat to slightly negative, while oil prices fell of a proverbial cliff (see figure 4.4) from about $112 per barrel to about $40.

It is noteworthy that agricultural exports during this period doubled from 3% to 6%, reflecting Russia's new status as the global leader in grain exports as of 2016. This reflects the rejuvenation of Russian agriculture, which has remained largely in private hands; growth in metals and machinery is also noteworthy, as shown by Russia's global dominance in raw nickel exports. When sanctions hit beginning in 2014, the Russian government had to find new places to peddle its products; it looked to China in particular to replace some European markets, with moderate success. The sanctions and counter-sanctions against European agricultural products have also had the effect of reviving some sectors of the

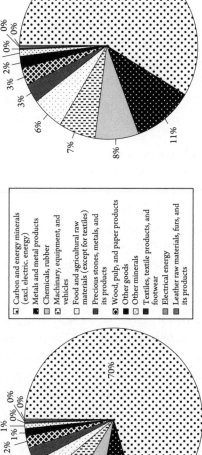

Structure of exports in 2013

Structure of exports in 2017

Carbon and energy minerals (excl. electric. energy)
Metals and metal products
Chemicals, rubber
Machinery, equipment, and vehicles
Food and agricultural raw materials (except for textiles)
Precious stones, metals, and its products
Wood, pulp, and paper products
Other goods
Other minerals
Textiles, textile products, and footwear
Electrical energy
Leather raw materials, furs, and its products

Figures 4.14a and 4.14b Structure of Russian Exports in 2013 and in 2017

Russian economy—for example, without European cheese imports, Russia developed its own cheese industry.

The State of Innovation: Russia Is Not a Start-Up Nation

While these are bright spots of the Russian economy, when we look at other indicators, the picture is not so rosy. Labor productivity, low in the late Soviet period, remained relatively low more than two decades later. Whereas in 1995, an American worker produced about $45 of GDP per hour worked, a Russian worker produced only $15 of GDP per hour. By 2019, a US worker was producing $71.78 of GDP per hour worked, while a Russian worker produced about $26.49 of GDP per hour worked—an improvement of only $11 of GDP per hour for a Russian worker, and of $26 for an American.[61] This and the relatively higher cost of labor than in many other transitional economies made Russia a less attractive venue for foreign investment in sectors other than resource extraction.

Another problematic characteristic of the post-communist Russian economy is the still significant degree of direct state interference and ownership—both legacies of the Soviet past, but also a result of the renationalization of privatized energy companies and growing protectionist tendencies under Putin.[62] This hurt competition in some sectors, and created high barriers to market entry for private actors—especially for those note linked closely to the Kremlin. But we should note that the degree of state involvement in an economy is difficult to assess because so many measures could be used, which too often are ill-defined in the popular press. In 2017, for example, without explaining precisely what was being measured, the *Moscow Times* reported that "[s]tate-owned companies controlled some 70 percent of the country's GDP in 2015, compared to 35 percent in 2005."[63] This type of description of the Russian economy has become pervasive, and is too often repeated without consideration or explication of what the terms "controlled" or "state-owned company" might mean in practice, or what exactly is being measured.[64] In order to properly assess the resilience and growth potential of the Russian economy as a factor in supporting Russia's resurrected global ambitions, it is important to understand the degree to which the state regulates and owns the economy, and whether that negatively affects GDP. Any estimation of state involvement must be consistent and mindful of the measures used. For example, should we look at the state's gross revenues or its spending as a percentage of GDP, its share in value added to GDP, or the number of people directly employed by the state? Is an enterprise considered state-owned if the share of ownership is less than 50%, or simply anything greater than 0%?

There is sometimes a misperception that any state ownership of enterprises will result in the misallocation of resources and distortions of market dynamics, not to mention kill innovation, deter investment, and hurt GDP. All of these certainly *can* result from too much state ownership. Robert Barro, however, notes that there is also evidence that higher state spending earlier in a country's economic transition or recovery can initially have a positive effect on growth, especially when rule of law and property rights protection are low. Barro also argues, however, that if the state retains high spending levels, the taxation rates on those private sector firms that do exist become unbearable and depress private investment and therefore growth.[65] This is often depicted as an inverted U curve for state investment over time. The ideal amount of state spending therefore differs between countries and over time within particular countries.

A second factor to consider is whether state involvement is better in some sectors than others. For example, it can hinder growth if the state controls access to capital by having a major presence in financial services (which was the case in Russia in 2017). Decisions about who receives financing and on what terms could become politically dependent, resulting in cronyism, as was the situation in Putin's Russia as it turned out. Further, as Andrei Shleifer argued in 1998, "private ownership should be preferred to public ownership when the incentives to innovate and contain costs are strong."[66] So, the state might not be good at developing high-tech products, for example, but might do better in drilling for oil, which requires a lot of capital, assuming the state has it. A third problem is that, depending on the sector, state ownership can limit competition and increase the concentration of the economy among a few large conglomerates.

Most of these concerns were taken into account in Russia's big privatization drives in the 1990s, when, by the estimates of the European Bank for Reconstruction and Development (EBRD), the share of the Russian state's value added in the economy relative to GDP (at PPP) went from 95% at the end of 1991 to 30% in 1997. By 2005, following the reverse privatizations (some may use the term "state confiscations") of companies like Yukos in the energy sector, this estimate rose to about 35% of GDP,[67] though this was similar to estimates for other transition economies at the same time. IMF analysts put this number at 33% of GDP in 2016; according to one study, "the breakdown of the state's value added in general government (supplying the actual functions of government) represented 13.5 percent of GDP in 2016 (slightly up from 13.1 percent of GDP in 2012) and state-owned enterprises (SOEs) accounted for 19.3 percent of GDP (also up from 18.8 percent in 2012)."[68] This was certainly a far smaller proportion of state involvement than the far higher numbers reported in the popular press, but it is still significant and problematic for the further development of the Russian economy.[69]

Further, partly as a result of the legacy of monopolies of the Soviet era, and partly because of a system of corrupt cronyism that has developed since 2000, the Russian economy has become highly concentrated, dominated by a few extremely large players. The OECD reported that the 100 largest enterprises in Russia accounted for 60% of its GDP by 2011.[70] These were familiar names: Gazprom, Lukoil, Alfa Group, Rosneft, Renova, Severstal, Norilsk Nickel, Evraz Group, Sistema, Rostechnologi, Mechel Steel, Tatneft, and Basic Element, for example. Notable too is that of the ten companies with the highest annual profits ($3 billion or greater) at the end of 2017, six were 50% or more state-owned, including Gazprom (natural gas), Sberbank (financial services), Rosneft (oil), Transneft (oil), Tatneft (oil), and VTB Bank (financial services).[71] A key part of the patronal political economy of Putin's regime is that these companies are also run by members of his inner circle. This will be discussed in greater detail in chapter 8.

Despite this, there has been growth in the number of small and medium business enterprises, which in 2011 comprised 21% of Russian GDP, according to the OECD.[72] The Global Entrepreneurship Monitoring Report (GEM) indicated that high-tech entrepreneurship in Russia had been increasing before the 2008–2010 economic downturn.[73] But Russian entrepreneurs faced an underdeveloped commercial financial system for getting loans for new businesses and very little venture capital was available for would-be entrepreneurs; it was state funds like Rusnano and programs like Skolkovo that helped incubate start-ups through funding and office space in the state-funded technology park. Following the financial crisis of 2014, there is evidence that it became harder to get credit to start Russian businesses; the legal and regulatory framework remained problematic for entrepreneurs, such that in a 2018 survey of 142 enterprises in 53 regions of Russia, one of the most frequently cited concerns was obtaining financing for short- or long-term loans. Another major challenge for Russian start-ups was a high tax burden at both provincial and federal levels.[74]

Although Putin has repeatedly declared his interest in Russia becoming a data storage hub of global importance, as well as calling for greater investment in new technologies such as artificial intelligence, by 2017 Russia was lagging in high-tech development. Relatively weak rule of law and uncertainties around property rights created barriers to domestic and foreign investment in the economy that might have promoted faster knowledge transfer inward from beyond Russian borders. Further, despite increased spending on higher education and an attempt to overhaul the Russian Academy of Sciences system (discussed in the context of the Russian educational system in chapter 5), research and business were still far apart—that is, most research still took place outside the private sector and was funded far more by the state than by private corporations.

Total Russian spending on research and development fell far behind that of the United States, China, and the EU, rising only to 1.13% of GDP by 2015 (see figure 4.15). Even when Russia's GDP was growing rapidly between 2003 and 2008, very little of this growth went into funding research in new technologies.

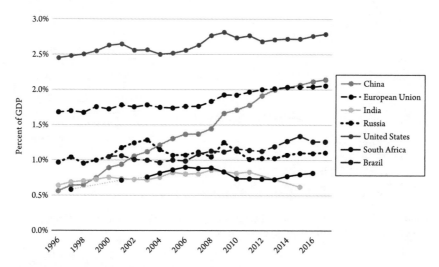

Figure 4.15. Research and Development Spending as a Percentage of GDP in BRICS, the EU, and the US, 1996–2017

In stark contrast, China's R&D spending went from a lower point than Russia's in 1996 (0.63% of GDP beside Russia's 0.96%) to match the rate of European spending at well over 2% of GDP. Russia's comparatively smaller growth in R&D spending, especially beside China and the United States, can also be explained by the fact that it is largely funded by the state rather than by private, profit-seeking corporations with in-house engineers and laboratories.

All of this presents serious obstacles to Russia's ability to become an economic challenger to the United States and China. This was also reflected in Russia's relatively poor performance in registering new patents compared to the United States and especially China, where patent registration has skyrocketed, even overtaking the US figure in 2015. As figure 4.16 indicates, however, Russia managed to increase its pace of patent registration after the lows of the early 1990s, and continued to register new patents far in excess of the average for the EU 28, Brazil, India, and South Africa. It would have to pick up the pace considerably, though, for new technology to become the basis of a more diversified Russian economy that might serve as a means to further expand its global power.

Is Russia's Economy a Stable Basis for Global Ambitions?

Despite its turnaround in the 2000s, gradual and modest economic diversification, and steady and disciplined macroeconomic and fiscal policy, the Russian economy retained a host of challenges in creating a framework for continued growth. Not least among these were high degrees of corruption and weak rule

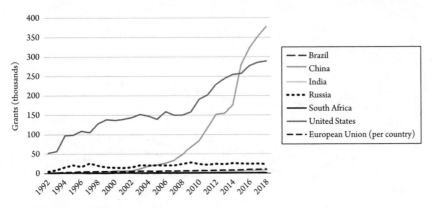

Figure 4.16. Total Patent Grants (Direct and PCT National Phase Entries) Originating from BRICS, the EU, and the US, 1992–2018

of law. As noted in this chapter's introduction, and in chapters 1 and 8, the Russian economy under Putin is a system of patronalism in which those in state service, who are supposed to act in the public interest, instead use the state as a vehicle for self-enrichment and for the benefit of their cronyistic networks. Post-Soviet Russia has consistently ranked high on various measures of corruption. Putin, after twenty years in power, is purported to be the wealthiest man in the world due to his own skimming from the riches of the Russian state.[75] Regardless of the accuracy of these accounts of Putin's personal wealth and that of his inner circle, virtually all available measures indicate that contemporary Russia suffers from high degrees of official corruption at various levels of government. While petty corruption that was endemic in the tumult of the 1990s, such as police shakedowns of vulnerable motorists, was largely tamed by 2019, higher-level corruption was certainly not a thing of the past. Too many of Russia's billionaires have had close long-term political connections with Putin himself, extending back to his adolescence in St. Petersburg. Their close ties to the Kremlin appeared to gain them lucrative contracts with the Russian government and preferential tax regimes, among other schemes, allowing them to make billions, most of which is thought to be held in offshore companies. The late opposition leader and former prime minister Boris Nemtsov and activist Vladimir Milov estimated in one study that there are "four sources of crony enrichment: privileged public procurement, stock manipulation, asset stripping, and privileged trade."[76] They estimate that in just the four years between 2004 and 2007, Gazprom alone transferred assets to Putin and his cronies that had a market value of $60 billion.[77] As explained further in chapter 8, Putin's close circle, many of whom were close friends and colleagues from his origins in St. Petersburg, have largely replaced the original seventeen powerful oligarchs of the 1990s, including the likes of Vladimir Gusinsky, whose empire was dismantled

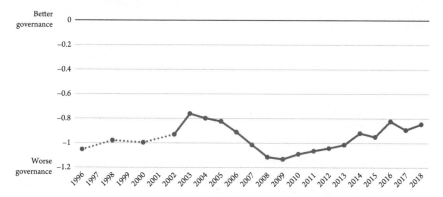

Figure 4.17. World Governance Indicators (WGI): Control of Corruption in Russia, 1996–2018

by Putin shortly after assuming the presidency in 2000; Boris Berezhovsky, who abandoned Russia to protect what assets he could in London, dying there in 2013; and Mikhail Khodorkovsky, Russia's richest man until his arrest and the confiscation of most of his Russian assets in 2003 (he was released from prison by a presidential pardon in December 2013 and quickly moved to Switzerland).

Figure 4.17 shows the World Bank's Governance Indicators for perceptions of a state's ability to control corruption. There are two interesting patterns. First, perceived control of corruption remained weak in the twenty-five years following the Soviet Union's collapse (from 1996 to 2017) in absolute terms, improving only from a low of −1.1 to −0.8. Within that period, there was slight improvement during the first three years of Putin's first presidential term, but as the economy expanded from 2003 through 2008, perceptions of corruption became far worse. Second, after Putin's return to the presidency in 2012, the perception of control over corruption increased only very slightly but still remained weak on this scale, moving from −1.12 to −0.9.

These patterns are echoed in the World Governance Indicators on perceptions of Rule of Law (see figure 4.18). Here too, we see a decline in perceptions of the state's ability to maintain rule of law in the 1990s, a slight improvement in the early 2000s, a slight decline during the economic boom years, followed by a modest improvement that brought perceptions back to about where they had been in 1996. Such numbers are problematic for investors who want to ensure legal protection for their investments. In a thriving market economy, the state has the ability to enforce rules and regulations, enforce contracts, protect property rights, and ensure that courts are capable of providing adequate and enforceable remedies to civil, criminal, and commercial disputes. The Russian state did not appear to change the perception that it was incapable of providing this crucial market scaffolding. International investors can, of course, choose to

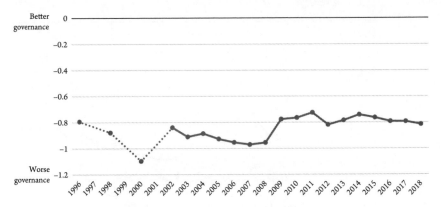

Figure 4.18. World Governance Indicators: Rule of Law in Russia, 1996–2018

start businesses elsewhere; innovatively minded Russians might do the same, where possible. Weak state enforcement of the rule of law, or even the perception thereof, means that "innovation promotion efforts will almost certainly fail if the overall investment environment is not conducive to long-term investment in new activities."[78]

Conclusion

Russia's economic development since the collapse of the Soviet Union has been uneven. Many of the features of the economy inherited from the Soviet system, such as low labor productivity, a tendency for a few outsized enterprises to dominate the economy, and corruption, have endured, along with other problems of the 1990s. All of these remained significant challenges for reliable economic development as a basis for Russia's extension of its renewed global influence.

Although the sanctions imposed on the Russian economy since 2014 in particular have not impeded economic growth as much as some may have expected, they were a hindrance in the development of a stable basis for future growth, particularly related to investment in oil and gas extraction infrastructure that would maintain and improve the efficiency of oil drilling in the Arctic and Russian Far East. Foreign direct investment from new partners in the Gulf States, India, and China, as noted in chapter 3, have helped to ameliorate this situation, but it is still a significant loss for future economic growth.

Further, relative to China or the United States, the Russian economy was low on innovation, and it underspent on R&D. The inherited structures of the Soviet economy were not helpful: the belief in gigantism to achieve economies of scale in production, accompanied by weak rule of law, has led to a highly concentrated economy dominated by a few actors closely tied to the state. The line between private business and public assets remains fuzzy, and opportunities for ravenous bureaucrats and elected officials to steal from the state have continued to abound.

Despite these very real problems, the Russian economy is not as weak as it is sometimes portrayed. Its ability to bounce back after successive crises should not be discounted when we evaluate the economy's role in the extension of Russian power. It should also be noted that many of the tools Russian leaders used between 2008 and 2017 to disrupt the politics of other countries did not especially tax the economy. In 2017, despite maintaining troops in Syria, the conflict simmering in Ukraine, and occupations in Georgia and Moldova, the Russian state still had low external debt-to-GNI, low unemployment, low inflation, high foreign reserves, and a well-capitalized sovereign wealth fund. Moreover, its economy was *still growing even under the most extensive sanctions* ever imposed on Russia by the West, and this was *outside the context of high global oil prices*. Russian policymakers have used its accumulated wealth to invest abroad, improve domestic infrastructure, raise standards of living, reform its military (see chapter 6), and improve some human development indicators (see chapter 5). Russian state-owned companies like Gazprom became instruments in an aggressive foreign policy, and were also used as investment tools in less-developed markets in Latin America, the Middle East, Asia, and sub-Saharan Africa (see chapters 2 and 3).

Some good policy decisions and disciplined implementation of them, as well as periodically high global prices for Russia's mineral exports, meant that within twenty-five years the Russian economy had more than recovered from the tremendous shock of the Soviet collapse. GDP had not only returned to pre-collapse levels, but soared far beyond; in some areas, like grain and nickel exports, Russian firms have become global market leaders. Still, while the Russian economy had recovered from its deep and successive economic crises of the 1990s, it was not a global economic front runner by virtually any measure. It remained only a fraction the size of China's economy, the United States', or the EU's. Nonetheless, Russia's economy, despite its clear limitations, has proven evidently not to be a hindrance to its resurgence in global politics. Whether the economy can sustain this resurgence and fuel President Putin's global ambitions, however, depends also on the health and demography of the Russian people. We turn next, therefore, from "money" to "men," —or the human development and demographic aspect of Russian power resources, assessing this area as a further means by which Russia has attempted to enhance its power in the new global order.

Russian Society as Power Resource or Constraint?

"If the nation is not capable of preserving itself and reproducing, if it loses it vital bearings and ideals, then it doesn't need foreign enemies—it will fall apart on its own."[1]

—Vladimir Putin, 2006

Any meaningful assessment of a state's means of power must look beyond merely the size of its population, but at the health, wealth, and general welfare and capacities of its people. This chapter adds human capital to the evaluation of Russia's relative power resources. In the quote that opens this chapter, Vladimir Putin himself indicates the importance of human capital to Russian power— a state cannot project power if its population cannot grow, is not long-lived, is not healthy, and lacks the skills and education to contribute to its economy and national security. All of these demographic trends have a direct bearing on who can contribute to the Russian economy and for how long. This includes considerations of who is active in a country's labor force, what their likely productive output will be (recalling from chapter 4 that Russia lags in GDP output per hour worked), and whether or not investments in updating the skills of older workers would produce a payoff in improved output over time.

In what follows, I examine first how the post-Soviet demographic decline in Russia threatened its economic recovery until about 2012. Despite significant improvements thereafter, under Putin's rule, Russia faces persistent challenges to further development of its human capital. These include improving, but still stubbornly low, life expectancy relative to countries with a similar GDP per capita; higher male mortality rates than peer countries; and an inefficient healthcare system that is poorly equipped to address these issues. In terms of population growth, the contemporary Russian government has struggled to improve a comparatively low fertility rate, which, in combination with relatively high mortality rates, contributed to negative population growth until roughly 2012, when the population recovered to at least a flat rate of growth. The ratio of immigration to emigration, while positive, is not sufficient to overcome years of population loss. Further, emigration of highly educated Russians to Europe and the United States may further detract from the accumulation of human capital. This, combined with younger Russians staying in the country but opting to have fewer or no children, has meant that Russia's labor force is aging. This will present challenges in developing a trained and productive labor force in the coming decades, not to mention providing the state pension benefits older Russians are accustomed to receiving. Despite what is often depicted as a dismal demographic, health, and human capital picture for contemporary Russia, however, Russian policymakers have had some success in addressing a few of the huge challenges of social development in the post-Soviet period. I provide a brief overview of Russia's anti-tobacco initiative as an example.

Second, beyond health and demographic challenges, this chapter also examines the effects of high Russian social inequality and wealth concentration on social mobility for young Russians. Third, and related, I also look into Russia's post-secondary educational reforms, and the degree to which the Russian labor force is prepared to further economic growth as a means of resurrecting Russian global power. Moreover, as with the economic means of Russian power, the human capital aspect has progressed significantly since the Soviet collapse in 1991, but it faces significant challenges if Russian power projection abroad is to expand.

Demographic Decline and Recovery

The massive challenges of radical political and economic transition faced by the fledgling Russian state from 1991 onward were made even more difficult and urgent by rapidly growing demographic problems. The USSR suffered a massive population decline during World War II, with an estimated almost 26 million people killed (almost 16,825,000 civilians and 8.7 million members of the military)—more than 15% of the population at the time.[2] Some historians estimate that Stalin's regime killed an additional 9 or so million people between the Ukrainian famine, imprisonment in the Gulag system of labor camps, and the Great Terror of the early 1930s.[3] The population recovered somewhat in a postwar baby boom, but by the 1960s, population growth had begun to slow. By the late 1980s, as noted in chapter 4, demographic trends were distinctly negative within the Russian Socialist Federative Soviet Republic (RSFSR) and throughout the Union as a whole. The severe recession under which the new Russian Federation began economic reform in 1992, at least initially, may have had a further negative demographic effect. The extensive communist system of cradle-to-grave social services had not been of high quality, but even scarcer resources meant that social support systems further declined in the early to mid-1990s. In 1992, the state healthcare system boasted an abundance of poorly trained doctors who had limited access to modern diagnostic equipment and prescription medications. Alcoholism, poor nutrition, and heavy smoking plagued the Russian population, and men in particular.

These were some of the factors that helped propel three main negative demographic trends. First, a decline in life expectancy for men and women (although more pronounced for men) from the 1990s through the first decade of the 2000s constrained the growth of the Russian labor force. Second, and relatedly, low birth rates relative to mortality led to negative to flat population growth. Third, as was the case with other upper-middle-income and even upper-income countries in Europe, Russia's population is aging. These are all concerning to Russian policymakers because if these trends continue, and if immigration does not help to ameliorate the resulting labor force decline, the prospects for economic growth and expansion would be further jeopardized. Indeed, until about 2012, demographic challenges were at risk of becoming bigger constraints on Russian conduct abroad than the economic or structural variables discussed in chapter 4, although the two are tightly intertwined.

An overview of Russia's comparative statistics on the United Nations Human Development Index (which measures "a long and healthy life, access to knowledge and a decent standard of living") indicates tremendous improvement for Russia over time on all three components of human development (see figure 5.1).[4] As with GDP, life expectancy, education, and gross national income show transitional U-shaped curves. That is, all of these measures declined initially (or started low, as in the case of education) in the early to mid-1990s, but began to inch up by the end of the decade and improved rapidly after about 1999. Within three decade of since the Soviet collapse, the United Nations reported that Russia had joined the group of 58 countries classified as having "very high human development" of the 189 countries included by the UN on the index (Russia had reached number 49).[5] For comparison, the United States was ranked number 13 and Portugal was ranked just above Russia at number 41 (recall from chapter 4 that this was Mr. Putin's developmental target by 2020), while other members of the BRICS economies all ranked considerably lower than Russia, falling in the "medium human development" group (Brazil at 79, China at 86, South Africa at 113, and India at 130).

Overall, then, Russian human development underwent dramatic improvement in the thirty or so years following the Soviet collapse. Particularly notable were the high rates of Russian schooling for men and for women (partly a Soviet inheritance), which could bode well for further diversifying and developing the

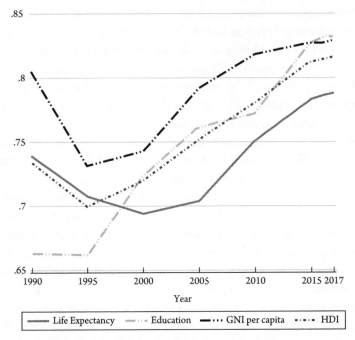

Figure 5.1. Trends in Russian Federation's HDI Component Indices, 1990–
2017 Source: United Nations Human Development Programme, Human Development Reports,
Russian Federation Human Development Indicators, available at http://hdr.undp.org/sites/all/
themes/hdr_theme/country-notes/RUS.pdf, accessed October 14 2020.

Russian economy as a stronger means of extending power abroad. Still, when
we look deeper at some of the individual measures of Russian demography,
some significant issues remain that may impede Russia's true resurrection as a
"great" power.

Life expectancy for Russian adults has remained a persistent problem. The
life spans of Soviet citizens had been declining over the last three decades of
the Soviet Union's existence, and within Russia itself, life expectancy at birth
plunged further in the immediate aftermath of the system's collapse. The Russian
government under Boris Yeltsin was embroiled in difficult political and economic transitions, so little could be done to stem the tidal wave of Russians dying
too young. The problem was particularly pronounced in men. Some theories
suggested that this may have been a direct result of economic reform and privatization in particular, processes which threw men into unemployment (not
a familiar position given that the Soviet system had guaranteed employment),
contributing to higher suicide rates and bad habits like higher vodka consumption.[6] In the first few years of the transition period alone, male life expectancy at
birth dropped from a high of 65 in 1988 (a few years before the Soviet collapse
in 1991), to a dismal 57.55 years in 1994 (on par with countries in sub-Saharan

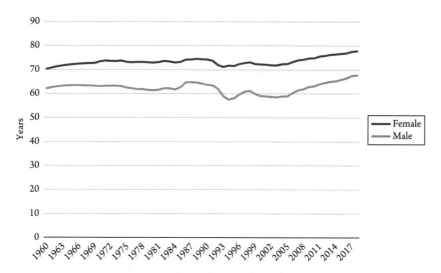

Figure 5.2. Life Expectancy of Men and Women in Russia, 1960–2018 Source: World Bank, https://data.worldbank.org/indicator/SP.DYN.LE00.FE.IN?locations=RU&view=chart, accessed July 5, 2020.

Africa that were suffering from the worst of the HIV/AIDS crisis), before gradually rising to a new peak of 67.8 years in 2018.[7] Since mass privatization took place between 1994 and 1996, the theory linking the trend to Russia's dismal male life expectancy does not seem to be supported by the trend in figure 5.2, which indicates that life expectancy rose during and after this first big phase of privatization. Other observers argued that it was actually an increase in alcoholism (especially the consumption of homemade alcohol, *samogon*, to which some Russians would resort to drinking in the face of high prices for name-brand vodka) that was depressing life expectancy.[8] We return to the alcohol issue later in this chapter.

In the same period, however, women fared much better than men in terms of life expectancy, declining from 74.53 in 1988 to 71.2 in 1993, and steadily increasing thereafter to end 2018 at an all-time high since the Soviet collapse of 77.81 years.[9]

Nonetheless, at 72.7 years, Russia men and women combined still stood at the lower end of comparative combined male/female adult life expectancy at birth. The EU and the United States reached 80.62 and 78.5 years, respectively, in 2018, but their citizens were not facing the type of economic and political upheaval that Russia endured after 1991, so it is not surprising that their average life expectancy soared far above Russia's. Notably, as indicated in figure 5.3, in 1990 average combined male and female Chinese life expectancy was very close to Russia's at about 68 years, but grew apace with its GDP to surpass Russia at over 75 years (as did Brazil's) in the thirty or so years thereafter. Only India and South

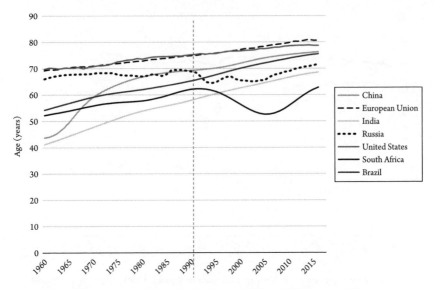

Figure 5.3. Life Expectancy at Birth in Russia and Selected Countries of Comparison, 1960–2018 Source: World Bank. "Life expectancy at birth (total), years." Data last updated September 21, 2019. https://data.worldbank.org/indicator/SP.DYN.LE00.IN

Africa maintained lower average combined life expectancy than Russia by 2018, though India did see steady improvement. While researchers have demonstrated that increases in Russian life expectancy have come with economic growth, some analysts have estimated that even with Russia's leaps in GDP per capita, life expectancy remained 6.5 years below other countries at a similar level of economic development.[10] Indeed, Russian women in 2018 lived about the same length of time as did Mexican women, but the GDP of Mexico is about 60% of Russia's. More striking was that Russian men in 2018 had the same life expectancy at birth as did men in São Tomé and Principe, where GDP was 0.02% of Russia's.[11]

The yawning almost eleven-year gap in life expectancy between men and women is also unique to Russia among the cases compared in this study, and also among *almost all other countries classified by the United Nations as having high or very high human development.* In the 58 countries in the category of very high human development, women live an average of just over six years more than men (almost half the gender gap that existed in Russia); by 2018 in these countries, average life expectancy hit 82.4 years for women (compared to Russia's 77.8), and 76.7 years for men (vs. 67.8 for Russian men). Upon his return to the presidency in 2018, Putin declared the goal of increasing life expectancy for both sexes to 76 years (from 72.7 years as noted above) by 2024, and to 80 years by 2030.[12] These targets are aggressive, but would put Russia more in line with countries at similar levels of economic development. The challenge for Russian policymakers has been to not only identify the causes of persistently low male life expectancy in particular, but also to devise public health interventions to ameliorate the problem, and to invest in these solutions.

Longevity for Russians is unlikely to continue to improve markedly without significantly more, and more effective, government investment in healthcare. Poor health for Russian men is primarily driven by cardiovascular disease, which, in turn, has been historically driven by high rates of vodka consumption, tobacco smoking, poor diet, and lack of physical activity. In the mid-2000s, the Russian government recognized these as major problems for labor force development, since men were becoming sick and dying when still in the prime of working age. By 2017, Russian men still made up the majority of the Russian labor force, with 71.8% of men working compared to 56.6% of women.[13] Further, as noted in chapter 4, while Russian labor productivity rose in the 2000s, it remained far lower than in the EU or the United States. Improvements in the health and longevity of Russian men could greatly boost Russian productive output. Recognizing this, and evidently acknowledging that previous efforts had been insufficient, in the spring of 2018, President Putin decreed the establishment of another new national health project to attack Russian demographic issues, including a focus on cardiovascular disease.[14]

As life expectancy measures hit their lowest points in the early to mid-1990s, the mortality rate reached its highest point, jumping from 12.6 per 1,000 people in 1992 to 15.9 in 1994, as indicated in figure 5.4. This was in stark contrast to

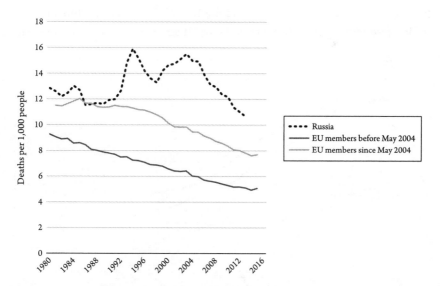

Figure 5.4. Age-Standardized Death Rates for Russia and EU Members, 1980–2016 Source: World Health Organization European Health Information Gateway. "SDR, All Causes, per 100,000." Data last updated June 15, 2018. https://gateway.euro.who.int/en/indicators/hfamdb_113-sdr-all-causes-per-100-000/

those countries that joined the EU after 2004 (in particular, Poland, the Czech and Slovak Republics, and the three Baltic States), where mortality rates *declined* steadily following the collapse of the Berlin Wall in 1989. Russia took far longer to get mortality under better control. Counterintuitively, in Russia, mortality rates actually increased again even as GDP rose between 1999 and 2003 (possibly a result of citizens having more disposable income to spend on bad habits like smoking and drinking), while elsewhere, they continued a steady decline. But from 2003 onward, the death rate in Russia followed a pattern more similar to its European neighbors. That noted, as figure 5.4 indicates, Russians, and especially Russian men, still died at a far faster rate (and younger) than most Europeans in the East or West.

At the same time that life expectancy declined and mortality rates increased, Russian women were having fewer children, as indicated in figure 5.5. The average number of children per family dropped from 1.545 children in 1990 to a low of 1.25 in 1995, during the depths of Russia's post-communist reform crisis period. The decline in fertility rates, at the same time as the increase in adult mortality rates, meant that Russia suffered negative population growth. But by 2017, Russia's population had recovered to flat growth and even a slightly positive increase (if one included Crimea as part of Russia, as President Putin did), reaching 146,780,720 by January 1, 2019 (about 144,480,000 without Crimea). While the good news for Russian policymakers was that life expectancy had increased since the dark days of the 1990s, it continued to lag well behind those of the United States, China, and the EU. While China and India needed to decrease fertility rates to increase GDP, Russia needed to do the opposite

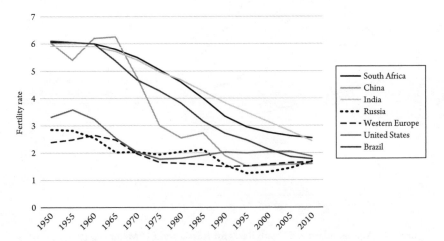

Figure 5.5. Total Fertility Rate in Russia and Selected Countries of Comparison, 1950–2010 Source: United Nations World Population 2017. "Total Fertility by Region, Subregion, and Country, 1950-2010 (Live Births Per Person)." Data last updated June 1, 2017. https://population.un.org/wpp/Download/Standard/Population/

in response to increased mortality and declining overall population. Notably, therefore, although the trends of declining fertility, life expectancy for men and women, and mortality had improved by twenty-five years after the demographic shocks of the early 1990s, sustaining this momentum would mean heavier, efficient investment in Russian public health. (It remains to be seen what the effect of the COVID-19 pandemic of 2020 will have on Russian demography. The Russian Federation in early May of 2020 was second only the United States in terms of the number of cases of the virus, but had a far lower reported death rate possibly because Russia has fewer very old people who proved particularly susceptible to the disease, but also likely as a result of the fact that at least initially, the Russian Health guideline was to include only those whose deaths that could be tied directly to COVID rather than any comorbidity in the total death count. Undoubtedly too, local officials were incented to underreport deaths due to the disease to promote the appearance that the Russian health system was outperforming others in containing the virus.[15])

Despite the bottoming-out of the demographic decline across these measures, Russia's population pyramid—its size and shape by sex and age—demonstrates the looming legacy of Soviet demography and the set of problems this has presented for its labor force development well into the twenty-first century. As noted earlier, Russia's population overall is aging, as is the case for many developed economies in Europe and Asia (especially Japan). The population pyramid graphic shown in figure 5.6 demonstrates that Russians are

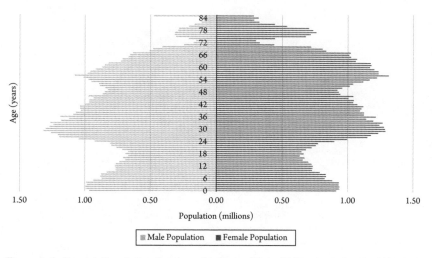

Figure 5.6. Russia's Population Structure by Sex and Age, 2017 Source: Russian Federal State Statistics Service (Rosstat). "Chislennost' naseleniia Rossiiskoi Federatsii po polu i vozrastu" [Population of the Russian Federation by sex and age]. Data last updated January 1, 2017. http://www. gks.ru/wps/wcm/connect/rosstat_main/rosstat/ru/statistics/population/demography/#

disproportionately female and over the age of 40. Based on the data, projections suggest that by 2030, there will be far more Russians of retirement age, and perhaps even more pensioners than workers (see figure 5.7). This is the case even after a controversial 2018 law stipulating a gradual rise in retirement age, to 60 for women and 65 for men, by 2028. While many countries' population structure resembles a pyramid, with a larger number of younger people than older, Russia's is more like an hourglass in shape, suggesting a bulge of older people in the coming decades.

Despite upward trends in life expectancy and GDP, and the fact that it has stemmed the bleeding in population growth by decreasing mortality rates and increasing fertility, Russia's still problematic demography can only be considered a constraint on the expansion of its global reach. A longer-lived and more productive population would be needed to transform the economy further, relieving its still disproportionately heavy reliance on natural resources in favor of more technological and knowledge-intensive industries. Further, as we will discuss in chapter 6, beginning in 2008, the Russian military underwent a significant reform and transformation to a professionalized force, but still relied to some degree on conscripted soldiers. A continued decline in birth rates would mean a decline in conscripts able to fulfill mandatory service requirements. To fuel President Putin's global ambitions, the number of Russian men of fighting (and working) age, and their general health, would have to increase dramatically, as would the number of children born to Russian couples overall.

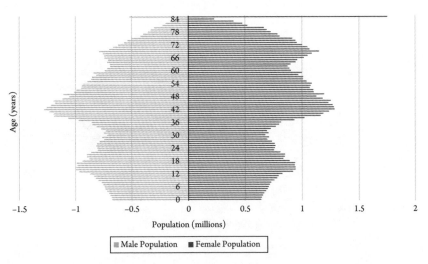

Figure 5.7. Russia's Population Structure by Sex and Age, 2030
(Predicted) Source: Russian Federal State Statistics Service (Rosstat). "Predpolozhitel'naia chislennost' naseleniia Rossiiskoi Federatsii" [Predicted population of the Russian Federation]. Data last updated October 3, 2018. http://www.gks.ru/wps/wcm/connect/rosstat_main/rosstat/ru/statistics/population/demography/#

Russian Policy Responses to Demographic Problems

Russian policymakers since 1992, made a variety of attempts to combat Russia's low life expectancy and high mortality rates with, as the improved measures in the Human Development Index indicated, some success. In 1993, the Russian government introduced Mandatory Health Insurance (MHI), a public health-care system funded by employers and regional governments. Public clinics were permitted to charge for services not covered by the MHI system. The MHI system was intended to provide a basket of guaranteed basic health services, but health-care costs became increasingly expensive for average Russians over time. In part, this was because corruption gradually crept into healthcare provision. According to one report, "In 2011, 34% of patients paying for outpatient visits indicated that they did so informally, whereas the proportion for inpatient services was 67%."[16]

By the mid-2000s, the Russian government under President Medvedev embarked on various public health reforms, which continued—with slight variation, and some aspects left uncompleted—into President Putin's third and fourth terms. Various initiatives focused on reducing vodka consumption and tobacco smoking, increasing the quality of healthcare in Russia by improving physician training and access to modern equipment, and providing easier access to healthcare across the country by increasing the number of clinics and hospital beds (although, in practice, more hospital beds just resulted in more people in the hospital, whereas a health policy focused on disease prevention might have targeted the root of the issue).

The problems in Russian health appear in adulthood, since Russia's infant mortality at 6.1 deaths per 1,000 live births by 2018 had steadily declined and was comparable to that of the United States at 5.6.[17] Further, deaths before the age of 5 years are the lowest of all the BRICS (at 7 per 1,000 live births) and more consistent with OECD countries.[18] Adult bad habits included some of the highest per capita rates of tobacco smoking in the world among both men and women, as well as consistently high rates of alcohol consumption. In 2008, more than 60% of Russian men over age 15 smoked; among Russian women, the rate of smoking rose from 5% in the mid-1980s to 12% in the mid-1990s to over 20% by 2012. It was at this time that the Russian government initiated a sweeping anti-tobacco policy that banned smoking in public places, increased taxes on cigarettes, banned certain forms of advertising, and strongly regulated point of sale of tobacco.[19] Since initiating this reform, smoking rates have declined from an average of 39% of all Russians over 15 years of age in 2009 to 31% by 2016. According to the Foundation for a Smoke-Free World, however, this still left Russians as the largest smoking population per capita in all of Europe.[20]

Alcohol consumption in Russia following the Soviet collapse was also problematic, but as with tobacco use, the Russian government endeavored to decrease

alcohol consumption with a series of policy changes from the early 2000s onward. These included restrictions on advertising, banning nighttime alcohol sales
and public drinking, and a minimum unit price policy. These efforts seem to have
had a significant effect, with the World Health Organization reporting a 43% decline in alcohol consumption between 2003 and 2016.[21] To illustrate the depth
of this health issue, note that Russians were designated the heaviest drinkers in
Europe in 2004, consuming an average of almost 17 liters of alcohol (primarily
vodka) per year, compared to a reported average of 13 liters per capita for EU citizens. By 2016, Russians were down to 13.5 liters per capita annually, compared to
about 12 liters in EU countries—a dramatic decline for Russians in a very short
period of time. While Russians were still out-drinking their European neighbors,
the overall decline had important demographic effects: recall from earlier in this
chapter that the United Nations reported a historic peak in life expectancy, which
reached almost 68 for Russian men and 78 for Russian women in 2018.[22] There
also has been a marked decline in mortality directly related to alcohol consumption for Russian men, from 62% to just over 30%.[23] While this number was still
well above the European average, the improvement is significant given the historical place of vodka consumption in particular in Russian culture.[24]

Despite these public health successes in curbing habits that were literally
causing Russians (men especially) to die in what should have been the prime
of life, the Russian government now spends less of its per capita GDP on health
than it has in the past. Higher health spending does not always lead to better
health outcomes, of course, but it is significant that by 2018, Russia also spent
less on health relative to other BRICS economies except India. India, however, has less to spend per person—its per capita GNI was a fraction of Russia's
($3,590 vs. $20,560, respectively[25]), which could explain the difference. Still,
Russian government spending on healthcare has not increased sufficiently to
overcome some of the country's pernicious public health problems.[26] Indeed,
Russian budgetary spending as a proportion of GDP on health and sport actually declined from 5% of GDP in 2011 to less than 4% by 2018.[27] There is also evidence that Russia's spending is not always efficient or directed to the right areas.
For example, the Russian Federation has far more doctors per capita (by a factor
of 400%) than other BRICS countries, yet Russians face a higher probability of
dying between the ages of 30 and 70 from preventable, noninfectious diseases
than residents of all of the other countries in the BRICS grouping.[28]

Outside of budgetary policy, a greater incentive for healthy lifestyles was seen
in the figure of the president himself. While photos of Vladimir Putin with his
shirt off on horseback, or saving Siberian tigers in the Russian wilderness, have
provoked amusement in the West, they play far better within Russia. Along with
lots of footage of Putin playing hockey or weightlifting with members of his
cabinet, both of which are routinely shown on Russian television, such images

encourage a healthier lifestyle and project a new image of Russian men as fit, strong, and living a sporting life well into their sixties. Of course, the extent of influence such images may have on the fitness of other Russian men is unclear, but the deliberate representation of Putin as a model of Russian manhood and physical prowess is just as centrally intended to symbolize political strength at home and abroad.

Immigration and Emigration

Beyond policies to improve the health and fertility rates of the population, immigration is another way in which other countries have changed what seemed to be their demographic destinies. Here, too, Russia has had a mixed record. (Figure 5.8 shows the pattern of migration into Russia since 1990, just prior to the Soviet collapse, through 2017, while figure 5.9 provides more detail on immigration and compares it to official emigration patterns through 2017.)

The establishment of fifteen separate states in the wake of the USSR collapse meant that there was considerable population movement across borders. Despite the difficult economic situation in Russia, immigration increased from 926,000 in 1992 to 1.2 million in 1994, and thereafter decreased steadily, bottoming out at 119,157 in 2004. Undoubtedly, through the 1990s, economic and political turmoil helped discourage immigration, but as Russia's economy boomed after 2004, immigration again increased steadily, with dips corresponding to the

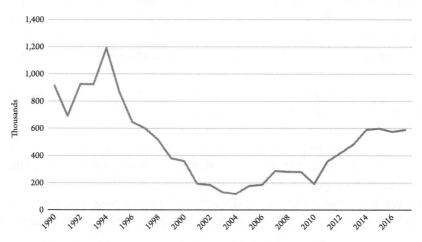

Figure 5.8. Total Migration into Russia from Foreign Countries, 1990–2016 Source: Russian Federal State Statistics Service (Rosstat). "Obshchie potoki naseleniia (po potokam peredvizheniia)" [Total population flows (by movement flows)]. Data last updated April 2, 2018. http://www.gks.ru/wps/wcm/connect/rosstat_main/rosstat/ru/statistics/population/demography/#

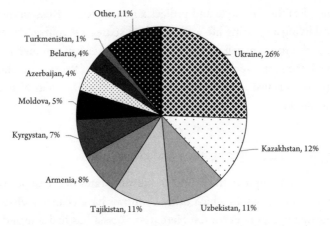

Figure 5.9. Top 10 Origin Countries for Immigrants to Russia, 2017 Source: Russian Federal State Statistics Service (Rosstat). "Mezhdunarodnaia migratsiia" [International migration]. Data last updated October 26, 2018. http://www.gks.ru/wps/wcm/connect/rosstat_main/rosstat/ru/statistics/population/demography/#

economic crisis of 2008–2009 and the recession of 2014; at the latter point, the flow of immigrants flattened out at about 600,000 per year for the next four years.

Most migrants into Russia by 2017 came from the near abroad—26% from Ukraine, and another 50% from Central Asia (led by Kazakhstan, Uzbekistan, and Tajikistan, with fewer from Kyrgyzstan and the isolated nation of Turkmenistan). Other migrants originated from Armenia, with fewer from Azerbaijan, Moldova, and Belarus. Only 11% of migrants into Russia came from elsewhere. Of these, the leading origin countries were China, accounting for about 8,000 people (about 1.4% of total immigration); North Korea, sending another 6,000 (about 1.2%); India, with 5,000 (about 1.00%); and Vietnam, sending just over 3,000 (less than 0.5%). Despite its ongoing military involvement in Syria, Russia welcomed very few Syrians fleeing from the conflict; the highest number, just over 1,000 people, arrived when Russia entered the war effort in Syria in 2015, and the influx decreased thereafter.[29]

Relatively speaking, Russia takes in very few immigrants overall, with a rate of about 590,000 annually since 2014, constituting an inflow of less than 0.5% of the country's total population per year. For perspective, according to the US Census Bureau, about 46.4 million immigrants entered the United States in the same period, and immigrants in 2017 constituted about 13.7% of the total population.[30]

A Brain Drain?

At the same time, there was reason for Russian policymakers to be concerned that some of their best-educated citizens were abandoning the country. The

Russian State Statistical Service reported that emigration of Russians abroad increased concurrently with the rising international flow of migrants into the country, thereby undercutting the net population gains from immigration. Figure 5.10 indicates that emigration had been decreasing through 2011, hitting a low of 36,774 Russians leaving, but then rapidly increased by almost tenfold, hitting 353,233 in 2014 and peaking at 377,155 by 2017. This meant that the net gain in population of immigrants to emigrants was just over 210,000 people in 2017, consistent with the statistics from the preceding three years.[31] If we consider that Russia's total population is 144,438,554 (without Crimea), that is a net increase in population from immigration of only 0.15% per year.

For the Russian government, a potentially problematic aspect of the uptick in emigration from Russia since 2012 is that official statistics may underestimate how many Russians have departed to live and work abroad. Some, for example, retained their citizenship and apartments in Russia while living permanently abroad.[32] It is unlikely that official state statistics would count such people as emigrants. Unfortunately for Russia, this trend may well represent a "brain drain," since many of those who have left Russia after 2014 are among the country's most highly educated, and their destinations are often in the tech industry in Silicon Valley or universities in the United States or Europe.[33]

Russia's already troubled demographics may be further damaged in future trends in the attitudes of Russian youth who indicated that they intended to permanently emigrate. As figure 5.11 indicates, the highly respected and independent Russian polling organization Levada Center has tracked a steady increase among 18–24-year-olds in Russia seeking to emigrate permanently. By

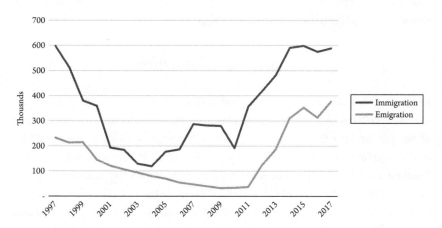

Figure 5.10. Total Immigration to Russia and Emigration from Russia, 1997–2017 Source: Russian Federal State Statistics Service (Rosstat). "Mezhdunarodnaia migratsiia" [International migration]. Data last updated October 26, 2018. http://www.gks.ru/wps/wcm/connect/rosstat_main/rosstat/ru/statistics/population/demography/#

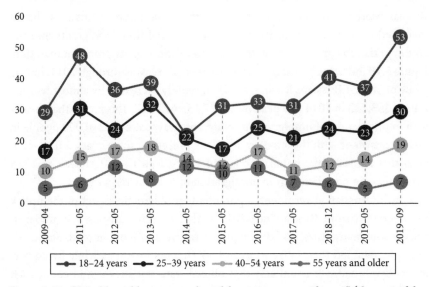

Figure 5.11. "Would you like to move abroad for permanent residence?" (the sum of the answers "Definitely yes" and "Rather yes" in %) Source: Levada Center, https://www.levada. ru/2019/11/26/emigratsionnye-nastroeniya-4/?fromtg=1

2019, this had reached a staggering 53% of respondents in this age category—a ten-year high in their polling.[34] The proportion of slightly older Russians in the 25–39-year-old category was also close to a 6-year high, at 31% of respondents. According to another study on what has been called the "Putin Exodus," the most desired destinations for these prospective émigrés were the United States and Western Europe.[35] Among the reasons given by those indicating a desire to leave Russia permanently were a desire for more career and educational opportunities abroad and a desire to better provide for their children.[36]

Inequality and Frustration

Young people's desire to emigrate, and a clear increase in youth political activism from 2014 onward, may be explained by frustration with the persistence or worsening of other problematic socioeconomic indicators, such as inequality and "grand" (high level) corruption. In March 2017, thousands of young Russians took to the streets of Moscow. Some protesters had not even reached their thirteenth birthdays; in some cases, these were the children of the Russians who had shown up in huge numbers to protest the Soviet system in 1990 and 1991, and Vladimir Putin's planned return to power in 2011 and 2012. This time, however, a younger generation of protesters—with no experience of the Soviet system or any political leader other than President Putin—were responding to mass corruption, as unveiled by social media. Specifically, a YouTube video produced by Russian opposition activist Alexei Navalny revealed what was alleged to be the extravagant, secret country home of former president and prime minister Dmitri Medvedev, using high-quality drone footage and damning investigative reporting. Protesters were fed up not only with reports of the endemic theft of state assets by public officials at the highest levels of the Russian government, but also with the everyday indignities tied to pervasive corruption. For younger Russians, this included being denied admission to a top school or university without paying a bribe to administrators, or losing out in favor of a seemingly less qualified candidate who turned out to be the child of a member of the economic or political elite.[37] Beyond this, the growing inequality in household income and access to education, healthcare, and employment presented a different challenge to the Russian economy as a firm basis for Russian power projection.

The promise of communism was the eradication of socioeconomic inequality, but in practice, the inequities of the old system were not necessarily measured in terms of differences in salaries or net wealth, but between Party elites and regular people. In the post-communist period, wealth and income inequality blossomed in large part because of the lack of established rule of law and the failure to regulate economic activity beginning in the 1990s. The practice of stealing from the state as it collapsed, and the ethos of "what is not clearly prohibited is permitted" in the rough-and-ready reform period, also helped create a new class of super rich, including the oligarchs, who became embroiled in politics under Boris Yeltsin. Many of the original oligarchs were brought to heel by Vladimir Putin in the early 2000s, as noted in chapter 4, but a new class of super rich quickly replaced them, further perpetuating socioeconomic inequality in wealth and income. At the end of 1991, about 24% of income was earned by the top 10% of Russians. But this proportion doubled by 1996 to over 48% of income going to the top 10% of earners, and hit an all-time high by the end of 2008, with over 50% of income going to this top group. The proportion declined slightly thereafter, but still hovered between 45% and 50%, while the bottom 50% of income earners claim less than 20% of the income distribution in post-communist Russia (see figure 5.12).

Russia's Gini coefficient—a measure of the concentration of income from 0 to 100, with 0 indicating perfect equality and 100 indicating perfect inequality—shows a similar pattern set in comparative context (see figure 5.13). Russia's Gini increased at the start of the reform period from 28 at the end of 1991 to 36 within just five years. It declined slightly through 2008, and by 2017 settled to hover around 36 (about where it was in 1995). But as problematic as inequality is for Russians, in 2017 it was lower than among citizens in the United States, China, Brazil, and especially South Africa. These comparisons, however, are unlikely to make the average Russian feel much better about his or her situation.

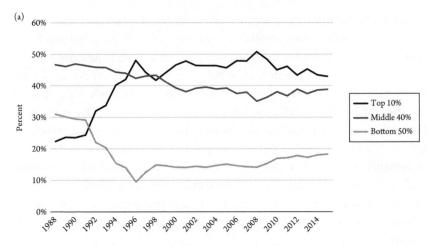

Figure 5.12. Distribution of Income among Top 10%, Middle 40%, and Bottom 50% of Russians Source: World Inequality Database. "World Inequality Database." Data last updated December 31, 2016. https://wid.world/data/

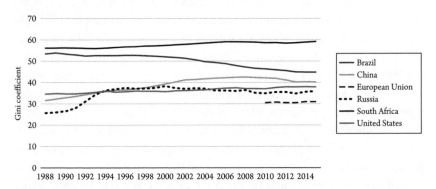

Figure 5.13. Gini Coefficients for BRICS, EU, and US, 1988–2014 Source: Frederick Solt. "Standardized World Income Inequality Database." Data last updated July 24, 2018. https://hdl.handle.net/1902.1/11992
The higher a Gini coefficient, the more unequal a country is.

The real problem for most Russian workers is the extreme concentration of wealth among Russia's top 1%. Figure 5.14 illustrates the yawning gap between Russia's ultra-rich and the rest of the population. The data available go back to 1995 (in the middle of Russia's first big privatization drive). At that point, the top 1% of the population claimed 21.5% of the country's total wealth, while the bottom 50% had about 8.5%. But as the very rich got much richer, their gains came at the expense of the bottom 50% of the population and the gap continued to widen, such that by 2000, the top 1% owned almost 43% of Russia's wealth while the bottom 50% had only about 6.2%. By 2017, the share

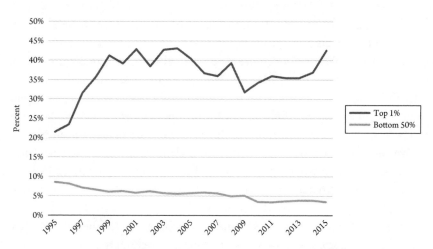

Figure 5.14. Distribution of Wealth among Top 1% and Bottom 50% of Russians, 1995–2015 Source: World Inequality Database. "World Inequality Database." Data last updated December 31, 2016. https://wid.world/data/

of the bottom 50% had declined to 3.5%, less than half what it had been two decades earlier.

These sorts of extremes in wealth and income inequalities may help fuel social unrest in Russia, but they may also be problematic for continued economic growth.[38] According to a 2014 OECD study, there is good evidence that higher inequality has a sizeable negative impact on growth.[39] But the literature is far less clear as to whether high levels of inequality actually cause lower growth, because there are so many intervening factors and variables.[40] In theory, inequality could actually be good for economic growth—it could make people work harder, invest in education, and take risks, especially if they see that those behaviors pay off for others; for example, if you believe that higher education is linked to higher incomes, then there is a clear incentive to go to university. But this assumes some sort of level playing field in terms of access to investment, markets, and education, and a legal and regulatory regime that would ensure that hard work and investment in education pay off. By 2017, these conditions did not consistently exist in Russia;[41] the path to success and wealth was not necessarily to play by the rules. Political power seemed more important for gaining economic privilege in post-communist Russia—not an entirely dissimilar dynamic from the communist system, although with different players and opportunities.[42] It was exactly this trend that young Russians were protesting in 2017.

Notwithstanding the potentially corrosive effects of socioeconomic inequalities in Russia on its long-term economic development, fewer Russians lived in poverty by 2017 than when Putin first entered the presidency in 2000. In the wake of the economic tumult of the 1990s and seventy years of communism before that, as many as 30% of Russians lived below the official poverty line in 1999. Less than twenty years later, however, this proportion had been cut in half. Comparatively, this was a better rate of poverty reduction than in Brazil or India, but was surpassed by China and South Africa in about 2012, as indicated in figure 5.15. Russia's progress in poverty reduction has come from overall improvement in the economy. The next big challenge from a policy perspective would be to tackle inequalities across regions in Russia. Where a Russian citizen is born or lives the greatest proportion of their lives determines their life expectancy and access to employment, education, and healthcare. In a study of regional inequalities in Russia, the World Bank reported vast regional disparities such that gross regional product differed by a factor of 17 in Russia's Far East, "Sakhalin oblast has a GRP per capita comparable to Singapore, whereas Ingush Republic [in the North Caucasus part of Russia] has one that is closer to Honduras."[43] The same study reported that Russia's spatial disparity exceeds that of comparison countries like Brazil, India, and China, for example. Regional poverty rates were also highly variable, ranging from 10% in resource-rich regions of Russia like Tatarstan and the big financial metropolises of Moscow and St. Petersburg, to 40% in the remote Siberian region of Tyva. Access to education, health services, and basic utilities like electricity also show high levels of variation, which, not surprisingly, is reflected in health outcomes like infant mortality rates and adult life expectancies. Many other large and diverse countries, like Brazil and India, for example, demonstrate high degrees of spatial inequalities too of course, but Russia is distinctive in the relative depth of its geographic inequalities.[44]

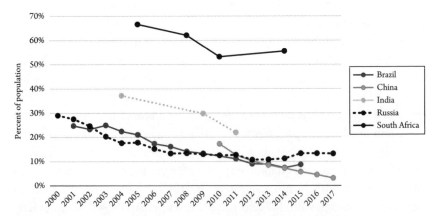

Figure 5.15. Poverty Headcount Ratio in BRICS Countries, 2000–2017 Source: World Bank. "Poverty headcount ratio at national poverty lines (% of population)". Data last updated January 30, 2019. https://data.worldbank.org/indicator/SI.POV.NAHC
The 2001 data for Russia was missing in the World Bank dataset. However, the World Bank Russia data is identical to Rosstat's poverty data, so the 2001 data point for Russia was copied into this chart from Rosstat's dataset.

Nonetheless, the World Bank reports that by 2017, Russia had made considerable progress between 2005 and 2015 in decreasing the degree of inequality in Russia in terms of real income per capita and poverty. This is in part due to federal transfers to fund social benefits for residents of poorer regions, but it does not completely ameliorate variation between regions. The World Bank has found that increased urbanization is positively associated with higher regional productivity, as well as the presence of medium- and high-tech industries, education levels and quality, and access to markets by air, rail, and sea.[45] All of these factors are available in Russia's larger cities, like St. Petersburg, Moscow, or Ekaterinburg, for example, but less so in more sparsely populated regions in the South and Far East. Further, there are significant barriers still to labor mobility in Russia—some of this is due to the variations in skills such that a young person from Chechnya may have a difficult time getting a high-paying job in Moscow given the generally lower-quality education in that area of Russia. Home and land ownership are another potential barrier to labor mobility— home ownership in poor regions of Russia is as high as 92% versus richer regions (80%). The system of privatization in the 1990s effectively gave Russians the apartments they already occupied at low or no cost, and in poorer regions of Russia the legacy of this has been a lack of liquidity in home real estate markets, creating a "house lock" phenomenon that tends to encourage people in poorer regions in particular to stay put where they at least have stable, no-cost housing.[46]

Education, Skills Matches, and the New Global Economy

Beyond demography, health, and socioeconomic well-being, the quality of a country's education system, and the proportion of the population that is able to access it and attain skills and employment as a result, is another key indicator of a nation's human capital. A clear asset that Russia's population had in 1992 was a high level of literacy and high-quality system of higher education inherited from the Soviet period. The Soviet era academic community had established a strong track record of research accomplishment internationally in some fields, especially the natural and physical sciences and mathematics. This provided the new Russia with a strong educational base in some areas, on which it might build. Largely as a result of this strong foundation, in 2017 Russia boasted the highest number of trained engineers in the world at 454,436, almost double that of the country with the next highest number, the United States, at 237,826.[47] The country also had a literacy rate near 100%, and the OECD reported that almost 58% of Russians aged 25–34 had some form of post-secondary education. For comparison, this number in the United States was 47.5%, and in Germany it was 30.5%, while other countries in transition recorded less than 20% of people in the same age group with post-secondary degrees.[48]

These statistics, however, reflect the *quantity* of Russian education, not its *quality*, or to what degree the skills and knowledge students gain, particularly in post-secondary institutions, match the needs of Russian employers. In 2013, as with health and demography, the Russian government instituted a national program for higher education called 5-100-2020—meaning that it strove to have five of its universities ranked in the top 100 in the world by QS Global Education Rankings by the year 2020. To accomplish this, some universities received targeted funding: to hire well-trained faculty from abroad or Russian faculty who were trained abroad; attract foreign students who would pay full tuition; enhance information technology; and provide other funding and grants as incentives to publish with foreign academics in English-language journals. Some post-secondary institutions were restructured and some were closed to focus state resources on what was hoped would be Russian education champions. By the time of writing, only Lomonosov Moscow State University had broken into the top-ranked universities, holding the 90th position.[49]

Despite this modest initial success, too little funding has been allocated to establish Russia as a desirable destination for foreign students or to afford it academic pre-eminence in almost any field. Figure 5.16 shows that the United States, which dominates in the QR index, spends more than double on education than Russia as a percentage of GDP—this with a much bigger GDP—and that this has been the case for decades. It would be difficult to make up the gap

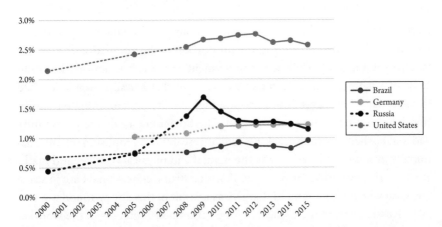

Figure 5.16. Higher Education Spending as a Percentage of GDP in Brazil, Germany, Russia, and the US, 2000–2015 Source: OECD. "Public spending on education." Data last updated January 1, 2017. https://data.oecd.org/edusource/public-spending-on-education.htm

in spending in a mere twenty-five years to be able to challenge US dominance in higher education rankings in particular (with 31 in the top 100 of the QS Scale).[50]

Russia's attempts to revamp its educational system are still young. A significant challenge is to better link technological education with industrial development. In Silicon Valley, for example, in the United States, there is a symbiosis between technology companies and Stanford University. This sort of relationship, as noted in chapter 4, could not exist in Russia given that the institutions belonging to the highly esteemed Russian Academy of Sciences conduct research independent of industry. In contrast to the Silicon Valley model, qualified academics in science, technology, engineering, and mathematics (STEM) in Russia do not freely float from one milieu to the other, because there is little ability or reward in doing so.

Under Dmitri Medvedev's presidency, Skolkovo represented an attempt to create a Russian version of this sort of symbiosis. The idea was to create a new kind of educational and research institution closely tied to technological innovation on a sprawling site just outside of central Moscow. Entrepreneurs could compete to get funding from Skolkovo and even take up residency there to bring new products to market. A graduate school in technological innovation and a business school were built on the site to provide training to aspiring Russian entrepreneurs. The project, however, was plagued initially with reports of corruption, and lost considerable steam in its continued development when Medvedev stepped out of the presidency in 2012. Still, Skolkovo continues to exist, although it is hard to point to a big-money idea that has come from it at time of writing.

While Skolkovo may have (thus far) failed to gain significant traction, Vladimir Putin has continued to articulate the importance of high-tech education for Russia. He has boasted of new initiatives for young people to compete in creative tech competitions like new business development and leadership.[51] Figure 5.16 shows that the Russian government has significantly increased its spending on higher education as a percentage of its GDP since 2000, although it is still far below higher education spending in the United States. Intriguingly though, it is close to the proportion of spending of GDP on education by the European powerhouse Germany. Further, Russia has a relatively high percentage of university graduates with STEM degrees—about 30% by 2016, in comparison to about 25% in the United Kingdom, and 18% in the United States, for example (see figure 5.17) . Further, Russia embarked on the National Technology Initiative in 2014, "NTI is a program designed to create Russian 'Champion' companies (from corporations to small and medium enterprises—SMEs) on fundamentally new markets and bring Russia to the global top of innovative and technological leaders by 2035" that

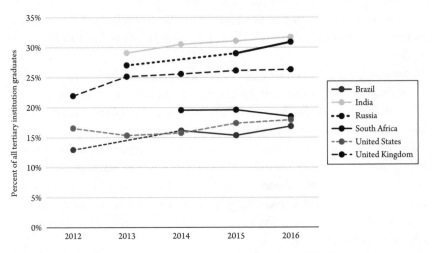

Figure 5.17. Percent of University Graduates with Degrees in STEM Fields in Brazil, India, South Africa, the US, and United Kingdom Source: United Nations Education, Scientific and Cultural Organization. "Percentage of graduates from Science, Technology, Engineering and Mathematics programmes in tertiary education, both sexes (%)." Data last updated September 1, 2018. http://data.uis.unesco.org/Index.aspx?DataSetCode=EDULIT_DS

Medvedev introduced in 2014.[52] Reportedly, this initiative has had some impact changing and updating curricula at some post-secondary institutions, but federal funding has been inconsistent. The challenge, however, is to create an "ecosystem" of companies, educational institutions, and students that can really propel the growth of innovative companies in significant numbers. In the case of Silicon Valley, this developed with the assistance of government funding, but private venture capital was vital, as was a reliable legal system that ensured property rights, including intellectual property, and that provided other legal protections ensuring the honoring of contracts that had long been in place. Thus, the business environment in Russia described in chapters 4 and 8, has proven to be an obstacle to fulfilling the promise of this sort of initiative in Russia, regardless of improvements in technical training among Russian students and nascent entrepreneurs.

Russians, however, have been quick and able adopters of information technology since the Soviet collapse. One study indicated that overall Internet penetration of the population in Russia is 76% (higher than South America at 73%, Southeast Asia at 63%, or Oceania at 69%) and that by 2019, there were 109.6 million Internet users in Russia.[53] Russians were also quick adopters of smartphones, such that 91% of the population have a smartphone, and 62% use it to go online for extended periods of time; the average user also has 4 separate messenger apps. Not surprisingly, people aged 16–19 are the most active Internet users.[54]

Nonetheless, despite a high proportion of STEM graduates, and high Internet usage, a common concern persists that there is a skills shortage or mismatch between the skills workers have and what Russian firms need. In 2014, Thomas Remington reported that "an RSPP survey found that 64% of firms considered the shortage of skilled labor to be one of the most severe problems facing them."[55] In an attempt to ameliorate this situation, and bring worker skills up to international levels, Russia joined WorldSkills,[56] and in 2014 "the government laid out a plan for reform of secondary vocational educational institutions that would increase the number of graduates by 2020 to 50,000 people 'who had demonstrated a level of training corresponding to the standards of WorldSkills.' In 2016, the government created a program called 'Worker Cadres for Advanced Technologies' and allocated 24 billion rubles to it."[57] This is one step forward, but better strategic partnerships between the public and private sectors, and between vocational schools and employers, are still needed in order to better allocate labor resources to firms that need certain sets of skills.[58] On the one hand, the Soviet system created a strong basis for technological training. But on the other hand, this system was not built to coordinate or support the development of technology with private companies. The process of reforming the legacy of the Soviet system of higher education to better match the needs of employers, especially in the tech sector, will continue to be challenging but crucial to the diversification of the post-Soviet Russian economy.

Conclusion

Undeniably, since the dark days of the 1990s, there have been significant improvements in Russian demographic indicators and health. Population decline has slowed or even stopped. Twenty-five years after the demographic catastrophe that ensued in the years immediately following the Soviet collapse, Russians were living longer and, generally speaking, living better, with a very few living far better than everyone else. That said, in order to enhance or maintain its current leadership's aspirations to (re-) establish Russia as a global power, positive trends in these areas must not only continue, but rapidly accelerate. Russian universities must continue to improve if they are to compete in quality with those in the United States or Europe; and young Russians in particular must see a future for themselves in their homeland so that emigration does not seem such an attractive option. The regime under Putin will have a difficult time increasing production or even finding labor for the large state conglomerates that are the powerhouses of the economy, and even of the patronalist political economy over which he presides, if these trends are not reversed. This will mean that Russian leaders will need to take seriously concerns among Russian youth of inequality and corruption. This chapter began with a quote from Vladimir Putin that referred not only to the importance of human capital in determining the power of a state, but that also mentioned the importance of "vital bearings and ideals." Young Russians in particular need to believe in Russia's national mission and *want to stay and invest* in their country if it is to be truly resurrected as a global power. We move next to look at hard, soft, and "sharp" means of Russian power that rely on the strength of the Russian economy, discussed in chapter 4, as well as Russia's improving, but still problematic, human capital resources discussed in this chapter.

6

Russian Hard Power

"Nobody should have any illusion about the possibility of gaining military superiority over Russia. We will never allow this to happen."
—Vladimir Putin, State of the Nation Address, December 2013

On March 1, 2018, days before he was to be elected to his fourth presidential term, Vladimir Putin strode confidently across a highly polished stage to deliver his annual address to Russia's Federal Assembly. The first half of his speech was devoted to the various accomplishments and challenges in continuing Russia's social and economic development, but he saved the real show for last—the introduction of no fewer than six new weapons systems. In front of a massive screen, he proudly described the capabilities of a hypersonic intercontinental ballistic nuclear missile that, he assured the audience, could fly at 10 times the speed of sound. Putin promised it would be too fast for any anti-missile system in the West to stop it: "It flies to its target like a meteorite, like a ball of fire. The temperature on its surface reaches 1,600–2,000 degrees Celsius." This new system, Putin claimed, was "invincible against all existing and prospective missile defense." He demonstrated what the weapon would be able to do with a simulation video that launched the missile from Russian soil over the North Pole to hit a target that looked suspiciously like Florida, the American state that was home to Mar-o-Lago, the winter retreat of President Donald Trump. Other new weaponry he described sounded like the stuff of science fiction. The new Poseidon nuclear-powered, nuclear warhead–equipped super-torpedo purportedly would be capable of creating 100-meter-tall waves as it crashed into an adversary's shore; the resulting tsunami would send flood waters up to 1,500 km into an opponent's territory, destroying everyone and everything in its path.

Speaking of a new nuclear-powered, intercontinental cruise missile (that could switch between conventional and nuclear warheads as needed), Putin proclaimed, "no other country has developed anything like this." He insisted that with these weapons, Russia intended only to maintain strategic parity with the United States. Putin's concluding remarks warned the West against further containment of Russia:

> And to those who in the past 15 years have tried to accelerate an arms race and seek unilateral advantage against Russia, have introduced restrictions and sanctions . . . aiming to restrain our nation's development, including in the military area, I will say this: everything that you have tried to prevent through such a policy has already happened. No one has managed to restrain Russia.[1]

Some of the systems Putin described in 2018 existed and had been deployed, others were still being tested, and at least a few were little more than ideas in the minds of Russian designers. Nonetheless, it was undeniable that Russia had indeed come a long way (if not all the way) back in resurrecting its once mighty military prowess, and in just under thirty years. Although the United States remains by far the most powerful military on earth, Russia is one of two states (the other is China) that could mount a serious challenge to it in certain crucial areas of operation. Russia alone, though, is the sole power on earth that truly represents an existential crisis for the United States due to its ability to deliver a nuclear-tipped missile to Washington, New York, or Los Angeles, among other valuable American targets, in under thirty minutes.

This chapter examines Russia's renewed defensive and offensive capabilities. We examine first Russia's "hard" power—its conventional and nuclear forces in comparison with those of the United States, China, and other leading states in the twenty-first-century international system.

It is not the case that Russia has regained the status or all of the hard power capabilities that the Soviet Union once had, nor is it at offensive parity in all respects with the United States. Nonetheless, Russia has formidable global reach in terms of its hard power resources. In some areas, as we shall see, Russia by 2020 was capable of seriously challenging and even exceeding NATO's combined capabilities, and for the most part overwhelming China's too.

For a country on its knees just three decades earlier, this is a remarkable recovery. As with its economy, and aspects of its social services and health sectors, when the Soviet Union collapsed in December 1991, its military effectively collapsed too. But the decline of the storied Soviet war machine had begun much sooner with Leonid Brezhnev's decision to invade Afghanistan in 1979, only to suffer a crushing defeat and casualties so high that it is sometimes referred to as the Soviet Union's "Vietnam War." Mikhail Gorbachev's decision to withdraw from Afghanistan narrowly preceded the collapse of the Berlin Wall, and with it the communist satellite regimes of Eastern Europe in 1989. Soviet military outposts across Eastern Europe, and after 1991 from virtually all other

Soviet military stations, were quickly abandoned. Soldiers returned home to insufficient housing, a collapsing economy, and an increasingly demoralized society. The once mighty Soviet navy was left to rust in port throughout the 1990s as Boris Yeltsin turned his attention instead to righting the ship of state. Russia inherited the Soviet nuclear arsenal, and while the weapons were kept secure following the collapse, modernization of the nuclear program languished until the twenty-first century.

The weakened Russian military participated in two wars in the tiny southern republic of Chechnya. The first was a near disaster lasting from 1994 to 1996, when underequipped, mostly young conscript soldiers were slaughtered by Chechen rebels who adeptly employed guerrilla tactics. Soldiers' mothers flocked to the front lines and begged Russian commanders to let their sons return home rather than face certain death. These scenes played out on Russian television, helping to make the first Chechen conflict, and Yeltsin, wildly unpopular by the time he stood for re-election against the background of an uncertain peace in 1996. The second Chechen conflict under President Putin (2000–2009) went better, though not because of improved Russian military performance against the Chechen fighters as much as the willingness of the new political leadership to employ a scorched-earth policy that ended in the flattening of Grozny, and the eventual cooptation of a few Chechen elites that finally ended the war.

In 2008, as noted in chapter 2, Russia managed to win the short five-day war with Georgia, but its conventional military capacity appeared dated even relative to the far weaker and far smaller Georgian forces.[2] As a result of this, and the fact that the Russian government could at that point afford it, a massive military reform—New Look—was announced in November 2008. Bettina Renz notes that the Soviet military had been designed for mass mobilization of a conscripted army to fight a conventional war in Europe.[3] The equipment that Russia had inherited from the Soviet military was so outdated and decrepit that Russia's new defense minister, Pavel Grachev, remarked in 1992 that it was "ruins and debris."[4] The Russian navy had suffered most from neglect and its forces had become so degraded that, "[a]part from a number of ballistic-missile submarines, which were consistently maintained as part of the nuclear triad, Russia had no real operational navy until the 2008 modernization plans addressed this situation."[5] The air force was similarly neglected, such that between 1993 and 2009, 55% of its equipment was purportedly out of commission and it received only a "handful" of new combat-capable aircraft.[6] This meant also that Russian pilots and sailors had very few training opportunities, and military exercises more generally did not take place. Recruitment into the military also suffered as former and potential new soldiers could make much more in the burgeoning private sector by the mid-2000s than they could in the military. As a partial result, and also because of the long-feared system of *dedovshchina* (brutal and sometimes violent hazing of conscripts by their superior officers), respect for the armed services sank to new lows such that Russian families who could do so bribed military recruiters or Duma members to gain exemptions for their sons from conscripted service.[7] This left only the poorest, and least healthy, of Russian young men to endure two years of required military service.

With this as background, the New Look military reform was announced by Defense Minister Serdyukov in autumn 2008. The fact that it was initiated at almost precisely the same time when Russian policymakers would also have to defend the economy from the effects of a global economic crisis is testament to the political priority that military reform had become by this time. The plan was nothing short of the complete transformation of a Cold War–era military force of mostly conscripted soldiers to a smaller, lighter, always ready and reactive, and largely professionalized force of about 1 million personnel. This radical remodeling was recognition of the fact that war of the type the inherited Soviet military structure had been designed to wage (against NATO in Europe) was not well suited to the guerrilla-type warfare of non-state actors that Russia had already encountered in Chechnya in the 1990s, for example, or to what the United States was waging in Iraq and Afghanistan in the early 2000s. The other factor that necessitated a redesign of Russian military personnel and training was demographic decline (as noted in chapter 5)—there were just not enough young men available anymore to populate a huge conscript-based military structure. The relatively poor and declining health of those eligible for conscription was also a problem, for "while at the end of 2007 the percentage of suitable recruits was 70.4% [of the conscripted pool of men between the ages of seventeen and twenty-seven years old], by the end of 2009 it was already down to 68.4%."[8]

New Look involved three main goals:

1. Modernizing weaponry across all branches of Russia's armed forces.
2. Increasing the efficiency and effectiveness of the military by decreasing the number of officers, reorganizing command structures, and creating a smaller, more rapidly reacting force structure.
3. Replacing the conscript system with a professionalized "contract" military of professional soldiers who would be well trained on new weapon systems.

Specific targets included, first, a reduction in the size of the Russian armed forces (in all services) from the ragged and officer-heavy organization that numbered 1.35 million men in 2008 to 1 million professional servicemen. Second, a massive reorganization reduced the number of units and military bases to dispense with the mass mobilization model to a professional (meaning paid on contract), tightly organized, and combat-ready force. This would also require decreasing the number of officers from 350,000 to 150,000 (although this number drifted up to 220,000, as it turned out) and established the goal of having 425,000 professional enlisted personnel in a permanent state of readiness by 2020.[9] Third, to support the goal of professionalization, military salaries and housing allowances were significantly increased, and the number of conscripts (who by that time served only one year) was reduced to about 150,000 annually, while *dedovshchina* was discouraged.[10] Fourth, an additional large organizational change would see six military districts reorganized into four joint strategic commands (JSCs), while maintaining the Strategic Rocket Forces, Aerospace Defense, and the Airborne Forces under a Central Command, with the latter two branches eventually combined into a single branch of service.[11] Personnel training was also reorganized and consolidated from sixty-five military training institutions to ten military universities; the Central Administrative staff and military command was similarly reduced in size. Fifth, and finally, the State Rearmament Program (GPV by its Russian acronym) adopted for the period 2011–2020 had the goal of having 70% of equipment either completely new or updated at a price of about 19 trillion rubles across nine or so years.[12]

The New Look reform was implemented swiftly initially by Serdyukov, and continued by Sergei Shoigu, his successor after Serdyukov's dismissal in 2012. The effort was pursued with clear political determination—possibly because of how poorly Russian armed forces looked in Georgia—and strong financial commitment in the wake of the growth of the economy the previous five years. Russia's force size after ten years of reform was estimated to be about 900,000, approaching the New Look goal of 1 million, with only about 142,000 conscripts.[13] It had a fully "contract-based" or professional non-commissioned officer corps, ensuring continuity of skills and training for new advanced weapon systems. Force structures had been reorganized, and the command organization streamlined. A first glimpse of Russia's New Look appeared in Crimea in 2014 in use by the "little green men" who appeared on the streets without any military insignia on their uniforms, but who were quickly identified as Russian (as described in chapter 2). Western reporters described the Russian soldiers assigned to guard Ukrainian military bases as "lean and fit, few if any seemed to be conscripts. Their uniforms were crisp and neat, and their new helmets were bedecked with tinted safety goggles. They were sober."[14] That the Russian military by 2014 had been "rebooted" was evidenced by other new high-tech pieces of equipment such as sophisticated new Pecheneg machine guns and push-to-talk, encrypted radio communications systems clipped to their uniforms, "including for soldiers on such routine duty as guard shifts beside machine-gun trucks."[15]

Similarly, Russia's military support a year later of President Bashar al-Assad in Syria's civil war provided another opportunity to display and test some new military capabilities and weapons systems. The words "competent, capable and professional had not been associated with the Russian military in a long time,"[16] remarked a group of American analysts, but that is what New Look appeared to have made of the Russian military. The US Chairman of the Joint Chiefs of Staff, General Joseph Dunford, had noticed the changes too, stating bluntly that

> the Russian military presents the greatest array of threats to US interests. Despite declining population, a shrinking economy, Russia has made a significant investment in military capabilities. Putin has recently fielded a wide range of systems to include new intercontinental ballistic missiles, aircraft, nuclear-powered submarines, tanks, and air defense systems.[17]

Clearly, by 2020, Russia's military capabilities were much improved relative to what they were at the time of the collapse of the Soviet Union, or even what they were in 2008. But how do Russia's renewed resources compare to those of the United States, China, or other strong international actors? Traditional approaches to evaluating state power projection capabilities suggest comparing among countries in terms of the number of military personnel, and annual state defense expenditures.[18] In what follows, this chapter examines these more quantitatively oriented measures in comparing Russia's military expenditures over time with those of the United States, China, and other emerging and traditional powers. We then move to comparing what those expenditures have actually bought Russia in terms of force structure and the quality of Russian weaponry relative to the United States as the world's undisputed leading military power. This comparison includes conventional weaponry as well as nuclear weapons. We then look at soft and sharp power capabilities in chapter seven, and how the Russian leadership has come to use hard, sharp, and soft power as a triad to support its foreign policy goals.

Russian Hard Power in Comparative Perspective

Defense Spending

I begin here with an examination of how much Russia's political leaders have chosen to spend on defense since the Soviet collapse. The defense "burden" of a country indicates the degree to which its military spending is prioritized by political leaders—that is, what the leadership *chooses* to spend versus what constraints the size of a country's economy may place on a defense "effort."[19]

Figure 6.1[20] shows the steep increase in Russian defense spending from 2008 through 2016 in trillions of rubles. In this period, annual spending on defense increased by more than 325% in ruble terms, from just under 1.4 trillion rubles

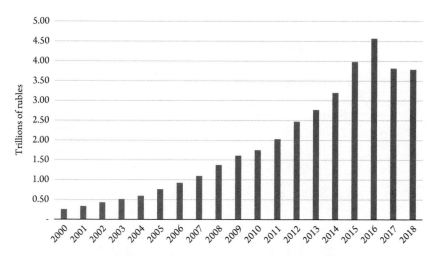

Figure 6.1. Russian Defense Effort 2000–2018 as Measured in Trillions of Rubles Source: SIPRI, 2019.

to 4.6 trillion per year. Between 2014 and 2015 alone, spending jumped up from 3.25 trillion to 4.05 trillion rubles—a remarkable increase in light of the fact that Western sanctions on parts of the Russian economy were imposed initially in the summer of 2014, and it was only in the fall of 2015 that Russia entered Syria when we might have expected an increase in spending to finance the effort. Although it seems as though spending then dropped off sharply between 2016 and 2017, in fact this dip was due to a one-time write-off of loans made to Russian defense manufacturers by the Ministry of Finance in 2016, making the change in spending between 2015 and 2016 seem much steeper than it actually was. These loans were to ensure that domestic weapons producers could fulfill equipment procurement orders on schedule, and the write-off was a recognition that the loans would in reality not be repaid to the banks the government had financed to make them. The defense budget actually fell in 2016 in real terms once the 685 billion rubles in write-offs are deducted.[21]

We can get a sense of how Russia's defense burden changed over time, and in comparison to other countries, by comparing military spending as a percentage of overall state spending, as shown in figure 6.2. In 1999, Russia was spending less (6.9%) on defense as opposed to other policy priorities than was the United States (at 8.9%), but far less than China (13.4%). But after 2001, American defense spending increased as it entered a war in Afghanistan, and then Iraq, peaking in 2011 at 11.8% of overall national government spending. China, in contrast, declined in the same period to 6.8%, perhaps reflecting the regime's commitment in that decade to policy priorities like education, infrastructure development, and other domestic policies. Russia's big leap in defense

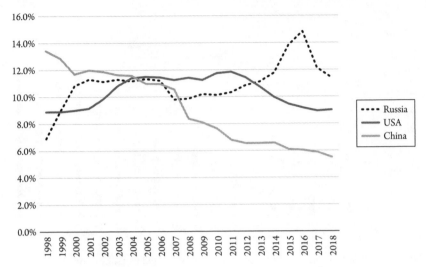

Figure 6.2. Military Spending as Percentage of Government Spending, 1998–2018 Source: SIPRI, 2019.

commitment relative to other priorities came between 2008 and 2016 (the peak years of New Look)—where it increased from 8.4% to a high of 14.8% of total annual government spending. Notably, this eclipsed the US high of 11.8% in 2011 and China's high in 1998 of 12.9% of all government spending. Because of the loan write-offs made in 2016, the graph makes it seem as though the proportion of its budget Russia spent on the military drastically declined in 2017 and 2018. In reality, it did not such that Russian military spending as a proportion of overall government spending still remained much higher than that of the United States or China in this period, reflecting its still high comparative priority for Putin's regime. Even while other policy priorities like social, health, and education spending were gaining ground in the Russian budget after 2016, defense remained of primary importance.[22]

Russian commitment to military reform is also evidenced by the fact that defense spending as a percentage of GDP increased over this period such that even as its GDP *decreased* between 2010 and 2015, military spending as a percentage of total state spending *and* as a percentage of total GDP *increased* year-on-year. The defense burden reached a high in 2016 of about 5.5% of GDP, but declined to about 4% by 2018—still higher than the United States (at about 3%, down from a high of about 4.8% in 1992), and China (down from a high of about 2.5% of GDP but steady at 2.0% from about 2010 through 2018). Some Russian analysts argued that 4.0% of GDP is the most that the Russian government should devote to military spending given other priorities like infrastructure and social spending needs, so the decline from 2015–2016 levels through 2017 and

2018 perhaps should not be viewed so much as reflective of Russia's overall economic environment (indeed, the economy was growing slightly at this time), as much as what was basically the proportion of spending intended by Russian policymakers.[23] Further, most of the initial costly goals of New Look had been achieved, so the flattening of spending reflected a shift to maintaining new and developing capabilities as opposed to further increases.

While the foregoing gives us some idea as to how much of a priority defense restructuring had become for Russia, it tells us nothing about actual spending on the military in absolute terms compared to the United States or China. There are debates as to how best to capture and compare Russia's relative defense burden to that of the United States in particular, and to other near-peer powers like China. The first and most common measure is comparative spending on defense across countries in standardized US dollars. In contrast to the Soviet period, in the twenty-first century, we now have some decent data by which to compare Russian military spending with other countries. Still, there are discrepancies in the ways in which numbers are reported, so consistent direct comparisons can be difficult. The most conservative measurement would look only at the specific chapter of the Russian government's annual federal budget entitled "Defense Spending" and not include military applicable spending that appears elsewhere in the budget. The most liberal interpretation of total Russian defense spending would include this chapter, plus spending from all possible areas in the budget that could have a defense-related application, as well as the full cost of using old weapons, and the full cost to the economy of mobilizing the economy in defense-related areas. This includes childcare, education of families, and so forth, as well as defense procurement programs and programs for the space launch centers. Because some of these programs are financed by other areas in the Russian state budget, and not by the Defense Ministry per se, they are not always included in total defense spending.[24] I will employ here a third method, however, used by the Stockholm Institute for International Peace (SIPRI), which provides estimates broader than simply the defense chapter of the federal budget alone, to include other parts of the Russian government involved in defense-related activities like military space activities, paramilitary forces, and aspects of the budget that cover the full costs of military personnel like pensions, social services, and healthcare, as well as arms procurement and military research and development.[25] But unlike the second method, SIPRI estimates do not include the even broader range of the cost of old weaponry, and an estimate of the total cost of mobilizing other parts of the economy in the service of defense. Moreover, SIPRI numbers hit a middle ground in terms of the upper and lower bounds of Russian defense spending, and they are also widely employed elsewhere to compare spending data across countries.[26]

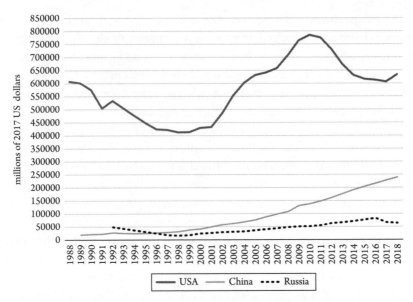

Figure 6.3. Russian Military Expenditure in Comparison to US and China, 1988–2018 (in millions of US dollars at 2017 standardized dollar) Source: SIPRI, MICEX

Figure 6.3[27] makes it immediately obvious that, although Russian defense spending clearly increased since 2008, the United States in fact still spent far more—a multiple of about 10 times—in standardized US dollars. In 2018, for example, the United States spent about $633.5 billion, while Russia spent only $62.2 billion. But for Russia, that was a dramatic increase from an all-time low of $16.2 billion in 1998 (the year of Russia's first big post-Soviet economic crisis described in chapter 4) to a high of $82.6 billion in 2016, before leveling off to an average of about $65 billion in 2017 and 2018 (although, recall that the drop is exaggerated between 2016 and 2017 because of the one-time loan write-offs). China, despite spending a lower proportion of its GDP on its defense burden, because of the astronomical growth of its GDP from 1999 onward meant that its actual spending increased dramatically from $19.3 billion to over $239 billion. Still, by this measure, Chinese and Russian military expenditures were fractions of that of the United States.

Figure 6.4 adds the spending in billions of standardized US dollars of France, Germany, and the United Kingdom to our comparison cases.[28] Again, the United States is the biggest spender on defense, by far eclipsing even the combined total spending of the other five countries. China (number 2 in global spending) and Russia (here third in spending by 2016) rank far behind the United States, as noted earlier. But the band representing Russia is similar in size to France, Germany, and the United Kingdom in this figure—on average,

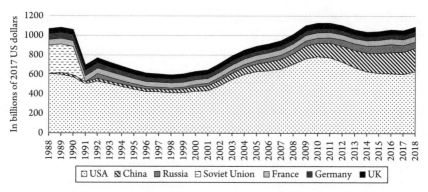

Figure 6.4. Russian Military Expenditures vs. Others 1992–2018 (US dollars) Source: SIPRI, MICEX

they are clustered around $65 billion in annual military spending by 2018. As others have noted, in a simple conversion of national currencies to billions of US dollars at a standardized rate, "economically, Russia is a European power."[29] If we left the analysis here, even this would be an impressive recovery given where Russia began in 1992. But one problem that immediately arises upon re-flection is that, by this measure of defense burden, Russia should have defensive capabilities that are also, at best, at rough parity to those of other European powers if it was spending the same amount and if military goods and services are assumed to cost the same. However, by 2018, the Russian government had dra-matically modernized and transformed its military while also waging a war in aid of Bashar al-Assad in Syria. How could this have happened if the Russian gov-ernment spent the same amount as France, the United Kingdom, or Germany? Clearly, and literally, Russia got more bang for its buck. Why?

Part of the answer lies in the variability of exchange rates between rubles and dollars. In the Russian case, this is particularly problematic following the global economic crisis in 2008, as well as after 2014, when the ruble-to-dollar exchange rates varied considerably.[30] The changes in military spending in dollar terms are often exaggerated relative to the growth year-on-year in defense spending in rubles during these periods.[31] To ameliorate this problem, and the fact that spending in rubles may buy more of the same goods and services than in dollars in the United States, some military analysts, like Richard Connolly and Michael Kofman, have argued convincingly for the use of a weighting instrument that reflects Russia's actual purchasing power.[32] A measure of military spending that uses a purchasing power parity weight acknowledges the fact that the same item may be much less expensive in one country than it is in another because the costs of inputs (land, labor, and capital) into a given product is lower. In the case of Russian defense spending, the costs of inputs differ radically from those in the United States, Russia, China, and elsewhere given the robustness of the Russian military industrial complex.[33] As one of the world's largest and most sophisticated producers of weapons, the Russian economy makes the military and defense products that the state budget purchases—it does not buy finished defense goods and services from abroad. (This is with the exception of a few components that, before sanctions in 2014, Russian producers sourced from Ukraine and Germany, and that they subsequently began producing domestically.[34]) Therefore, production and purchasing of weaponry and defense-related equipment and services, as well as personnel costs, are all in rubles at local prices.

In his examination of Russia's comparative defense burden, Connolly explains the concept of purchasing power parity using what the *Economist* magazine first cheekily called in 1986 the "Big Mac Index." If, for example, you were to go to McDonald's in Pushkin Square in Moscow to purchase a Big Mac in January 2020, the cost of your burger would be 135 rubles, but if you quickly flew to New York or Washington, DC, the cost of the same burger would be $5.67. This implies that the ruble-to-dollar exchange rate was R135:$5.67 = 23.81 R/$, but in fact the official exchange rate was 61.43R to the dollar in January 2020.[35] Indeed, the International Monetary Fund uses an implied purchasing power exchange rate that is close to the Big Mac Index of 25.37 R/$, or an increase in purchasing power of 2.6 times.[36] Figure 6.3 compares Russia's defense spending at purchasing power parity using the IMF multiplier rate in annual market exchange rates of local currency to US dollars. The difference between this method of comparing relative defense burdens versus just using an annual US dollar comparison is striking. Purchasing power parity weighting shows Russia's peak spending was more in the neighborhood of $100 billion per year from 2009 to 2013 (vs. $50–66.7 billion at non-PPP). It then jumped to $150 billion in 2014 and 2015 (versus 71.5 and 77.0 billion at non-PPP) and was well over $200 billion in 2016 (vs. 82.6 billion at non-PPP), before settling at about $150 billion annually in 2017 and 2018 (vs. $66.5 and $64.2 billion, respectively, at non-PPP). Using purchasing power parity helps to explain how it is that the Russian military was able to have completed a sweeping modernization program on seemingly the same amount of standardized dollars that France and the United Kingdom spent on their militaries, which, as we will see, are not in fact military rivals to Russia at all. Russia modernized equipment, including new conventional and nuclear missile systems, transitioned to a predominantly contract based professional military rather than relying on conscripts, and added air, land, and sea capabilities while engaged in significant conflict in Syria, and a smaller defense commitment in Ukraine.

Figures 6.5 and 6.6 illustrate this difference further by comparing defense spending in the five biggest defense spending nations at international market exchange rates (figure 6.5), and then versus their relative spending using PPP and

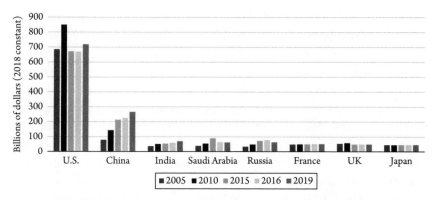

Figure 6.5. Military Expenditures in Russia vs. World Highest Defense Spenders (Market Exchange Rate) Source: Stockholm International Peace Research Institute. "Military expenditure by country, in constant (2018) US$ m." Data last updated January 1, 2020. https://www. sipri.org/databases/milex

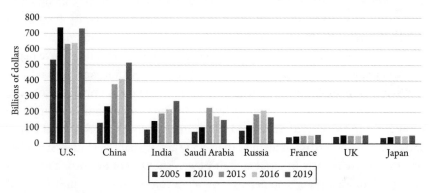

Figure 6.6. Military Expenditures in Russia vs. World Highest Defense Spenders (Purchasing Power Parity) Sources: Stockholm International Peace Research Institute, International Monetary Fund. "Military expenditure by country, in local currency"; "Implied PPP conversion rate". Data last updated January 1, 2020. https://www.sipri.org/databases/milex, https:// www.imf.org/external/pubs/ft/weo/2019/02/weodata/index.aspx

a converted market exchange rate annual US dollars (figure 6.6).[37] Notably, even at purchasing power parity, Russian spending levels still *were not anywhere near the equivalent of what the United States spent annually* or what China spent in the same period. That said, however, both China and Russia at their peak spending years were much closer to US spending levels by this method (its high was about $700 billion in 2010) than at market exchange rates alone, with China spending $450 billion at PPP when it peaked in 2018 and Russia spending about $205 billion at PPP at its apex in 2016. The purchasing power comparison shows Russia consistently in the top five of the globe's highest military spenders (with the United States, China, Saudi Arabia, and India), and some years in the top three behind only the United States and China. (Recall from chapter three that China and India were supplied their weaponry by Russia, and Saudi Arabia is among the largest customers of the United States, although it has begun to buy from Russia as well.) This methodology also helps to explain why Russia has been able to afford its sweeping defense modernization program, including developing the weapons systems Putin so proudly described in 2018, while appearing to spend the same amount as the United Kingdom or France by conventional constant dollar pricing (about $65 billion), neither of which undertook anything similar in terms of military reform or modernization. The reality is that military goods and services simply cost less in real terms in Moscow and Beijing than in London or Paris, and using PPP methodology reflects this.

Conventional Capabilities in Comparison

We can be even more confident that comparing Russian military spending to that of other top spending countries at purchasing power parity provides a better picture of Russia's actual defense capacities when we look more deeply into what that spending has actually bought for the Russian military. We begin by comparing Russian conventional force changes over time, and then relative to other countries. In terms of direct comparisons by the numbers of soldiers, ships, aircraft, and other equipment, by 2018 Russia had become the only true competitor to the United States and China in virtually all areas of hard power and occasionally surpassed them both in a few areas. That the United States has superiority particularly in naval and air power, should not be surprising given how much more it spends on defense overall in comparison to both Russia and China even in per capita terms. But the capabilities gap is definitely closing.

Russian Military Personnel in Comparative Perspective

Table 6.1 provides a quick comparison of some major indicators of the relative size of the military forces of the world's major powers.[38] In terms of the number of active personnel, Russia's military at 900,000 is smaller than the United States at 1,359,450, China at 2,035,000, and India at 1,444,500. However, when reservists are added to total personnel for each country, Russia has 2,900,000 total personnel—more than any other military force in the world. Recall, however, that a key aspect of the New Look reforms was to create a smaller, more efficient, and effective military force, so Russia deliberately decreased its total personnel from an estimated 4,000,000 inherited largely conscript-based force in 1992 to a professional contract-based force of 900,000 in a state of high readiness, only about 140,000 of whom would be conscripts serving twelve-month rotations.

Comparative Land-Based Combat Capabilities (Selected)

In terms of its key land systems, Russia has far more combat-ready battle tanks than the United States, although fewer than China or India still. Notably, though, Russia had far more armed infantry vehicles than any other country on earth. This is significant in any European-based conflict, as explained later in this chapter. Finally, Russia has become very competitive with the United States in terms of number of artillery pieces, although it still trails China and India (see table 6.1). Total personnel and key land force comparisons between Russia, France, and the United Kingdom support the argument made earlier in this chapter regarding the best way to compare Russian defense spending to other countries. The Russian military in all respects clearly dwarfs those of the United Kingdom and France, Europe's other leading powers. This is true of naval and air capabilities as well, as indicated later in this chapter. Seventy percent of equipment in Russia's conventional forces and 82% in its nuclear arsenal were modernized as of 2020, so Russia's superiority over France and the United Kingdom is not merely a legacy of the Soviet military. Moreover, *even if its spending as measured in billions of dollars renders it a European power, Russia's actual military capabilities far exceed that of any other European country in practice.* Another chilling observation is that should China and Russia combine forces to challenge NATO in Europe or elsewhere, they would outnumber, and outgun, the West.

Numbers alone, however, do not tell the whole story concerning weapons systems. With 70% of its ground combat forces modernized, the capabilities of newer Russian tanks and armored vehicles in terms of firepower and the

Table 6.1 **Total Personnel (All Services) and Key Land Forces (Some Comparisons) as of 2018**

	Active Personnel	*Reserve Personnel*	*Total Personnel (active + reserve)*	*Main Battle tanks*	*Armed Infantry Vehicles*	*Artillery*
Russia	900,000	2,000,000	2,900,000	3,110	6,221	5,325
United States	1,359,450	845,000	2,204,450	2,833	3,419	6,883
China	2,035,000	510,000	2,545,000	5,800	5,060	8,954
India	1,444,500	1,155,000	2,599,500	3,565	3,100	9,719
France	203,900	36,300	240,200	200	627	273
UK	148,350	80,000	228,350	227	623	637

Tables 6.1, 6.2, and 6.3 are drawn from *The Military Balance* (London: International Institute for Strategic Studies, 2019), 26–27.

distance from which they can attack targets exceed that of the weaponry of NATO countries in the European theater.[39] For example, the Koalitsiya, a self-propelled howitzer, can be mounted on a tank platform (either the new Armata or T-90) or a very large truck, with a 152 mm caliber gun capable of hitting targets 70 km (43 miles) away. The United States, in contrast, operates a Paladin model that can fire only 18 miles. The Koalitsiya can reportedly fire 15–20 rounds per minute versus the Paladin's rate of 8 rounds per minute.[40] More generally, Russian artillery is also very flexible in terms of size and the range of its warheads.

Adding to its conventional land capabilities, introduced in 2015, the T-14 Armata battle tank is also a new capability for Russia and represents a departure from the Soviet emphasis on numbers of units over the survivability of the crew in an attack, as well as demonstrating new firepower. Further, the new T-15 armored vehicle, which also emphasizes crew survivability, is capable of keeping up with a tank to deploy troops rapidly. The T-15 is unusually heavy, armed with a 30 mm cannon, and also anti-tank missiles with ranges of between 8–10 km that can fire on multiple targets simultaneously. Reportedly, "as in the case of the T-14 fourth generation battle tank, the United States and its European partners have no alternative of their own to the T-15 at present."[41]

Reorganized Russian ground combat units have the ability to conduct what are known as "combined arms maneuvers," meaning that ground force brigades can rely on having their own joint intelligence and surveillance capabilities rather than having to coordinate with other military branches, as does the US Army, for example.[42] The Defense Intelligence Agency reported that the Russian ground forces have about 350,000 personnel (as of 2017).[43] As a RAND analysis noted, "although they may not be equal to Western forces on a soldier to soldier or platform to platform basis, their ability to conduct combined arms maneuvers . . . would pose serious challenges to the United States or NATO units in a conventional conflict."[44]

Wargaming studies focused on the Baltics have concluded that NATO would be in significant trouble should, for example, the Russian military opt to use some of these conventional land capabilities to invade one or all three Baltic countries. This is because Russia would have a geographic advantage in rapidly positioning its forces even with NATO's rapid reaction forces stationed in the Baltics since 2014, and an overwhelming numerical advantage over NATO in terms of ground forces. Even with US and NATO air power in play, without sufficient ground troops, artillery, and tanks that could take on the new Russian weaponry, NATO forces would be unable to stop a Russian attack. In one study, it was estimated that because of the ability to concentrate a range of forces in the region, it would take approximately 60 hours or less for Russian soldiers to reach Riga and Tallinn, and months if not years for NATO to force them out.[45]

Russian Naval Combat Capabilities in Comparative Perspective

The navy, although significantly reformed since 2008, is the weakest link in Russia's military array of forces. It is weaker in terms of pure numbers of surface ships and submarines, as reported in table 6.2, than is the United States, but falls behind China in some important areas of naval strength as well. This makes sense given that less spending has gone to the navy (about 23.5%) than to personnel (46%), although the Russian air force received less (about 11%) as a proportion of total military spending.[46] Nonetheless, Russia's New Look naval spending focused primarily on rebuilding its ballistic missile submarine capabilities, giving it more boats in a better-powered fleet than in the past. This has included increasing in number or modernizing some of the best and hardest-to-detect diesel-powered submarines in the world, including the Kilo and Lada classes that are reportedly fast and stealthy and that are able to carry torpedoes and missiles. Nuclear-powered submarines, which can remain submerged longer than diesel-powered subs, are slightly fewer in number in the Russian navy (10) than the American (14). But this is not a huge or insurmountable edge, especially given that "Russia's nuclear attack submarines like the Yasen are potent. . . . The newer versions are equipped with long-range conventional cruise missiles that could conceivably attack distant land targets in Western countries. . . . This is a serious capability."[47] Despite the asymmetry in terms of quantity of ships, it is these sorts of advanced capabilities, coupled with new submarine-launched ballistic missiles that are more accurate and heavily equipped than were their Soviet predecessors, that "[put] the Russian navy in the top tier of foreign navies."[48]

At the time of writing, Russia still lacked amphibious assault ships relative to the United States (where the former had 5 and the latter had 32), but is on par here with China. The cancellation of the Mistral contract with France in 2014 hurt Russia's capabilities in this regard. Reportedly, however, Russian naval commanders have grown very creative in compensating for this shortcoming, even resorting to the use of a few icebreakers to transport troops to Syria.[49]

The United States has a unique global capability in aircraft carriers—with 11 total as compared to 1 each in all of the other powers reported below. Russia has a single aircraft carrier, the diesel-powered Admiral Kuznetsov that can accommodate 22 strike aircraft and 17 attack helicopters. However, it is no match for any of the 11 US aircraft carriers and was damaged in port in 2019. Russia's paucity of aircraft carriers, however, as indicated in table 6.2, is more the norm than the exception globally. The fact that other countries have far fewer of them than the United States may have more to do with American geography and history of combat locations that are not near the homeland rather than serving as an indicator of relative global force projection capability. Arguably, too, Russia's four main areas of sea access (the Northern Pacific Ocean, Arctic, Baltic, and Black

Table 6.2 **Sea Forces (Key Selected Systems) as of 2018**

	Attack Submarines	Ballistic Missile Nuclear-Powered Subs	Frigates, Cruisers, and Destroyers	Amphibious Ships	Patrol/Coastal Combatant	Aircraft Carriers	Icebreakers
Russia	49	10	33	5	105	1	46
United States	53	14	101	32	?	11	5
China	54	4	86	5	?	1	3
India	15	1	27	1	?	1	—
France	6	4	23	3	?	1	—
UK	6	4	19	—	?	1	—

Note: Finland has 10 icebreakers, Canada 7, Sweden 7, Denmark 4, and others including Norway and Germany have 5 total. Heritage Dakota Woods, 211

Seas) are not well suited to the kind of deep and relatively warm water ports a fleet of aircraft carriers would require, so there is likely no particular urgency in building these massive and expensive platforms. Further, given its location between Europe and Asia, Russia's force projection can be done easily into Europe, the Middle East, Central and South Asia, and North America (over the North Pole or across the Atlantic) with submarines, conventional land-based weapons systems, aircraft, and missiles. Since 2014, the Russian military has reportedly transformed the annexed Crimean Peninsula into a "virtual aircraft carrier," moving significant weaponry there, including surface-to-air, cruise, and Iskandr dual conventional/nuclear-capable missile systems that can project hard power easily into the Middle East and Southern and Eastern Europe.[50]

The renewed Russian navy is organized into four fleets: the Northern, the Pacific, the Baltic, and the Black Sea, with a smaller flotilla in the Caspian Sea. Of the four fleets, the Northern Fleet is the most capable, with seven ballistic missile submarines that form the basis of Russia's nuclear sea force. The Northern Fleet also provides counterpiracy patrol boats for the Horn of Africa, and other vessels from the Kola Peninsula base of the Northern Fleet aid in projecting Russian power along the North Atlantic coasts of the United States and Canada, as well as into the Caribbean.[51] Further, although not part of the Northern Fleet, to support its push into the Arctic and the establishment of a Northern Sea Route, and also to support energy exploration and mining projects there, Russia has invested in the world's largest fleet of icebreakers (46), including six that are nuclear-powered.[52] Thus, Russia's icebreakers have both a civilian (trade) and military purpose in keeping shipping lanes clear in a treacherous environment.

Indeed, Russia has greatly expanded its Arctic military operations since 2012. Russia's Arctic coastline is strategically important in the wake of climate change that is creating new sea routes there between the Atlantic and Pacific Oceans. This enables easier and faster movement of ships between the Northern and Pacific Fleets, and compensates somewhat for a delay in shipbuilding in that it provides for faster mobilization and maneuverability of the existing fleet. The establishment and control of a North Sea Route to facilitate trade from China in particular, discussed in chapters 3 and 4, is another motivation for the establishment of Russian military bases in the Arctic region. Further, as Katarzyna Zysk notes, another key driver of Russia's militarization of the Arctic is the region's natural resource riches. In the spring of 2014, Putin himself pointed to the potential of the energy reserves in the Arctic, which well exceed 1.6 trillion tons.[53] Clearly, Russia's leadership views the Arctic region as a treasure trove of its future energy wealth. To guarantee access to the oil and natural gas reserves in that region, and to establish oversight of the Northern Sea Route, required the increased presence of Russian naval forces, particularly since climate change has made it easier for other littoral nations to establish claims to the region and its riches as well. Thus, Russia's military has prepared to defend its claims to the region (some of which overlap with those of Canada and Denmark and the Norwegian archipelago of Svalbard) in anticipation of future conflict there.[54] This has meant the addition to the Northern Fleet of up to eight new Borei class submarines, and new nuclear attack submarines of the Severodvinsk class, as well as the modernization of older Akula class and Oskar class submarines. Surface ships have also been added to the Northern Fleet to supplement Arctic defenses, including smaller, icebreaking-capable patrol boats that will also purportedly be capable of hosting Kalibr cruise missiles.[55] But the navy is not the only service of the Russian military in place to defend the Arctic region—air defenses, including S-300 and S-400 air defense systems, have been installed on Novaya Zemlya, Franz Josef Land, Severnaya Zemlya, and the New Siberian Islands, as well as in settlements in Yakutia and the Kola Peninsula. Other branches of the Russian military like the air force have established bases in the Arctic region, or modernized former Soviet bases, and Russia has inserted ground forces known as Arctic Brigades near Russia's borders with Norway and Finland.

While much of Russia's Arctic focus concerns the Northern Fleet, the Pacific Fleet, Russia's second largest naval command, is also part of the establishment of the Northern Sea Route. The Pacific Fleet has a base in the Petropavlovsk-Kamchatskiy Peninsula to aid with this mission, but is headquartered in Vladivostok. The Pacific Fleet has not received as much attention as the Northern Fleet in terms of upgrading and maintenance, but it houses both diesel- and nuclear-powered submarines with nuclear ballistic missiles capable of hitting targets in the American West. It comprises more than 70 combat ships, including 50 warships, more than 20 submarines, and some of Russia's nuclear-powered icebreakers.[56] Moreover, due to the military deterrent Russia has placed in the Pacific Fleet, combined with its conventional forces in the Eastern Military District on land, Russian forces "should prove capable of repelling any unlikely attack from either a state or nonstate actor in the region."[57] Even with China's growing military presence in the Pacific, Admiral Harry B. Harris Jr., the US Pacific Fleet commander, still considers the "Russian forces in the Pacific a formidable threat."[58]

Since its annexation of the Crimean Peninsula, the Russian Ministry of Defense has focused its spending on systems to patrol and dominate the Black Sea region. In 2015, new submarines and surface combat ships arrived to strengthen the fleet, along with the Kalibr land-attack cruise missile system (to be discussed further). According to the US Defense Intelligence Agency, the Black Sea Fleet may also receive six new attack submarines and six new surface ships that can help the Russian navy further exert control over the Black Sea as well as operating in the Mediterranean Sea.[59]

The Baltic Fleet, based in the tiny Russian enclave of Kaliningrad, has supported missions in the Eastern Mediterranean Sea related to the Syrian conflict and in the Horn of Africa. It also houses surface vessels with Kalibr cruise missiles, and since 2016 it "presents a significant long-range precision conventional and theater nuclear strike threat to Western Europe."[60] The Russian navy's flotilla in the Caspian Sea has been armed since 2015 with vessels capable of launching Kalibr cruise missiles that were initially fired into Syria. The Caspian flotilla also possess the capability of hitting targets in Central Asia, further into the Middle East, and also parts of Southern Europe.[61] The ubiquitous Kalibr is a very significant new Russian military capability and "is profoundly changing its ability to deter, threaten, or destroy adversary's targets."[62]

The Russian navy has invested heavily in attack submarines, and by 2018, with 49 in its fleet, approached parity with China (54) and the United States (53). It had also added to its fleet of nuclear-powered submarines carrying nuclear-capable ballistic missiles, again almost reaching parity with the United States. They have been observed with increased frequency in the Pacific theater, according to the US navy commanders operating in that area since 2016.[63] There are plans for more new ships and submarines in the 2020s, but the Russian navy will still need to rely on its older Soviet era ships in some regions. Nonetheless, the American Defense Intelligence Agency reported that "despite this, Russia is still capable of deploying its assets worldwide."[64]

Russian Air Combat Capabilities in Comparative Perspective

As we compare Russian and American air power capabilities in terms of sheer numbers (see table 6.3), the United States has overwhelming superiority in tactical aircraft, bombers, attack helicopters, transport helicopters, transport aircraft, air tankers, early warning aircraft, and probably drones (designated in the table as heavy unmanned aerial vehicles). These numbers, however, do not tell the whole story of Russia's relative air power projection capacity relative to the United States.

As part of the New Look reforms, the Russian Air Forces and its Aerospace Defense Troops were merged to create a new entity, the Russian Aerospace Forces, in 2015. The combined force (known by the Russian acronym VKS) has about 148,000 personnel and includes Long Range Aviation, Military Transportation Aviation, as well as Space Troops tasked with conducting space launches, maintaining the missile early warning system, Russia's satellite control network, and surveillance and identification of space objects.[65] Long Range Aviation is Russia's bomber force, possessing both conventional and nuclear weapons. The Defense Intelligence Agency reported in 2017 that Russian heavy

Table 6.3 **Air Forces (Key Selected Systems) as of 2018**

	Tactical Aircraft	Bombers	Attack Helicopters	Transport Helicopters	Transport Aircraft	Tanker Air	Early Warning & Control Aircraft	Heavy Unmanned Aerial Vehicles
Russia	1,146	139	383	374	178	15	18	"some"
United States	3,421	157	928	2,665	682	530	111	514
China	1,932	193	278	383	85	18	29	19
India	756	—	19	12	37	6	4	13
France	250	—	70	158	48	15	7	6
UK	191	—	50	108	47	14	6	9

bombers (the TU-95MS) were being remodeled to accommodate the Kalibr (Kh101/102) cruise missiles.[66]

By all accounts, Russia has one of the world's best air defense systems, including radar, surface-to-air missiles (SAMs), an integrated command-and-control system, as well as electronic warfare equipment that can jam the enemy's communications systems. The S-300 and S-400 missile air defense systems are particularly potent components of Russia's air capabilities. They can be ground-launched from trucks, can track multiple targets simultaneously, and can also fire several missiles at targets simultaneously. The newer S-400 system can accommodate four types of missiles (vs. two types for the S-300), with ranges up to 250 miles, and are thought to be able to target US F-22s or F-35s. Both the S-300s and S-400s are pervasive in the Russian force structure.[67]

Russia has also developed an attack helicopter that rivals the US Chinook in speed, and that possesses 30mm guns, 80mm unguided rockets, and anti-tank missiles, again matching the capabilities of the Chinook or Apache in the US arsenal. Another aspect of the modernized Russian air forces includes the development of a hypersonic anti-ship missile that could be fired from a MiG-31 jet. If this were to become operational, then it would be too fast for other anti-missile defense systems to stop, and would have the ability to strike American warships and aircraft carriers with crippling force.[68] Other aircraft upgrades on the Su-27 and Su-35 jets have brought improvements in engines, munitions, and electronic sensors, and they are "substantially more capable than the systems they have superseded."[69] They too have been outfitted with new and more effective air-to-air missiles. Training has expanded since 2012, the results of which were evident in Syria, where Russian pilots gained even more experience with their aircraft.[70] Similarly, the Kalibr long-range cruise missiles can be air-launched from retrofitted heavy bombers, as well as from sea or land with conventional or nuclear warheads. They fly at low altitude, below infrared or radar range.[71]

Although the table shows that Russia has only "some" heavy unmanned vehicles, it has poured resources into the development of tactical reconnaissance systems or mini-UAVs. It is also reportedly working on unmanned combat aerial vehicles (drones), although information on the prevalence of these systems was limited at the time of writing.[72]

Finally, the Russian navy and air force have invested heavily since 2008 in an estimated 700 combat fighter and bomber aircraft systems. The capabilities of some of Russia's newer aircraft, in combination with its missile defense systems, would present a worrisome problem for the United States and NATO forces in the European and Middle Eastern theaters in particular.[73]

Although not all of Russia's new weapons programs have come to fruition, and others have been slow to develop, Russia's modernization efforts have given it significant new capabilities such that in overall quality and reach, "the US military advantage over Russia is eroding."[74]

Readiness

Weapons, soldiers, sailors, and pilots are only as good as their training. Any comparison of the Russian military to others should look not just at the quantity of weapons or soldiers each country possesses, but also at the quality—in military parlance, "force readiness." Russian active military personnel are fewer in number than China, India or the United States, but have had active training in Syria since 2015, and in a range of regular and comprehensive military exercises since about 2012. Given the size and complexity of Russian training exercises, its overall force readiness is likely rivaled only by the United States. This too is a start contrast to the 1990s, when training across the Russian military was cut by a reported 70%.[75] Russian military exercises were held frequently and with increasing complexity following the New Look reforms. They included all branches of the armed forces individually and together, and at different locations meant to simulate varied conflict scenarios. One analyst reported that in the fourteen-month period between July 2013 and September 2014 alone, six major exercises were held from Kaliningrad to the Kuril Islands and from the Arctic to Russia's southern borders.[76] There has also been an increase in the number of snap exercises, some of which appear to have been in preparation for the Crimean annexation in February 2014, and on the western border during the upheaval in neighboring Ukraine. Similarly, before the start of the Syrian campaign in September 2015, warships from the Black Sea Fleet were deployed for drills.[77]

The Arctic has been a particularly good area in which to conduct exercises for the Russian military. In 2015 the Arctic coast was the site of snap exercises that included 45,000 personnel, approximately 3,000 vehicles, 40 surface ships, submarines, and 110 aircraft deployed to positions in Novaya Zemlya and Franz Josef Land.[78] By the time the exercise concluded, it had expanded to the Far North, and included a reported 80,000 personnel, 65 warships, 15 submarines, and 220 aircraft. This was small, however, compared to the 2014 Vostok exercise in Russia's Far East, which involved 150,000 personnel. In 2016, Russian paratroopers practiced landing on icebergs in the Arctic Ocean, and Aerospace Forces drilled landings on Aleksandra Land Arctic Airfield. Search-and-rescue exercises using the battle cruiser *Pyotr Velikii* took place as early as 2012 to practice protecting the North Sea Route.[79] Another exercise in 2015 called Arktika rehearsed an oil spill scenario that brought in forces from different military services as well as the Northern Fleet, Ministry of Transport, Emergency Ministry, the Russian Coastguard, Gazprom, and Lukoil. These are but a few examples of the large, complex, and very regular exercises of the new Russian military.

Russian Nuclear Weapons in Comparative Perspective

Despite significant improvements in its conventional hard power capabilities by 2020, the crown jewel of Russia's military capacity remained its nuclear arsenal. This aspect of Russian hard power has also been modernized and upgraded since 2008, although the strategic rocket forces were relatively well maintained in comparison to other parts of the armed forces that atrophied in the 1990s. By December 2018, Defense Minister Shoigu announced that more than 82% of Russian nuclear forces had been modernized.[80]

The United States became the world's first nuclear power in the summer of 1945, and it used its new capabilities to drop atomic bombs on Hiroshima and Nagasaki in August of that year. By 1949, the Soviets had conducted their first nuclear explosion. The United Kingdom followed in 1952, France in 1960, and China in 1964. The Soviet Union and the United States, of course, built up huge nuclear arsenals during the Cold War, eventually signing a series of arms control agreements in the 1970s, 1980s, and early 1990s intended to limit what each accumulated. After the fall of the Soviet Union, all nuclear weapons that were in the former Soviet republics of Belarus, Kazakhstan, and Ukraine were transferred to Russia. By 2020, Russia and the United States together still owned 90% of the world's stockpile of nuclear weapons.

There is some variation in exact numbers of missiles and warheads reported across sources, but the New START (Strategic Arms Reduction Treaty, signed between the United States and Russia in 2010) reporting obligations provide consistent data on at least strategic nuclear-capable systems, although not on shorter-range, non-strategic (or tactical) nuclear weapons. The data on non-strategic weapons varies somewhat depending on the source; however, the numbers in table 6.4 provide the best available estimates at the time of writing.

In terms of total warheads, Russia led the world with a combined total of 6,490 strategic and tactical nuclear warheads, while the United States had 6,185. They both far outpaced all other nuclear powers like China (with only 290), France (300), the United Kingdom (200), and the smaller nuclear states of Pakistan, India, Israel, and North Korea. Of Russia's 6,490 total warheads, an estimated 2,000 have been retired, leaving about 4,490 operational warheads. Of these, an estimated 1,820 are non-strategic (tactical) warheads and not included in New START, which sets limits only on strategic weapons. New START has set an upper limit on 1,550 *deployed* strategic warheads on both the United States and Russia, which both countries were to meet by February 5, 2018. Russia's

Table 6.4 **Russia's Nuclear Weapons vs. Other Nuclear Powers, 2019**

Nuclear State	Total Warheads	Retired	Total Operational (Strategic and Non-Strategic Warheads)	*Of which x Strategic Deployed*	Total Operational	*Strategic Warheads in Storage*	Total Operational	*Of which x are non-Strategic*
Russia	6,490	2,000	4,490	*Of which* 1,461 *Strategic deployed*	4,490	1,070	4,490	1,820
United States	6,185	2,385	3,800	*Of which* 1,365 *Strategic deployed*	3,800	2,115	3,800	230
France	300	—	300	*Of which* 280 *deployed*				
China	290	—	290	*Of which* 290 *deployed*				
UK	200	—	200	*Of which* 120 *deployed*				
Pakistan	160	—	150–160					
India	140	—	130–140					
Israel	90	—	80–90					
North Korea	30–40*estimated	—	30–40*estimated					

These estimates are from a combination of Kristensen and Korda, "Russian Nuclear Forces," 73; Arms Control Association, "Nuclear Weapons: Who Has What at a Glance," updated July 2019, available at: https://www.armscontrol.org/factsheets/Nuclearweaponswhohaswhat, accessed April 22, 2020; Hans M. Kristensen, "World Nuclear Forces: Russia," *SIPRI Yearbook, 2019*, 4, available at: https://www.sipri.org/yearbook/2019/06, accessed April 10, 2020; and Hans M. Kristensen and Matt Korda, "United States Nuclear Forces, 2019," *Nuclear Notebook, Bulletin of the Atomic Scientists* 75, no. 3 (2019): 123, available at https://doi.org/10.1080/00963402.2019.1606503, accessed April 23, 2020.

deployed strategic warheads by 2019 were reported to be 1,461. The United States reported 1,365, giving Russia an advantage of almost 100 deployed strategic warheads. However, the United States has a greater number in total when one adds non-deployed warheads to the mix.

It is, however, the Russian arsenal of 1,820 shorter-range, non-strategic or "tactical" nuclear warheads that gives its military a very serious nuclear advantage over the United States or any other country on the planet. Before the end of the Cold War and the arms reduction agreements signed by Mikhail Gorbachev and George H. W. Bush, the Soviet Union and the United States had combined arsenals of 20,000–30,000 of these shorter-range, lighter-payload nuclear weapons. By 2020, however, there were about 2,500 non-strategic nuclear warheads in total in existence, 2,050 of which are owned by either Russia or the United States. But Russia has a disproportionate number (1,820) as opposed to the United States (230)—an almost 8:1 ratio.

This is potentially very problematic for a number of reasons. First, because the range of these weapons, although shorter than intercontinental ballistic missiles (which are a strategic weapon intended to fly long distances in short times and carry payloads capable of destroying huge targets like cities), is still sufficient to deliver tremendously destructive nuclear payloads to a variety of targets in both Eastern and Western Europe, the Middle East, and North and South Asia, and when put on ships, submarines, or bombers, into North America, South America, and the remainder of Africa too. A second concerning issue, then, is that because tactical nuclear weapons can be launched from a number of air-, land-, and sea-based platforms, they are extremely difficult to find by satellite or other surveillance systems in order to map, count, or destroy. This is unlike silo-based ICBMs (intercontinental ballistic missiles, a strategic nuclear weapon), that cannot be moved or hidden from aerial surveillance very easily. Third, after the demise of the Intermediate Nuclear Forces (INF) Treaty in August 2019, there are no limits to the number of these types of weapons allowed on European soil for either Russia or the United States. There is also no treaty that limits their launching from sea-based platforms, from the air, or as part of missile defense systems. Finally, there is some debate (and concern) as to whether Russia's nuclear doctrine has evolved such that tactical nuclear weapons would be used in actual combat to compensate for shortcomings in conventional weapons relative to the United States and NATO.[81]

The 2014 update to the 2010 Russian military doctrine stated:

> The Russian Federation shall reserve the right to use nuclear weapons in response to the use of nuclear and other types of weapons of mass destruction against it and/or its allies, as well as in the event of aggression against the Russian Federation with the use of conventional weapons when the very existence of the state is in jeopardy.[82]

What would constitute a situation that would endanger "the very existence of the state" is nowhere defined in the doctrine itself, however, and that has left it open to interpretation, perhaps by design.[83] Does it mean the survival of the current political regime led by Vladimir Putin, or is it meant to be a strictly territorial definition of "the state"? A 2020 decree signed by Putin on Russian nuclear deterrence policy seemed to lower the threshold for use of nuclear weapons to include situations where its "territorial integrity" was under threat.[84] This implies that an assault by foreign forces on any part of the territory of the Russian Federation, such as newly annexed Crimea, for example, could trigger a nuclear response from the Kremlin. Alternatively, this ambiguity could be a form of deterrence such that purposeful fuzziness about the threshold for the use of nuclear weapons (especially non-strategic) is a strategy to dissuade potential adversaries from attacking Russia with conventional weapons. That is, merely threatening to use any type of nuclear weapon in a combat situation would escalate a conflict that Russia is losing by conventional means, but doing so would serve to de-escalate the situation and leave Russia in a better bargaining position. This has become known in US military vernacular as "escalate to de-escalate." The alternative interpretation, however, is that the Russian strategy *is not simply to escalate from conventional conflict with the threat to use tactical nuclear weapons,* only to de-escalate in order to negotiate from a stronger position, *but actually meaning to resort to first use of a tactical nuclear weapon.*

The 2018 US Nuclear Posture Review published by the Department of Defense interpreted the wording of the doctrine to mean that Russian decision-makers *would* indeed resort to a limited first use of tactical nuclear weapons in order to improve their negotiating position in a war with the United States or NATO:

> Most concerning are Russia's national security policies, strategy, and doctrine that include an emphasis on the threat of limited nuclear escalation, and its continuing development and fielding of increasingly diverse and expanding nuclear capabilities. Moscow threatens and exercises limited nuclear first use, suggesting a mistaken expectation that coercive nuclear threats or limited first use could paralyze the United States and NATO and thereby end a conflict on terms favorable to Russia. Some in the United States refer to this as Russia's "escalate to de-escalate" doctrine. "De-escalation" in this sense follows from Moscow's mistaken assumption of Western capitulation on terms favorable to Moscow.[85]

Many analysts, however, see this as a fundamental misreading of Russia's policy, and that the 2010 doctrine and its updated 2014 version are in fact a scaling-back of much stronger and more concerning statements in its earlier military doctrines that seemed to indicate a lower threshold for the use of nuclear weapons. Crane, Oliker, and Nichiporuk argue for example that Russia's 2000 Military Doctrine set a lower threshold than what was published in 2014. The 2000 Military Doctrine indicated that Russia could resort to the use of nuclear weapons in the case of "large-scale aggression by conventional weapons in situations deemed critical to the national security of the Russian Federation."[86]

Still, Putin has at other times seemed to resort to more ambiguous language regarding the usability of nuclear weapons in war. In a 2015 interview for a documentary marking the first anniversary of Russia's annexation of Crimea, Putin claimed that he was ready to use nuclear weapons and had put defensive missiles on high alert.[87] The Russian ambassador to Denmark, Mikhail Vanin, in a 2015 op-ed published by *Jyllands-Posten*, a Danish newspaper, warned Denmark that if it were to join NATO's missile defense, "Danish warships will become targets for Russian atomic missiles."[88] Russia's 2017 Naval Doctrine further confuses the matter, stating that "under conditions of escalating military conflict, a demonstration of readiness, and will to use force, including with non-strategic nuclear weapons, is an effective deterrent factor."[89] But by 2018, Putin himself insisted that Russia would not resort to a pre-emptive first nuclear strike and that Russia's nuclear policy was "launch on warning."[90]

The kinds of weapons and quantity of non-strategic warheads, in particular, that Russia has been building since the beginning of the New Look program, however, indicate that their purpose is more than simply as deterrents to possible aggression against the homeland. Earlier sections of this chapter that looked in detail at the naval, land, and air branches of Russia's armed forces reviewed the quantity of some of Russia's new delivery systems, but it is worth briefly reviewing some of what the newer strategic and non-strategic weapons that Russia possesses can actually do, and that should be cause for concern for the United States in particular.

Table 6.5[91] presents a direct comparison of the Russian and American strategic nuclear arsenals as of the end of 2019 (the most recent year available at time of writing), subject to the New START agreement. This includes intercontinental ballistic missiles (ICBMs), submarine-launched ballistic missiles (SLBMs), and bomber aircraft. The United States had a greater number of launching platforms in all three categories (706 in total) over Russia (with 546). It had more ICBMs (400) with a total of 800 warheads, more SLBMs (with 240) with 1,920 total warheads, and two fewer bombers (66) compared to Russia (68), but with 850 warheads compared to 786 for Russia.

In sum, the United States had a greater number of total launching platforms and warheads, as indicated in the table, but fewer deployed warheads (1,365) than did Russia (1,461). That said, should it become necessary, the United

Table 6.5 **Russian and American Strategic Nuclear Forces**

Type of Strategic Nuclear Weapon	Russia		Russia	United States	United States
	No. of Launching Platforms		Total Nuclear Warheads	No. of Launching Platforms	Total Nuclear Warheads
Intercontinental Ballistic Missiles (ICBMs)	318 1–10 warheads per missile (depending on model) SS-18 M6 Satan SS-19 M3 Stiletto SS-19 M4 SS-25 Sickle SS-27 Mod 1 (mobile) Topol" SS-27 Mod 1 (silo)" Topol-M" SS-27 Mod 2 (mobile) "Topol-M" SS-27 Mod 2 (silo) "Yars" SS-X-27 Mod? (rail) "Barguzin" SS-X-28 (mobile) "Yars-M" "Rubezh" SS-X-29 (silo) "Sarmat"		1,165	400 1–3 warheads, (depending on model) LGM-30G Minuteman III Mk-12A Mk-21/SERV	800
Submarine Launched Ballistic Missiles (SLBMs)	10 160 missiles each; 3–6 warheads depending on boat. SS-N-18 M1 Stingray SS-N-23 M1 Sineva SS-N-32 Bulava		720	240 1–8 warheads UGM-133A Trident II D5 Mk-4 Mk-4A Mk-4A Mk-5	1,920
Bombers/weapon	68 Bear-H6 Bear-H16 Blackjack		786	66 B-52s B2A	850
Total	**546**		**2671**	**706**	**3,570**
Total Deployed			**1,461**		**1,365**
Total Stockpiled			669		1,505

Data from Bulletin of the Atomic Scientists, Nuclear Notebook, "Russia and the United States," 2019

States could draw quickly from its higher number of 1,505 stockpiled (vs. Russia's 669) warheads. Russia's advantage in ICBM nuclear warheads (1,165 vs. 800 for the United States) is considerable—at least on paper. It is important to realize, however, that this part of the Russian nuclear arsenal is most vulnerable to a first strike from the United States, given that most of those warheads are on siloed missiles, and therefore easy to locate and destroy before they are launched. One study indicates that between 41–47% of Russian ICBMs are mobile (on rail platforms, or launched by sea from submarines), with the remainder being siloed. But if we were to include its submarine-launched ballistic missiles, then an estimated two-thirds or so of Russia's strategic nuclear weapons could be on first-strike survivable systems. This is important, since Russia's satellite-based early warning system was apparently not well maintained in the years following the Soviet collapse, and so the proportion of Russian strategic nuclear missiles that are based in silos makes the operability of the warning system particularly important to its strategy. But if this warning system is unreliable, then creating systems that are mobile or capable of evading US missile defense systems would be of special importance to Russian nuclear policy going forward.[92] This is part of what we see in its modernization programs.

Russia's Upgraded and New Nuclear Systems

According to studies in the Bulletin of the Atomic Scientists, Russia's ICBM capabilities eroded over the first twenty-five or so years following the collapse of the Soviet Union, but was on course to update about two-thirds of its strategic arsenal by the early 2020s.[93] The new weapons that Putin outlined in his March 2018 speech include a new powerful silo-based ICBM, the Sarmat (SS-29), called "Son of Satan," by the American military because it is an updated version of the SS-18 missile that the United States had dubbed "Satan" due to the destructive capacity of its nuclear payload. It is a hypersonic ICBM that purportedly can carry up to fifteen glide warheads that can move independently and that can evade US ballistic missile defense systems. According to Putin, they are so fast that "missile defense systems are useless against them, absolutely pointless."[94] The Sarmat is through the testing phase, and large-scale production of this weapon was expected in 2020.

Two other strategic missiles were developed as part of Russia's modernization program. Barguzin is a road mobile ICBM, and the Rubezh is a road mobile ICBM with "independently guided warheads designed to break through missile defense shields," but their deployment may have been postponed beyond 2027.[95] The Avangard is a new hypersonic glide re-entry vehicle that is designed to fit onto a ballistic missile and can maneuver around defense systems to deliver its nuclear payload. Putin reported that it could reach speeds of Mach 20. This system was deployed initially in 2019 on SS-19 missiles.[96]

The Burevestnik or SSC-X-9 (which NATO calls "Sky Fall") is another new strategic weapon in development for the Russian arsenal that is a cruise missile with a small nuclear engine and bearing a nuclear payload. It too is intended to be able to bypass missile defense systems by being able to fly at a relatively low altitude while maneuvering easily at hypersonic speeds. Putin boasted in his March 1, 2018, speech to the Federal Assembly that "no other country has developed anything like this." This, however, is probably for very good reason: the US military views this kind of weapon as particularly dangerous, since the technology has historically been unstable. Indeed, it is believed that there was an accident in the testing of the Burevestnik in northern Russia at a site on the White Sea in August 2019 that involved a relatively small, but detectable, release of radiation, and resulted in the death of seven Russian scientists.[97] Finally, the Kinzhal (meaning "dagger") is a new air-launched ballistic missile with sea-based vessels as its intended targets. As with many of Russia's other new weapons, it is both nuclear and conventionally capable. The Kinzhal has a range of over 2,000 km and can allegedly travel at Mach 10, and is movable throughout its flight so that it can dodge incoming defensive missiles in getting to its target.[98]

Russia's sea-based strategic nuclear arsenal has also received new weapons. One is the Poseidon—a long-range nuke-powered "torpedo" (also described as a self-navigating drone) that can travel a distance of 10,000 km, at a depth of 1,000 m, at a speed of 100 knots to deliver a 200-megaton warhead.[99] It would cause a tsunami once it exploded in the ocean, flooding the shores of the nearest land, and spreading its radioactive fallout indiscriminately. Putin has rightly claimed of Poseidon torpedoes that "there is simply nothing in the world capable of withstanding them."[100] The United States has nothing in its arsenal that would overwhelm or stop it. The Poseidon (which is dual nuclear/conventional capable) has reportedly been deployed on a small number of Russia's nuclear submarines. In early 2020, the Russian navy also successfully tested a surface-launched hypersonic anti-ship missile, the Tsirkon, and had plans to test it from submarines later that year. It is thought to be capable of hitting targets on land or sea that are as much as 1,000 km away at a speed of up to Mach-6, although some estimates are higher (up to Mach-9).[101]

As powerful as some of these new strategic nuclear weapons are, a bigger threat may come from Russia's non-strategic (tactical) nuclear arsenal (see table 6.6). As the 2018 American Nuclear Posture Review noted, "Russia possesses significant advantages in its nuclear weapons production capacity and in non-strategic nuclear forces over the United States and its allies."[102] (Recall that the United States reports having only 230 non-strategic nuclear weapons, while Russia is estimated to have between 1,820–2,000 weapons in its arsenal.[103])

Table 6.6 **Russian Non-Strategic Nuclear Weapons, 2019**

Type of Non-Strategic Nuclear Weapon	No. of Launching Platforms/Type	Total Nuclear Warheads
ABM/Air/Coastal defense missiles	~1,000 S-300/S-400 (SA-20/ SA-21); 68 53T6 Gazelle; 8 SSC-1B Sepal (Redut); 48 SSC-5 Stooge (SS-N-26)	386
Land-based air Bombers/fighters	300 (Tu-22M3/Su-24M/Su-34/ MiG-31K)	530
Ground-based	144 SS-21 Scarab SSM (9K79, Tochka) SS-26 Stone SSM (9K720, Iskandr-M) SSC-7 GLCM (9M728) SSC-8 GLCM (9M729)	
Naval	16 Submarines/surface ships/air	820 Land to Air CMs; SLCMs; Torpedoes
Subtotal non-strategic and defensive forces		1820
Total deployed		**1,820**

The Russian navy is thought to have most of the country's tactical nuclear weapons, with 820 warheads. These can be launched from submarines, frigates, cruisers, and destroyers. Russia has on its land-based air systems an estimated 530 tactical nuclear weapons, with an additional 380 or so on its air defense systems.

Among the most problematic for Russia's adversaries is the Kalibr cruise missile, known as the Kh101 in its conventional variant and Kh102 when it is armed with a nuclear warhead. As noted in the discussion of the Russian navy, the Kh102 can be launched from submarines (the Yasen/M nuclear attack submarine can reportedly accommodate between 32–40 Kh102 cruise missiles).[104] In November 2017, Dan Coates, then US director of national intelligence, testified to the US Senate that Russia's testing of the SSC-8 (which is the Kh102) at distances under, but also over, 500 km on land, violated the Intermediate Nuclear Forces (INF) Treaty, because it is dual capable and is a ground-launched cruise missile.

The INF was an agreement signed by the United States and the Soviet Union in 1987 with the intention of eliminating nuclear and conventional ground-launched ballistic and cruise missiles with a range of 500–5,500 km (both nations could still have weapons with ranges of less than 500 km, however). By June 1991 the Soviet Union and the United States had destroyed 2,692 short-, medium-, and intermediate-range missiles. Since the United States at the time had naval and air capabilities from which to launch shorter-range nuclear weapons into Europe and the Soviet Union, the INF proved to be more of a constraint on the Soviets and Russia as the successor state to the Soviet era agreements. Russian military leaders since the mid-2000s became increasingly concerned about China's having such weapons, and presumably that is why they developed the Kh102, which has a more powerful warhead than its predecessor and a more advanced guidance system. It is this weapon that caused the United States ultimately to abandon the INF in August 2019. It is difficult to see how Russia would not have understood this to be an INF violation, but perhaps developing the Kh102 was an effort to get the United States to abandon the treaty, such that together Russia and the United States could move to establish a new intermediate forces treaty that would include limits on China's development and deployment of these weapons too.

In addition to the versatile Kh101/102 cruise missile, Russia has also introduced the dual conventional/nuclear capable SS-26 Iskandr missile that has a 350 km range, a tripling of the range of its predecessor, the SS-21. The Iskandr also has double the firepower of the SS-21.[105] Finally, the ubiquitous S-300 and S-400 anti-ballistic missile defense systems are also now dual nuclear/conventional capable.

In sum, Russia has maintained nuclear parity with the United States. Indeed, through its modernization efforts, it even has a few powerful strategic and non-strategic weapons that exceed what the United States and NATO have in their combined arsenals. In combination with its reformed and professionalized conventional forces, Russia has regained its footing as a global leader in hard power capacities. It does not have the most soldiers, sailors, or airmen, nor does it have the most or even the best of every weapon system—nuclear or conventional; but it has rebuilt formidable military capabilities that would seriously challenge the United States and China pretty much anywhere, and at any time.

Conclusion

There are clear power asymmetries in some areas and not others between Russia and the United States, and China in particular. In terms of the sheer size of its military, the United States is obviously and clearly without parallel. It outspends

Russia by a ratio of almost ten to one. China too spends far more on its military in gross terms. Some of the asymmetry in conventional power between Russia and the United States, and China, however, is made up by Russia's nuclear weaponry. Perhaps unusable in war, Russia's leaders view it as a guarantee of sovereignty, as well as, if we take Putin literally and Russian nuclear doctrine at face value, usable in certain circumstances.

Russia has managed to rebuild and maintain its nuclear arsenal, significantly upgrade and modernize its conventional forces, and create a disruptive fighting capacity that has served to increase its global influence, as noted in chapter 2 (Ukraine and Georgia) and chapter 3 (in Syria), as examples. The Russian government under Putin persisted in its military modernization at a time when the economy went from an economic high to an economic low, demonstrating its deep commitment to upgrading its hard power capabilities. We turn next to the final category of the means of power to be assessed in this study, Russia's soft and sharp power capabilities, and examine the ways in which Russia under Putin has combined conventional hard power and soft and sharp power capabilities—on their own, and sometimes in combination—to extend its global reach in the twenty-first century.

Russian Soft and Sharp Power Resources

"The liberal idea has become obsolete. It has come into conflict with the interests of the overwhelming majority of the population."
—Vladimir Putin, June 2019[1]

Russia's hard power capabilities—its conventional and nuclear forces—have unquestionably gone through radical restructuring and modernization since 2008, as demonstrated in chapter 6. Beyond these areas of power projection, modern Russia has also developed some new abilities and redeployed certain Soviet-era techniques to battle the West for hearts and minds around the globe. Over the last decade in particular, the triad of Russian hard, soft, and sharp power has become particularly potent as the Putin regime's foreign policy goals have crystallized. The tools that decision-makers have employed abroad to project Russian influence have become more sophisticated, diverse, and effective. Moreover, beyond its formidable renewal of hard or coercive instruments of power projection, Russian "soft" and "sharp" power resources have assisted in extending its global reach and influence over societies in other states, rather than just economic and political elites.

Russian policymakers employ soft power resources as part of their foreign policy toolkit to further state interests and attract the citizens and leadership of other states to Russia's international preferences. Soft power, as noted in chapter 1, was first defined by Joseph Nye as a country's ability to pull rather than push a country to do what it might otherwise not. For Nye, "[i]n international politics, the resources that produce soft power arise in large part from the values that an organization or country expresses in its culture, in the examples it sets by its internal practices and policies, and the way it handles its external relations with others."[2] In addition to tactics that in the past might have been called propaganda, Russia's soft power resources include an array of tools of goodwill, including the provision of aid and emergency services to foreign countries during natural disasters, the establishment of cultural centers in Europe and the United States, and the use of pan-Slavism and the Russian Orthodox religion. Russian leaders understand soft power not as a passive force of attraction, as Nye does, but an active campaign to "wage friendship" in the service of specific interests.[3] Soft power, then, in contrast to the threat or use of force in the purview of hard power, is supposed to be the power of attraction—"getting others to want the outcomes that you want."[4]

"Sharp" power is a more recently coined term meant to capture the ways in which some authoritarian states, like Russia and China, have employed coercive techniques that do not fit the definition of "hard" power, but do not quite fit what Nye would recognize as "soft" either. Christopher Walker and Jessica Ludwig argue that sharp power techniques are intended to manipulate, confuse, and distract the target population. For instance, blurring the lines between "soft" and "sharp" power, the Russian leadership has established new media resources that present news and information from a distinctly pro-Russian, usually anti-Western perspective. Russian policymakers realized that "they did not need to convince the world that their autocratic system was appealing in its own right. Instead, they realized that they could achieve their objectives by making democracy appear less attractive."[5] As such, Russia has used more traditional media resources along with social media and cyber-based platforms to influence and often distort its adversaries' information environments, the most notorious example being the 2016 US presidential election. Examples of sharp power include tactics like stealing information and releasing it publicly through a trusted intermediary at a time thought to be most damaging to the adversary; planting false stories and using fake social media accounts to launder and amplify the message until it is picked up by a targeted group; and interrupting information flows through denial of services attacks. Broadly speaking, while soft power can win support and pull populations toward a sympathetic view of another country and its culture, sharp power is both a "push"—as a manipulation of the informational ecosystem in the target population, for example—and a "pull," presenting alternate narratives that are more favorable to Russian interests. Sharp power, therefore, is designed to "pierce, penetrate or perforate the political and information environments in the targeted countries."[6] This chapter provides an overview of Russian uses under Putin's regime of soft and sharp power as means of winning allies and sowing discord abroad.

Russia's Soft Power and the Soviet Legacy

The Soviet Union's soft power usage centered on providing the ideology of Marxism-Leninism as a key alternative to that of Western liberalism and capitalism. At various points, soft power proved quite effective in extending Soviet power globally. In the 1930s, for example, young Americans and Europeans saw in the Soviet Union a social system that appeared to be trying to overcome the failings of capitalism that were painfully evident in the wake of the Great Depression.[7] The communist society being built in the Soviet Union seemed far more equitable and humane than the market forces that, at the time, had let them down in many Western countries. Most of these young travelers, however, were ultimately disappointed by what they saw in Stalin's purges and prison camps of the 1930s and 1940s. As chapter 3 noted, Soviet soft power, as perpetuated through ideology, education, and aid, was also attractive to leaders of the independence movements of sub-Saharan Africa in the 1950s and 1960s. But the international soft power of the Soviet Union waned as it proved to have built not a better society, but a highly repressive, failing system of government and economic stagnation by the 1980s.

There was not much in the 1990s to attract foreign audiences to a Russia struggling to overcome the challenges of its tumultuous economic, political, and social transition in the aftermath of the Soviet collapse. But by the mid-2000s, under Vladimir Putin, Russian foreign policy developed both soft and sharp power resources to challenge the dominance of the West by pointing to its flaws and offering an alternative to liberal democracy. By Nye's definition, however, soft power is hard for a state to guide, not only because the production of cultural resources (television shows or films, for example) is not always within a government's control, but also because the effects of soft power "depend heavily on acceptance by the receiving audiences." Thus, Nye concludes, "soft power resources are slower, more diffuse, and more cumbersome to wield than hard-power resources."[8]

The Russian perspective on soft power, however, is different. Some of the tools that have been developed since the mid-2000s are intended to transcend the more passive influence of Nye's conceptualization of soft power.[9] Instead, they are used to reinforce hard power where needed (as, for example, in Ukraine in 2014) and to pursue broader foreign policy goals in place of hard power. According to one of Putin's decrees on the implementation of Russian foreign policy, "soft power is a set of instruments and methods used to achieve foreign policy goals without resorting to military means, but with the help of information and other instruments of influence."[10] The usage of soft power under Putin's regime stems from the leadership's perception that the West has used soft power to mischaracterize Russia's global role as pernicious and malevolent, especially following the Georgian war of 2008 and the seizure of Crimea six years later. Indeed, Russia's Foreign Policy Concept of 2013 noted that one of its goals was to "improve the informational support of foreign policy activities in the interests of an objective perception of the Russian Federation in the international arena."[11]

Instruments of influence are thus designed to present Putin's Russia as a seemingly reasonable and attractive alternative to the West. Often, however, these methods blur the line between the attraction component of soft power and the coercive, manipulative aspects of sharp power.

Efforts to tailor Russia's international image were intensified following Vladimir Putin's return to the Russian presidency in 2012, when Russian policymakers made concerted efforts to present the system over which he presided as a bulwark of Eurasian social conservatism that could stand strong against the flood of malign influences that swept the globe as a result of the purported decline of European and American liberal societies. From this perspective, Western liberalism was no longer the only desirable mode of political and economic development, as it had been in the years immediately following the collapse of the Soviet empire. As Putin himself argued in the quotation that opened this chapter, in the twenty-first century, Western liberalism no longer provides an unequivocal model of success.[12] Especially after the Arab Spring uprisings in the Middle East and North Africa in 2011 and the civil wars that followed in Syria and elsewhere, anti-immigrant sentiment ran high in the European countries that had taken them in, terrorism was on the rise, and the EU project was seen as under threat. With those developments, Anna Matveeva observes, "the perceived weakness of the West has become an asset to Russia."[13]

Soft power became a particularly favored foreign policy tool to appeal to former Soviet populations in the Baltics, Ukraine, Georgia, Kyrgyzstan, and Moldova, states that had either joined the EU or aspired to do so, and saw the EU and the West as more attractive global models than Russia, their near neighbor. The CSTO, Shanghai Cooperation Organization, and Eurasian Economic Union were other ways in which Russian policymakers aimed to more closely integrate the former Soviet space, as noted in chapter 2. Through these various non-military means, soft power became an intentional, instrumental method of pushing forward Russia's foreign policy aims.[14] Just as the Kremlin has used energy dependence and trade to shore up its political and economic goals around the globe, it has also made use of culture, religion, and access to international clubs to extend its global reach and influence.

Russian "policy" on soft power, such as it is, has several dimensions and varies depending on whether the target population is in the post-Soviet space or other parts of the world. Following the Georgian and Ukrainian conflicts, there was increased emphasis in former Soviet republics on ensuring ongoing Russian influence among not only elites, but also their broader societies, since history had shown that elites could be toppled. A strong connection and perception of cultural kinship could be produced by broadcasting Russian media into neighboring countries, and further bolstered with the establishment of cultural centers to promote Russian arts, literature, language, and the Russian

Orthodox religion, particularly the Moscow Patriarchy, in those countries.[15] Efforts to ensure avenues to educate young people in the Russian language have been particularly important in maintaining a strong cultural connection to Russia as the regional economic, political, and cultural hegemon. The regime hoped that the Russian language would become a desirable alternative to English in countries seeking to join the EU based on the availability of programs for learning Russian and the broadcast of entertaining Russian-language television programs.[16]

In addition to the "near abroad," under Putin, Russia has worked to promote pan-Slavism in its Eastern European neighbors, especially Slavic countries such as Serbia, by investing in religious areas, such as the reconstruction of Orthodox churches.[17] Indeed, the Russian Orthodox Church has effectively become a tool of the Russian state abroad. For instance, the Church has been aided by the Russian Ministry of Foreign Affairs in purchasing property in Paris, and in return has helped to gather members of the French diaspora and to ensure that Russian culture and history are celebrated and advanced along with current policies.[18] In Bosnia and Herzegovina, Russia promotes cultural and religious ties with Republika Srpska, even opening a "humanitarian center"—similar to one it established in Serbia—that is supposed to help with natural disasters like fires or floods.[19] As noted in chapter 3, in other countries with large Russian-speaking diasporas, like Israel, pension payments have been paid to elderly former Soviet citizens who served in World War II.

Another tool of Russian soft power is education at Russian universities, whether funded completely by Russian government scholarships or made available at significantly reduced rates. Foreign students can get a degree paid for by the Russian government at some of Russia's top universities, including Moscow State University, St. Petersburg State University, and the Higher School of Economics, as well as newer institutions like Skoltech at the Skolkovo research park outside of Moscow. These opportunities are available for students from former Soviet republics, but also those from African countries, Europe, Latin America, and elsewhere.

The presidential administration has also funded the Valdai Discussion Club since 2004 as a way to shape the narrative on Russia for foreign analysts. Every year, about 100 non-Russian academics and journalists who focus on Russia are invited to this conference to listen to presentations on Russian identity, local politics, the economy, and Russian foreign policy. President Putin usually graces the three-day gathering at an intimate dinner that has at times become an "ask-me-anything" session. The events are well-planned and professional, but most presentations unsurprisingly feature a pro-Russian perspective, presenting Russia as not without problems, but nonetheless fundamentally misunderstood in the West.

Establishing research centers abroad has furthered Russia's soft power strategy in various ways, whether focusing on education, civil society, or humanitarian endeavors. In 2008, for instance, the Institute on Democracy and Cooperation, founded by the Russian government though evidently not funded by it, opened a branch in New York City led by Andranik Migranyan, a former advisor to Boris Yeltsin. The goal of the Institute, according to Migranyan, was to monitor and improve the human rights situation in the United States—clearly a dig at US-based organizations seen as interfering in Russian society by targeting Russian human rights violations. The institute evidently accomplished this goal by 2015, when it closed,[20] though a Paris branch still existed at the time of writing. The Russian International Affairs Council (RIAC) is a more successful, government-funded research organization that pursues Russia's foreign relations through high-quality publications, conferences, and collaboration with foreign partners. RIAC is modeled loosely on the Council on Foreign Relations in New York, and chaired by former Russian minister of defense Igor Ivanov. Beyond educational and research aspects of Russian soft power, the Russian Ministry of Foreign Affairs in 2010 established the Gorchakov Public Diplomacy Support Fund to fund civil society organizations and forge people-to-people contacts in various countries, particularly in bordering states like Ukraine, Belarus, and the Baltics. These groups, in turn, connect with Russian government–backed civil society organizations in related fields.[21] Other Russian government–sponsored organizations are the Russkii Mir Foundation and Rosstrudnichestvo, which have opened about twenty or so centers in different parts of Belarus and Ukraine, for example, to promote language, culture, science, and technology.[22] These organizations loosely resemble China's Confucius Institutes, although they do not appear to be as well funded or numerous.[23]

The geographic domain of Russian soft power projection, including humanitarian aid and debt relief, was covered in various regions in chapter 3. But this sort of soft power tool, along with financial and political incentives, has spread to other parts of the globe as well. For example, in the spring of 2020, as Italy was quickly overcome with coronavirus (Covid-19) infections and short of supplies to treat people who were infected, the Russian government sent no fewer than nine transport aircraft with supplies of personal protective equipment, along with about 100 military personnel to help transport and distribute those supplies to Italian hospitals, all under the banner "From Russia with Love."[24] Photographs of Russian and Italian military commanders planning the distribution were released widely by the Russian Ministry of Defense. The Russian military was able to deliver these supplies to Italy within twenty-four hours of Vladimir Putin's offer of help to Italian prime minister Giuseppe Conte. This was notable considering that at the same time, Italy's neighbors, Germany and France, were prohibiting the export of face masks, while offers of help from the

United States and other NATO members were non-existent. A few days later, President Putin also arranged, through a direct phone call with Donald Trump, to sell scarce medical supplies to the United States as it too struggled to contain the virus and treat its victims. The irony was that the supplies were made by a Russian company under US sanctions for Russia's annexation of Crimea. In purchasing them—even at the allegedly below-market price which Trump deemed "a very nice offer"—the United States violated its own sanctions. A recording of a New York air traffic controller thanking the Russian pilot for "all the help you are delivering" was broadcast back home in Russia as well as on US media.[25]

Another form of soft power involves the representation of Russian wealth and success on the international stage, as with Russia's hosting of mega sports events like the 2014 Winter Olympics in Sochi and the 2018 Football (soccer) World Cup. Both events showcased Russia to the world as a developed, modern, and capable country. While the Sochi Olympics were a successful exercise in Russian soft power in that they came off without major hitches, the host country did face some critiques, notably due to the discomfort of gay athletes in the context of Russia's recent law prohibiting "homosexual propaganda," as well as the high cost of the games, which was (allegedly) inflated by corruption. Beyond this, much of the international goodwill generated by the Sochi games was quickly squandered as the Ukraine crisis unfolded at almost precisely the same time—illustrating the perhaps contradictory nature of Russian soft and hard power strategies.[26] (The Games themselves and the annexation of Crimea, however, both proved very popular within Russia, as indicated in chapter 1, so from a domestic politics perspective, both were huge successes.) Further, in the ensuing years, many Russian athletes were accused of taking part in a state-sponsored doping program that involved an elaborate scheme to substitute dirty urine samples with clean ones. The result was a suspension of Russian athletes from international competitions, and Russian competitors who had won events in Sochi had to return their medals. The FIFA International World Cup in 2018, for its part, proved to be well organized and showcased soccer matches in well-appointed stadiums in various cities across Russia. Still, despite the overall success of the event, accusations of corruption in the regime's successful bid for the event hovered on the sidelines, especially given the arrest and accusation of bribery of Sepp Blatter, the president of FIFA.[27]

Beyond the strong smell of corruption wafting over these events, the soft power gains of the Sochi Olympics or the World Cup have been repeatedly undermined in the wake of high-profile bad press for Putin's Russia abroad. Key incidents include the polonium-210 poisoning of Sergei Litvinenko, a former Russian spy-turned-informant, by Russian agents in London in 2006; the officially "unsolved" murder of Boris Nemtsov, former deputy prime minister and opposition leader, steps from the Kremlin gates in 2015; a coup attempt orchestrated by Russian intelligence agents in Montenegro in 2017 to prevent its joining NATO; and the attempted poisoning of Sergei Skripal, a former Russian military intelligence operative turned double agent for the United Kingdom, and his daughter, by Russian agents in the British town of Salisbury in 2018, which was caught on street cameras.

A tactic that further blurs the line between soft and sharp power, and one that has risen in prominence and international scrutiny in the Internet age in particular, is the use of traditional and digital media to influence target populations abroad. Most prominent among such media outlets are RT and Sputnik, which French president Emmanuel Macron described as "organs of influence and propaganda," even as he stood next to President Putin in Paris in 2017.[28] In 2005, the Russian government founded an international broadcast network called *Russia Today* (reintroduced as the more subtly titled RT in 2008). The goal of this media mechanism was to generate a different perspective on the West and on Russia, effectively blunting the impact of American and European soft power at home, in the neighborhood, and farther abroad. Essentially, RT was the Kremlin's response to what Putin and his government perceived as America's guiding hand behind the color revolutions in Georgia in 2003 and Ukraine in 2004.

RT has gained significant traction around the globe. By 2020, RT broadcast in 100 countries, across five continents, and on social media platforms including YouTube, and claimed 16 million subscribers. Broadcasting in English, French, Arabic, and Spanish, the network reported a weekly audience of 100 million television viewers, with its largest regional audience in Europe (43 million), as well as 11 million in the United States and an additional 11 million in fifteen countries across the Middle East and North Africa. It also claims to be among the ten most popular television channels in Latin America. In a direct shot across the bow of Western news sites, its website bragged, "Online, RT is the top *non-Anglo-Saxon* [emphasis added] TV news network in terms of traffic: in 2019, RT websites, collectively, had more than 175 million monthly visits, according to SimilarWeb."[29] RT's slogan is "Question More"—deemed ironic by some, since it only encourages audiences to question claims made by other sources—and according to its mission statement, it "creates news with an edge" because it "covers stories overlooked by the mainstream media, provides alternative perspectives on current affairs and acquaints international audiences with a Russian viewpoint on major global events."[30] The network uses a range of tactics, from high production value to foreign, often English-speaking "expert" interviewees—to make the Russian viewpoint appear objective.

Similarly, Sputnik News, a radio and online news network, was created in 2013 from what had been Radio Moscow and RIA Novosti, the Russian international news agency. Together, after Putin's return to office as president in 2012, "RT and Sputnik would be the nucleus of an assertively aggressive pro-Russian, anti-Western information network; RT in the mold of a more traditional cable network, and Sputnik as its outspoken, flashy younger sibling."[31] Sputnik broadcasts in ninety cities around the world and in the United States, and, like RT, tends to cover stories on the extremes of American politics. It employs reporters who formerly worked for Breitbart, the right-wing online news site, and features the views of far-right conspiracy theorists like Alex Jones. In February 2020, Sputnik was newly on three radio stations in Kansas City, Missouri, broadcasting for six hours per day in a three-year contract. It had started broadcasting in the Washington, DC, area at the end of 2017. The deficiencies of the US political system are a constant drum beat in RT and Sputnik programming, although, like the Russian government itself, both were ardently pro-Trump. Indeed, one commentator on Sputnik described the US Senate's impeachment trial of Donald Trump in January 2020 as "a Jewish coup."[32]

While both networks most prominently feature right-wing voices, their journalists and stories are designed to gain credibility among local audiences across the political spectrum. In particular, RT-America, based in Washington, DC, has hired journalists who speak excellent English, including a number of well-known former journalists from CNN (like Larry King), and a former foreign correspondent for the *New York Times*. It even featured a show hosted by WikiLeaks founder Julian Assange. Regardless of political slant, the network's programs and stories tend to highlight the downsides of life in the United States such as racism, poverty, and inequality, along with issues that divide Americans, like, for example, the disproportionate number of crimes purportedly committed by undocumented immigrants. RT also used this strategy in Germany with the "Lisa case" described in chapter 3, in which the story of a young girl allegedly kidnapped and raped by undocumented refugees from the Middle East stirred mass outrage (the story was quickly proven false). Typically, RT programs present themselves as platforms to air " 'dissident voices' currently missing from the mainstream media, [and] discussions that can't be heard anywhere else."[33] So slick and Westernized is the presentation platform that a viewer may have no idea that they are hearing global news filtered through the lens of the Russian government.

Generally, RT and Sputnik focus on vulnerable elements of targeted societies, putting forward what one analyst has called a "grievance narrative," aimed at those who feel they have been left behind by globalism, and who are increasingly disenchanted with what they see as Western moral hypocrisy in Iraq, Afghanistan, Europe, and elsewhere.[34] The goal is to exacerbate cleavages that might already exist and to confuse the information landscape, making it difficult to distinguish truth from lies. In presenting Russia's point of view as a cohesive, alternative narrative, these networks are attempting "to demonstrate that those tired of Western liberal moralizing have found a pole to rally around."[35]

To the extent that there is an ideology attached to this narrative, it is one of social conservatism, traditional family values and gender roles, spirituality, and a rejection of the political correctness of the excessively permissive West. It is blended with an economic ideology that is more nationalist than globalist, explicitly anti-American, and Euro-skeptical. This message has found supporters on the extreme right and left in Europe, the United States, parts of the Middle East, and beyond.

The success of RT and Sputnik in spreading divisive narratives indicates their importance not just as propaganda, but also as a means of driving specific policy. They have been used to amplify the populist policies of Hungarian president Viktor Orbán, as noted in chapter 3, and to drive a wedge into Western alliances, in particular the EU, both for trade purposes and with the goal of having sanctions on Russia lifted, ideally with the support from some EU members persuaded by the Russian narrative.[36] In these ways, RT and Sputnik are much more than media outlets promoting soft power messaging; they are sharp power tools with real impact on policy and opinion, in societies around the world and in political circles that offer clear connections and benefits to Russian government interests.

When Soft Becomes Sharp: Russia's Information Wars

RT and Sputnik, in combination with other aspects of Russia's modern information technology, are clearly more than mere instruments of propaganda: they are important components of Russia's developing practice of "misinformation" warfare against the West. Making efforts to alter the enemy's information landscape is not particularly new to warfare in general, and the Soviet Union was an outstanding practitioner of the art of misinformation. During the Cold War, the Soviets used techniques known as *dezinformatsiya* (disinformation) or *aktivnyie meropriyatia* (active measures) to sow social discord and discredit adversaries with deception. The historical use of these tactics surely set the scene for their prevalence today.

As Thomas Boghardt explains regarding these practices in Soviet times, "The term *dezinformatsiya* denoted a variety of techniques and activities to purvey false or misleading information that Soviet bloc active measures specialists sought to leak into the foreign media."[37] One infamous late Soviet example was the story concocted by the KGB that the United States had purposely fabricated the HIV/AIDS virus.[38] This narrative capitalized on Ronald Reagan's leadership early in his presidency: he had proven himself a hawk where the Soviet Union was concerned, and his administration was slow to realize the deadliness of the AIDS virus. Moreover, many countries also harbored lingering distrust of

the US government's military-industrial complex, especially given its development of biological weapons during the Vietnam War. It was thus no great leap in
logic for KGB operatives to create a false connection between these unpopular
weapons programs and the mysterious new disease. In articles first planted in a
newspaper in India, and in a Soviet newspaper in 1985, facts from open sources
regarding how the disease spread were mixed with fiction, this blend of truth and
lies being "an essential ingredient of a successful disinformation campaign."[39]
The KGB then enlisted the East German intelligence service, the Stasi, to push
the story using a respected East German scientist, Jakob Segal, who authored
a pamphlet lending legitimacy to the false narrative provided by the KGB.[40] In
1986, a document written by Segal that refuted the evidence that the African
continent was the origin of the HIV/AIDS virus was circulated at a non-aligned
nations conference in Harare, Zimbabwe. It met with a warm reception among
the 100 or so leaders from developing countries in Africa and elsewhere in at-
tendance. Segal's story that AIDS originated in a bioweapons lab in the United
States was picked up by other German authors in the East and West, and repeated relentlessly through the later 1980s by Soviet state media. Boghardt
reports that by 1986 a gay men's magazine in New York was openly calling for
congressional investigations; by late 1987, the story had run in eighty countries,
over 200 periodicals, and twenty-five languages,[41] with many publications, including the British *Sunday Express* and *Daily Telegraph*, reporting the story
without questioning it.

As the story spread, it became increasingly politicized. The KGB gradually
embellished the story with additional detail; one mistruth was that the United
States had developed the virus to help South Africa's apartheid regime eliminate non-whites. This was a dual-purpose attempt to attach the United States to
the unpopular South African regime of the time, as well as sow suspicion of the
US government among African Americans within the United States, a community increasingly hard hit by HIV/AIDS. Similar to more recent disinformation
campaigns, this was a strong display of the technique of targeting an existing
cleavage and injecting false information to exacerbate social tension and, as
much as possible, destabilize the political system. The KGB's "active measures"
regarding the HIV/AIDS story ended in 1988, as the virus began to spread more
widely within the Soviet Union itself. Needing collaboration with American
medical experts to combat the spread of the disease, Soviet experts disavowed
the claim that the United States had created the disease as part of its bioweapons
program.[42]

More than thirty years later, the lessons of Soviet "active measures" in the
HIV/AIDS story are particularly instructive, helping us understand not only
how disinformation campaigns operated in the Soviet past, but also tactics still
used by Putin's regime in the present. Although technology and social media

platforms have helped to advance disinformation more rapidly, the structure of such methods are strikingly similar. In particular, the Soviet technique of mixing false narratives with kernels of truth has been adopted by Russian practitioners of disinformation, while cyber tools that were not available to their Soviet predecessors enable them to quickly and precisely target their adversaries.

The coordinated blending of social media messaging with traditional media like RT and Sputnik to target an adversary was developed gradually, beginning in about 2008 with the Georgian war, perfected against Ukraine by 2014, and being masterfully unleashed against the United States in the presidential election of 2016. During the election cycle, many stories circulated with the intent of damaging the candidacy of Hillary Clinton. Among them was "Pizzagate," a story traced back to Russian trolls, which claimed that Clinton ran a pedophilia ring in the basement of Comet Ping Pong Pizza, a pizza restaurant popular with Democratic staffers. The Pizzagate story made its way through Reddit, 4chan, and Twitter, and was retweeted by Alex Jones, among others. It culminated when a twenty-eight-year-old man drove from North Carolina to Washington, DC, and appeared at the pizzeria bearing an AR-15 rifle, intending to investigate for himself and free the children if needed. Like the HIV/AIDS story three decades earlier, the Pizzagate story was false, but the way in which it made its way through fringe news sites and right-wing media demonstrated the heightened potency of disinformation campaigns in the age of the Internet.[43]

Russian cyber warriors, like those who promoted Pizzagate and other anti-Clinton narratives throughout the 2016 election cycle, engage tools of information disruption that complement the efforts of RT and Sputnik. They amplify and "launder" news stories through repetition, making the original source difficult to trace. The stories are picked up and repeated by "bots"—automated fake social media accounts on platforms such as Twitter—or trolls—fake personas and social media accounts staffed by actual people.[44] As these items "trend," they can be picked up by real Twitter users, unaware that the story may be fake, partially true, or an almost direct repetition of a Russian government talking point. Eventually, these witting or unwitting "useful idiots"—real people who have no idea that the story was created by agents of a foreign government to agitate and confuse the targeted population—may even come to believe the story (as evidently happened with Pizzagate), in part because it reinforces a negative perception they already have. As Keir Giles notes, Russian troll armies "interact directly with readers of media and in online discussion boards and therefore [act] as a force multiplier for driving home the Russian message."[45]

Creating stories and using social media to target vulnerable groups is one of several ways in which Russian actors have used cyber weapons. Other methods include denying access to the Internet to coerce or send a message to political leaders in other countries that Putin's regime would like to influence. This technique includes *distributed denial of service* (DDoS) attacks, which Russian hackers initiated as early as 2007 in Estonia and 2008 in Georgia, used repeatedly in 2015 and 2016 in Ukraine, and have continued regularly through the time of writing. The December 2015 Ukrainian DDoS attack temporarily shut down parts of the country's energy infrastructure in the dead of winter, affecting the electricity grid, transport, media, and financial infrastructure, and impacting hundreds of thousands of Ukrainians. The December 2016 attack was similar, but lasted less than an hour.[46] The point of such attacks is to destabilize the economic and political landscape and coerce political elites in the target country to stop efforts to integrate with the West and turn to Russia instead. They could also be intended to turn local populations against elites, replacing them with more pro-Russian regimes. If this was the goal in Ukraine, evidently it did not succeed.

Another popular technique—and one not exclusive to Russian hackers, of course—is that of the *phishing attack*, which Russian actors acting on behalf of the Putin regime used to steal and then reveal private information in 2016. Phishing involves sending an email that seems to be from a trusted source in order to get an unwitting user to click on an embedded link, which then creates an opening for a hacker to steal data or introduce malware into the user's system. This technique enabled Russian hackers to steal emails from John Podesta, the chairman of Hillary Clinton's presidential campaign, in April 2016. These emails were then released through the fake online personas DCLeaks and Guccifer 2.0, and eventually by WikiLeaks (which never identified exactly where the email dump came from), coinciding with the real scandal around Donald Trump's offensive remarks about women in the *Access Hollywood* tapes. In the case of the Podesta emails, this hack-and-dump tactic served to distract cyber conversations and mainstream media from focusing exclusively on the Trump story, thus potentially diluting its impact on the electorate, and led to an explosion of stories about the alleged scandals within the Clinton campaign. Such stories were further distributed by bots and trolls on Twitter, Facebook, and other social media platforms to embarrass Clinton and ultimately damage her campaign.

At about the same time, the Democratic Congressional Campaign Committee (DCCC) and the Democratic National Committee (DNC) were similarly infiltrated through phishing attacks. The DNC infiltration resulted in a dump of emails showing that DNC chairwoman Debbie Wasserman Schultz strongly favored Clinton in the primaries for the Democratic candidacy over Bernie Sanders. The release of this information was designed to inflame Sanders supporters and perhaps suppress Democratic voter turnout. That email dump resulted in Schultz's resignation as DNC chairwoman just prior to the Democratic National Convention that would officially nominate Clinton as the Party's candidate.[47]

While Russian hacking, phishing, disinformation, and other cyber tactics are perhaps most notorious surrounding the 2016 US presidential election, other countries have been similarly attacked. France and Germany in particular, as two leaders in the EU, have been targeted with malware and other campaigns by Russian sources. In May 2017, Emmanuel Macron's French presidential campaign was the victim of a hack-and-dump campaign later traced to Russian operatives, who sought to improve the chances of the Russian government's preferred candidate, the far-right populist-nationalist leader Marine Le Pen. As with the hack-and-dump operations in 2016 against the Clinton campaign, the DCCC, and the DNC, members of Macron's campaign team had been victims of phishing attacks that enabled malware to steal troves of email. Evidently, these were not juicy enough for the cyber espionage group to make public, and Macron's team claimed that several emails had been doctored with references to fake offshore bank accounts storing Macron's alleged ill-gotten millions. Still, these stories were picked up by bots and trolls and circulated on social media, and expanded by WikiLeaks dumps and stories on RT-France and Sputnik, to further amplify the narrative that Macron was corrupt. The hack-and-dump operation was executed within the forty-four-hour blackout period before French polls closed, during which candidates are not permitted to make public statements, making it harder for Macron to rebut the material. Nonetheless, he won the election with 66.1% of the vote, demonstrating that not all cyber-based information warfare operations succeed.[48]

Another phishing scheme targeted Germany in May 2015, inserting malware onto computers belonging to the German Bundestag (Parliament). This malware spread through the Bundestag's network, stealing passwords, grabbing a reported sixteen gigabytes of data from the mailboxes of Parliament members—as well as Chancellor Angela Merkel's—and eventually "rendering its online services and external website inaccessible."[49] Almost five years later, the German Federal Police identified the attack and data theft as having been orchestrated by a Russian hacker from Unit 26165 within Russian military intelligence (the GRU) known as APT 28 or "Fancy Bear." Fancy Bear was the same unit that would later be identified in the US special counsel's investigation, also known as the Mueller Report, as responsible for the hacking of the Democratic National Committee.[50]

These are only a few of many, many examples of Russia's sharp power projection, illustrating the extent to which Russian government agencies are involved in distorting the information environment of its perceived adversaries. The purchase of hundreds of inexpensive advertisements on Facebook and Twitter is another technique that Russian government–financed agencies employed in the 2016 US presidential elections. Russian operatives used fake personas on these platforms to amplify pro-Trump and anti-Clinton messages.[51]

Russian military intelligence is similarly involved in trolling on Western cyber platforms, sometimes in concert with "private" firms and sometimes in competition with them, as well as other branches of government and the military. Troll farms, like the well-known Internet Research Agency (IRA), work in the shadows on government-connected information operations. Officially, the IRA was privately owned by Putin crony Yevgeny Prigozhin and operated out of St. Petersburg. Like the GRU unit "Fancy Bear," the IRA was named in the Mueller Report as integral to the cyber operation aimed at the Clinton campaign and some of its employees specifically indicted by Mueller. It is one of many similar operations within Russia.

Beyond manufacturing bots and employing trolls to amplify and launder fake stories, as well as distributed denial of service and phishing attacks, Russian hackers have also managed to infiltrate state- and county-level American voting records and steal data.[52] There is no evidence that records were altered, but clear Russian footprints were left behind. The purpose of such cases may have been to investigate sensitive voting data or merely to demonstrate Russia's cyber capabilities to infiltrate, and may have been intended to threaten or warn the targets or prepare for an attack at some point in the future.

Generally, Russian strategies to alter information environments are employed in a triad. First, cyber actors attack information infrastructure, for example, through hacking or phishing attacks to get into an adversary's network to steal or manipulate information. Second, they focus on content, pursuing the goal of disrupting a narrative or planting messaging that is in Russian interests. Third, bots, trolls, and other online actors get others to pick up and perpetuate their targeted messaging, whether wittingly or unwittingly, so that it spreads through an adversary's information environment.[53] While these tactics have emerged in various forms, the far-reaching impact of Russia's sharp power tools has been made clear time and time again.

Soft, Sharp, and Hard: Russia's Hybrid Tactics

Under Putin's leadership, especially since 2012, Russia's confluence of soft, sharp, and hard tactics of power projection is an effective and dangerous combination. A variety of terms have been employed to describe the tactic, including "hybrid warfare"—the use of both violent and nonviolent means against an adversary. Such hybrid tactics operate in a "gray zone" between peace and conflict.[54] In particular, Russia's use of cyber and information technologies has clear military applications, and some analysts have pinpointed ways in which Russian information environments are coordinated with other forms of deception. The "Gerasimov Doctrine" is another term used to characterize the combination of information warfare, deception, and hard power. It is named for the Russian Chief of the General Staff of Russia's Armed Forces, General Valerii Gerasimov, who explained the usefulness of information as a weapon of warfare in a 2013 article. Neither term, however, is without controversy. Indeed, after coining the term "Gerasimov Doctrine," Mark Galeotti appears to have retracted his attribution of the idea of information technology in warfare to Gerasimov alone, and reconsidered its innovativeness as a part of Russia's military arsenal.[55] As for the term "hybrid warfare," leaders in the Russian military itself use this phrase not to refer to their own way of war, but to that of the United States and NATO. They describe their own mixed-use methods of violence and nonviolence as "nonlinear" or "asymmetric" warfare. Others inside the Russian military call these methods "active measures"—recycling the Soviet-era term—or "*spetsoperatsii*," special operations.[56]

Regardless of the term we apply, it is clear that Russian military leaders use information technology as a weapon in their arsenal just as they employ tanks, submarines, and bombs. The importance of information technology was even written into Russia's official Military Doctrine of 2010: "This Military Doctrine reflects the Russian Federation's adherence to the utilization of political, diplomatic, legal, economic, environmental, informational, military, and other instruments for the protection of the national interests of the Russian Federation and the interests of its allies."[57]

Clearly, for Russia's military leaders, information is increasingly crucial to the conduct of modern warfare. This is partly because hard power weapons have become more digitized and automated.[58] Given that advanced weapons systems depend on the secure flow of information, disrupting that flow with electromagnetic jamming can change the facts of war on the ground. The ability to plant malware to cause a malfunction, disrupt communications among troops and commanders, alter messages, or steal information on the battlefield are among many ways a modern military can gain a tactical advantage over an adversary.

While Western analysts and media often portray Russia as an unprovoked aggressor, especially in the realm of information warfare, Daniel Bagge notes that Russia sees its activities as defensive as much as offensive because it perceives that its adversaries use media to attack Russia in the same way.[59] Indeed, in the 2015 National Security Strategy, the Russian leadership noted the interconnectedness of its various tools of strategic deterrence:

> In order to order to provide strategic deterrence, to protect the sovereignty and territorial integrity of the Russian Federation, and to prevent military conflict, interconnected political military, military technical, diplomatic, economic, informational and other measures will be used.[60]

In Putin's Russia, we can conclude, the realm of information—bridging both soft and sharp power tactics—can be regarded as "a strategic asset reaching the significance of nuclear arsenals in the past—for the ability to alter strategic stability on a global scale."[61] Notably, this disruptive asset costs far less than most hard power investments, whether the development of a new nuclear weapon system or the reorganization of personnel under New Look. Yet aimed at the right target, soft and sharp power tools can be just as devastating. Beyond the impressive modernization of Russia's hard power capabilities and the adept maneuverability of its new and renewed soft and sharp power instruments, what is particularly notable about the confluence of these hybrid power resources is the willingness of Vladimir Putin's regime to use them. Chapter 8 explores why this has happened by examining the links between Russian domestic politics and its power projection abroad.

THE PURPOSES BEHIND RUSSIAN POWER PROJECTION ABROAD

The Domestic Determinants
of Russia's Resurrection

"The President is the guarantor of the Constitution, or simply put, the guar-
antor of the country's security, domestic stability and, as I said before, ev-
olutionary development—I repeat, evolutionary development, because we
have had enough revolutions. Russia has fulfilled its plan when it comes to
revolutions."[1]

—Vladimir Putin, March 10, 2020

In the thirty years following the collapse of the Soviet empire, as the preceding
chapters confirm, contemporary Russia has resurrected many instruments of
global power projection. It has not fully re-established the geographic domain of
power of the Soviet Union, but neither is it merely a local or regional power. Far
more than merely the hegemon in the former Soviet space alone, contemporary
Russia now has global reach in a variety of spheres.

In the global economy, Russia is now a significant actor—sometimes the most
significant actor—in a number of crucial sectors, including oil and gas (not only
in sales, but also control over crucial pipelines), nuclear energy, aluminum, grain,
precious metals, and the production and sale of conventional weapons, to name
only a few areas. It has become an international donor, after being a debtor only
a decade earlier. While the economy needs to diversify further, it has proven surprisingly resilient even under the extensive American and European sanctions
imposed in 2014. The leadership has built new trade relationships to get around
those economic penalties, and it has recovered time and again after successive
crises. Geopolitically, Russia's range has extended far beyond the former Soviet
space—into the Middle East and North Africa in part due to Putin's ongoing
support of Bashar al-Assad in Syria; the use of the military and mercenaries in
Libya; and the development of trade and strong diplomatic relationships with
Iran, Saudi Arabia, Egypt, and Israel. Russian militias have popped up in sub-
Saharan Africa to settle civil conflicts and help market precious metals (for a

fee), and the Russian footprint can be discerned in Europe, Latin America, and elsewhere, as well. The Russian military, too, has been reformed and revived into a professionalized force with a host of new conventional and nuclear weapons. It has gained combat experience and changed the facts on the ground in Syria, effectively edging the United States out of any future settlement of the conflict. Finally, under Vladimir Putin's rule, Russia has used its soft and formidable sharp power resources to covertly and overtly influence elites and societies across the globe, especially in the United States and Europe.

To be sure, despite these areas of recovery, Putin's Russia continues to face serious developmental challenges, including the need to open and expand its economy and to address lingering societal and demographic challenges. Its population growth teeters between flat and slightly positive; life expectancy has improved, but still falls considerably below the OECD average. The healthcare system, as highlighted by the Covid-19 crisis of 2020, is uneven at best.

Yet Russia's policy weight in key sectors of the global economy; its extended geographic domain of influence; and the military, soft, and sharp means of power its leadership has used willingly and relentlessly in recent years indicate that, as Vladimir Putin noted in the 2002 quotation that started chapter 1: "Russia is never as weak as she looks." Indeed, conceptualizing Russian power projection abroad across various dimensions demonstrates that Russia is not merely playing a weak hand well; rather, it has some strong cards to play. Even with an uneven hand, however, the ways in which Russian power has been employed, and the willingness of the political regime under Vladimir Putin to be disruptive and assertive in international politics, has contributed to Russia's resurrection as a global power. Clearly, Russian power resources do not have to be the best in the world across all three dimensions of geographic domain, policy scope, and material means examined in this study; they can have ample effect in shaping a new global order if they are merely "good enough" when combined with the *desire* and *ability* of Russian leaders to use what they have. The United States, despite the superior strength of its economy, conventional military, and size of its population, was utterly unable (or unwilling) to challenge meaningfully Russian action in Ukraine in 2014, or Syria in 2015. The U.S. has "more" than Russia on virtually every dimension of power, yet its polarized political system at times renders it unable or unwilling to use it.

The broader conceptualization of power that I have adopted in this study, then, underscores the fact that contemporary conflicts are no longer determined by the size of a country's military, population, or wealth alone, but, as James Scherr writes, "by the conversion of national attributes (moral and material) into useable power."[2] Contemporary Russia's *useable* power resources are indeed considerable and appear at least sufficient for the purposes of its current leadership.

Russian Power and Its Purposes

But what are the purposes of the contemporary Russian regime's increasingly formidable and functional power? To answer this question, we must shift focus and look within Russia, and in particular at state-society relations. In doing so, I argue that power projection abroad—especially after 2012 and Putin's return to the Kremlin—has become necessary to maintain regime support at home. A focus on regime politics draws attention to the fact that there is something distinctive—and not inevitable—about the strategic and tactical choices behind contemporary Russian power projection. In other words, Russia's resurrection in global politics is not determined by the calculus of great power realpolitik alone. Rather, it is influenced as much or more by domestic political exigencies. The regime that has developed under Putin has become highly dependent on the need for social stability to undergird a "patronal" autocratic political economy in which access to the state and its resources are shared among a small group of elites.[3] It is a system with Putin at the apex of a pyramid of relations among a coterie of close associates whose control over Russian state resources revolves around self-enrichment. The purpose of Russian power abroad, then, is as much to support this system as it is to defend or assert Russian national interests. While it is too easy to conflate Russian national interests with the narrow interests of Putin's patronal autocratic regime, both purposes are key in understanding Russia's projection of power in the twenty-first century.

This argument contrasts with other explanations of Russia's resurgence in international politics. One popular explanation views Russian power projection under Putin as essentially reactive to provocations against Russia by the United States and Europe, such as NATO and EU expansion toward Russian borders. From this standpoint, the international system is essentially a war of all against all, and peace in the international system comes about only when power among states is in a balanced equilibrium. Thus, there is every incentive for states to maximize power. This realist perspective on international relations is dependent on the realist definition of power (described in chapter 1), which narrowly focuses on means—specifically "men, military, and money." The greater a state's means, the greater its influence relative to other states in the international system. Changes in the balance of power among states cause conflict, so for most realists, domestic political considerations are important only to the extent that they may alter a state's available means of power (the size of its military, strength of its economy, and size of the population). The key strategic goal of power maximization, however, remains the same.

But just as a traditional realist approach has often led to an underestimation of Russian power, it also leads to a misspecification regarding the purpose of

Russian power projection. Although realist arguments on the reasons for Russia's resurrection in global politics do shed some light on what might motivate Russian power projection, I argue that these explanations are ultimately unsatisfactory for two reasons. First, they imply that any Russian regime would make the same decisions faced with the same conditions in twenty-first-century global politics. Second, they ignore the fact that following the collapse of the Soviet Union, Russia became increasingly integrated into international institutions such as the WTO, G-8 nations, and Council of Europe, and until 2014, was set to join the OECD.[4] As such, post-communist Russia's relations with the West were not always adversarial. It follows, therefore, that domestic factors might better explain why Russian power projection abroad appears to have changed, after 2012 in particular. After examining these realist arguments verses domestic political motivations, I conclude with a discussion of why the West and Russia need not be inevitable adversaries in a new "cold war."

The Realist Explanation of the Purposes of Russian Power—What's Wrong with This Picture?

The West on Offense, Russia on Defense

A particularly prominent realist argument, represented by John Mearsheimer and Stephan Walt, among others, explains Russia's exercise of power abroad as primarily reactive to perceived challenges to its sovereignty and authority by other states.[5] In this view, Russia has been provoked by the West into defending itself and its historical sphere of influence, most notably by the incursion of NATO and the EU into Ukraine, Georgia, and the Baltic States. For Walt, "relations with Russia deteriorated largely because the United States repeatedly ignored Russian warnings and threatened Moscow's vital interests."[6] In other words, the apparent threat to infiltrate the buffer states of the former Eastern Bloc has made it inevitable that "Russia" (led presumably under a democratic system or not) would react eventually.

By this logic, it would not matter what kind of regime ruled Russia— communists, democrats, or an autocrat—because any leader would recognize that Russia's national security has always depended on its unchallenged control of this geographic region. Proponents of this perspective perceive the EU's plans to incorporate Ukraine in 2013 and 2014 as unnecessarily provocative, making it the "West's fault" that Putin's Russia annexed Crimea and has kept Ukraine's eastern border unstable since 2014. As Mearsheimer writes, "No Russian leader would tolerate a military alliance that was Moscow's mortal enemy until recently, moving into Ukraine. Nor would any Russian leader stand idly by while the West helped install a government there that was determined to integrate Ukraine into the West."[7]

Notable in this explanation of Russian government actions, specifically regarding Ukraine in 2014 onward, is a lack of agency on the part of Ukrainians. The assumption is that they were unwitting pawns in a struggle between two great powers—not a sovereign state with an elected government, but a piece of property condemned to being a perpetual battleground between two powerful adversaries. It was this way in the imperial period, in the Soviet period, and so is not surprising now: "Geopolitics 101: great powers are sensitive to potential threats."[8] In the ongoing game of great power politics, other countries are consigned to the role of chess pieces. Observing American-Russian relations in 2018, Walt declared, "Great power competition had returned with a vengeance."[9]

These kinds of explanations also paint a picture of Russian power projection in the twenty-first century as following a long historical arc, stemming from the invasion of Kyivan Rus' by the Mongol Horde in the thirteenth century through Hitler's invasion of the Soviet Union in the twentieth. In other words, contemporary Russia's foreign policy follows a long lineage of defensive reaction to the incursions of other states. By this account, Russia's geography—its size and the number of borders shared with other states—has helped generate an enduring and seemingly inevitable wariness of foreign invasion among its leaders.[10] In the imperial period, foreign policy was driven by the clash between Russia and other empires over territory and resources. This meant constant wars against the Swedish Empire, Austro-Hungarians, Ottomans, Persians, occasionally the British Empire, and, of course, Napoleon's armies in 1812. The Russian and Japanese empires clashed in the east in the early twentieth century, and Operation Barbarossa brought Hitler's forces smashing through the Soviet Union's western borders right to the gates of Moscow and Leningrad during World War II. By this version of events, Russia has always been under siege by one foreign invader or another, and its contemporary power projection abroad under Putin's leadership should be understood as purely reactive to other powers and a result of inherent security vulnerabilities. As Bobo Lo claims, "geography has nourished a security outlook dominated by threat perceptions and geopolitical calculus."[11] Historian Stephen Kotkin argues that "Russia's foreign policy orientation, in other words, is as much a condition as a choice."[12] With this historical trajectory in mind, in the twenty-first century, the West should not "fear Russia," but should not provoke it either.[13] According to this account, the Russian seizure of Crimea in 2014 was a predictable (and justifiable) reassertion of Russian interests in a traditional zone of influence, and the leader of any "great" power would have done the same. As Mearsheimer writes, "The West's triple package of policies—NATO enlargement, EU expansion, and democracy promotion—added fuel to a fire waiting to ignite."[14]

Within Russia itself, a similar realpolitik narrative prevails. The notion of Russia's need to defend itself against persistent Western aggression is based on a perception of accumulated grievances since the purportedly harsh settlement of the Cold War. Some leading Russian analysts of international affairs have used the metaphor of Germany's reaction to the Treaty of Versailles between the first and second world wars in justifying Russia's annexation of Crimea as a "natural" reaction to Western provocations:

> The West's approach to Moscow objectively was a mild version of the Versailles policy even though this was never stated openly as a goal, and most politicians in Europe probably did not even suspect that. There were no scoffing, annexations, or contributions, but there was a policy of "victors," who consistently drove the "defeated party" to bay, seeking to control its economic, political, and military interests. However, Russians did not feel defeated and the policy of NATO expansion engendered the Weimar Syndrome.[15]

Other influential Russian commentators have picked up the grievance narrative to justify Russia's aggression in Ukraine: "The US treated Russia as if it were a loser country, although it was Russia that put an end to the Soviet empire and the Cold War."[16]

These analysts paint a picture of the United States as villain and Russia as victim in the 1990s. According to this view, Russia's economic chaos was exacerbated by malevolent or incompetent advisors from the United States, and harsh terms imposed by the American-dominated International Monetary Fund and unforgiving Paris Club. NATO took advantage of Russia's temporary military weakness to bomb Russia's Serbian allies in 1999, and as though that were not provocative enough, according to Putin, "then, they hit Afghanistan, Iraq, and frankly violated the UN Security Council resolution on Libya, when instead of imposing the so-called no-fly zone over it they started bombing it too."[17] The perception that the United States and NATO were out to absorb Russia's sphere of influence was heightened by the series of color revolutions, seen as American-inspired and -controlled, including in Serbia in 2000, Georgia in 2003, and Ukraine in 2004. By 2011, the West was evidently behind the popular uprisings that swept the Middle East and overturned dictatorships in Egypt, Tunisia, and Libya, and threatened the Assad regime in Syria, creating continued instability in the region that turned the "the Arab Spring . . . into the Arab Winter."[18] The deployment of missile defense systems in Poland, the Czech Republic (abandoned by the United States initially in 2009, but replaced with new systems in 2016 in Poland and Romania), despite being intended to protect European targets from Iran—were seen by Putin's regime as violating Russia's "traditional sphere of influence."[19] A complaint that surfaced intermittently too was NATO's expansion into formerly communist Eastern Europe, contradicting Russian claims of American promises to Gorbachev not to go farther East.[20]

From this perspective, Russia has been the eternal target of the aggressive and dishonest West. While the United States inflicted disorder across the globe, Russia was duped and its interests disregarded. Putin has argued that, despite America's global rampage, "Russia strived to engage in dialogue with our colleagues in the West. We are constantly proposing cooperation on all key issues; we want to strengthen our level of trust and for our relations to be equal, open and fair. But we saw no reciprocal steps."[21] Eventually, Russian patience snapped, starting with Ukraine in 2014. Putin justified the annexation of Crimea to Russian lawmakers that March by referring to the gamut of past mistreatment by the West, insisting:

> They are constantly trying to sweep us into a corner because we have an independent position, because we maintain it and because we call things like they are and do not engage in hypocrisy. But there is a limit to everything. And with Ukraine, our western partners have crossed the line, playing the bear and acting irresponsibly and unprofessionally.[22]

From this perspective, the mobilization of Ukrainians on the streets of Kyiv was nothing more than a product of Western manipulation and democracy promotion efforts, orchestrated not by the protesters themselves, but by such agencies as the CIA, US Department of State, and National Endowment for Democracy.[23] And, far from helping sovereign, formerly communist countries turn their economies around, Putin saw Europe seeking to promote its own interests yet again, *against* Russia:

> [I]n the framework of the EU Eastern Partnership Program there have been attempts to tear states which had been parts of the former USSR off Russia and to prompt them to make an artificial choice between Russia and Europe. The Ukrainian crisis has become a high point of these negative trends. We repeatedly warned the USA and its western allies about harmful consequences of their interference in Ukrainian domestic affairs but they did not listen to our opinion.[24]

In sum, this realist argument boils down to three main complaints:

1. In a world divided into spheres of historical influence, each dominated by one great power or another, Russia's traditional control over buffer states has been unjustly and overtly challenged by unchecked, unified foreign aggressors.

2. Russia has been ignored, not dealt with as an "equal" partner, and lied to repeatedly by the United States and the EU.
3. The inevitable cycle of Russian history, by 2014, had completed another
   revolution.

This national grievance narrative, however, and the parallel to the German
Weimar Republic, are fundamentally flawed. First, there was no treaty to
end the Cold War, as the Versailles Treaty ended World War I, and no harsh
postwar terms *imposed* on Russia following the Soviet Union's collapse. In
fact, as documented in chapter 1, the United States and Russia constructively
cooperated to the benefit of both in the late 1980s as they negotiated arms control and reduction treaties under Presidents Reagan and Gorbachev. There was
also cooperation on trade and financial assistance in the 1990s under George
Bush, Bill Clinton, and Boris Yeltsin; on the fight against global terrorism early
in the presidencies of both George W. Bush and Vladimir Putin; and agreements
on trade and security between Barack Obama and Dmitri Medvedev between
2008 and 2012. NATO expansion had stopped in 2009 following the accessions
of Albania and Croatia—neither of which were former republics of the Soviet
Union—so by 2014, when Russia annexed Crimea, a full five years had passed
since any state had joined NATO. Further, NATO membership was not part of
the EU's accession agreement with Kyiv in November 2013, when the Euro-
Maidan demonstrations began. Indeed, it was not a politically palatable subject
within Ukraine at that time and had not been for a number of years.[25]

Second, the West did *not* sabotage the Russian economy by saddling it with
a post–Cold War "settlement" designed to keep a defeated Russia down. Unlike
Weimar Germany, post–Cold War Russia rose from the ashes of the failed political and economic system of communism. Communist leaders were not tossed
out as a byproduct of military defeat; they were replaced, in many cases by their
own citizens, through open elections, and some became democratic presidents
of independent states. Political and economic systems were not reordered based
on settlement terms in a treaty, and Russia, as the Soviet successor state, was not
stripped of its military power or punished under a heavy debt load imposed by
Cold War victors (indeed, some debts were forgiven, but most were paid off by
the mid-2000s). The extent of Russia's resurgence, and its cooperation and relatively cordial relations with the West, especially prior to Putin's return to the
Kremlin in 2012, clearly show the shortcomings of the argument that the West
was "out to get" Russia.

Western actors cooperated with and supported Russia on a number of fronts
following the Soviet collapse. In the economic sphere, Germany and the United
Kingdom, among others, were huge investors in Russia from the early 1990s.
Recall that the United States supported Russia's entry into the G-8 in 1998,

even though its economy was in no way one of the world's biggest, and also strongly supported Russia's application to join the WTO in 2012 (it was Putin who slowed that process previously). Regarding military cooperation, Russia was invited into the NATO Partnership for Peace; cooperated with the United States in getting troops and supplies into Afghanistan; signed the JCPOA regarding Iran's nuclear program with the United States, Germany, and the UK; and, notably, signed the New START strategic arms control agreement with the United States in 2011. Moreover, far from ignoring Vladimir Putin's complaints regarding US behavior abroad in his 2007 Munich speech, the Obama administration responded with a policy of "reset" in 2009 to address, in Obama's words, the "dangerous drift" in US-Russian relations.[26]

While realists typically paint the United States as constantly undermining Russian power and interests, the reset of their bilateral relations between 2009 and 2012 was generally successful, as the United States and Russia reestablished cooperation on the national security issues noted earlier and established other new mechanisms of collaboration, including a bilateral presidential commission with sixteen working groups on space, health, nuclear energy, sports, culture, civil society, and even intelligence sharing. Military-to-military cooperation included anti-terrorism work and anti-piracy operations off the Somalian coast. Trade and investment by US companies increased in aerospace industries, food manufacturing, and oil and gas exploration. In the area of high technology, the American semiconductor giant Cisco Systems pledged $1 billion over ten years for projects at the Russian innovation center, Skolkovo. Finally, a bilateral visa regime was instituted that made it easier and faster for Russians to obtain long-term visas to the United States, and for Americans to get multi-year, multi-entry visas to Russia.[27]

Most of these developments took place under Dmitri Medvedev's presidency and the "reset." Upon leaving office in the spring of 2012, Medvedev personally thanked President Obama for their work together:

> And of course, Barack, I would like to take the opportunity to say how much I enjoyed the cooperation we had with you. And I believe that it really was the highlight of the previous years. And due to the high level of cooperation, we managed to resolve various complicated issues bilaterally. . . . And I hope that the same high level of our relations will remain between the United States of America and the Russian Federation when the new President steps in office.[28]

After Medvedev left office, economic ties and international events show that relations between Russia and the West remained at least cordial. In 2013, Rosneft and the American oil company Exxon Mobil signed a series of agreements valued at roughly $500 billion to explore oil and natural deposits—reserves of an estimated 12.3 billion tons of oil and 15.2 trillion cubic meters of gas—in the Russian Arctic, Siberia, and the Black Sea.[29] When President Putin hosted the Sochi Olympic Games in February 2014, mere weeks before the escalation of conflict in Ukraine and annexation of Crimea, Russia appeared to be a modern, stable country on the upswing—hardly the story of the Weimar Republic in interwar Germany. As chapters 5 and 6 demonstrated, Russia's people were richer, healthier, and wealthier than they had ever been in the country's history.

This is far from an exhaustive list of areas of collaboration and cooperation, but it is sufficient to demonstrate that the West was not trying to kick Russia to the mat and hold it down; they had been partners. There were serious disagreements, but there was little reason for Russia to fear the West, nor the West, for that matter, to fear Russia.[30] The so-called realpolitik perspective, then, ignores the reality that policy decisions are not historically and geographically predetermined. It was not inevitable that any Russian regime would react to a social uprising in Ukraine by invading and annexing part of its territory, especially given the context of years of cooperation and integration with Europe and the United States that preceded Russia's invasion.

Given all this, it is difficult to understand the Crimean annexation as a successful defense of Russia's national interests. To present a counterfactual, had the regime under Vladimir Putin's leadership not annexed Crimea and maintained a low-boil conflict in Eastern Ukraine for years afterward, then Russia would likely not have faced years of economic sanction from Europe and the United States. If anything, the invasion of Ukrainian territory made Russia less secure, not more: its neighbors became more interested in joining the EU and NATO than ever, and NATO responded to the annexation by creating a Very High Readiness Joint Task Force (VJTF) with a rotating contingent of about 20,000 NATO troops deployed in the Baltic republics and Poland, designed to quickly respond to any further incursions from Russia.[31] Given these details of cooperation giving way to renewed conflict, the realist argument that Russia has been playing defense to the West's offense quickly loses credibility.

Russia on Offense?

A second argument sees Russia's projection of power abroad as aggressive rather than defensive. In this argument, Russia under Putin—characterized as an evil but strategic genius—is seeking to re-establish its place within the global balance of power. Now that Russia has recovered from the shock of communism's collapse, which led to that balance tipping in the West's favor, the resurgent state is challenging the United States and Europe to regain its proper place in the international system as a "great power." To simply restore the balance, however, is not enough: as US General Breedlove testified in the House Arms Services Committee in February 2016, "Russia does not want to challenge the agreed rules of the international order. It wants to rewrite them."[32]

This line of argumentation posits that a reinvigorated Russia has naturally—and again, inevitably—become more assertive in its power projection abroad, largely due to the objective of regaining the status it lost with the fall of the Soviet Union. For Walter Russell Mead, Russia, along with China and Iran, did not accept the settlement of the global order that followed the Cold War, and they are now trying to revise it.[33] Mead insists that "Russia wants to reassemble as much of the Soviet Union as it can," regaining its former status, sphere of influence, and place as a leader in the international system.[34] Russian policy, therefore, is not purely defensive; it challenges the current status quo with the aim of establishing a new global order in which Russia will once again be indispensable, exceptional, and the overlord of its own Eurasian sphere of influence.[35] Whether Russia is a rising or declining power is not as important as the idea of changing the balance of power, and with the perception of the United States as fading hegemon, China—and now, evidently, Russia—are emerging as revisionist powers with their own interests and spheres of influence.

Regardless of whether one sees Russia as acting in self-defense or on offense, the logic of realpolitik suggests that *any regime type* in Russia, whether a monarchy, democracy, or autocracy, would behave the same way in seeking to project power abroad. According to both perspectives, the *individual leaders* in any type of political regime matter far less than national interests, which have been defined largely by history and geography. In this sense, while the manner in which Russian interests have been pursued after 2012 has changed, the goals of great power politics have remained constant.[36] The preferences of other states caught in between (like Ukraine) are either overlooked or deemed unimportant: they are mere objects over which great powers fight in a strategic game of global domination. As well as explaining Russia's use of hard power as in line with the assertiveness due to a great power, this argument contextualizes Russia's use of sharp power during the 2016 elections as an attempt to destabilize the United States—if relations between them are a zero-sum game, an American loss is a Russian win. With a divided and weak United States, Russia will be left alone to thrive.

But is realpolitik the only purpose of Russian power? While aspects of so-called great power geopolitics, as Robert Legvold says, "may offer some broad insight into the context within which the confrontation is unfolding . . . [they] explain little of the dynamic within this confrontation."[37] Indeed, the realist approach overlooks the influence of Russian internal politics on how its power resources are used abroad. In other words, the purposes of Russian power projection abroad may be as much endogenous as exogenous.

While a lens of geography, national history, and culture may contribute to how different leaders determine what is in the national interest, precisely how key interests are pursued depends on the nature of the domestic political regime. In considering the role of regime politics, it is tempting to focus on leadership alone—in this case, that of Vladimir Putin. Indeed, there is much scholarship on Vladimir Putin's background that provides insight into his worldview, which is merited given how centralized the political system has become during his primacy in Russian politics since 2000. No doubt, understanding how he thinks and what his priorities may be is important in divining a Russian "grand strategy." Still although Putin is tremendously influential to the nation's political system, he does not completely control it. We must, therefore, also consider how the political milieu in which Putin operates might influence Russian power projection across borders.

From the Soviet period, we know that ideology at times defined Soviet strategy on power projection abroad—communism was inherently expansionist, not strictly defensive.[38] It was spreading an ideology "scientifically derived" to end the exploitation of man by man, after all. Soviet grand strategy was not (at least initially) aimed at realpolitik; it was aimed at the emancipation of the proletariat from mistreatment by capitalists worldwide. The type of regime that ruled *mattered* in determining the purpose of its power abroad. The extent to which the regime was over-institutionalized also impacted the degree of risk its leadership was willing to undertake in its foreign policy, as institutional constraints like the Politburo prevented general secretaries after Stalin from making rash decisions. Communist leaders resisted direct military confrontations, ensuring that the Cold War with the West remained cold and fought through proxies. In contemporary Russia, however, few institutional constraints exist to prevent the president from making dangerous decisions; informal norms instead govern the system. Nor do the regime's decisions reflect a greater ideological purpose, a new model of human development, or even perhaps the national interest. Their primary role, rather, is to serve the patronalist autocratic regime over which Putin presides.

Patronal Regime Politics and the Purposes of Russian Power

From 1991 to the start of Putin's fourth term as president in 2018, Russia transitioned from an unsteady quasi-democracy to a highly personalized autocracy—as Steven Fish characterizes it, "the gold standard for contemporary autocracies."[39] A parade of terminology to capture the spirit of "Putinism" has evolved over time from "managed" democracy early in his second term; followed by "competitive authoritarianism" with a political economy of "cronyism" and "kleptocracy"; and eventually, post-2012, a "personalistic, autocratic, conservative, populism," or simply a "dictatorship."[40] In common among these labels is the idea that formal institutions of competitive politics exist—like political parties, parliaments, and elections—but they do not determine the true distribution of power, instead merely endorsing and legitimizing decisions from above. Electoral outcomes are not left to chance; indeed, after twenty years of Putin in power, perhaps the only surprise about Russian elections is that they have taken place at all. Moreover, courts are not free to decide cases of any great importance independently; property rights and rule of law have become flexible and negotiable.

Clearly, this system of domestic politics has implications for understanding contemporary Russian behavior in the global order of the twenty-first century.[41] That Russia has devolved into an autocracy is not in doubt: a highly centralized, increasingly personalistic, *patronal* system of governance and political economy. Patronal systems are defined not by formal institutions, but as a "politics of individual reward and punishment,"[42] in which power is distributed through patron-client networks. In the Russian case, Vladimir Putin sits at the apex of a pyramidal network composed of elite relationships that divide state resources among themselves and control who gets what. Further, as Henry Hale argues, "ultimate power in patronalistic societies can be used not only to push for policies one supports, but also to direct favors to allies and to target opponents for punishment."[43] But this system is inherently fragile. Its main vulnerability is at the summit of power—if the leader were to change, then the value of networks and elites' access to state resources might decline or even disappear. Thus, those in power have every incentive to maintain the status quo. This requires the support of clients within the network and a steady flow of favors from patrons to supporters, with a share of financial rewards flowing back to patrons.

But patronal systems also require stability within elite groups *and* within society more broadly; instability caused by social mobilization against the inequalities of wealth and access to state resources generated by patronalism is its biggest potential threat. Thus, Putin views his role as Russia's president as making him its "guarantor of social stability and evolutionary development," as he explains in the quotation that opened this chapter. Development must be *evolutionary* to pacify society, but not revolutionary—because serious social protest would threaten the regime's very existence.

The popularity of the autocrat (in patronal autocracies, the biggest patron in the system) is a valuable and important power resource, as Samuel Greene and Graeme Robertson have also noted.[44] There is ample evidence that autocrats are sensitive to public opinion, and Putin is purportedly an avid consumer of his own polling data.[45] If public approval is in a sense genuine—whether encouraged by ideology, a cult of personality, state-controlled messaging through the media, or a combination thereof—then social control is easy to maintain. (Stalin's funeral witnessed outpourings of true loss and hysterical devotion from the Soviet people, after all.) While the use of force and selective application of the law against any opposition to the regime are other available tools, the Russian regime is aware that social support is equally important, and ultimately more effective. After all, the fates of Egypt's Hosni Mubarak, or Libya's Muamar Gaddafi following the Arab Spring of 2011, can attest to the fact that even autocrats with the seemingly unfettered ability to use state-sponsored violence to impose their wills on the people can be overthrown by their own societies.

Within contemporary Russia, despite the concentration of power within Putin's hands, there are still many good examples of his autocratic regime adapting to demands from Russian society—even changing policies that provoked street demonstrations. Two notable examples are the 2005 social benefits reform and the 2018 pension reform. In the former, the federal government was attempting to eradicate social subsidies like free public transportation, subsidized housing, prescriptions, and telephone services for millions of veterans, retirees, and people with disabilities, instead providing those eligible with a small monthly cash payment—which was slow to arrive and insufficient to cover the costs of the previous benefits. Facing widespread street protests led by the elderly and disabled, Putin appeared on television to make modifications that softened the program's effects.[46] Similarly, in 2018, tens of thousands of protesters rallied to oppose a law that would raise the federal pension age for men and women, as described in chapter 6. Again, the regime retreated and the law was modified (though not eradicated) in an attempt to quell social unrest. Although the reforms were altered but not eliminated in both cases, it is significant that the regime was compelled to substantially scale back the original versions of the policies due to street protests across the country. Putin's popularity, too, was damaged: in 2018, it dropped fifteen percentage points between April (82% approval) and August (67% approval), a time punctuated by street demonstrations against various regime policies nationwide. The irony of the Putinist autocracy, then, is that despite its outwardly strong and repressive appearance, its durability is still hostage to a notable degree of public approval. This contradiction has played a key role in the consolidation of autocracy under Putin's leadership.

Tightening Autocracy and the Domestic Purposes of Power

Domestic politics underwent a dramatic change beginning with Putin's return to the Kremlin in 2012, and with that change came a shift in the purposes of how

Russian power is used abroad. As Russia's autocracy became more entrenched, the system not only became more repressive, but also more willing to use its power abroad. How did this happen? Answering this question takes us to the economic boom of Putin's first two terms, but has roots even earlier.

With the collapse of the global economy in 2008 and 2009, and the fact that Russia was not subsequently able to regain the high growth rates of the preceding period, Russia's leadership could no longer rely on the growing economy as a source of social legitimacy. Announcing his return to the presidency in the autumn of 2011, Putin was met not by popular enthusiasm, but by huge social protests against him that continued past his inauguration in 2012. On the streets were precisely those sectors of society that had most benefited from Russia's recent economic growth—middle-class urbanites. As Seymour Martin Lipset's modernization theory would have predicted, following a notable improvement in material circumstances, here were members of the country's emergent middle class, filling the avenues of Russia's largest cities to demand open politics and "Russia without Putin."[47] It is precisely this kind of challenge that a patronalist system cannot tolerate. The economy can modernize—to a certain extent— but people cannot be permitted to mobilize against the regime.[48] Social protest against the regime is deemed an existential threat; the Russian "street" is thus far more threatening to Putin's patronalist autocracy than NATO or the EU.

In response, a new phase of autocratization began soon after Putin took up residence again in the Kremlin in the spring of 2012. First, as his approval ratings declined, mechanisms of greater social repression were introduced. One major change targeted non-governmental organizations, as the laws regulating them were amended to require NGOs that were involved in political activities and accepting money from abroad to re-register with the Ministry of Justice as "foreign agents"—a politically charged term from the Soviet era associated with espionage. Since there were few alternative funding sources for many Russian NGOs, especially those whose activity was focused on protecting human rights and freedoms from abuse by the state, this would effectively cause their closure. In addition, the rule of law came down hard on protesters who had taken to the streets to oppose Putin's return to the presidency. Accused of inciting violence, many young people who had been victims of the police were given long jail sentences. The leaders of Russia's relatively small liberal opposition were frequently jailed for legally demonstrating.

It was not by chance that the Kremlin grew increasingly assertive in its foreign relations at the same time that politics at home were becoming more repressive. No longer able to rely on economic growth to ensure social compliance, the regime sought a new legitimacy story. It was a narrative that would lean on the historical mythology of a Russia again under siege, coupled with an appeal to

Orthodox nationalist sentiments to protect Russian society from the aggressions of an overly permissive, liberal West.

This marked a departure from the implicit social contract that had developed between the people and the emerging autocracy under Putin in his first two terms: "You tolerate a rollback of rights and freedoms of the 1990s and I will ensure that the country is stable and the economy is growing." In the early 2000s, Putin's regime legitimacy initially came from the contrast between leaders, with Putin a younger, seemingly more capable and decisive president than the elderly and ill Boris Yeltsin. This legitimacy grew as revenues from the rise in global oil prices pumped money through the economy, especially during the tremendous economic boom between 2003 and 2008, and Russian standards of living increased. At the same time, freedoms of the press, speech, and association, as well as rule of law, steadily declined, without much in the way of popular opposition.

The winnowing of the already weak representative institutions that had existed under Yeltsin began not long after Putin's first term as president in 2000. Indeed, the methodical approach to disassembling the checks on the state's control over society during Putin's first administration reads like an autocrat's "playbook" on how to undermine institutions of democracy and accountability. The first target was the Russian media. In the 1990s, formerly Soviet state-owned TV channels and newspapers were bought up by a small group of wealthy businessmen—the original Russian oligarchs described in chapter 4, who had made their money through the vagaries of the privatization process. Most prominently, Boris Berezovsky and Vladimir Gusinsky created huge media conglomerates, and naturally used their positions to influence the editorial line and ideally bend state policy in their favor as a result. Shortly after Vladimir Putin's rise to the presidency, both oligarchs—who, in Putin's estimation, had become far too influential over Russian politics and the economy—were forced to leave their positions in the face of state investigations, enabling Putin's new administration to establish control of the traditional media, thus gaining control over the flow of information and messaging to the Russian public.

The second step in dismantling competitive politics targeted political pluralism by establishing the supremacy of a ruling party that would tame the Duma, Russia's lower house of parliament. Although the Russian constitution grants the executive branch extraordinary powers relative to the legislative branch,[49] Yeltsin faced stiff opposition throughout his presidency, even from the new Duma that he created in 1993, which effectively held the executive branch in check. This would not be the case under Putin, whose party of choice—initially known as Unity, but renamed United Russia by 2004—managed to dominate the Duma, rendering it largely irrelevant as an alternative locus of political influence to the Kremlin. This was a significant move, since patronal regimes cannot survive and thrive when there are too many competing sources of power. In the early to mid-2000s, opposition parties were systematically undermined and other forms of political accountability eroded through, for example, the creation of administrative hurdles for opposition candidates to register in local and federal elections; unequal access to the media for approved versus opposition candidates; and the cooptation of parties remaining in the legislature such as the LDPR and CPRF. When deemed necessary to ensure a win, there has also been outright fraud in favor of United Russia at the polls.[50]

The third step in the dissolution of popularly accountable government was to eradicate the patchwork system of Russian federalism that had evolved under Yeltsin. In the 1990s, powerful elected governors had wrestled preferential tax arrangements and other special privileges from Yeltsin's administration. With Putin's ascent to the presidency, Federal Districts were put in place as a new layer of central bureaucracy to prevent governors from dealing directly with the president and his administration, thus blocking their efforts to cut special deals for their regions. Further, governors would no longer be members of the upper house of parliament, the Federation Council, which they had often held hostage to their agendas. Instead, the presidential administration would appoint full-time "senators" in consultation with regional legislatures and governors. In practice, the senators became more dependent on the Kremlin than on the regions they were appointed to represent. The final blow to Russian federalism involved the selection process of governors themselves. The pretext was a 2004 domestic terrorist attack in the southern Caucasus town of Beslan that was badly handled by local authorities, tragically resulting in the deaths of hundreds of children and their parents. Based on this mismanagement (or at least using it as a pretext), local governors would no longer be elected; they, too, would be appointed by the presidential administration as part of the regime's "vertical of power."

In parallel with derailing Russia's already flagging democratic development, Putin also assumed the task of rearranging the economy to construct a patronal system of control over state resources. The oligarchs of the 1990s were told that the rules by which business had influenced politics were changing under Putin's administration: if they stayed out of politics, then the state would stay out of their businesses.[51] It was too late for Gusinsky, one of the top media magnates, but others got the message and managed to survive with their businesses largely intact, or fled abroad while they could.[52] The wealthiest among them, Mikhail Khodorkovsky, however, continued to finance opposition parties and civil society organizations, in addition to owning some of the jewels of the Russian economy. He was taken down by the regime's selective application of the law in 2003, when he was charged with tax evasion, fraud, and embezzlement. The state quickly dismantled his Yukos empire and repossessed most of the rest of his businesses, including oil and gas holdings, banks, and media. His ten-year sentence to a Siberian labor colony served as an example to others: fail to comply with the unofficial rules of the new regime and lose everything.[53]

Putin's taming the oligarchs of the 1990s proved to be a very popular move within Russian society. Most average Russians felt little sympathy for Khodorkovsky, Gusinsky, and Berezovsky, for example, who had made billions while most of the rest of society suffered the full financial brunt of the collapse of communism and Yeltsin's uneven reforms. On the back of this strike against the oligarchs, and in a stroke of luck for Putin's young regime, by 2003, global oil prices began a multi-year climb, as illustrated in chapter 4. The revenue that flowed into the country's economy rapidly increased economic growth and the incomes of average Russians. Putin's personal public approval soared in this period, reaching a high for the preceding three years of 86% only a month or so after Khodorkovsky's arrest in late October 2003.

Putin's taming of the oligarchs of the 1990s not only tightened his own hold on business and politics; it also proved popular within Russian society. Most average Russians felt little sympathy for men who had made billions while most of society suffered the full financial brunt of the collapse of communism and Yeltsin's uneven reforms. With the multi-year climb in global oil prices starting in 2003 bolstering the incomes of average Russians, Putin's personal public approval soared, reaching a three-year high of 86% about a month after Khodorkovsky's arrest.

Ironically, perhaps, Putin's approval ratings rose ever higher as he implemented the final step in establishing a political economy of patronalism. With the oligarchs swept aside, his closest associates—some from his childhood and university days in St. Petersburg, others from his career in the KGB—moved into plum positions controlling huge portions of the re-nationalizing economy. They moved freely between government and business in the absence—or in open violation—of conflict-of-interest laws that may have inhibited them privately benefiting from holding public office. Putin's patronal politics was taking shape.

Patronal Purposes: Enrichment and Regime Stability

The purposes and methods of projection of Russian power in the twenty-first century have been largely guided and determined by Vladimir Putin. Without going into his biography, which is well known and covered in depth elsewhere,[54] it is important to note certain details that have shaped his leadership. Experiences that shaped his worldview, such as his youth in St. Petersburg or stationing in Dresden as a Lieutenant Colonel in the KGB in the mid-1980s, are important, of course, but more central to the current argument is the network he developed upon his return to St. Petersburg a few months after the collapse of the Berlin Wall.[55] It is this network that forms the basis of contemporary Russia's patronal political economy.[56]

Putin's path to presidency was paved by these connections. After returning from Dresden in 1990, Putin was hired to advise his old law professor, Anatoly Sobchak, with his work on the Leningrad City Council, subsequently serving as deputy while Sobchak was St. Petersburg mayor from 1991 to 1996, when Sobchak lost his bid for re-election. After a brief stint out of work, Putin landed an enviable job in Moscow thanks to some of his St. Petersburg contacts, quickly climbing the ranks from deputy director of the Presidential Administration's International Property Division, to KGB head, to the office of prime minister in August 1999. By then, Boris Yeltsin was looking for a reliable successor—one who would protect Yeltsin once out of office as much as a competent leader. In a surprise telecast at midnight on December 31, 1999, Yeltsin announced that he was resigning the presidency effective January 1, 2000, and that Vladimir Putin would become acting president. Three months later, Putin was formally elected with 54% of the vote.

With him to the Kremlin came the network of friends from St. Petersburg. Many had already used their proximity to Putin and his position in the deputy mayor's office, which enabled him to control licenses for foreign trade, to enrich themselves—and Putin too, as most observers strongly suspect. With their arrival in Moscow and Putin's rapid rise to the presidency, the opportunity to control the resources of the entire Russian state now lay before them. Putin installed members of his inner circle as heads of new quasi-state entities like Rosneft and Gazprom, while others oversaw the vast resources of the presidential administration or led power ministries like defense, the Security Council, and state investigative agencies like the State Security Service (or FSB, by its Russian acronym). A third group of Putin's close friends became owners of sprawling conglomerates that gained preferential access to state contracts, which would make them billionaires over Putin's long reign.[57] As Karen Dawisha explains, "It is this kleptocratic tribute system underlying Russia's authoritarian regime that the US government sought to expose and punish beginning in March 2014. The names of the sanctions list read like a Who's Who of Team Putin."[58] In sum, she observes:

> Political leaders close to Putin have become multimillionaires, and the oligarchs around them . . . have become billionaires. . . . And these billionaires, far from being titans of industry motoring the modernization of the Russian economy, have secured and increased their wealth by relying on and bolstering the centralized power of the state.[59]

In this system, she continues, the state "absorbs" or "nationalizes" the risk "but continues to privatize the rewards to those closest to the president in return for their loyalty," by "provid[ing] state funds for investment, and giv[ing] those close to the Kremlin massive monetary rewards."[60] Alena Ledeneva refers to the regime as "Sistema," Anders Åslund calls it "crony capitalism," and Brian Taylor describes it as operating according to the "Code of Putinism."[61] Regardless of the terminology, descriptions of the system converge on one key point: "that its inner logic was focused on the protection of the wealth of those closest to the Russian president."[62]

This mixing of public and private interests has fueled Russia's vast inequalities in wealth accumulation. Russia is by far the most highly wealth-concentrated country in the world: in 2019, the top 1% purportedly owned 57% of the country's wealth—down, however, from over 60% in 2016. While this figure was about 48% in the next highest country, Brazil, in 2019, it was still much higher than in many Western countries (24% in the UK, for example).[63] Seen a slightly different way, the top decile of wealth holders owns 83% of household wealth in Russia, versus 60% in China and 76% in the United States.[64] According to the 2019 Credit Suisse Global Wealth Report, Russia is ranked ninth in the world in its number of ultra-high-net-worth individuals (with assets over $50 million), despite its relatively middle-range per capita GDP.[65]

In order to maintain the social stability required for the system to function, even as inequality and elite corruption through the siphoning of state assets increased, Putin's regime had to keep the Russian people pacified. Media control certainly aided with this crucial task by controlling the flow of information to the public, as did the elimination of any true electoral opposition in the Duma. But political scientists have demonstrated credibly that Putin's popular approval ratings have often been genuine—ironically, even as Russians themselves lost individual rights and freedoms.[66] For those weary of the instabilities of the 1990s and the inequalities that Yeltsin's privatization and macroeconomic policies created, Putin's commitment to a "dictatorship of law," as he called it, and his early emphasis on political, social, and economic stability, were most welcome. The trade-off between living better and living with fewer rights and freedoms did not seem to be that difficult for a vast majority of Russians.

But the question that threatens all patronal systems stalked the last year of Putin's second term: Who could succeed the man at the top of the pyramid? The Russian constitution limited the presidency to two consecutive terms; by 2008, Putin would legally have to step down. As the Russian political system had become more autocratic and patronal, however, it also became increasingly centralized, de-institutionalized, and personalistic—dangerously so. Hale notes that patrons must match clients' expectations that benefits will continue to flow in return for loyal support: there is a mutual dependency despite the hierarchy.

If clients sense the patron is weakening or departing, then instability and competition for wealth and access to resources may follow. Rather than stepping out of politics in 2008, therefore, Putin stepped sideways—to the office of prime minister—and the system remained intact as he effectively remained in charge.

The patronal regime had become precariously dependent on the personal legitimacy, or charisma, of Vladimir Putin.[67] This was a resource that it turned out he could not transfer to a successor. Although Dmitri Medvedev had been a reliable client to Putin throughout his career in St. Petersburg and Moscow, he could not rule Russia the same way. Medvedev could neither reassure clients in Putin's patronal network that their access to state resources would not be threatened by his own clients, nor did he manage to carry the same appeal for most of the Russian public without Putin to stand beside him. Despite some political liberalization under Medvedev between 2008 and the end of 2011, and warming relations in that period with the West, as described earlier, for all intents and purposes, Putin was still in control of the regime and of Russia's patronal political economy.

By the autumn of 2011, with economic growth again lagging, Medvedev's presidential term was drawing to a rocky conclusion. Once again, the succession question loomed. In patronal systems, the de-institutionalization of domestic politics makes the regime particularly vulnerable to leadership changes, especially as informal norms of decision-making are more important than formal rules. This has made Vladimir Putin's personal legitimacy fundamental to the regime's durability: only Putin as supreme patron could maintain the status quo that created opportunities for the few to the disadvantage of the many. As former deputy chief of staff and Duma speaker Vyacheslav Volodin proclaimed to an international audience, "There is no Russia today if there is no Putin."[68]

The goal of the elites at the top of this system is to maintain domestic stability and preserve the status quo. They understand that the only real threat to this system that benefits them at the expense of society comes not from NATO or foreign invasion: the real threat to the current Russian regime comes from within. In a democracy, legislative and executive checks and balances, independent courts, the consistent application of rule of law through an independent judiciary, and a free and independent press are the key mechanisms that constrain the state from infringing on the personal rights and freedoms of members of society. But in the Putinist patronal system, society is subordinate to the state, and the state is subordinate to Putin and the networks of patrons and clients that flow downward from him. The resources that average Russians generate for the state, through labor and taxation, flow to a self-enriching network that sends some portion back for the private gain of Putin himself. To maintain this arrangement, the regime tracks Putin's approval and trust ratings relentlessly—not only to monitor social stability, but also to demonstrate to the networks below him that Putin as head patron is indispensable to the system.[69] Clients remain loyal to their patrons as long as their expectations are managed; if the future is more or less known, then it does not pay for clients to collectively challenge their patron. Anything that might mobilize Russian citizens or competing pyramids of power—like a functioning parliament, opposition parties, or other elite networks—must be prevented at all costs.

This helps explain how Putin's patronal autocracy has used Russian power abroad—particularly since his return to the presidency in 2012. Presumably, the goal of any regime in Russia or elsewhere is to stay in power. Whereas in a democracy, this means winning elections in a free and fair competition, in a patronal autocracy, where elections matter little, the ability to remain in office must come from elsewhere. This is why regime type matters to the projection of Russian power abroad. A patronal autocracy makes very different choices as to what serves the "national" interest than would a more open and accountable political system. Indeed, Putin's patronal system of government has effectively fused the national interest with the interest of the regime, but they are not always the same. A different regime type would pursue—and at times even define— Russian national interests rather differently.

The Effects of Patronalism on Domestic and Foreign Policy

How do we know that regime type matters to Russia's conduct abroad? A key case study is Russia's policy in its near abroad. As discussed in chapter 2, the breadth and depth of Russia's policy influence in crucial sectors like energy, and its huge market for the goods and services of surrounding states, mean that Russia cannot help being an important influence over the politics, societies, and economies of its neighbors. This somewhat resembles the influence of the United States over Canada and Mexico—it is dominant in so many areas that, as former Canadian prime minister Pierre Trudeau once said of his neighbors to the south, "Living next to you is in some ways like sleeping with an elephant. No matter how friendly and even-tempered is the beast, . . . one is affected by every twitch and grunt."[70] Given the asymmetry of their power resources along virtually every dimension, it would be laughable for the United States to invade the province of Ontario on the pretext of protecting American sovereignty from Britain; in the same way, Putin's annexation of Crimea on the pretext of protecting Russian sovereignty from Ukraine's joining the EU is comparably absurd. The position that it was in "Russian" interests, as opposed to those of the Putinist regime, to retain influence over the former Soviet states thus rings false;

another government would more likely have pursued a policy to ensure influence without annexing territory.

Daniel Treisman, Michael McFaul, and others provide convincing accounts that Russia's annexation of Crimea in March 2014 was not a predictable response to NATO expansion.[71] The hypothesis that Putin harbors imperial ambitions to reconstitute the Soviet Union, as Mead and others have claimed, also fails to hold water.[72] Nor was he pursuing a cultural quest to reunify Crimea and Russia. The mythology surrounding Crimea that Putin spun following the annexation in the spring of 2014 was, to a significant degree, manufactured. Most Russians, as Greene and Robertson note, would have some knowledge of Crimea's place in Russian religious history as the land of "ancient Chersonesus" where "Holy Prince Vladimir was baptized" in the tenth century, bringing Christianity to the region, although other historical and military links to the region were likely too obscure for most people—even for some Russian historians.[73] Other arguments explaining the annexation also fall flat: some observers suggest that Russian military leaders feared losing access to the Black Sea Fleet under the new anti-Russian government in Ukraine, but this seems an unwarranted concern given the weakness of any new regime in Kyiv and the difficulty it would have in practice in prying Russia from its bases[74]—not to mention Ukraine's dire economic circumstances, which would make the income from Russia's lease payments desirable to the new regime.

Although a clear national interest of any Russian regime would be maintaining sovereignty, there was no such threat in 2014. Instead, what was at risk was a Ukrainian regime that looked strikingly like a miniature version of the patronal autocracy that governed Putin's Russia, making it a very comfortable neighbor. Yet the difference between Russia under Putin and Ukraine under Viktor Yanukovych was not just in scale, but also the nature of state-society relations: Ukrainians gathered in Maidan Square in 2014, as they had in 2004, yet again standing up to a corrupt regime and, evidently, winning! Not only was this destabilizing for the Yanukovych regime; if it succeeded, it could also prove destabilizing to Putin's regime in Russia. For the very survival of Putin's regime, then, the popular uprising against Yanukovych could not be perceived as successful to Russians watching back home; social mobilization against corruption must not spread to Russia itself. Thus, a vital cause of what turned out to be an unplanned and impromptu Russian military intervention was the leadership's fear of a spillover demonstration effect from Ukraine to Russians at home.[75]

The domestic political context by 2014 is important to recall. In the autumn of 2011, Putin had dramatically announced that he would be swapping places with Dmitri Medvedev. While the constitution stipulated that no one could hold more than two consecutive terms in the presidency, there was nothing that forbade Putin from taking a four-year break before returning to the Kremlin in

2012. But as noted earlier, the decision was not greeted with as much enthusiasm as Putin may have anticipated, and people across the country took to the streets to protest the waning of political choice in Russia—manifested in Putin's decision to return to the presidency, and also the rigging of the Duma elections on December 4, 2011, in favor of United Russia. In the street rallies that began that winter and extended through spring 2012, tens of thousands of average Russians, from the tiny enclave of Kaliningrad in the west to Vladivostok in the far east, marched through hundreds of cities, many carrying placards with slogans like "Russia without Putin"; "the rats should go"; "swindlers and thieves, give us our elections back!"; and "Putin is a thief."[76] Hundreds of protesters and some of the main leaders were arrested. US secretary of state Hillary Clinton condemned the 2011 Duma election results as "dishonest and unfair," which Putin latched onto as a sign that the United States was encouraging the protesters to oust him from power, rather than a typical statement by a democratic leader delivered to any country where election results are suspect.[77]

The rallies and marches against Putin's return to the presidency initiated a second wave of autocratization within Russia. Even legal protests against the regime were met with force from police, and protesters young and old were given long prison sentences, sometimes in labor camps, to deter others who might consider opposing the regime. NGOs were classified as "foreign agents," and American and European organizations engaged in the development of political parties were prohibited from operating within Russia. The narrative of Russia "under siege" by the West began in earnest, with a new legitimacy narrative claiming that these sorts of liberal uprisings were not indigenous to the Russian nation, but bad influences from the West. One study of Russian state-society relations notes that until Putin's return to the Kremlin in the spring of 2012, "ideological ambiguity and peaceful co-existence had been the name of the game . . . the goal was to keep politics away from the people and the people away from politics."[78] But the popular mobilization that confronted the regime in late 2011 and 2012 initiated a change in strategy, with new tactics developed to more actively marshal segments of Russian society in favor of Putin's patronal autocratic rule.

Greene and Robertson demonstrate convincingly that Putin's strategists aimed to demobilize opposition through the exploitation and activation of existing social "wedge" issues in Russian society—specifically, religion and gay rights. Infamously, the Pussy Riot affair in 2012 helped further this agenda.[79] A trio of radical feminist artists performed an anti-Putin "punk prayer," lasting about thirty seconds, on the altar of the Cathedral of Christ the Savior in central Moscow, and subsequently posted the footage on YouTube. It took about two weeks for the regime's tacticians to understand the performance as a political gift to be exploited and issue arrest warrants for the three women. They were quickly convicted of "hooliganism motivated by religious hatred" and sentenced to two years in prison camps. The real consequence of the incident was the amount of national press coverage it received—especially on state-owned TV networks, the preferred source for news of the majority of Russians. Public opinion consolidated quickly around the view that the performance was blasphemous to the Russian Orthodox Church. The media coverage of the trial—which, by no coincidence, took place in the early months of Putin's new term—was unrelenting, since "the goal was to ensure that as many Russians as possible felt personally offended by what Pussy Riot had done."[80] The more the Western press and American or European officials and public figures condemned the trio's conviction and imprisonment, the more the narrative of Russia under siege from the liberal West penetrated Russian society.

Soon after the women's trial, the Duma passed a law "on the protection of feelings of religious believers." Another law passed shortly thereafter prohibited the perpetration of positive images of the "gay lifestyle" to children. A Pew Research Survey indicated that in 2013, 74% of Russians thought homosexuality should not be accepted by society, so in adopting laws that criminalized homosexuality, the regime was following rather than leading public opinion. Greene and Robertson argue that the use of religion and sexuality "as wedge issues did exactly what it was designed to do: it widened the ideological divide between the pro-Putin majority and the oppositional minority in the country."[81] In other words, the regime weaponized legislation in order to separate out the liberal, Western-leaning segment of the population that comprised the opposition from more conservative Russians—some of whom may have supported the protests against Putin's return to the Kremlin, but drew the line on such divisive issues as religion and sexuality.

A further strike against supporters of the liberal opposition involved harsh jail sentences for some of their key leaders and for dozens of young protesters. These punishments were handed out slowly over a three-year period after the 2012 protests, while "perpetrators" were held in prison without bail. Some ended up in labor camps for several years, a disturbing parallel to the treatment of dissidents in the Soviet era. The effect of this, too, was to divide society further and deflate enthusiasm for future public demonstrations against the regime.[82]

Thus, when the uprisings began in Ukraine after President Yanukovych announced his decision not to sign the EU accession agreement in November 2013, Russian domestic politics were already unsettled. In response, the Russian media spread reports that Ukrainian fascist groups were attacking ethnic Russians in Ukraine, drawing parallels to Ukrainian nationalists who had fought alongside Hitler's SS against the Soviets, like Stepan Bandera, during World War II. This narrative slyly invoked a precious national memory—the Soviet defeat of fascist Germany—to denigrate the "Revolution of Dignity," as the popular uprisings were called within Ukraine. The media fueled anger with vivid, violent stories, such as the report that Ukrainian fascists had crucified a Russian child in Slavyansk in Eastern Ukraine.[83] Despite being completely fabricated, such stories produced the desired effect in Russians watching back home. According to this narrative, Putin's regime was patriotically duty-bound to defend ethnic Russians in Eastern Ukraine, as well as in Crimea. His approval rating shot up by twenty points between the end of February and the end of March 2014.[84] The real political danger was not fascist Ukrainian usurpers, but the possible contagion of social protest; such narratives ensured that this would not be the case in Putin's Russia.

The West, and especially the United States, was painted as the guilty party in Ukraine, and this scapegoating proved useful on other fronts as well. The narrative that Ukraine, Russia's "brother country," was destroying itself—all due to American intervention—was promoted as an example of the instability that could take root in Russia if not for Putin's regime. The Arab Spring in 2011 and 2012, with huge demonstrations and ensuing violence in autocratic Egypt, Syria, and Libya, were presented as further evidence of the destabilizing effects of Western meddling. At almost the same time, a new American ambassador, Michael McFaul, arrived in Moscow in January 2012—who, according to state media, had the goal of starting a revolution in Russia as well. A campaign against him as an agent of the United States, specifically tasked to organize insurrection and instability in Russia, fit well into the Kremlin's emerging legitimacy story.[85] McFaul proved a convenient foil for further fueling anti-American nationalist sentiment.

In addition to enabling a narrative that bolstered regime legitimacy and popular support, the projection of Russian power in Ukraine provided a side benefit for clients in the patronal system: opportunities to use the state to gain access to lucrative deals. Specifically, the integration of the Crimean Peninsula into Russia would require building new infrastructure. The construction of the Kerch Strait Bridge connecting the peninsula to the Russian mainland, for example, provided contracts worth billions of dollars to Putin's closest clients.[86] Boris and Arkady Rotenberg, two of Putin's dearest and oldest friends from St. Petersburg, reportedly won major Russian government contracts worth $9 billion in 2014; contracts to build structures for the 2014 Sochi Olympics provide a similar example.[87]

Indeed, much of the projection of power abroad that emerged during Putin's third term served the purposes of the patronal system. Many such contracts offered opportunities for enrichment as well as supporting Russia's national interests—at least, those interests as defined by Putin's regime. Another prime example is that of the ostensibly private businessman Yevgenyi Prigozhin, known sometimes as "Putin's caterer," whose personal ties to Putin stem from St. Petersburg. Prigozhin seems to have his fingers in a number of pies with unsavory connections to state power: as noted in chapter 7, he controlled the Internet

Research Agency, and was indicted in the Mueller Report for interference in the 2016 US presidential elections; his companies have valuable contracts to supply food services to the Russian Defense Ministry; and he controls the Wagner Group, the private militia that Putin's regime has employed on missions in Syria, Libya, and various parts of Africa, described in chapter 6. He was specifically named in US sanctions in 2014, as were the Rotenberg brothers. These are but a few of many, many examples of friends of Putin who have benefited from their access to him as patron.[88] Indeed, a Forbes Russia 2016 study found that four out of the top five businesses that gained state contracts worth more than $15 billion were very closely tied to Putin. Putin's close friends, therefore, "form a distinctive group that is more successful than any other."[89] As the tactics both at home and abroad to maintain stability and legitimacy demonstrate, these beneficiaries are keen to preserve their hold on power at all costs.

How regime type matters in the exercise of Russian power

If we had understood Ukraine as a reactive move purely in defense of national interests, designed to prevent Ukraine from joining NATO and the EU, then it could be considered an abject failure. Ukraine's newly elected president, Petro Poroshenko, pursued the EU accession agreement after 2014; the United States sent advisers and offensive weapons to the Ukrainian military; and Russia's economy still faces heavy sanctions at the time of writing. Russia seems to have fully lost control over Ukrainian politics with the election of a political outsider, Volodymyr Zelensky, in 2019, despite the regime's best efforts to continue to influence Ukraine's internal politics.

However, seen from the perspective of Russian domestic politics within a patronal autocracy, the operation has been an unqualified success. True, the annexation of Crimea and continued funding of militias in the East continued to destabilize Ukraine. But more important for the domestic status quo, not only did Putin's internal public approval and trust ratings within Russia improve immediately following the March 2014 annexation of Crimea, but his approval remained over 80% until about March 2018, when he was re-elected president for a fourth term, set to last until 2024 (and perhaps beyond as explained below). The "rally 'round the flag" payoff from the Ukraine operation was further bolstered by the introduction of various populist techniques and new media policies.[90] State-controlled media cast opposition figures as out-of-touch intellectuals funded by foreigners; in contrast, a highly polished, adoring, two-and-a-half-hour documentary, *Prezident*, appeared on Russian television in April 2015 to celebrate fifteen years of Putin's rule.[91] The Internet was another battleground: pro-Kremlin bloggers were unleashed to project the regime's message, and the state employed denial-of-service attacks against opposition websites. The Kremlin also coopted some of the largest Internet providers, and effected a takeover of the Russian version of Facebook, VKontakte. A flood of new legislation enabled regulators to block any online content that published "extremist" content (a term left largely undefined, but often used to penalize voices of opposition).[92]

The narrative of "Putin's Russia saves the world" would be bolstered by the operation in Syria that began in September 2015. Gleb Pavlovsky, a former consultant to Yeltsin, Putin, and Medvedev, argued that "de-escalation in Ukraine meant escalation in Syria." Media was again flooded with stories about the Russian military succeeding where "the West" had failed in defeating ISIS in the Middle East. In the fall of 2015, the coverage of Ukraine that had blanketed Russian television coverage was replaced by images of Russian aircraft bombing terrorist targets in Syria. The highlight of the narrative that Russia was bringing peace to the Middle East was a concert in Palmyra by St. Petersburg's Mariinsky Orchestra (featuring Putin's childhood friend, cellist Sergei Roldugin), conducted at a theater that ISIS had used to execute prisoners.[93] Driving the point home that Russian intervention was a force for good globally, Defense Minister Sergei Shoigu declared that, thanks to Russia, "[t]he chain of 'color revolutions' spreading across the Middle East and Africa had been broken."[94]

To complement Russia's military projection of power abroad, political strategists learned that Russia's conservative moral narrative could also be internationalized. In defying NATO and the EU in Ukraine in 2014, Gulnaz Sharafutdinova writes, "Putin had shifted from a defensive position vis-à-vis the West, with Russia trying to coin its own version of a 'sovereign democracy,' into an offensive stance associated with the claim that Russia represents the last bulwark for defending traditional . . . values."[95] This perspective spread into Europe and even into the United States, and was soon being used in support of far-right populism. And in the Middle East, Putinist "selective bigotry" in the form of conservative morality resonated with anti-gay and largely anti-feminist Muslim societies, especially when contrasted to the overly tolerant liberal West.[96] This posturing as a great power and defender of conservatism abroad and at home dominated the domestic narrative on Russian interests and actions, but this trajectory should not be viewed as inevitable.

Two Russias Counterfactual: The Power of Regime Type

The exercise of imagining a different kind of regime in Russia in the twenty-first century is useful in illustrating that the use of Russian power resources abroad is not predetermined by great power politics, geography, or history. Had Russia remained on a path of democratization after 2000, it would not have worried about NATO or EU incursion on its sovereignty or sphere of influence, and incidents targeting liberalizing former Soviet republics—Estonia in 2007 and thereafter; Georgia in 2008; Moldova with consistency; and Ukraine, initially after the Orange Revolution in 2004 and again from 2014—would have been unthinkable. This hypothetical Russia might have seen these states not as enemies, but as allies. Indeed, an alternative direction for an open Russia may have seen it becoming a member of the EU, or at least on a path of more amicable and productive association with it.

Moreover, if Russia was governed by a more open and accountable government, then its power projection into the Middle East and elsewhere beyond its neighborhood might have looked quite different. A different regime might not have seen the overthrow of dictatorships in Libya, Egypt, or Tunisia as engineered by the United States, nor as potentially contagious and damaging to Russia's domestic politics. On the contrary, a more open and accountable regime might have worked with the United States and Europe against ISIS across the Middle East. With a Russian regime as an ally to the United States and the EU, there would have been no need to waste resources in trying to undermine French, German, or American elections, or in supporting Brexit. Improved relations with the United States would not only enable both to invest less in new conventional and nuclear weaponry in favor of social and infrastructure investment, but would also allow them to create a united front against the rise of China.

In terms of the economy, Russia could have pursued growth through investment from Europe and the United States, especially if rule of law could protect investors' property rights. Greater foreign investment might have allowed Russia to diversify its economy away from oil and gas dependence, and rendered relationships based on oil revenues with rogue regimes like Venezuela utterly unnecessary; joint ventures with Exxon, Chevron, and British Petroleum, for example, would produce far better financial opportunities. Finally, American and European democracy and humanitarian assistance could proceed more smoothly without being seen as intended to undermine Russia's domestic political process. Power projection abroad might have remained on a path of cooperation with the United States and Europe.

In sum, Russian national interests in economic prosperity, sovereignty, and national security could have been better met with a different type of regime. Those who have pushed the Weimar Russia analogy to claim the inevitability of a Russian reaction to the West should try to imagine instead a Russia that looks more like contemporary Germany today—the democratic, undisputed economic and political leader of Europe, arisen from the ashes of defeat in World War II only fifty years earlier.

Too often, however, analysts accept and adopt the Kremlin's line in conflating the *Russian national interest* with the *interest of maintaining the personalistic patronal autocracy under Vladimir Putin.* Just as attempting rapid neoliberal policies over a more gradual approach was not the only way to approach economic reform in the 1990s, aggression against NATO, the United States, and Europe was not the only way to defend Russian national security in 2014 and beyond. Those actions were policy choices, not natural or inevitable reactions to external provocations. A Russian leader in a more open political system might have made a different decision in addressing upheaval in Ukraine, perhaps choosing the side of those who wanted to overthrow Yanukovych; remaining active in NATO's partnership for peace; or perceiving, instead of a unified "West" behind the protests on Ukraine's streets, a frustrated population revolting against a corrupt, cronyistic regime.

Moreover, leaders, and the political and social milieux within which they operate, matter not only to the definition of the national interest, but also to the policies employed to pursue it. As Vladimir Putin and clients in his network have used access to the state's resources for personal gain, the real wages of Russian citizens have declined since their peaks a few years ago, along with quality of life and access to social services. To be sure, even after the "rally 'round the flag" effect fostered from 2014 onward, some began to weary of the increasingly obvious inequalities within Russian society. As noted in previous sections of this book, protests emerged in the spring of 2017 against inequality and graft, and in response to pension reform in 2019, while more than half of Russian youth surveyed expressed plans to permanently emigrate for better opportunity. Notably, the blame is usually shifted to the government, instead of placed on Putin personally. For example, in August 2018, 66% disapproved of the government, but Putin retained 67% approval—lower than the 80%-plus of a year earlier, but far higher than his prime minister and ministers. His berating of government officials on television for not fulfilling his decrees on development was evidently enough to convince average Russians that the lack of follow-through was not his fault—no matter that he had appointed the government that was to blame.

As declining approval ratings and attempts to maintain control demonstrate, personalistic, patronal regimes such as Russia's by 2020 are inherently vulnerable. A major reason for this is the lack of a genuinely competitive and institutionalized succession process, along with the lingering threat of alternative sources of power that could arise from society or other elite networks when the patron-in-chief leaves office. This might explain the furious rush in January 2020 to initiate sweeping constitutional reforms to enable Putin to remain Russia's president, possibly for life. In the summer of 2019, Vladimir Putin's approval ratings hovered between 68% and 70%, while almost 50% of respondents to

Levada surveys indicated that the country was moving in wrong direction. The steady decrease in Putin's personal approval rating, in combination with Medvedev's consistently low approval rating (in the fall of 2019, near an all-time low of 38%), appeared to be the impetus for drastic changes in government. By the end of 2019, something had to be done. As the regime well knew, *popularity is a power resource against rival elites*, a means of keeping clients loyal as well as an indicator of social stability. Putin's proposal to amend the constitution opened the option of his remaining in power until 2036, and in this way demystified what would happen to the regime after his term was to have expired in 2024. The move thus served to reassure invested wealthy cronies that a plan was in place to maintain the status quo, regardless of growing social disapproval. There would be evolutionary development in Putin's Russia, but no revolutions.

Conclusion: A Strong Hand and the Will to Use It

This study has proposed two central corrections to the ways in which analysts and policymakers understand Russia's role in the world in the twenty-first century. First, I have sought to present a multidimensional understanding of Russian power resources beyond the traditional means of men, military, and money. Instead, this framing of power resources also includes geographic domain and policy scope and weight. When examined in this way, it appears that Russia by almost thirty years after the Soviet collapse was not playing a weak hand of cards well in the international arena, as some have suggested, but rather, that a resurrected Russia had gained a few strong cards with which to challenge other players in the construction of a new global order.

Second, I have endeavored to link Russia's emerging *willingness* and *ability* to employ these power resources abroad to the nature of its domestic political regime. This second argument makes the case that the use of Russian power abroad is not determined by realpolitik alone, nor by supposed geographical or historical path dependencies that will always pit Russia against "the West," broadly speaking. Rather, this power projection is specific to Putin's autocratic patronal regime. As such, conflict between Russia and the West is not inevitable; we need not think of the current tensions as predestined or permanent. Russia's behavior abroad is very much determined by the political regime at home, so if the nature of domestic politics were to change, then the way in which Russian leaders employ its power abroad would change in kind. Just as Russian capabilities have been underestimated because the wrong measures of power tend to be employed, there is a similar misunderstanding of the role regime type has played in determining the purposes of Russian power projection abroad under Vladimir Putin's long tenure at the head of its political system.

This argument implies that enduring hostile relations between Russia and its more politically liberal neighbors are not predetermined by history, geography, or culture. Indeed, as pointed out in chapter 1 initially, the period at the end of the Cold War under Mikhail Gorbachev saw some of the most substantial arms control agreements with the West in history. Similarly, Boris Yeltsin maintained cooperation with Europe and the United States on a range of security issues in the 1990s, despite times of disagreement, such as Kosovo in 1999. Moreover, during Putin's first term from 2000 to 2004, and Medvedev's term from 2008 to 2012, there was tremendous cooperation between Russia and the West, with 64% of Russians surveyed in November 2011 indicating favorable attitudes toward the United States.

The conflation of Russian national interest with the interests of a personalistic patronal autocratic regime has sometimes led to false comparisons of Russian-Western relations after 2014 to the Cold War—a relationship that was tense and adversarial, with violence implied, but not directly employed. The term "cold war" also suggests two cultures and ideologies in fundamental opposition to one another, and infers that enmity between post-Soviet Russia and the West is inevitable. This metaphor insinuates, therefore, that a return to normalcy is a return to conflict; the short period of cooperation was the irregularity in Russian-Western relations, not the norm. But this too is misleading: Russia's aggressive behavior abroad has become more pronounced only as the patronalist autocratic regime under Putin has become more threatened by the prospect of internal instability. Under Putin's aging regime, a willingness to project power abroad, I have argued, might have some root in a misperceived sense of danger to national security, but more crucially, it is based on the desire to buttress a narrative of regime legitimacy designed for internal consumption by Russian society and elites.

The patronal political and economic system Putin has built is vulnerable, but not because it is threatened from abroad. NATO's small, rotating contingent of troops in Eastern Europe is not going to bring it down: only Russian society will be able to do that. Russia itself is not fragile, however, and the Russian Federation as nation-state is more than the regime alone. Russia is *not* Putin. Confrontation with the West is neither inevitable nor desirable—at least, for the Russian people. Every time Russians have been given the opportunity to choose their leaders freely and fairly, they have seized it with both hands. There is no cultural allergy to democracy and no universal desire for strongman rule. As Russians demonstrated in 1917, 1991, 2011, 2012, 2017, and 2019, they are not afraid to take to the streets to demand better governance.

As far as the country has come in the close to thirty years since the Soviet Union collapsed, it could have come farther with an honest, open and inclusive political system. A free press would have exposed and curbed endemic elite corruption; fewer state resources might have been diverted to the military, and more may have been spent to improve health and education; leaders might have dedicated more energy to diversifying the economy, improving Russians' standard of living and even lifespan. The fact that so many young Russians want to emigrate permanently shows that the regime is struggling; if their votes at the ballot box don't matter, people will vote with their feet.

Russia is hugely changed since December 1991 and the demise of the Soviet Union. As far as the country has come, however, Putin's patronal autocracy is holding it back from developing even further.[97] The demands of a changing Russian society will eventually overwhelm the capabilities of the regime that he has constructed. When—not if—that willingness to challenge the patronal system takes permanent root, then we can expect that a different form of governance will alter how Russia projects its power abroad. But only when its power has been put to the purpose of serving its people will Russia truly be resurrected.

NOTES

Chapter 1

1. Putin was paraphrasing the famous saying, attributed variously to Otto von Bismarck, Klemens von Metternich, Charles Maurice de Talleyrand, and Winston Churchill, among others: *"Russia is never as strong as she looks; Russia is never as weak as she looks."* See Mark N. Katz, "Is Russia Strong or Weak?," Washington, UPI, July 10, 2006, available at: www.upi.com/Business_News/Security-Industry/2006/07/10/Policy-Watch-Is-Russia-strong-or-weak/39541152565695, accessed December 1, 2015.

2. Source is the International Monetary Fund, World Economic Outlook Database. Statistics on gross domestic product as shares of the global economy can be found at: http://www.imf.org/external/pubs/ft/weo/2017/01/weodata/index.aspx, accessed May 2, 2017.

3. World Bank, http://data.worldbank.org/indicator/SP.POP.TOTL. Data are as of 2018.

4. Stockholm International Peace Research Institute (SIPRI) Military Expenditure Database. Figures are for 2018 and available at: https://www.sipri.org/databases/milex, accessed November 2, 2019. Throughout this book, any dollar-denominated currency totals are in US dollars unless otherwise noted.

5. David Baldwin, "Power and International Relations," ch. 11 in *Handbook of International Relations*, ed. Walter Carlsnaes, Thomas Risse, Beth Simmons (Los Angeles: SAGE Publications, 2013), 277.

6. Valerie Bunce made a similar observation about the collapse of communism in Eastern Europe in 1989 in *Subversive Institutions: The Design and Destruction of Socialism and the State* (New York: Cambridge University Press, 1999).

7. See, for example, Timothy J. Colton, *Dilemma of Reform in the Soviet Union* (New York: Council on Foreign Relations, 1986) for a serious, but in the end positive, assessment of the chances for the Soviet Union's continued survival, published only five years before the regime collapsed.

8. Anders Åslund, *How Russia Became a Market Economy* (Washington, DC: Brookings Institution, 1995), 41–50.

9. "Russia's Economic Revival," in *The Russia Balance Sheet*, ed. Anders Åslund and Andrew Kuchins (Washington, DC: Peterson Institute for International Economics and Center for Strategic and International Studies, 2009), 44.

10. Angela Stent, *The Limits of Partnership: US-Russian Relations in the 21st Century* (Princeton: Princeton University Press, 2014), 69.

11. See Condoleezza Rice, *Democracy: Stories from the Long Road to Freedom* (New York: Grand Central Publishing, 2017), especially chapters 2 and 4; and Michael A. McFaul, *Cold War, Hot Peace: An American Ambassador in Putin's Russia* (New York: Penguin, 2018), on the change in Putin's perspective on the West following the color revolutions in Georgia and Ukraine.

12. Andrei Shleifer and Daniel Treisman, "A Normal Country: Russia after Communism," *Journal of Economic Perspectives* 19, no. 1 (Winter 2005): 151–174.

13. Ibid., 152.
14. Dominic Wilson and Roopa Purushothaman, "Dreaming with the BRICs: The Path to 2050," *Goldman Sachs Global Economics Paper 99*, http://www.goldmansachs.com/our-thinking/archive/archive-pdfs/brics-dream.pdf, accessed November 16, 2015.
15. Ibid., 5.
16. The next six paragraphs draw from Kathryn Stoner and Michael McFaul, "Who Lost Russia (This Time)?: Vladimir Putin," *Washington Quarterly* 38, no. 2 (September 2015): 167–187.
17. Aron Bernstein, "Is President Obama Reducing the Probability of Nuclear War?" *MIT Faculty Newsletter* 22, no. 4 (March/April/May 2010), http://web.mit.edu/fnl/volume/224/bernstein.html.
18. Kenneth Katzman, *Afghanistan: Post-Taliban Governance, Security, and US Policy* (Washington, DC: Congressional Research Service, April 2013), 31.
19. "Ethnic Uzbeks Flee Violence in Kyrgyzstan," *New York Times*, slideshow, June 14, 2010, http://www.nytimes.com/slideshow/2010/06/14/world/0614-Kyrgyzstan.html?_r=0.
20. Gorbachev did not try to stop the first Gulf War, but the US response there, in cooperation with many other countries, was in response to Iraqi intervention in Kuwait.
21. "Trade in Goods with Russia," US Census Bureau, available at: https://www.census.gov/foreign-trade/balance/c4621.html.
22. Medvedev's comments can be heard in Russian at: http://www.nato.int/nato_static/assets/audio/audio_2010_11/20101120_101120f-01.mp3, accessed June 9, 2015.
23. Medvedev press conference, Seoul, South Korea, March 27, 2012, transcript available in English at: https://obamawhitehouse.archives.gov/the-press-office/2012/03/26/remarks-president-obama-and-president-medvedev-russia-after-bilateral-me, accessed June 19, 2020.
24. The 2014 Russian Military Doctrine is available in English at: https://www.offiziere.ch/wp-content/uploads-001/2015/08/Russia-s-2014-Military-Doctrine.pdf; the NATO threat reference is in Article II, point 12, "Main External Military Dangers."
25. Steven J. Pifer, "Putin's Nuclear Saber-Rattling: What Is He Compensating For?" *Brookings Blog*, June 17, 2015, available at: http://www.brookings.edu/blogs/order-from-chaos/posts/2015/06/17-putin-nuclear-saber-rattling-pifer, accessed November 16, 2015. The documentary is called *President* and aired on Rossiya TV One on April 26, 2015. Episodes can be viewed in Russian at: http://www.liveleak.com/view?i=c7f_1430284031 and in English at: http://www.stankovuniversallaw.com/2015/05/president-putins-15-years-in-power-en-subtitles-video. Both sites were accessed November 16, 2015.
26. For statements by General Selva and General Dunford, see Paul McLeary, *Foreign Policy*, July 14, 2015, available at: http://foreignpolicy.com/2015/07/14/more-pentagon-generals-line-up-to-proclaim-russia-existential-threat-to-u-s, accessed August 12, 2015. For Odierno's statements, see Kristina Wong, "Top US General: Russia Is Most Dangerous Threat," *The Hill*, August 12, 2015, available at: http://itk.thehill.com/policy/defense/250962-odierno-russia-is-the-most-dangerous-threat-to-us, accessed August 12, 2015.
27. General Philip Breedlove, public address at Stanford University, November 9, 2015, Stanford, California.
28. Vladimir Putin, speech to expanded meeting of the Federation Council on Russia's Development Strategy through 2020, February 7, 2008, available at: http://archive.kremlin.ru/eng/speeches/2008/02/08/1137_type82912type82913_159643.shtml, accessed October 28, 2015.
29. Knowledgeable readers will think of Russia's participation in peacekeeping in Kosovo in 1999, but this was not an offensive mission as was the 2015 mission in Syria. Russia participated in Kosovo as part of a NATO-Russian coalition.
30. David E. Sanger and Eric Schmitt, "Russian Ships Near Data Cables Are Too Close for US Comfort," *New York Times*, October 25, 2015, available at: http://www.nytimes.com/2015/10/26/world/europe/russian-presence-near-undersea-cables-concerns-us.html?_r=0, accessed September 7, 2016.
31. For more on recent changes to Russian nuclear doctrine, see, for example, Stephen Blank, ed., *Russian Nuclear Weapons: Past, Present and Future* (Carlisle, PA: Strategic Studies Institute, US Army War College, 2011), available in PDF format at: http://www.strategicstudiesinstitute.army.mil/pdffiles/pub1087.pdf; and for more on nuclear doctrine,

see http://www.nti.org/learn/countries/russia/nuclear, accessed September 7, 2016. The updated document detailing Russian deterrence policy, "Foundations of State Policy of the Russian Federation in the Field of Nuclear Deterrence," is available at: http://publication. pravo.gov.ru/Document/View/0001202006020040?index=0&rangeSize=1, accessed June 30, 2020. See the excellent analysis of the nuclear deterrence policy in Russia stemming from the June 2 "Foundations of State Policy" document by Nicolai Sokov, "Russia Clarifies Its Nuclear Deterrence Policy," June 3, 2020, available at: https://vcdnp.org/russia-clarifies-its-nuclear-deterrence-policy, accessed June 30, 2020. For nuclear war in the Russian media, see, for example, Steven Ennis, "Russian Media Learn to Love the Bomb," *BBC Monitoring*, February 23, 2015, available at: http://www.bbc.com/news/world-europe-31557254, accessed September 7, 2016.

32. The doomsday clock timeline is available at: https://thebulletin.org/doomsday-clock/?gcl id=EAIaIQobChMI0Me6862q6gIVnB-tBh01-AnPEAAYASAAEgIHG_D_BwE, accessed June 30, 2020.

33. President Vladimir V. Putin's interview with *Al-Ahram* newspaper, February 9, 2015, available at: http://en.kremlin.ru/events/president/news/47643, accessed August 3, 2015. A representative Russian perspective on Russia's complaints against the United States by Sergei Karaganov can be found at: http://eng.globalaffairs.ru/number/ Russia-and-the-US-A-Long-Confrontation-16990.

34. See Organization for Cooperation and Economic Development (OECD) Data, GDP per hour worked available at https://data.oecd.org/lprdty/gdp-per-hour-worked.htm#indicator-chart, accessed October 1, 2020.

35. OECD website: https://data.oecd.org/lprdty/gdp-per-hour-worked.htm#indicator-chart, accessed October 1, 2020.

36. For data on foreign direct investment see the World Data Bank, World Development Indicators, available at: http://databank.worldbank.org/data//reports.aspx?source=2&cou ntry=RUS&series=&period=, accessed August 12, 2020.

37. Numbers are current GDP per capita at purchasing power parity in current international dollars. Data available at: http://data.worldbank.org/indicator/NY.GDP.PCAP.PP.CD, accessed October 9, 2019.

38. "Russia Economic Report," no. 42, December 4, 2019, available at: https://www.worldbank. org/en/country/russia/publication/rer.

39. For more on Russian comparative life expectancy and mortality trends in comparison to other countries, see United Nations, Human Development Index, available at: http:// hdr.undp.org/en/content/2019-human-development-index-ranking, and https://data. worldbank.org/indicator/SP.DYN.LE00.MA.IN?locations=RU, both accessed December 19, 2019.

40. See "Table 1: Human Development Index and Its Components," in *2015 UN Human Development Report*, 208–211, available at: http://hdr.undp.org/sites/default/files/hdr_ 2015_statistical_annex.pdf, accessed September 7, 2016.

41. Joseph S. Nye Jr., *Soft Power: The Means to Success in World Politics* (New York: Public Affairs, 2003), 1.

42. The data are available at the Levada Center website at: http://www.levada.ru/en/2017/01/ 09/russia-as-a-great-power, accessed May 2, 2017.

43. Robert A. Dahl, "The Concept of Power," *Behavioral Science* 2, no. 3 (July 1957): 202–203.

44. Ibid., 203.

45. Hans Morgenthau, *Politics among Nations* (New York: Knopf, 1948); Kenneth Waltz, *Theory of International Politics* (New York: McGraw-Hill, 1979); John Mearsheimer, *The Tragedy of Great Power Politics* (New York: W. W. Norton, 2001); and Steven Walt, *The Hell of Good Intentions: America's Foreign Policy Elite and the Decline of US Supremacy* (New York: Farrar, Straus & Giroux, 2018).

46. Baldwin, "Power and International Relations," 277.

47. Ibid., 275.

48. Mikhail S. Gorbachev, "West Spreads Its Democracy like Coffee in Bags, but People Need to Make Own Choice," *Russia Today*, August 19, 2016, available at: https://rt.com/gorbachev, accessed August 22, 2016.

49. John Mearsheimer, "Why the Ukraine Crisis Is the West's Fault," *Foreign Affairs*, September/October 2014, available at: https://www.foreignaffairs.com/articles/russia-fsu/2014-08-18/why-ukraine-crisis-west-s-fault.

50. See Anna Andrianova, "Russian GDP Plunges 4.6%," *Bloomberg Business*, available at: http://www.bloomberg.com/news/articles/2015-08-10/russian-economy-shrinks-4-6-as-oil-slump-risks-deeper-recession, accessed August 12, 2015.

51. See "Putin's Philosopher: Ivan Ilyin and the Ideology of Moscow's Rule," *Foreign Affairs*, September 20, 2015, available at: https://www.foreignaffairs.com/articles/russian-federation/2015-09-20/putins-philosopher, accessed September 2, 2016.

52. See, for example, Robert Legvold, "The Three Russias: Decline, Revolution and Reconstruction," in *A Century's Journey: How the Great Powers Shape the World*, ed. Robert A. Pastor (New York: Basic Books, 1999), 139–190.

53. Henry Hale refers to this system as "patronalism" in *Patronal Politics: Eurasian Regime Transitions in Comparative Perspective* (New York: Cambridge University Press, 2014). I describe the system in greater detail in chapter 8.

54. Vladimir Putin, Address to the Federal Assembly, March 10, 2020.

55. See, for example, Steven Levitsky and Lucan A. Way, "Elections without Democracy: The Rise of Competitive Authoritarianism," *Journal of Democracy* 13 (April 2002): 51–65; see also their book *Competitive Authoritarianism: Hybrid Regimes after the Cold War* (Cambridge, UK: Cambridge University Press, 2010); Timothy J. Colton, "Regimeness, Hybridity, and Russian System Building as an Educative Project"; and M. Steven Fish, "What Has Russia Become?," both prepared for a special issue of *Comparative Politics* (April 2018), edited by Kathryn Stoner; Anders Åslund, *Russia's Crony Capitalism: The Path from Market Economy to Kleptocracy* (New Haven: Yale University Press, 2019); and Karen Dawisha, *Putin's Kleptocracy: Who Owns Russia?* (New York: Simon & Schuster, 2014).

56. Legvold makes this argument regarding Russian foreign policy and the legacy of authoritarianism in "The Three Russias," for example.

57. The data here come from the Levada Center, http://www.levada.ru/eng/, accessed September 7, 2015.

58. Andrei Tsygankov, *Russia's Foreign Policy: Change and Continuity in National Identity*, 4th ed. (Lanham, MD: Rowman and Littlefield, 2016); on the influence of culture on Russian foreign policy, see also Robert Nablandov, *Not by Bread Alone: Russia's Foreign Policy under Putin* (Lincoln: Potomac Books, University of Nebraska Press, 2016).

59. Stent, *The Limits of Partnership*.

60. Nikolas Gvosdev and Christopher Marsh, *Russian Foreign Policy: Interests, Vectors and Sectors* (London: Chatham House, 2014). See also Jeffery Mankoff, *Russian Foreign Policy: The Return of Great Power Politics* (New York: Council on Foreign Relations, 2012).

61. Bobo Lo, *Russia and the New World Disorder* (Washington, DC: Brookings Institution, 2015).

62. See Dmitri Trenin, *Post Imperium: A Eurasian Story* (Washington, DC: Carnegie Endowment, 2007) and *Should We Fear Russia?* (New York: Polity Press, 2016).

63. A perusal of recent titles of books on Russian politics demonstrates the emphasis on Putin alone. See, for example, Steven Lee Meyers, *The New Tsar: The Rise and Reign of Vladimir Putin* (New York: Vintage Books, 2015) and Fiona Hill and Clifford Gaddy, *Mr. Putin: Operative in the Kremlin* (Washington, DC: Brookings Institution, 2013).

64. Fish, *What Has Russia Become?*

65. A simple Google search of this phrase brings up literally dozens of references.

66. Joseph Nye coined the term "soft power." See, for example, Joseph S. Nye Jr., *Soft Power: The Means to Success in World Politics* (New York: Public Affairs, 2004).

67. Christopher Walker, "What Is 'Sharp Power'"? *Journal of Democracy* 29, no. 3 (July 2019): 9–23.

Chapter 2

1. Cf. chapter 1, David Baldwin, "Power and International Relations," 4, 2012.

2. See Angela Stent, *Putin's World: Russia against the West and with the Rest* (New York: Twelve, 2019), 34–36, regarding Eurasianism.

3. "The Geopolitics of Russia: Permanent Struggle," April 15, 2012, available at: https://www.stratfor.com/analysis/geopolitics-russia-permanent-struggle and https://www.cia.gov/library/publications/the-world-factbook/geos/rs.html, accessed June 27, 2016.

4. Border countries and length of borders with Russia are as follows:

> Azerbaijan 338 km, Belarus 1,312 km, China (southeast) 4,133 km, China (south) 46 km, Estonia 324 km, Finland 1,309 km, Georgia 894 km, Kazakhstan 7,644 km, North Korea 18 km, Latvia 332 km, Lithuania (Kaliningrad Oblast) 261 km, Mongolia 3,452 km, Norway 191 km, Poland (Kaliningrad Oblast) 210 km, and Ukraine 1,944 km, from https://www.cia.gov/library/publications/the-world-factbook/geos/rs.html, accessed June 27, 2016.

5. The governments of all three had fought actively against the Bolsheviks following the revolution of 1917.

6. James S. Corum, *The Security Concerns of the Baltic States as NATO Allies* (Carlisle, PA: Le Tort Papers, Strategic Studies Institute, US Army War College, 2013), 18.

7. Corum, *The Security Concerns of the Baltic States as NATO Allies*, 35.

8. Agnias Grigas, "Legacies, Coercion and Soft Power: Russia's Influence in the Baltic States," Briefing Paper (London: Chatham House, August 2012), 2, available at: http://irsociety.org/wp-content/uploads/2014/09/Legacies-Coercion-and-Soft-Power-Russian-Influence-in-the-Baltic-States.pdf.

  The May 2007 oil supply delay came during the Bronze Soldier riots by ethnic Russians against the relocation of a soldier commemorating Soviet/Russian resistance to the Nazis during World War II. After several months energy flows were reinstated without Estonia backing down on statue relocation. See Grigas, 5–6.

9. Ibid., 4.

10. "Completion of North Stream-2 to Strengthen European Energy Security—FM," Sputnik, April 2, 2016, available at: https://sputniknews.com/europe/201602041034192225-russia-north-stream-2-eu.

11. Grigas, "Legacies, Coercion and Soft Power," 7.

12. Ibid., 11.

13. Ibid., 2.

14. Daunis Auers, *Comparative Politics and Government of the Baltic States: Estonia, Latvia and Lithuania in the 21st Century* (London: Palgrave Macmillan, 2015), ii.

15. See Table 2.1.

16. Grigas, "Legacies, Coercion and Soft Power," 3.

17. Ibid., 10–11.

18. See United Nations data on ethnic population distribution in Estonia at https://www.unodc.org/balticstates/en/about/country-profiles/estonia.html, accessed October 1, 2020.

19. Stephen Herzog, "Revisiting the Estonian Cyber Attacks: Digital Threats and Multinational Responses," *Journal of Strategic Security* 4, no. 2 (2011): 49–60.

20. Ibid., 53.

21. In an intriguing twist of fate, Saakashvili gave up his Georgian citizenship to avoid extradition from Ukraine, and in an odd twist, in May 2015 Petro Poroshchenko, Ukraine's new president (and a personal friend to Saakashvili from their days as students at Taras Shevchenko National University in the early 1990s), appointed Saakashvili governor of the Ukrainian province of Odessa. Not long thereafter, Saakashvili became a critic of Poroshchenko's government, and resigned from his post as governor in November 2016; he was then stripped of his Ukrainian citizenship and deported to Poland. In a further odd turn of events, he returned to Ukraine and was appointed in May 2020 by Ukraine's new president, Vladimir Zelinsky, to the country's National Reform Council.

22. "Bucharest Summit Declaration," NATO, Bucharest, April 3, 2008, article 23, available at: www.nato.int/cps/en/natolive/official_texts_8443.htm, accessed August 3, 2016.

23. Dmitri V. Trenin, *Post-Imperium: A Eurasian Story* (Washington, DC: Brookings Institution Press, 2012, Kindle Edition), 32–33.

24. Vladimir Putin, Speech to the Russian Duma and Senate, March 18, 2014, available in English at: http://en.kremlin.ru/events/president/news/20603.

25. For more on the transfer of Crimea to the Ukrainian SSR, see Mark Kramer, "Why Did Russia Give Away Crimea Sixty Years Ago?" Cold War Project, March 19, 2014, available at: https://www.wilsoncenter.org/publication/why-did-russia-give-away-crimea-sixty-years-ago, accessed August 19, 2016.

26. Condoleezza Rice, *Democracy: Stories from the Long Road to Freedom* (New York: Hachette Book Group, 2017), 132.

27. This account of Ukrainian/Russian gas wars comes primarily from Anders Åslund, *Ukraine: What Went Wrong and How to Fix It* (Washington, DC: Peterson Institute for International Economics, 2015), 75–77, and Margarita Balmaceda, *The Politics of Energy Dependency: Ukraine, Belarus, and Lithuania between Domestic Oligarchs and Russian Pressure* (Toronto: University of Toronto Press, 2013).

28. Åslund, *Ukraine*, 94.

29. This account is drawn from ibid., 96–97.

30. Åslund makes this point also, at ibid., 101.

31. For a more detailed account of the Euromaidan protests and Yanukovych's moves and counter moves, see the report prepared by one of the key instigators of the protests, Mustafa Nayem, in "Uprising in Ukraine: How It All Began," Open Society Voices, April 4, 2015, available at: www.opensocietyfoundations.org/voices/uprising-ukraine-how-it-all-began, accessed August 20, 2016; and Timothy Snyder, "Fascism, Russia and Ukraine," *New York Review of Books*, March 20, 2014.

32. Office of the United Nations High Commissioner for Human Rights, *Report on the Human Rights Situation in Ukraine 16 February to 15 May 2016*, 6, available at: www.ohchr.org/Documents/Countries/UA/Ukraine_14th_HRMMU_Report.pdf, accessed August 20, 2016.

33. For Russian troop deaths, see Aleksei Erkomenko, "Russia's Classified Crisis Death Toll Appears to Have Leaked," NBC News, August 16, 2015, available at: www.nbcnews.com/storyline/ukraine-crisis/russias-classified-ukraine-crisis-death-toll-appears-have-leaked-n416206, accessed August 20, 2016.

34. See comparisons between December 2013 (as Maidan started) and December 2014 (after Maidan and Russia's seizure of Crimea) of Ukrainian public opinion on EU member-ship versus Eurasian Union membership, indicating a jump in support for EU accession, jumping from 46.4% in 2013 to 57.3% in 2014. Available at: www.razumkov.org.ua/eng/poll.php?poll_id=919, accessed September 20, 2016.

35. Trenin, *Post-Imperium*, 2.

36. Charles King, *The Moldovans: Romania, Russia, and the Politics of Culture* (Stanford, CA: Hoover Institution Press, 2000), 117.

37. Ibid., 139.

38. See Trans-Dniester Profile, BBC News, available at: www.bbc.com/news/world-europe-18284837, accessed August 29, 2016.

39. See Humphrey Hawksley, "Ukraine Crisis: Could Trans-Dniester Be Next," BBC News, March 20, 2014, available at www.bbc.com/news/world-europe-26662721, accessed August 29, 2016.

40. See EU-Republic of Moldova Relations, at http://eeas.europa.eu/factsheets/news/eu-moldova_factsheet_en.htm, accessed August 29, 2016.

41. See Freedom House's assessment of Armenia at https://freedomhouse.org/country/armenia/nations-transit/2020, accessed October 2, 2020.

42. Trenin, *Post-Imperium*, 26.

43. Ibid., 46.

44. See Vitali Silitski, "Contagion Deterred: Preemptive Authoritarianism in the Former Soviet Union (the Case of Belarus)," in *Democracy and Authoritarianism in the Postcommunist World*, ed. Valerie Bunce, Michael McFaul, and Kathryn Stoner-Weiss (New York: Cambridge University Press, 2010), 274–299.

45. Ibid., 283.

46. For more on the Eurasian Economic Union, see the Union's website, available at: www.eaeunion.org/?lang=en#about-history, accessed September 20, 2016.

47. See Trenin, *Post-Imperium*, 46 and 156.

48. Silitski, "Contagion Deterred," 20.
49. Aleksandr Lukashenko's address to the Third All-Belarusian People's Assembly, 2 March 2006, *Sovetskaya Belorussiya*, March 3, 2006.
50. Although in August of 2020, Belarusians took to the streets by the thousands to protest his re-election to the presidency, claiming fraudulent results. Lukashenko, however, drove many members of the opposition out of the country, and used his formidable security forces to beat and jail others as well as protestors in an effort to cling to power. Nonetheless, protests continued for weeks on the streets of Minsk and elsewhere, At the time of writing, Lukashenko remained in power with a security guarantee from Moscow should protests spin out of Lukashenko's control.
51. Silitski, "Contagion Deterred," 33.
52. See Margarita Balmaceda, *Belarus: Oil, Gas, Transit Pipelines and Russian Foreign Energy Policy* (London: BMG Publishing, 2006), 13–14.
53. Trenin, *Post-Imperium*, 46.
54. Ibid., 11.
55. Ibid., 152.
56. Ibid., 112.
57. See, for example, Gabrielle Tétrault-Farber, Andrei Makhovsky "Putin Says Russia Has Set Up Force to aid Belarus Leader if Needed, Reuters, August 27, 2020, available at https://www.reuters.com/article/us-belarus-election-russia/putin-says-russia-has-set-up-force-to-aid-belarus-leader-if-needed-idUSKBN25N1Q3, accessed October 1, 2020.
58. James Nixey, "The Long Goodbye: Waning Russian Influence in the South Caucasus and Central Asia" (London: Chatham House, 2012), 2, available at: https://www.chathamhouse.org/publications/papers/view/184065, accessed July 7, 2016.
59. Ibid., 5.
60. Sam Butia, "Unpacking Armenia's Resilient Economic Growth," Eurasianet, Nov. 6, 2019, available at: https://eurasianet.org/unpacking-armenias-resilient-economic-growth, accessed October 2, 2020.
61. Ownership and loan figures come from Nixey., 5. More trade and Russian FDI data regarding Armenia can be found in *Future Armenia: Connect, Compete, Prosper. A Systematic Country Diagnostic*, The Word Bank Group, November 2017. http://documents1.worldbank.org/curated/en/716961524493794871/pdf/Armenia-SCD-in-Eng-final-04192018.pdf, accessed October 2, 2020.
62. Nixey., 5.
63. The CSTO had its roots in 1992 under the framework of the Commonwealth of Independent States as the Treaty on Collective Security. In 2002 its name was changed to the Collective Security Treaty Organization and was represented as a potential counterweight or interlocutor with NATO. It is led by Russia, and its other members include Belarus, Armenia, Kazakhstan, Kyrgyzstan, and Tajikistan. Its stated goal is to provide a security community and interact with other multilateral institutions like the United Nations and NATO. It is discussed in greater detail later in this chapter.
64. Nixey, "The Long Goodbye," 6. Nagorno-Karabakh was the object of a war between Azerbaijan and Armenia after the collapse of the Soviet Union. The region was left effectively under Armenian control in a treaty signed in 1994. The treaty did not resolve the region's status, however, and disputes have erupted between ethnic Armenians and Azeris intermittently since. It is considered a "frozen" conflict, although one that heats up from time to time. Most recently, conflict erupted between Armenia and Azerbaijan as this book went to press in the autumn of 2020. For short explanations of the Nagorno-Karabakh conflict, see www.bbc.com/news/world-europe-18270325, accessed September 21, 2016 and also https://www.bbc.com/news/world-europe-54324772, accessed October 2, 2020.
65. Alexander Cooley, *Great Games, Local Rules: The New Great Power Contest in Central Asia* (New York: Oxford University Press, 2012).
66. Ibid.
67. Nixey, "The Long Goodbye," 5.
68. Cooley, *Great Games, Local Rules*.

69. Amie Ferris Rotman, "Fearing Afghan Instability, Russia Mulls Border Troops," Reuters, May 17, 2013.

70. UN Office on Drugs and Crime, *Drug Report* (New York: UNODC, 2011).

71. Ibid., 72–73.

72. World Drug Report, 2019, United Nations Office on Drugs and Crime, p. 19 available at https://wdr.unodc.org/wdr2019/prelaunch/WDR19_Booklet_1_EXECUTIVE_SUMMARY.pdf, accessed October 3, 2020.

73. See Stephen Blank, "Anti-Drug Trafficking Light Goes On in the Kremlin, but It's Low Wattage," available at: www.eurasianet.org/node/66502, accessed June 23, 2014.

74. World Drug Report, 2019, United Nations Office on Drugs and Crime, pp. 15–16.

75. See Freedom House, Map of Freedom in the World, 2020. The data are from 2019, but published online in 2020 at: https://freedomhouse.org/explore-the-map?type=fiw&year=2020, accessed July 2, 2020.

76. Angela Stent, *The Limits of Partnership: US-Russian Relations in the 21st Century* (Princeton: Princeton University Press, 2014), 98.

77. See ibid., 236–237, on the Menas case and Cooley.

78. Cooley, *Great Games, Local Rules*, 24.

79. Nixey, "The Long Goodbye," 13.

80. Trenin, *Post-Imperium*, 80.

81. Cooley, *Great Games, Local Rules*, 55.

82. Ibid., 57–58.

83. Article 7 of the Charter of the Collective Security Treaty Organization, available at: www.odkb-csto.org/documents/detail.php?ELEMENT_ID=1896, accessed September 26, 2016.

84. Charter of the Collective Security Treaty Organization (emphasis is the author's), available at: www.odkb-csto.org/documents/detail.php?ELEMENT_ID=1896, accessed September 26, 2016.

85. Albert Hayrapetyan, "Why the Collective Security Treaty Organization Is a Pale Replica of NATO," *Russia Direct*, September 8, 2016, available at: www.russia-direct.org/opinion/why-collective-security-treaty-organization-just-pale-replica-nato, accessed September 26, 2016.

86. Neil MacFarquhar, "Russia and Two Neighbors Create Economic Union That Has a Ukraine-Sized Hole," *New York Times*, May 29, 2014, available at: www.nytimes.com/2014/05/30/world/europe/putin-signs-economic-alliance-with-presidents-of-kazakhstan-and-belarus.html?_r=1, accessed September 26, 2016.

87. The Eurasian Economic Union has an excellent website that contains its founding documents, as well as the areas of trade, finance, and economics to be integrated. See https://docs.eaeunion.org/ru-ru, accessed October 3, 2020.

88. See Freedom House, *Nations in Transit*, map 2.1.

89. Bakytzhan Sagintayev, the first deputy prime minister of Kazakhstan and lead negotiator, as quoted in MacFarquhar, "Russia and Two Neighbors."

90. Nixey, "The Long Goodbye," 11.

Chapter 3

1. As quoted in Scott Wilson, "Obama Dismisses Russia as 'Regional Power' Acting out of Weakness," *Washington Post*, March 25, 2014, available at: https://www.washingtonpost.com/world/national-security/obama-dismisses-russia-as-regional-power-acting-out-of-weakness/2014/03/25/1e5a678e-b439-11e3-b899-20667de76985_story.html, accessed September 10, 2019.

2. Angela Stent, *Putin's World: Russia against the West and with the Rest* (New York: Twelve, 2019), 32–33.

3. See, for example, Alexander Dallin, "The Domestic Sources of Soviet Foreign Policy," in *The Domestic Context of Soviet Foreign Policy*, ed. S. Bialer (Boulder, CO: Westview Press, 1981), 335–408, where he argues that ideology seemed ever flexible in justifying both expansion and coexistence with the West. Certainly, there were adaptations made to ideology to fit circumstances, but it is hard to maintain the argument that ideology did not matter in Soviet foreign policy. This is also discussed usefully in Stent (2019), 37.

4. Odd Arne Westad, *The Cold War: A World History* (New York: Basic Books, 2017), 226, emphasis mine.

5. Ibid., 324.

6. For an excellent overview of the Sino-Soviet split, see ibid., 233–259.

7. Chapters 6 and 7 provide further evidence of how Putin's regime has used hard, soft, and sharp means of power abroad to disrupt international politics, and compares their relative means in these areas to China and the United States—its two "near peer" powers.

8. Since Estonia, Latvia, and Lithuania were formerly members of the Soviet Union proper, and not "Eastern European satellites" of the Soviet Union, I am not including them in the total count of former East European communist states that joined the EU in 2004. Their 2004 accession is covered in chapter 2.

9. Mitchell Orenstein, *The Lands in Between: Russia vs. the West and the New Politics of Hybrid War* (New York: Oxford University Press, 2018).

10. James Goldgeier and Michael McFaul, *Power and Purpose: US Policy toward Russia after the Cold War* (Washington, DC: Brookings Institution, 2003), in chapter 10 describe the difficult negotiations between Boris Yeltsin and Bill Clinton and their intermediaries on Kosovo, and in chapter 8 they provide an expansive discussion on NATO enlargement and Yeltsin's concerns in particular about his own domestic political standing should NATO expand prior to his re-election in 1996.

11. Dave Majumdar, "Newly Declassified Documents: Gorbachev Told NATO Wouldn't Move Past East German Border," *The National Interest*, December 12, 2017, available at: https://nationalinterest.org/blog/the-buzz/newly-declassified-documents-gorbachev-told-nato-wouldnt-23629, accessed September 12, 2019. For access to the archived documents indicating that Gorbachev may well have made such a promise, see Svetlana Savranskaya and Tom Blanton, "NATO Expansion: What Gorbachev Heard—Declassified Documents Show Security Assurances against NATO Expansion to Soviet Leaders from Baker, Bush, Genscher, Kohl, Gates, Mitterrand, Thatcher, Hurd, Major, and Woerner," Briefing Book #613, December 12, 2017, available at: https://nsarchive.gwu.edu/briefing-book/russia-programs/2017-12-12/nato-expansion-what-gorbachev-heard-western-leaders-early#. WjAX9r_XxYI.twitter, accessed September 12, 2019. See also Goldgeier and McFaul, *Power and Purpose*, 184–186 in particular.

12. See Roger Cohen, "Yeltsin Opposes Expansion of NATO in Eastern Europe," *New York Times*, October 2, 1993, available at: https://www.nytimes.com/1993/10/02/world/yeltsin-opposes-expansion-of-nato-in-eastern-europe.html, accessed September 12, 2019.

13. Goldgeier and McFaul, *Power and Purpose*, 184.

14. See ibid., chapter 8. And see Anatol Lieven, "Russian Opposition to NATO Expansion," *The World Today* 51, no. 19 (October 1995): 196–199, available at: https://www.jstor.org/stable/40396653?seq=2#metadata_info_tab_contents, accessed September 12, 2019.

15. Vladimir Putin, "Speech and the Following Discussion at the Munich Conference on Security Policy," February 10, 2008, available at: http://en.kremlin.ru/events/president/transcripts/24034, accessed September 12, 2019.

16. Angela Stent, *The Limits of Partnership: U.S.–Russia Relations in the Twenty-First Century*, (Princeton: Princeton University Press, 2014), 47.

17. Vladimir Putin, "Excerpts from Transcripts from a Press Conference for Russian and Foreign Journalists, July 18, 2001," transcripts available at: http://en.kremlin.ru/events/president/transcripts/21291, accessed July 3, 2020.

18. See Nikolai Sokov, "Why Russia Calls a Limited Nuclear Strike 'De-Escalation,'" *Bulletin of Atomic Scientists*, March 13, 2014, available at: https://thebulletin.org/2014/03/why-russia-calls-a-limited-nuclear-strike-de-escalation, accessed September 13, 2019. In June 2020, a presidential decree tried to clarify Russia's nuclear deterrent posture, and appeared to lower the threshold for the use of nuclear weapons. See chapter 6 for more detail.

19. F. Stephen Larrabee, Stephanie Pezard, Andrew Radin, Nathan Chandler, Keith Crane, and Thomas Szayna, "Russia and the West after the Ukraine Crisis: European Vulnerabilities to Russian Pressure," RAND (2017), 5.

20. Interview at Fort Irwin, August 2019.

21. A similar point is made by Mark Leonard and Nicu Popescu, "A Power Audit of EU-Russia Relations," Policy Paper (London: European Council of Foreign Relations, 2007).

22. Larrabee et al., "Russia and the West after the Ukraine Crisis," 18.

23. Ibid., 22.

24. For more examples affecting other German and French manufacturers, see ibid., 22.

25. Ibid., 23–24.

26. Orenstein, *The Lands in Between*, 113.

27. Ibid.

28. Larrabee et al., "Russia and the West after the Ukraine Crisis," 25.

29. Ibid., 27.

30. Ibid., 31.

31. "The Druzhba Pipeline Crisis: Lessons for Europe and for Russia," Oxford Institute for Energy Studies, Oxford, UK, June 19, 2019. Available at: https://www.oxfordenergy.org/wpcms/wp-content/uploads/2019/06/The-Druzhba-Pipeline-Crisis-The-Lessons-for-Russia-and-for-Europe.pdf, accessed August 29, 2019.

32. Larrabee et al., "Russia and the West after the Ukraine Crisis," 33.

33. See https://ec.europa.eu/eurostat/statistics-explained/index.php/Archive:Trade_in_energy_products.

34. Larrabee et al., "Russia and the West after the Ukraine Crisis."

35. Simon Pirani, Jonathan Stern, and Katja Yafimava, "The Russo-Ukrainian Gas Dispute of 2009: A Comprehensive Assessment," Oxford Institute for Energy Studies, February 2009, available at: https://www.oxfordenergy.org/wpcms/wp-content/uploads/2010/11/NG27-TheRussoUkrainianGasDisputeofJanuary2009AComprehensiveAssessment-JonathanSternSimonPiraniKatjaYafimava-2009.pdf, accessed September 9, 2019.

36. Orenstein, *The Lands in Between*, 65.

37. See Morena Skalamera, "Revisiting the Nabucco Debacle: Myths and Realities," *Problems of Post Communism* 65, no. 1 (2018): 20; Rawi Abdelal, "The Multinational Firm and Geopolitics: Europe, Russian Energy, and Power," *Business and Politics* 17, no. 3 (2015): 553–576; Rawi Abdelal, "The Profits of Power: Commerce and *Realpolitik* in Eurasia," *Review of International Political Economy* 20, vol. 3 (2013): 421–456; Adrian Dellecker and Thomas Gomart, eds., *Russian Energy Security and Foreign Policy* (New York: Routledge, 2011).

38. Katinka Barysch, "Should the Nabucco Pipeline Project Be Shelved?" *Policy Brief*, Centre for European Reform, May 2010; Pavel Baev and Indra Overland, "The South Stream versus Nabucco Pipeline Race; Geopolitical and Economic (Ir)rationales and Political Stakes in Mega-projects," *International Affairs* 86 (2010): 1075–1090; Frank Umbach, "The Black Sea Region and the Great Energy Game in Eurasia," in *The Eastern Partnership in the Black Sea Region: Towards a New Synergy*, ed. Adam Balcer (Warsaw: Demos Europa, Center for European Strategy, 2011), 55–88.

39. Orenstein, *The Lands in Between*, 112.

40. "TurkStream: Another Russian Gas Pipeline to Europe," Congressional Research Service, April 2019, available at: https://fas.org/sgp/crs/row/IF11177.pdf, accessed September 16, 2019.

41. See Charles K. Bartles, "Getting Gerasimov Right," *Military Review*, January/February 2016, 30–38, available at : http://fmso.leavenworth.army.mil/documents/Regional%20security%20europe/MilitaryReview_20160228_art009.pdf, accessed September 11, 2019.

42. Mitchell Orenstein and Peter Kreko, "A Russian Spy in Brussels?: The Case of KGBela—And What It Means for Europe," *Foreign Affairs*, May 29, 2014, available at: https://www.foreignaffairs.com/articles/hungary/2014-05-29/russian-spy-brussels, accessed September 11, 2019.

43. Orenstein, *The Lands in Between*, 35.

44. Alina Polyakova, Marlene Laruelle, Stefan Meister, and Neil Barnett, "The Kremlin's Trojan Horses: Russian Influence in France, Germany and the United Kingdom," Atlantic Council, November 2016, available at: www.atlanticcouncil.org/images/publications/The_Kremlins_Trojan_Horses_web_0228_third_edition.pdf.

45. Orenstein, *The Lands in Between*, 38.

46. See Stefan Meister, "The Lisa Case: Germany as a Target of Russian Disinformation," *NATO Review Magazine*, July 27, 2016, available at: https://www.nato.int/docu/review/2016/ Also-in-2016/lisa-case-germany-target-russian-disinformation/EN/index.htm, and Damien McGuinness, "Russia Steps into Berlin 'Rape' Claim Storm, Claiming German Coverup," BBC News, January 27, 2016, available at: https://www.bbc.com/news/blogs-eu-35413134, both accessed September 11, 2019.

47. See *Freedom in the World, 2020, Hungary* country report (Washington, DC: Freedom House, 2020), available at: https://freedomhouse.org/country/hungary/freedom-world/2020, accessed July 3, 2020.

48. Lionel Barber and Henry Foy, "Vladimir Putin Says Liberalism Is Obsolete," *Financial Times*, June 27, 2019, available at: https://www.ft.com/content/670039ec-98f3-11e9-9573-ee5cbb98ed36, accessed July 1, 2020.

49. *Nations in Transit*, 2020 Freedom House. Available at: https://freedomhouse.org/country/ serbia/nations-transit/2020, accessed October 3, 2020

50. Igor Delanoe, *Russie: Les enjeux du retour au Moyen-Orient* (Moscow: L'inventaire/ L'observatoire franco-russe, 2016), 32, as cited in Dmitri Trenin, *What is Russia up to in the Middle East?* (Cambridge, Polity Press, 2018), 21.

51. Trenin, 2018, 23.

52. Ibid., 25.

53. James Sladden, Becca Wasser, Ben Connable, and Sarah Grand-Clement, "Russian Strategy in the Middle East" (Los Angeles: RAND Corporation, 2017), 2.

54. Ibid.

55. Ibid.

56. Igor Ivanov, "Forward" in *Russia-Iran Partnership: An Overview and Prospects for the Future*, Russian International Affairs Council (Moscow: 2016), 6.

57. Andrei Kortunov, "Iran, Russia and the West," in *Russia-Iran Partnership*, 2016, 37, and Sladden et al., 2017.

58. This information was provided in a personal communication on June 23, 2020, to the author by Michael A. McFaul, who served at the time (2009–2011) as the senior director for Russia and Eurasia in the National Security Council of the United States during the Obama administration. He later became the American ambassador to Russia, serving from 2012 to 2014.

59. Vladimir Sazhin, "Iran-Russian Strategic Partnership at a New Stage: What Could We Propose to Each Other?" in *Russia-Iran Partnership*, 2016, 12, and see www.rusexporter.ru/research/ country/detail/4239 for more current figures.

60. Alexei Khlebnikov, "Iran, Russia, and the Impact of US Sanctions," Middle East Institute, July 17, 2019, available at: https://www.mei.edu/publications/iran-russia-and-impact-us-sanctions, accessed September 17, 2019, and "Russia and Iran Turn to Barter Trade," Radio Farda (RFE/RL Iran), June 19, 2019, available at: https://en.radiofarda.com/a/russian-and-iran-turn-to-barter-trade-/30008556.html, accessed September 17, 2019. Note that there was some disagreement as to whether the arrangement was sustained and operational for long. See Michael Lipin and Danila Galperovich, "No Evidence of Russia Buying Iran's Oil in Claimed Defiance of US Sanctions," Voice of America News, July 16, 2019, available at: https://www.voanews.com/middle-east/voa-news-iran/no-evidence-russia-buying-irans-oil-claimed-defiance-us-sanctions, accessed September 17, 2019.

61. According to Stockholm International Peace Research Institute (SIPRI) data, available at http://armstrade.sipri.org/armstrade/page/values.php, accessed September 17, 2019. Market size based on SIPRI data and author's calculations of Importer/Exporter Total Values from 2000 to 2010.

62. SIPRI, TIV of arms exports to Iran 2000–2018, generated September 17, 2019, at http:// armstrade.sipri.org/armstrade/html/export_values.php.

63. David M. Herszenhorn, "Putin, Trolling Trump, Says Saudi Arabia Should Buy Russian Air Defense System," *Politico*, September 16, 2019, available at: https://www.politico.eu/article/ putin-trolling-trump-says-saudi-arabia-should-buy-russian-air-defense-system, accessed September 17, 2019.

64. Peter Zwack and Marie-Charlotte Pierre, *Russian Challenges from Now in the Next Generation: A Geostrategic Primer*, (Washington, D.C.: Institute for National Strategic Studies, National Defense University, 2018), 19.

65. Transcript "Special Representative for Syria Engagement Jeffrey Interview with RIA Novosti and Kommersant," November 21, 2018, available at: https://ru.usembassy.gov/special-representative-for-syria-engagement-jeffrey-in-interview-with-ria-novosti-and-kommersant, accessed September 18, 2019.

66. Dimitar Bechev, "Russia's Pipe Dreams Are Europe's Nightmare," *Foreign Policy*, March 12, 2019, available at: https://foreignpolicy.com/2019/03/12/russia-turkstream-oil-pipeline, accessed September 16, 2019.

67. Ruslan Mamedov, "After the Caliphate: The Prospects of Russia-Iraq Relations," Working Paper #46 (Moscow: Russia International Affairs Council, 2019), 5–6.

68. Ruslan Pukhov and Sergei Denisentsev, "Nashe oruzhie snova v Irake," *Voennoe obozrenie*, July 5, 2015, available at: https://topwar.ru/78238-nashe-oruzhie-snova-v-irake.html, accessed September 20, 2019.

69. Ibid.

70. Mamedov, "After the Caliphate," 15.

71. Ibid.

72. Şaban Kardaş, "Turkey-Russia Energy Relations: The Limits of Establishing Cooperation through Economic Interdependence," *International Journal* 67, no. 1 (Winter 2011–2012): 81–100.

73. Dimitar Bechev, "Russia's Pipe Dreams Are Europe's Nightmare" .

74. Pinar Tank, "Turkey's Turn toward Russia," Carnegie Endowment for International Peace, May 16, 2017, available at: https://carnegieendowment.org/sada/69981, accessed May 2, 2018.

75. Vladimir Putin, as quoted in ibid.

76. Joshua Krasna, "Moscow on the Mediterranean: Russia and Israel's Relationship," Russia Foreign Policy Papers, Foreign Policy Research Institute, June 2018, 9–10.

77. "Putin Awards Soviet WWII Veterans in Israel Lifetime Benefits," December 31, 2017, available at: https://tass.com/society/983700, accessed October 4, 2019.

78. Krasna, "Moscow on the Mediterranean," 10, and also *Moscow Times*, "Russia to Pay $83 Million to Israeli Pensioners in 2017," June 8, 2016, available at: https://www.themoscowtimes.com/2016/06/08/russia-to-pay-to-83m-to-israeli-pensioners-in-2017-a53205, accessed October 4, 2019.

79. Krasna, "Moscow on the Mediterranean," 7.

80. Ibid., 12, citing the Israeli ambassador to Russia, Magen.

81. Mark N. Katz, "Putin's Pro-Israel Policy," *Middle East Quarterly* 12, no. 1 (Winter 2005): 51–59.

82. Benjamin Netanyahu, March 9, 2017, "Meeting with Prime Minister of Israel Benjamin Netanyahu Vladimir: Putin Met at the Kremlin with Prime Minister of Israel Benjamin Netanyahu, Who Is in Russia on a Brief Working Visit," website of the President of the Russian Federation, available at: http://en.kremlin.ru/events/president/news/54016, accessed October 4, 2019.

83. Anna Borshchevskaya, "Putin's Self-Serving Agenda: Why Russia Now Recognizes West Jerusalem as the Capital," *Foreign Affairs*, April 13 2017, available at: https://www.foreignaffairs.com/articles/israel/2017-04-13/putins-self-serving-israel-agenda, accessed October 4, 2020.

84. Vladimir Putin, Speech to the 70th Session of the UN General Assembly, September 28, 2015, available at: http://en.kremlin.ru/events/president/news/50385, accessed October 3, 2020.

85. Sladden et al., "Russian Strategy in the Middle East," 6–7.

86. Federica Saini Fasinotti, "Russia and Libya: A Brief History of an On-Again-Off-Again Friendship," (Washington, D.C.: Brookings Institution), 2016.

87. Ibid and Tarek Megerisi and Mattia Toldi, "Russia in Libya: A Drive for Escalation," (Washington, D.C.: Carnegie Endowment for International Peace, December 8, 2016.

88. Tarek Megerisi and Mattia Toldi, "Russia in Libya"

89. Ibid.

90. "35 Russian Mercenaries Killed in Libya," October 9, 2019, VOA News, available at: http://voanews.com/Africa/reports-35-russian-mercenaries-killed-Libya, accessed October 27, 2019.

91. Stanley Reed, "Russia and OPEC Draw Closer on Oil, Joining Other Producers to Manage Market," *New York Times*, July 2, 2019, available at: https://www.nytimes.com/2019/07/02/business/energy-environment/opec-russia.html, accessed November 2, 2019.

92. This figure comes from the United States Energy Information Administration, https://www.eia.gov/tools/faqs/faq.php?id=709&t=6, accessed December 19, 2019.

93. Sladden et al., "Russian Strategy in the Middle East," 7.

94. Henry Foy, "Russia-Saudi Arabia Rapprochement Reshapes More than the Oil Market," *Financial Times*, October 29, 2018, available at: https://www.ft.com/content/aa39b74c-4f0c-11e8-ac41-759eee1efb74, accessed October 2, 2020.

95. Euronews, "Saudi Arabia and Russia Sign Arms Deal," October 6, 2017, available at: https://www.euronews.com/2017/10/06/saudi-arabia-and-russia-sign-arms-deal, accessed October 3, 2020.

96. Stockholm International Peace Research Institute, Arms Transfer Database, March 11, 2019, available at: https://www.sipri.org/research/armament-and-disarmament/arms-transfers-and-military-spending/international-arms-transfers, accessed November 2, 2019.

97. Sladden et al., "Russian Strategy in the Middle East," 10.

98. Mehmet Cem Ogulturk, "Russia's Renewed Interests in the Horn of Africa as a Traditional Rising Power," Rising Powers Quarterly, vo. 2, issue 1, February 2017, 127.

99. Aleksandra Arkhangelskaya and Vladimir Shubin, "Russia's Africa Policy," Occasional paper no. 157, Global Powers and Africa Programme, South African Institute for International Affairs, October 2013, 21.

100. Ibid, 9

101. Ibid 2015, 10.

102. "The Concept of Foreign Policy of the Russian Federation (approved by President of the Russian Federation V. V. Putin on November 30, 2016)" (Ministry of Foreign Affairs of the Russian Federation, published December 12, 2016), 30, point 99.

103. Keir Giles, "Russian Interests in Sub-Saharan Africa," (Carlisle, PA: Strategic Studies Institute, US Army War College, 2013).

104. Arkhangelskaya and Shubin.

105. Arkhangelskaya and Shubin, 16. See also Anton Troianovski, "'A New Message': Russia Trains Its Propaganda Machine on Africa," *New York Times*, October 29, 2019, available at: https://www.nytimes.com/2019/10/29/world/europe/africa-russia-sochi.html, accessed November 25, 2019.

106. Arkhangelskaya and Shubin, 17.

107. Ibid., 19.

108. Henry Foy, "Putin Seeks Friends and Influence at First Ever Russia-Africa Summit, https://www.ft.com/content/f20dbcc2-f17b-11e9-ad1e-4367d828119S, accessed October 4, 2020, and Tamas Gerocs, "The Transformation of African-Russian Economic Relations in the Multi-Polar World System," *Review of African Political Economy*, vol. 46, issue 160, 2019, 317–335.

109. Both quoted in Troianovski, "'A New Message.'"

110. Ibid.

111. See Kimberly Marten, "Russia's Use of Semi-State Security Forces: The Case of the Wagner Group," *Post-Soviet Affairs* 35, no. 3 (2019): 181–204. See also Tarek Megerisi and Mattia Toaldo, "Russia in Libya, A Driver for Escalation?" (Washington, D.C.: Carnegie Endowment for International Peace), December 8, 2016.

112. Dionne Searcey "Gems, Warlords and Mercenaries: Russia's Playbook in Central African Republic," *New York Times*, September 30, 2019, available at: https://www.nytimes.com/2019/09/30/world/russia-diamonds-africa-prigozhin.html, accessed October 3, 2019

113. See Michael Schwirtz and Gaelle Borgia, "How Russia Meddles Abroad for Profit: Cash, Trolls and a Cult Leader," *New York Times*, November 11, 2019, available at: https://www.google.com/search?q=russia+madagascar+nyt&oq=Russia+mada&aqs=chrome.2.69i57j0 l5.4633j0j7&sourceid=chrome&ie=UTF-8, accessed November 25, 2019.

114. Shelby Grossman, Dan Bush, and Renee DiResta, "Evidence of Russia-Linked Influence Operations in Africa," Stanford Internet Observatory, October 29, 2019, available at: https://fsi-live.s3.us-west-1.amazonaws.com/s3fs-public/29oct2019_sio_-_russia_ linked_influence_operations_in_africa.final_.pdf, accessed December 19, 2019.

115. See Arne Westad, *The Cold War: A World History*, (New York: Basic Books, 2018).

116. Zwack and Pierre, 45.

117. Ibid.

118. Carl Meacham, "Is Russia Moving In on Latin America?" CSIS, March 25, 2014.

119. See Diana Villiers Negroponte, "What's Putin's Game in the Western Hemisphere," *Americas Quarterly*, Winter 2015, available at: https://www.americasquarterly.org/content/whats-putins-game-western-hemisphere, accessed November 25, 2019.

120. Hearing to Receive Testimony on the United States Northern Command and Southern Command in Review of the Defense Authorization Request for 2019 and the Future Years Defense Program before the US Senate Armed Services Committee, 115th Congress (2018), February 15, 2018 (Statement of Admiral Kurt W. Tidd, Commander, United States Southern Command), .6, available at: https://www.armed-services.senate.gov/hearings/18-02-15-united-states-northern-command-and-united-states-southern-command, accessed October 5, 2019.

121. As cited by "Russo-Latin American Arms Sales," in *Americas Quarterly*, Winter 2015, available at: https://www.americasquarterly.org/content/russo-latin-american-arms-sales; accessed October 4, 2020.

122. Clifford Krauss, "Russia Uses Its Oil Giant Rosneft as a Foreign Policy Tool," *New York Times*, October 29, 2017, available at https://www.nytimes.com/2017/10/29/business/energy-environment/russia-venezula-oil-rosneft.html, accessed October 4, 2020.

123. Ibid.

124. Ryan C. Berg, "Is Russia Gearing Up for a Conflict with the United States in the Caribbean?," *Foreign Policy*, October 9, 2019, available at: https://foreignpolicy.com/2019/10/09/russias-putin-venezuela-evade-oil-sanctions-preparing-conflict-united-states, accessed October 11, 2019.

125. Douglas Farah and Kathryn Babineau, "Extra-regional Actors in Latin America: The United States Is Not the Only Game in Town," *PRISM: The Journal of Complex Operations* 8, no. 1 (February 26, 2019), available at: https://cco.ndu.edu/News/Article/1767399/extra-regional-actors-in-latin-america-the-united-states-is-not-the-only-game-i, accessed November 25, 2019.

126. Hearing to Receive Testimony on the United States Northern Command and Southern Command in Review of the Defense Authorization Request for 2019 and the Future Years Defense Program before the US Senate Armed Services Committee, 115th Congress (2018), February 15, 2018 (Statement of Admiral Kurt W. Tidd, Commander, United States Southern Command), .7, available at: https://www.armed-services.senate.gov/hearings/18-02-15-united-states-northern-command-and-united-states-southern-command, accessed November 3, 2019.

127. Daniel R. Coats, "Statement for the Record: Worldwide Threat Assessment of the United States Intelligence Community," for the United States Senate Select Committee on Intelligence, January 29, 2019, 17.

128. See, for example, Leon Aron, "Are Russia and China Really Forming an Alliance?: The Evidence Is Less than Impressive," *Foreign Affairs*, April 4, 2019, available at https://www.foreignaffairs.com/articles/china/2019-04-04/are-russia-and-china-really-forming-alliance, accessed December 9, 2019.

129. See Dmitri Trenin, "How Cozy Is Russia and China's Military Relationship?," Carnegie Endowment for International Peace, November 19, 2019; Lora Saalman, ed., "China-Russia Relations and Regional Dynamics: From Pivots to Regional Diplomacy," Stockholm International Peace Research Institute (SIPRI), (Stockholm, March 2017), 26; and Coats, "Statement for the Record," 37, supporting the points regarding military technological superiority, as well as material in chapter 6 of the current study. Russia's arrangements

with OPEC via Saudi Arabia described earlier in this chapter also support the point of its increased weightiness in the oil sector.

130. Nadege Rolland, "A China-Russia Condominium Over Eurasia," 7, available at https://www.iiss.org/publications/survival/2019/survival-global-politics-and-strategy-februarymarch-2019/611-02-rolland, accessed October 4, 2020.

131. Aron, "Are Russia and China Really Forming an Alliance?," citing SIPRI data.

132. A. V. Lukin and V. B. Kashin, "Russian-Chinese Cooperation and Security in the Asia Pacific Region," *Comparative Politics Russia* 10, no. 2 (2019): 135–151 (in Russian), available at: https://doi.org/10.24411/2221-3279-2019-10021, accessed December 13, 2019.

133. Trenin, "How Cozy Is Russia and China's Military Relationship?"

134. SIPRI 2017, 26 and Ray Silvius, "Chinese-Russian Economic Relations: Developing the Infrastructure of a Multi-Polar Global Political Economy?" *International Politics* 26 (2019): 622–638.

135. Katie Stallard-Blanchette, "Putin and Xi's Buddy Act Could Blow Up East Asia," *Foreign Policy*, July 31, 2019.

136. See Varvara Pertsova, "Neft' i politika: kak Rossiya zakhvatyvala rynok chernogo zolota pri Putine," *Forbes Russia*, March 23, 2018, available at: https://www.forbes.ru/biznes/359015-neft-i-politika-kak-rossiya-zahvatyvala-rynok-chernogo-zolota-pri-putine, accessed November 5, 2019, and Alexey Khlebnikov, "Iran, Russia, and the Impact of US Sanctions," The Middle East Institute, July 17, 2019, available at: https://www.mei.edu/publications/iran-russia-and-impact-us-sanctions, accessed December 9, 2019.

137. Georgi Kantchev, "China and Russia are Partners – and Now Have a \$55 billion Pipeline to Prove It" , *Wall Street Journal*, December 1, 2019, available at https://www.wsj.com/articles/china-and-russia-are-partnersand-now-have-a-55-billion-pipeline-to-prove-it-11575225030, accessed October 4, 2020.

138. See "Russian-Chinese Joint Declaration on a Multi-Polar World and the Establishment of a New International Order," Ministry of Foreign Affairs of the Russian Federation, 1997; Lora Saalman, ed., *China-Russia Relations and Regional Dynamics: From Pivots to Peripheral Diplomacy* (SIPRI, March 2017), available at https://www.sipri.org/publications/2017/other-publications/china-russia-relations, accessed October 4, 2020.

139. See President of Russia, "Presenting the Order of St. Andrew the Apostle to President Xi," July 4, 2017, available at: http://en.kremlin.ru/events/president/news/54973, accessed December 9, 2019.

140. Reported by Reuters, "China's Xi Awards 'Best Friend' Putin Friendship Medal, Promises Support," June 8, 2018, available at https://www.reuters.com/article/us-china-russia/chinas-xi-awards-best-friend-putin-friendship-medal-promises-support-idUSKCN1J41RO, accessed October 4, 2020.

141. Aron, "Are Russia and China Really Forming an Alliance?"

142. Westad, *The Cold War: A World History*, 438 (electronic version).

143. Russian International Affairs Council (RIAC), *Report - 70ᵗʰ Anniversary of Russia-India Relations: New Horizons of Privileged Partnership*, (Moscow: 2017, 14.

144. Ibid., 34.

145. Ibid., 34.

146. Ibid., 23.

147. Pieter Weseman et al., "Fact Sheet: Trends in International Arms Transfers, 2019" Stockholm International Peace Research Institute (SIPRI), March 2020, available at https://sipri.org/sites/default/files/2020-03/fs_2003_at_2019.pdf, accessed October 4, 2020.

148. *70ᵗʰ Anniversary of Russia-India Relations, 2017*, 14.

149. "What's India Doing in Russia's Far East?" *The Diplomat*, October 9, 2019. Online; trade statistics are from the International Monetary Fund Direction of Trade Statistics available at: https://data.imf.org/regular.aspx?key=61013712, accessed December 10, 2019.

150. Shruti Godbole, "Future of the India-Russia Relationship post Sochi Summit," Brookings Blog, July 2, 2018, available at: www.brookings.edu/blog/up-front/2018/07/02, accessed June 30, 2019.

Chapter 4

1. Karen Dawisha, *Putin's Kleptocracy: Who Owns Russia?* (New York: Simon & Schuster, 2014); on kleptocracy, crony capitalism, and organized crime in Russia, also see also Anders Åslund *Russia's Crony Capitalism: The Path from Market Economy to Kleptocracy* (New Haven: Yale University Press, 2019), and work by Mark Galeotti, David Hoffman, Dylan Myles-Primakoff, and others.

2. https://data.worldbank.org/country/russian-federation and official 2018 report available at: https://openknowledge.worldbank.org/handle/10986/31158.

3. "Recession and Growth Under the Shadow of a Pandemic," Russia Economic Report, no. 43, July 6, 2020. (Washington, DC: World Bank), available at https://www.worldbank.org/en/country/russia/publication/rer, accessed October 4, 2020.

4. Dawisha, *Putin's Kleptocracy*, 1–4. See also Anders Åslund, *Russia's Crony Capitalism*.

5. This is not to suggest that Russian entrepreneurs did not create new, dynamic tech and information companies, including, for example, Kaspersky Labs, Yandex, Odnoklasniki, V Kontakte, and Telegram, among others. These, however, were minuscule in comparison to Google, Facebook, and WhatsApp. I discuss some of Russia's leading companies later in this chapter.

6. Russia Monthly Economic Developments Report, January 2019. World Bank. Available at: http://documents.worldbank.org/curated/en/397961548429146766/Russia-Monthly-Economic-Developments.pdf, accessed September 18, 2019.

7. On the development of the banking system in the late Soviet Union and early Russian economy, see, for example, Juliet Johnson, *A Fist Full of Rubles: The Rise and Fall of the Russian Banking System* (Ithaca, NY: Cornell University Press, 2000). See also Anders Åslund, *How Capitalism Was Built: The Transformation of Central and Eastern Europe, Russia, and Central Asia* (Cambridge, UK: Cambridge University Press, 2008).

8. Mikhail S. Gorbachev, *Memoirs* (New York: Doubleday, 1995), 165.

9. Timothy Colton, *The Dilemma of Reform in the Soviet Union* (New York: Council on Foreign Relations, 1986), 47.

10. Ibid., 35.

11. Ibid., 51.

12. Åslund, *How Capitalism Was Built*, 147; see also János Kornai, *The Socialist System: The Political Economy of Communism* (Princeton: Princeton University Press, 1992).

13. Åslund, *How Capitalism Was Built*, 71.

14. Yegor Gaidar, *The Collapse of an Empire: Lessons for Modern Russia* (Washington, DC: Brookings Institution, 2007), 61, 108–109; this quotation is from Gaidar's speech at the American Enterprise Institute, "The Soviet Collapse," November 13, 2006, available at: http://www.aei.org/feature/the-soviet-collapse, accessed July 8, 2019.

15. Gaidar, speech at the American Enterprise Institute, 2006.

16. Gaidar, *The Collapse of an Empire*, 242.

17. Ibid., 95.

18. Colton, *The Dilemma of Reform in the Soviet Union*, 52.

19. These estimates are from the International Monetary Fund, "The Economy of the former USSR in 1991," *Economic Review* (Washington DC, 1992), 76.

20. Gaidar, *The Collapse of an Empire*, 99

21. See Colton, *The Dilemma of Reform in the Soviet Union*, and cf. chapter 5 on demographic trends overall.

22. Colton, *The Dilemma of Reform in the Soviet Union*, 36.

23. David Lipton and Jeffrey Sachs, "Russia's Prospects for Economic Reforms," *Brookings Papers on Economic Activity*, no. 2 (1992): 220.

24. Ibid., 224.

25. Anders Åslund, *Russia's Capitalist Revolution: Why Market Reform Succeeded and Democracy Failed* (Washington, DC: Peterson Institute for Economic Studies, 2007), 91.

26. Lipton and Sachs, "Russia's Prospects for Economic Reforms," 219.

27. Ibid.

28. See, for example, Åslund, *Russia's Capitalist Revolution*; Lipton and Sachs, "Russia's Prospects for Economic Reforms."

29. See Figure 4.6, p. 135 and also chapter 5, table 5.15, p. 171 of this book for more on Russian poverty rates.

30. See Åslund, *Russia's Capitalist Revolution*; Daniel Treisman, "Russia's Billionaires," *American Economic Review* 106, no. 5 (May 2016): 236–241; Timothy J. Colton, *Russia: What Everyone Needs to Know* (Oxford: Oxford University Press, 2016); Richard Sakwa, *Putin and the Oligarch: The Khodorkovsky-Yukos Affair* (London and New York: I. B. Tauris & Co. Ltd., 2014).

31. International Monetary Fund, World Economic Outlook Database. Statistics on gross domestic product as shares of the global economy available at: http://www.imf.org/external/pubs/ft/weo/2017/01/weodata/index.aspx, accessed May 2, 2017.

32. https://www.imf.org/external/datamapper/GGXWDG_NGDP@WEO/OEMDC/ADVEC/WEOWORLD/RUS.

33. https://www.imf.org/external/datamapper/GGXWDG_NGDP@WEO/OEMDC/ADVEC/WEOWORLD/RUS/USA.

34. https://www.worldbank.org/en/country/russia/brief/international-development and https://www.oecd.org/russia/russias-official-development-assistance.htm.

35. https://data.oecd.org/oda/net-oda.htm.

36. Vladimir Putin, "Russia at the Turn of the Millennium" (*Rossiia na rubezhe tysiacheletii*), December 29, 1999, available at: www.ng.ru/politics/1999-12-30/4_millenium.html, accessed September 10, 2019.

37. Ibid. Putin does not indicate whether these numbers refer to the volume of foreign investment in 1999 or since the collapse of the Soviet Union.

38. https://data.worldbank.org/country/france?view=chart and https://data.worldbank.org/country/united-kingdom?view=chart, accessed June 24, 2019.

39. Vladimir Putin, Inaugural Address, May 6, 2000, Radio Free Europe/Radio Liberty Russia Reports.

40. *OECD Reviews of Innovation Policy, Russian Federation* (Paris, OECD, 2011), 12, available at: https://www.oecd-ilibrary.org/science-and-technology/oecd-reviews-of-innovation-policy-russian-federation-2011_9789264113138-en, accessed June 28, 2019.

41. Ibid., 77.

42. Ibid., 68.

43. Ibid, 71

44. Maggie McGrath, "2017 Global 2000: These Are the Largest Companies in Russia," *Forbes* (May 24, 2017), available at: https://www.forbes.com/sites/maggiemcgrath/2017/05/24/the-2017-global-2000-these-are-the-largest-companies-in-russia/#7f94794d62af, accessed September 18, 2019.

45. "PM Medvedev Wants Russia to Achieve GDP Growth Higher Than That of Global Economy," *TASS* (September 8. 2017), available at https://tass.com/economy/964755, accessed September 18, 2019.

46. Vladimir Putin, interview with the *Financial Times*, June 27, 2019, available at https://www.ft.com/content/670039ec-98f3-11e9-9573-ee5cbb98ed36, accessed September 18, 2019.

47. OECD (2011), p. 79.

48. Ibid.

49. See OECD, "Investment Policy Reviews: Russian Federation 2008, Strengthening the Policy Framework for Investment" (Paris: OECD, 2008).

50. Ibid.

51. Author's notes from attending Medvedev's address at Stanford University, June 23, 2010.

52. Kontseptsiia dolgosrochnovo sotsial'no-ekonomicheskogo razvitiia Rossiiskoi Federatsii (Concept of the Long-Term Socio-Economic Development of the Russian Federation to 2020). September 2007, available at www.economy.gov.ru/wps/wcm/myconnect/economylib/mert/welcome/economy/macroeconomy/administmanagementdirect/doc1202863991297, cited in Andrew Kutchins et al., *Russia's 2020 Strategic Economic Goals and the Role of International Integration, July 2008, Center for Strategic and International Studies*

(*CSIS*), www.ifpa.org/confrncNworkshp/confrncNworkshpPages/usRussiaMarch2011/Russias%202020%20Strategic%20Goals.pdf, accessed June 30, 2019.

53. OECD Investment Policy Reviews, "Russian Federation, 2008: Strengthening the Policy Framework for Investment" (Paris: OECD, 2008).

54. See https://unctad.org/en/PublicationsLibrary/webdiaeia2013d6_en.pdf.

55. For patterns of FDI in this period, see https://www.ceicdata.com/en/indicator/russia/foreign-direct-investment, accessed July 12, 2019.

56. For an interesting argument regarding the nil effect of these sanctions on the Russian economy, see Stacy Closson, "Diminishing Returns: How Effective Are Sanctions against Russia?" PONARS Eurasia Policy Memo no. 567, January 2019, available at www.ponarseurasia.org/memo/diminishing-returns-how-effective-are-sanctions-against-russia, accessed September 19, 2019.

57. https://tradingeconomics.com/russia/foreign-direct-investment.

58. Data are from https://data.oecd.org/fdi/fdi-stocks.htm.

59. "The Rise of BRICS FDI and Africa," Global Investment Trends Monitor, United Nations UNCTAD (March 25, 2013), 6, available at https://unctad.org/en/PublicationsLibrary/webdiaeia2013d6_en.pdf, accessed July 12, 2019.

60. "The Rise of BRICS FDI and Africa," 8.

61. See Organization for Cooperation and Economic Development (OECD) Data, GDP per hour worked available at https://data.oecd.org/lprdty/gdp-per-hour-worked.htm#indicator-chart, accessed October 1, 2020.

62. See, for example, the 2019 Index of Economic Freedom, available at https://www.heritage.org/index/country/russia.

63. "The Kremlin Named as Biggest Threat To Competitive Russian Economy," *The Moscow Times*, February 2, 2017. https://www.themoscowtimes.com/2017/02/08/kremlin-named-as-biggest-threat-to-competitive-russian-economy-a57077.

64. DiBella, Dynnikova, and Slavov make this excellent point and note articles that appeared in Project Syndicate and CNN, among others. Gabriel DiBella, Oksana Dynnikova, and Slavi Slavov, "The Russian State's Size and Its Footprint: Have They Increased?" International Monetary Fund Working Paper 19/53 (March 2, 2019), 3, fn. 1, available at https://www.imf.org/~/media/Files/Publications/WP/2019/WPIEA2019053.ashx, accessed July 12, 2019.

65. Robert Barro, "A Cross Country Study of Growth, Saving, and Government," National Bureau of Economic Research, (1991).

66. See, for example, Maxim Boycko, Andrei Shleifer, Robert Vishny, *Privatizing Russia* (Cambridge, MA: MIT Press, 1993).

67. European Bank for Reconstruction and Development (EBRD), as cited in DiBella, Dynnikova, and Slavov, "The Russian State's Size and Its Footprint," 12. Their methodology uses the EBRD's definition of State-Owned Enterprises and controls for the possible under specification of the subsidiaries of SOEs of the twenty biggest non-financial state conglomerate enterprises like Gazprom, Rosneft, Transneft, etc.

68. DiBella, Dynnikova, and Slavov, "The Russian State's Size and Its Footprint," 12.

69. For more on this, see the interesting discussion in Åslund, *Russia's Crony Capitalism*, 212–217.

70. OECD, Reviews of Innovation Policy, Russian Federation, 2011, available at https://read.oecd-ilibrary.org/science-and-technology/oecd-reviews-of-innovation-policy-russian-federation-2011_9789264113138-en#page22.

71. Maggie McGrath, "How Much of Russia's Biggest Banks and Drillers Does the Kremlin Own?" *Forbes*, May 24, 2017, available at https://www.forbes.com/sites/maggiemcgrath/2017/05/24/heres-how-much-of-russias-biggest-banks-and-drillers-the-kremlin-owns/#56b9b0713fea, accessed July 15, 2019, and also "Регстр предприятий, находящихся в собственности РФ, госкорпораций, хозобществ, акции (доли) которых находятся в собственности РФ" (Register of enterprises owned by the Russian Federation, state corporations, property and shares of which are the property of the Russian Federation), http://esugi.rosim.ru/Section/OpenInfo/Browser/Index/849b732a-d0b2-4742-8f3f-b592d5ff3bb4, accessed July 15, 2019.

72. OECD (2011), 23.

73. OECD, Reviews of Innovation Policy, Russian Federation, 2011.

74. D. B. Kuvalina, A. K. Moiseeva, and Yu. V. Zinchenkoa, "Russian Enterprises at the End of 2018: Analysis of Global Sustainable Development Goals and Difficulties in Obtaining Bank Loans," *Studies on Russian Economic Development* 30, no. 3 (2019): 334–345. The survey was conducted by the Institute for Economic Forecasting at the Russian Academy of Sciences in November–December 2018. In total, 142 companies were involved in the survey in a wide variety of sectors (power engineering; ferrous and nonferrous metallurgy, chemistry, mechanical engineering, the building-materials industry, the timber industry, woodworking and the pulp and paper industry, light, food, pharmaceuticals, printing, perfumery, and the medical industry; agriculture, construction, transport, and sanatorium resort sphere) for fifty-two regions of Russia.

75. See Dawisha, *Putin's Kleptocracy*, and Åslund, *Russia's Crony Capitalism*, especially chapter 6.

76. As summarized in Åslund, *Russia's Crony Capitalism*, 154.

77. As cited in ibid. Chapter 8 of the current study goes into greater depth on how patronalism functions.

78. OECD (2011), 119.

Chapter 5

1. Vladimir Putin, Annual Address to the Russian Federal Assembly, May 10, 2006, available at: http://en.kremlin.ru/events/president/transcripts/23577, accessed January 20, 2020.

2. The numbers vary depending on the source, but the official Soviet estimate was 8.7 million soldiers, while other sources indicate that number may have been as high as 10 million. The estimate of Soviet civilian deaths in World War II appears in a number of sources, including https://worldpopulationreview.com/country-rankings/world-war-two-casualties-by-country. For readers interested in the total death toll by country in World War II, a fascinating video with interactive charts, "The Fallen of WWII," is available at: http://www.fallen.io/ww2, accessed July 5, 2020.

3. Timothy Snyder, *Bloodlands: Europe between Hitler and Stalin* (New York: Basic Books, 2012), 21–58; and see also Timothy Snyder, "Hitler vs. Stalin: Who Killed More?" *New York Review of Books*, March 10, 2011, available at: https://www.nybooks.com/articles/2011/03/10/hitler-vs-stalin-who-killed-more, accessed July 5, 2020, where he estimates that between 1930 and 1953, Stalin's regime killed an additional approximately 9 million between famines (particularly in Ukraine, where 3.3 million died), the Gulag, and the Great Terror.

4. Human Development Indices and Indicators: 2018 Statistical Update Briefing note for countries on the 2018 Statistical Update Russian Federation, available at http://hdr.undp.org/sites/all/themes/hdr_theme/country-notes/RUS.pdf, accessed July 22, 2019.

5. See United Nations Human Development Index Rankings, 2017, available at: http://hdr.undp.org/en/data, accessed January 20, 2020.

6. See, for example, John S. Earle and Scott Gelbach, "Mass Privatization and the Post-Communist Mortality Crisis: Is There a Relationship?," *Upjohn Working Papers and Journal Articles*, 2010.

7. United Nations Human Development Index, 2018; in 2019 it dropped back slightly to 66.9 years, UN Human Development Index, Russian country profile 2020, available at http://www.hdr.undp.org/en/countries/profiles/RUS, accessed October 6, 2020.

8. For rates of alcoholism in Russia from the 1960s onward, see World Health Organization, Russian Country Profile, Global Alcohol Report, available at: https://www.who.int/substance_abuse/publications/global_alcohol_report/profiles/rus.pdf?ua=1, accessed December 21, 2019.

9. Female life expectancy would dip slightly in 2019 to 77.6 years. Russian Country Profile, UN Human Development Index, 2020.

10. See Vladimir M. Shkolnikov, Evgeny M. Andreev, Rustam Tursun-zade, and David A. Leon, "Patterns in the Relationship between Life Expectancy and Gross Domestic Product in Russia in 2005–15: A Cross-Sectional Analysis," *The Lancet Public Health* 4, Issue 4 (April 2019): e181–e188, available at: https://www.sciencedirect.com/science/article/pii/S2468266719300362, accessed July 29, 2019.

11. In 2018, Mexico's GDP was 2.574 trillion current US dollars, Russia's was 4.193 trillion, and São Tomé and Principe's was 852.7 million, World Bank, https://data.worldbank.org/

indicator/NY.GDP.MKTP.PP.CD?contextual=similar&locations=MX-RU-SA-MD-ST, accessed July 5, 2020.

12. Decree of the President of the Russian Federation on National Goals and Strategic Objectives of the Development of the Russian Federation for the Period to 2024, issued May 7, 2018. A condensed version is available at: http://en.kremlin.ru/events/president/news/57425, accessed January 20, 2020.

13. For more on gender and labor force participation in Russia, see https://www.theglobaleconomy.com/Russia/Female_labor_force_participation, https://www.theglobaleconomy.com/Russia/Male_labor_force_participation, and http://datatopics.worldbank.org/gender/country/russian-federation. All accessed December 21, 2019.

14. See Nana Pogosova and Olga Sokolova, "Governmental Efforts for Cardiovascular Disease Prevention in the Russian Federation," National Research Center for Preventative Medicine, Moscow, Russia, February 27, 2017, available at http://dx.doi.org/10.21037/cdt.2017.03.01, accessed December 21, 2019. See also Decree of the President of the Russian Federation on National Goals and Strategic Objectives up to 2024, May 7, 2018, no. 404. Available at Presidential Library of the Russian Federation, https://www.prlib.ru/en/item/1155783, accessed December 21, 2019.

15. For more on the course of COVID-19 in Russia through 2020, see https://www.worldometers.info/coronavirus/country/russia/, accessed October 6, 2020. On the possibility of underreporting deaths due to COVID see Jake Cordell, "Six Months into the Corona Virus Outbreak, Russia's Statistics Still Provide More Questions than Answers, " *The Moscow Times*, August 11, 2020, available at: https://www.themoscowtimes.com/2020/08/11/six-months-into-the-coronavirus-outbreak-russias-statistics-still-provide-more-questions-than-answers-a71069, accessed October 6, 2020.

16. Robert Marten, Diane McIntyre, Claudia Travassos, Sergei Shishkin, Wang Longde, Rinath Reddy, and Jeanette Vega, "An Assessment of the Progress towards Universal Health Coverage in Brazil, Russia, India, China, and South Africa (BRICS)," *The Lancet* 384 (December 13, 2014): 2165–2166, Available at https://www.thelancet.com/journals/lancet/article/PIIS0140-6736(14)60075-1/fulltext, accessed July 29, 2019.

17. Mortality rate, infant (per 1,000 live births)—Russian Federation, United States, France, Japan, Kazakhstan, Ukraine, available at https://data.worldbank.org/indicator/SP.DYN.IMRT.IN?end=2018&locations=RU-US-FR-JP-KZ-UA&start=2018&view=bar, accessed December 21, 2019.

18. See "Mortality Rate, Under-5 (per 1,000 live births)" in the World Bank indicators, available at: https://data.worldbank.org/indicator/SH.DYN.MORT, accessed December 21, 2019. Brazil's rate of under-5 mortality per 1,000 was 14, China's was 9, and India's was a staggering 37, while South Africa's was similarly high at 34. The world average is 38.6 per 1,000 live births.

19. These figures are drawn from the Russian Longitudinal Monitoring Surveys, as cited in the *Global Anti-Tobacco Survey, Russia* (2012), 22.

20. See "State of Smoking in Russia," Foundation for a Smoke-Free World, available at https://www.smokefreeworld.org/global-smoking-landscape/country-profiles/state-smoking-russia, accessed July 29, 2019.

21. "Alcohol Policy Impact Case Study: The Effects of Alcohol Control Measures on Mortality and Life Expectancy in the Russian Federation," 2019, World Health Organization, 8, available at: www.euro.who.int/en/health-topics/disease-prevention/alcohol-use/publications/2019/alcohol-policy-impact-case-study-the-effects-of-alcohol-control-measures-on-mortality-and-life-expectancy-in-the-russian-federation-2019, accessed October 1, 2019.

22. World Health Organization, "Alcohol Policy Impact Case Study," 16, and World Health Organization, Russian Country Profile, Global Alcohol Report. Available at: https://www.who.int/substance_abuse/publications/global_alcohol_report/profiles/rus.pdf?ua=1, accessed December 21, 2019 and United Nations Human Development Index, 2019.

23. Country Success Stories, in World Health Statistics, World Health Organization 2017, 44, available at: https://www.who.int/gho/publications/world_health_statistics/2017/EN_WHS2017_Part3.pdf#page=8, accessed October 1, 2019.

24. See, for instance, Mark Lawrence Schrad, *Vodka Politics: Alcohol, Autocracy, and the Secret History of the Russian State* (Oxford: Oxford University Press, 2014).

25. These statistics from Marten et al., "An Assessment of the Progress towards Universal Health Coverage in Brazil, Russia, India, China, and South Africa (BRICS)," 2166 and 2168.

26. V. V. Moiseev, A. B. Savin, T. V. Oleynik, and R. A. Khalturin, "Economy of Russia: Possibility of Breakthrough Development 2025," *Advances in Social Science, Education and Humanities Research (ASSEHR)* 312 (April 2019), available at https://www.atlantis-press.com/proceedings/tphd-18/55916703, accessed July 29, 2019.

27. Ministry of Finance of the Russian Federation. "Kratkaia informatsiia ob ispolnenii federal'nogo biudzheta" [Summary of information on the fulfillment of the federal budget], available at https://www.minfin.ru/ru/statistics/fedbud, accessed February 22, 2019.

28. Marten et al., "An Assessment of the Progress towards Universal Health Coverage in Brazil, Russia, India, China, and South Africa (BRICS)," 2165.

29. Russian Federal Statistics Service. Data available in Russian at https://www.fedstat.ru/indicator/43514, accessed July 23, 2019.

30. See Steven A. Camarota and Karen Zeigler, "Record 44.5 Million Immigrants in 2017," Center for Immigration Studies (September 15, 2018), available at https://cis.org/Report/Record-445-Million-Immigrants-2017, accessed July 23, 2019.

31. For more on brain drain and references, see Russian Federal Statistics Service. See also John Herbst and Sergei Erofeev, "The Putin Exodus: The New Russian Brain Drain," The Atlantic Council, February 2019, Available at https://www.atlanticcouncil.org/in-depth-research-reports/report/the-putin-exodus-the-new-russian-brain-drain-3, accessed December 19, 2019.

32. Sergei Guriev, Chief Economist, European Bank of Reconstruction and Development, in conversation with the author, Stanford, California, April 23, 2019.

33. Herbst and Erofeev, "Putin's Brain Drain, 16."

34. Levada Center, "Emigration Attitudes," November 26, 2019, available at: https://www.levada.ru/2019/11/26/emigratsionnye-nastroeniya-4/?fromtg=1, accessed January 20, 2020.

35. Earlier data and reports available at: https://www.levada.ru/2019/02/04/emigratsionnnyenastroeniya-3, accessed July 23, 2019. See also, Vladimir Milov and Olga Khvostunova, "Russian Youth: A Look Inside the Black Box," (Moscow: Free Russia Foundation, 2019), available at: https://www.4freerussia.org/wp-content/uploads/2019/05/Russian-Youth_web_eng.pdf, accessed, September 30, 2019.

36. Levada Center, "Emigration Attitudes."

37. Author's conversations with young protesters on the streets of Moscow, March 2017.

38. See Federico Cingano, "Trends in Income Inequality and Its Impact on Economic Growth," Social, Employment and Migration Working Papers, no. 163 (Paris: OECD Publishing, 2014), available at: https://www.oecd-ilibrary.org/social-issues-migration-health/trends-in-income-inequality-and-its-impact-on-economic-growth_5jxrjncwxv6j-en, access July 23, 2019.

39. Ibid., 17.

40. For more on the relationship between inequality and growth, see S. N. Durlauf, "The Rise and Fall of Cross-Country Growth Regressions," *History of Political Economy* 41 Supp. (2009): 315–333.

41. See Cingano, "Trends in Income Inequality and Its Impact on Growth."

42. Thomas Remington, "Closing the Skills-Jobs Gap: Russia and China Compared," Basic Research Program Working Papers, *Political Science*, no. 53, 2017, National Research University Higher School of Economics, Moscow. See also Stephen White, Brian McCallister, and Alexander Munro, "Economic Inequality and Political Stability in Russia and China," *Europe-Asia Studies* 69, no. 1 (January 2017): 1–7.

43. The World Bank Group, "Rolling Back Russia's Spatial Disparities: Reassembling the Soviet Jigsaw under a Market Economy" (2018), 10, available at: https://openknowledge.worldbank.org/bitstream/handle/10986/29866/126805-WP-WBrollingback-PUBLIC.pdf?sequence=8, accessed December 19, 2019.

44. The comparison between states is available in ibid., 11.

45. Ibid., 40.

46. Ibid., 53.

47. See "Countries That Produce the Most Engineers," World Atlas, available at: https://www.worldatlas.com/articles/countries-with-the-most-engineering-graduates.html, accessed July 24, 2019. "Engineer" is a very broad term, and in the Russian context in particular, but here it is taken to mean students graduating in programs that teach civil (construction), industrial, electrical, chemical, and biomedical engineering, as well as engineering physics.

48. "Population with Tertiary Education," OECD. Data last updated January 1, 2017, available at: https://data.oecd.org/eduatt/population-with-tertiary-education.htm, accessed January 6, 2019. (Germany is used as a proxy for the EU.)

49. QS World University Rankings 2019, available at https://www.topuniversities.com/university-rankings/world-university-rankings/2019, accessed October 3, 2019.

50. Ibid.

51. See Presidential Address to the Federal Assembly, February 20, 2019, available at: http://en.kremlin.ru/events/president/news/59863, accessed December 18, 2019.

52. Ivan V. Danilin and Zaur A. Mamedyarov, "National Technology Initiative (NTI): New Start or *déjà-vu* of Russian Innovation Policy?" in *Year of the Planet: Yearbook, 2016 edition*, ed. B. Baranovsky and E. Solovyev, Primakov Institute of World Economy and International Relations (Moscow: Idea-Press, 2016), 2.

53. Alyssa Yorgan, "10 Key Statistics on Internet Usage in Russia (2019)" (February 20, 2019), available at: https://russiansearchmarketing.com/internet-usage-russia-2019-10-key-statistics, accessed January 20, 2020.

54. "Media consumption in Russia 2019: Key Trends," Deloitte CIS Research Center (Moscow, September 2019), available at: https://www2.deloitte.com/ru/en/pages/technology-media-and-telecommunications/articles/media-consumption-in-russia.html, accessed January 20, 2020.

55. Thomas F. Remington, "Closing the Skills-Jobs Gap", 6.

56. WorldSkills is an international competition to help young people around the world gain and then showcase vocational training skills. For more on WorldSkills see: https://worldskills.org/about/#vision-mission.

57. Ibid., 9.

58. Ibid., 16 and 25.

Chapter 6

1. Vladimir Putin, "Presidential Address to the Federal Assembly of Russia," March 1, 2018, available at: https://en.kremlin.ru/events/president/news/56957, accessed April 7, 2020.

2. Bettina Renz, *Russia's Military Revival* (Medford, M.A.: Polity Press, 2018), 50.

3. Ibid., 53.

4. As quoted in James Sherr, "Russia and the West: A Reassessment," *The Shrivenam Papers*, no. 6 (January 2008): 28.

5. Renz, *Russia's Military Revival*, 56.

6. Mikhail Barabanov, Konstantin Makienko, and Ruslan Pukhov, "Military Reform: Toward the New Look of the Russian Army," Valdai Discussion Group Analytical Report, Moscow, July 2020, available at: http://vid-1.rian.ru/ig/valdai/Military_reform_eng.pdf, accessed April 9, 2020; and Renz, 55.

7. Aleksandr Golts and Tonya L. Putnam, "State Militarism and Its Legacies: Why Military Reform Has Failed in Russia," *International Security*, vol. 29, no. 2, Fall 2004, 136 and 153. and Dale Herspring, "Vladimir Putin and Military Reform in Russia," *European Security*, vol. 14, issue 1, 2005, 140, describing the dismal life of Russian conscripts at the time and 146 on conscription avoidance.

8. Barabanov et al., "Military Reform," 12.

9. Russian Military Power Report 2017, Defense Intelligence Analysis, 2017, 12.

10. Renz, *Russia's Military Revival*, 65.

11. Barabanov et al., "Military Reform," 14.

12. See Russian Military Power Report 2017; Keith Crane, Olga Oliker, and Brian Nichiporuk, "Trends in Russia's Armed Forces: An Overview of Budgets and Capabilities" (Santa Monica,

CA: RAND Corporation, 2019). See also Kommersant, https://www.kommersant.ru/doc/3467573, accessed April 9, 2020.

13. Crane, Oliker, and Nichiporuk, "Trends in Russia's Armed Forces," 60.

14. C. J. Chivers and David Herszenhorn, "In Crimea, Russia Showcases a Rebooted Army," available at: https://www.nytimes.com/2014/04/03/world/europe/crimea-offers-showcase-for-russias-rebooted-military.html, accessed April 20, 2020.

15. C. J. Chivers and M. S. Herzenhorn, "Crimea Offers Showcase for Russia's Rebooted Military," *New York Times*, April 2, 2014, available at: https://www.nytimes.com/2014/04/03/world/europe/crimea-offers-showcase-for-russias-rebooted-military.html?action=click&module=RelatedCoverage&pgtype=Article&region=Footer, accessed April 27, 2020.

16. Crane, Oliker, and Nichiporuk, "Trends in Russia's Armed Forces," 1.

17. "Meeting Today's Global Security Challenges" with General Joseph F. Dunford, Center for Strategic and International Studies, Washington, DC, March 29, 2016, available at: https://www.csis.org/events/meeting-todays-global-security-challenges%C2%A0-general-joseph-f-dunford, accessed April 9, 2020.

18. https://correlatesofwar.org/data-sets/national-material-capabilities.

19. Susanne Oxenstierna, "The Economy and Military Expenditure," in *Russian Military Capability in a Ten-Year Perspective, 2019*, ed. Frederick Westerlund and Susanne Oxenstierna (Stockholm: FOI [Total Defense Research Institute], December 2019), 102, available at: https://www.foi.dr/russia, accessed April 30, 2020. See also Richard Connolly, "Russian Military Expenditure in Comparative Perspective: A Purchasing Power Parity Estimate," CNA Analysis and Solutions, October 2019, 5, available at: https://www.cna.org/CNA_files/PDF/IOP-2019-U-021955-Final.pdf, accessed March 1, 2020.

20. These data are from Stockholm International Peace Research Institute (SIPRI) Military Expenditure Database, 2019, available at https://www.sipri.org/databases/milex, accessed July 2, 2020.

21. Crane, Oliker, and Nichiporuk, "Trends in Russia's Armed Forces," 3 and 5. See also Connolly, 2019 and K. Zysk chapter 14, "Russia's Strategic Underbelly: Military Strategy, Capabilities and Operations in the Arctic," in Stephen Blank, ed., *The Russian Military in Contemporary Perspective* (Carlisle, PA: United States Army War College Press, 2019), 687–723.

22. This is also demonstrated in Susanna Oxenstierna, "The Economy and Military Spending," in *Russian Military Capability in a Ten-Year Perspective, 2016*, ed. Frederick Westerlund and Susanne Oxenstierna (Stockholm: FOI [Total Defense Research Institute], December 2019), 135–136.

23. Barabanov et al., "Military Reform."

24. For more on this, see Crane, Oliker, and Nichiporuk, "Trends in Russia's Armed Forces," and Oxenstierna, "The Economy and Military Expenditure" 2016, 143.

25. Oxenstierna, "The Economy and Military Expenditure," 102. See also Connolly, "Russian Military Expenditure in Comparative Perspective," 2019, 5.

26. For more on the debate regarding which measures of spending to use, see Oxenstierna, 2019, 102–3, where she notes that a fourth method of evaluating Russian spending on defense is in using figures provided to the United Nations by the Russian government, but she argues that these data are inconsistent over time with Russian budget data, and can over- and underestimate, depending on the year, military spending because what items are reported annually to make up these numbers appears to vary.

27. Data are from the SIPRI Military Expenditure Database, 2019.

28. Data are from the SIPRI Military Expenditure Database, 2019.

29. Crane, Oliker, and Nichiporuk, "Trends in Russia's Armed Forces," 28.

30. Connolly, "Russian Military Expenditure in Comparative Perspective" .

31. See ibid, 9. For more detailed information on Russian military budgeting see Oxenstiena, "The Economy and Military Expenditure," 2019.

32. Connolly, "Russian Military Expenditure in Comparative Perspective." See also Michael Kofman and Richard Connolly, "Why Russian Military Expenditure Is Much Higher Than Commonly Understood (as Is China's)," War on the Rocks, December 16, 2019, available at: https://warontherocks.com/2019/12/why-russian-military-expenditure-is-much-higher-than-commonly-understood-as-is-chinas.

33. For more on the Russian military industrial complex, see the fascinating and comprehensive account in Crane, Oliker, and Nichiporuk, "Trends in Russia's Armed Forces," 19–26, including a useful description of Putin's creation of "national champions" through the consolidation of enterprises into large state-owned conglomerates like the United Aircraft Corporation, United Shipbuilding Corporation, and Russian Helicopter Company, among others.

34. Crane, Oliker, and Nichiporuk, "Trends in Russia's Armed Forces," 34.

35. This comparison is used in Connelly, "Russian Military Expenditure in Comparative Perspective," but numbers here were updated to January 1, 2020, data using the *Economist's* calculating tool available at: https://www.economist.com/news/2020/01/15/the-big-mac-index, accessed April 14, 2020. A full description of the Big Mac Index concept is also available at this website.

36. IMF Data Mapper, Implied PPP Conversion Rate; see https://www.imf.org/external/datamapper/PPPEX@WEO/OEMDC/ADVEC/WEOWORLD, accessed April 13, 2020.

37. Data for both tables are from the SIPRI Military Expenditure Database, 2019 with purchasing power parity conversion done according to the IMF multiplier for each year.

38. Tables 6.1,6.2 and 6.3 are drawn from data in *The Military Balance* (London: Institute for Strategic Studies, 2019), 26–27.

39. Crane, Oliker, and Nichiporuk, "Trends in Russia's Armed Forces," 59; International Institute for Strategic Studies, *The Military Balance* (London: IISS, 2018), 172–179.

40. Logan Nye, "Here are Seven Dangerous Russian Weapons to Watch Out for on the Battlefield," Business Insider, November 26, 2018. https://www.businessinsider.com/here-are-7-deadly-russian-weapons-to-watch-out-for-on-the-battlefield-2018-11#7-hypersonic-anti-ship-missiles-7 and https://www.globalsecurity.org/org/overview/history.htm.

41. Quotation is from https://militarywatchmagazine.com/article/russia-s-massive-new-t-15-fighting-vehicle-why-the-second-armata-platform-poses-a-considerable-threat-to-the-country-s-adversaries. But see also https://nationalinterest.org/blog/the-buzz/the-russian-armys-super-weapon-beware-the-t-15-heavy-19184.

42. Crane, Oliker, and Nichiporuk, "Trends in Russia's Armed Forces," 35.

43. Defense Intelligence Agency, *Russian Military Power* (2017), 50.

44. Crane, Oliker, and Nichiporuk, "Trends in Russia's Armed Forces," 34.

45. David Shlapak and Michael Johnson, "Reinforcing Deterrence on NATO's Eastern Flank: Wargaming the Defense of the Baltics" (Santa Monica, CA: RAND Corporation, 2016), available at: https://www.rand.org/pubs/research_reports/RR1253.html, accessed June 20, 2020.

46. Crane, Oliker, and Nichiporuk, "Trends in Russia's Armed Forces," 13.

47. Ibid., 42.

48. Defense Intelligence Agency, *Russian Military Power*, 66.

49. Dakota Woods, ed., *2020 Index of U.S. Military Strength* (Washington, DC: Heritage Foundation, 2020), 203.

50. Rose Gotemoeller, former deputy general secretary of NATO, in conversation with the author, Stanford University, April 14, 2020.

51. Defense Intelligence Agency, *Russian Military Power*, 67.

52. Woods, ed., *2020 Index of U.S. Military Strength*, 213, see fn. 172.

53. Katarzyna Zysk, "Russia's Strategic Under Belly: Military Strategy, Capabilities and Operations in the Arctic," ch. 14 in *The Russian Military in Contemporary Perspective*, ed. Stephen Blank (Carlisle, PA: US Army War College and Strategic Studies Institute, 2019), 692–693.

54. Ibid., 694.

55. Ibid., 699.

56. Far more detail on the Pacific Fleet's force composition can be found in Richard Weitz, "Russian Military Power and Policy in the Far East," ch. 20 in *The Russian Military in Contemporary Perspective*, ed. Stephen Blank (Carlisle, PA: US Army War College and Strategic Studies Institute, 2019), in Blank, ed., 925–932.

57. Richard Weitz, "Russian Military Power and Policy in the Far East," 2019, 951.

58. Ibid., 951.

59. Defense Intelligence Agency, *Russian Military Power*, 68.

60. Ibid., 68.

61. Ibid., 68.

62. Ibid., 70.

63. Author's interview with commander of USS *Karl Vincent* during a trip to the ship in August 2016.

64. Defense Intelligence Agency, *Russian Military Power*, 70.

65. Ibid., 60.

66. Ibid., 59.

67. Crane, Oliker, and Nichiporuk, "Trends in Russia's Armed Forces," 37.

68. Logan Nye, "Here Are 7 Dangerous Russian Weapons to Watch Out For on the Battlefield," *Business Insider*, https://www.businessinsider.com/here-are-7-deadly-russian-weapons-to-watch-out-for-on-the-battlefield-2018-11, accessed April 20, 2020.

69. Crane, Oliker, and Nichiporuk, "Trends in Russia's Armed Forces," 37.

70. Ibid., 36.

71. Defense Intelligence Agency, *Russian Military Power*, 36; Crane, Oliker, and Nichiporuk, "Trends in Russia's Armed Forces," 36–37.

72. Defense Intelligence Agency, *Russian Military Power*, 65.

73. Ibid. *The Military Balance 2019*, "Comparative Defense Statistics," ch. 2 at 23, available at https://doi.org/10.1080/04597222.2019.1561026, accessed October 5, 2020. Also see Crane, Oliker, and Nichiporuk.

74. Elbridge Colby, as cited in Woods ed., 202. Also note that RAND study of wargaming in Baltics indicates NATO would be outgunned.

75. Isabelle Facon, "Military Exercises: The Russian Way," ch. 5 in *The Russian Military in Contemporary Perspective*, ed. Stephen Blank (Carlisle, PA: US Army War College and Strategic Studies Institute, 2019), 219.

76. Ibid., 220.

77. Ibid., 221

78. Ibid., 223, and Zysk, "Russia's Strategic Under Belly."

79. Zysk, "Russia's Strategic Under Belly," 704–705.

80. Quoted in Hans M. Kristensen and Matt Korda, "Russian Nuclear Forces," *Nuclear Notebook, Bulletin of the Atomic Scientists*, no. 2 (2019): 73–84, available at https://doi.org/10.1080/00963402.2019.158089, accessed April 22, 2020, at 75. Dakota Woods, ed., *2020 Index of U.S. Military Strength*, 202.

81. See, for example, the discussion in Stephen Blank, ed., *The Russian Military in Contemporary Perspective*, 2019, "Introduction," ch. 1, 1–48.

82. The Military Doctrine of the Russian Federation, Approved by the President of the Russian Federation on December 25, 2014 No. Pr-2976, chapter 3, paragraph 27, available in official English translation at the website of the Embassy of the Russian Federation to the United Kingdom and Northern Ireland at: https://rusemb.org.uk/press/2029, accessed April 20, 2020.

83. Russian military strategists evidently have pondered what the threshold would be, but it is not codified in current doctrine. For more on this, see Kristen Bruusgard, "Russian Strategic Deterrence," *Survival* 58, no. 4 (August–September 2016): 12. In June 2020, the Russian government produced a fascinating document that in one place for the first time explained its deterrence policy. See "Foundations of State Policy of the Russian Federation in the Field of Nuclear Deterrence," Government of Russia, available at: http://publication.pravo.gov.ru/Document/View/0001202006020040?index=0&rangeSize=1, accessed June 30, 2020. For a detailed analysis of the policy relative to the 2014 and 2000 military doctrines, see Nicolai Sokov, "Russia Clarifies Its Nuclear Deterrence Policy," Vienna Center for Arms Control and Nuclear Security, June 3, 2020, available online at: https://vcdnp.org/russia-clarifies-its-nuclear-deterrence-policy, accessed June 30, 2020.

84. See the excellent analysis of this by Sokov, 2020. The "territorial integrity" threshold is mentioned in paragraph 4 of the Decree of June 2, 2020, "Foundations of State Policy."

85. US Department of Defense, Office of the Secretary of Defense, Nuclear Posture Review, February 2019, 30, available at: https://media.defense.gov/2018/Feb/02/2001872886/-1/-1/1/2018-NUCLEAR-POSTURE-REVIEW-FINAL-REPORT.PDF, accessed April 20, 2020.

86. Security Council of the Russian Federation, "Military Doctrine of the Russian Federation, 2000" Approved by Order of the President of the Russian Federation on April 21, 2000, as cited in Crane, Oliker, and Nichiporuk, "Trends in Russia's Armed Forces," 45. See also Kristen Ven Bruusgard, "The Myth of Russia's Lowered Nuclear Threshold," War on the Rocks, 2017, available at: https://warontherocks.com/2017/09/the-myth-of-russias-lowered-nuclear-threshold.

87. Adam Withnall, "Vladimir Putin Says Russia Was Preparing to Use Nuclear Weapons If Necessary," *The Independent*, March 15, 2015, available at: https://www.independent.co.uk/news/world/europe/vladimir-putin-says-russia-was-preparing-to-use-nuclear-weapons-if-necessary-and-blames-us-for-10109615.html, accessed July 1, 2020.

88. "Russia Threatens Denmark with Nuclear Attack," available at: https://www.thelocal.dk/20150321/russia-threatens-denmark-with-nuclear-attack, accessed April 23, 2020.

89. "Basis of Russian Federation Government Policy in the Area of Military-Naval Activity for the Period until 2030, Decree No. 327," July 20, 2017, as cited in Crane, Oliker, and Nichiporuk, "Trends in Russia's Armed Forces," 47, and Zysk, "Russia's Strategic Under Belly," 90. See also the Nuclear Threat Initiative extensive website coverage of Russia, which also provides helpful information on the evolution of Russian nuclear doctrine since 1993, at https://www.nti.org/learn/countries/russia/nuclear, accessed April 23, 2020.

90. Vladimir Putin, as quoted in Zysk, "Russia's Strategic Under Belly," 89.

91. Data are from Kristensen and Korda.

92. Crane, Oliker, and Nichiporuk, "Trends in Russia's Armed Forces," 42.

93. For more detail on old and newer systems, see Kristensen and Korda, 76.

94. Putin, March 2018 speech, 30.

95. Dmitri Gorenburg, "Russia's Military Modernization Plans," Program on New Approaches to Russian Security (PONARS), Policy Memo 495, November 2017, available at: https://www.ponarseurasia.org/memo/russias-military-modernization-plans-2018-2027, accessed April 27, 2020; Kristensen and Korda, 77.

96. Kristensen and Korda, 76.

97. David E. Sanger and Andrew E. Kramer, "U.S. Officials Suspect New Nuclear Missile in Explosion that Killed 7 Russians, *New York Times*, August 12, 2019, available at https://www.nytimes.com/2019/08/12/world/europe/russia-nuclear-accident-putin.html, accessed October 6, 2020.

98. Putin, March 2018 speech, and Congressional Research Service, 2020, 19.

99. Congressional Research Service, 202, 23.

100. Putin, March 2018 speech, 31.

101. Mark Episkopos, "Is Russia's Hypersonic Cruise Missile Really a Big Deal?" *The National Interest*, February 20, 2020, available at: https://nationalinterest.org/blog/buzz/russias-tsirkon-hypersonic-cruise-missile-really-big-deal-125421, accessed April 27, 2020; Xavier Vavasseur, "Analysis: Russia's Tsirkon Hypersonic Missile Trials Enter Final Stage, *Naval News*, March 3, 2020, available at: https://www.navalnews.com/naval-news/2020/03/analysis-russias-tsirkon-hypersonic-missile-trials-enter-final-stage-part-2, accessed April 27, 2020; and "Russian Nuclear Weapons, Doctrine, Forces and Modernization," Congressional Research Service, updated January 2, 2020, available at: https://fas.org/sgp/crs/nuke/R45861.pdf, accessed April 27, 2020.

102. *The Nuclear Posture Review of the United States*, 2018, 9.

103. See Kristensen and Korda. Note that the Congressional Research Service claims Russia may have closer to 2,000 non-strategic weapons.

104. Kristensen and Korda, 80–81.

105. Ibid., 81.

Chapter 7

1. Vladimir Putin, transcript of interview with Lionel Barber and Henry Foy, *Financial Times*, June 26, 2019, available at: https://www.ft.com/content/670039ec-98f3-11e9-9573-ee5cbb98ed36, accessed June 27, 2019.

2. Joseph Nye, *Soft Power: The Means to Success in World Politics* (New York: Public Affairs, 2004), 19.

3. This is a term used also by James Sherr, "The New East West Discord: Russian Objectives and Western Interests," (Clingendael, Netherlands Institute for International Relations, 2015, and James Sherr *Hard Diplomacy and Soft Coercion: Russia's Influence Abroad*, (London: Chatham House, 2013).

4. Nye, *Soft Power*, 19.

5. Christopher Walker and Jessica Ludwig, "The Meaning of Sharp Power: How Authoritarian States Project Influence," *Foreign Affairs*, November 16, 2017, available at: https://www.foreignaffairs.com/articles/china/2017-11-16/meaning-sharp-power.

6. Ibid, 3.

7. See, for example, Timothy Tzouliadis, *The Forsaken: An American Tragedy in Stalin's Russia* (New York: Penguin Press, 2008); and the classic by John Scott, *Behind the Urals: An American Worker in Russia's City of Steel* (New York: Cambridge University Press, 1942).

8. Nye, *Soft Power*, 94.

9. Nye himself has pointed out Russian policymakers' misuse of the term in Joseph Nye, "What China and Russia Don't Get about Soft Power," *Foreign Policy*, April 29, 2013, available at: https://foreignpolicy.com/2013/04/29/what-china-and-russia-dont-get-about-soft-power, accessed May 4, 2020.

10. Vladimir Putin, "On Measures to Implement the Foreign Policy of the Russian Federation," May 7, 2012, available at: http://kremlin.ru/acts/news/15256, accessed May 1, 2020.

11. "The Foreign Policy and Diplomatic Activity of the Russian Federation in 2013," Russian Ministry of Foreign Affairs, available at: https://www.mid.ru/activity/review, 3.

12. Barber and Foy, *Financial Times* interview with Vladimir Putin, 2019.

13. Anna Matveeva, "Russia's Power Projection after the Ukraine Crisis," *Europe Asia Studies* 70, no. 5 (July 2018): 719.

14. Peter Rutland and Andrei Kazantsev, "The Limits of Russia's 'Soft Power,'" *Journal of Political Power* 9, no. 3 (2016): 395–413, has additional insights from Putin's speeches and writings on soft power and how it should be used in promoting Russian interests.

15. This appears in Putin, 2012.

16. For more on this, see Vasile Rotaru, "Forced Attraction?: How Russia Is Instrumentalizing Its Soft Power Resources in the Near Abroad," *Problems of Post Communism* 65, no. 1 (January–February 2018): 38–39.

17. Dakota Woods, ed., *The 2020 Index of US Military Strength* (Washington, DC: Heritage Foundation), 217.

18. See for example the activity on the site of the Institute of Democracy and Cooperation in Paris. The Institute was founded by the Russian government: www.idc-europe.org/en/The-Institute-of-Democracy-and-Cooperation, accessed October 7, 2020.

19. Woods, ed., *The 2020 Index of Military Strength*, 218.

20. Rosie Gray "Pro-Putin Think Tank Based in New York Shuts Down," Buzzfeed News, June 30, 2015, available at https://www.buzzfeednews.com/article/rosiegray/pro-putin-think-tank-based-in-new-york-shuts-down, accessed October 7, 2020 andhttps://www.rferl.org/a/In_The_Heart_Of_New_York_Russias_Soft_Power_Arm_Gaining_Momentum/1493429.html.

21. Antoaneta Dimitrova, Matthew Frear, Honorata Mazepus, Dmiter Toshkov, Maxim Boroda, Tatsiana Chulitskaya, Oleg Grytsenko, Igor Munteanu, Tatiana Parvan, and Ina Ramasheuskaya, "The Elements of Russia's Soft Power: Channels, Tools, and Actors Promoting Russian Influence in the Eastern Partnership Countries," *EU-Strata Working Paper Series*, no. 4 (July 2017): 17, available at: http://eu-strat.eu/wp-content/uploads/2017/07/WP4.pdf, accessed May 1, 2020.

22. Dimitrova et al., "The Elements of Russia's Soft Power," 17; Sergei Lavrov "Russian World: Steering Towards Consolidation," November 3, 2015, Rossiiskaya Gazeta and in English available https://www.rbth.com/opinion/2015/11/03/rusian-world-on-the-path-to-consolidation_536865, accessed October 7, 2020; also, James Sherr, "The New East West Discord,", 2015, 54.

23. Rutland and Kazantsev, "The Limits of Russia's 'Soft Power,'" 402.

24. Yaroslav Trofimov, "Viruspolitik at Play as Moscow Sends Soldiers to Help Italy: Russia's President Sent Aircraft Full of Medical Supplies to Italy to Aid in Combating the Coronavirus When Help from Europe and the US Is Scarce," *Wall Street Journal*, March 31, 2020, available at: https://www.wsj.com/articles/russian-soldiers-in-italy-contain-the-coronavirus-and-mark-a-political-shift-11585647002?mod=searchresults&page=1&pos=6, accessed April 1, 2020.

25. See Jennifer Hansler and Kylie Atwood, "Russian Coronavirus Aid Delivery to US Prompts Confusion and Criticism," CNN, April 2, 2020, available at: https://www.cnn.com/2020/04/02/politics/russia-medical-supplies-us-propaganda/index.html, accessed May 6, 2020. Note that there was some debate as to whether or not the equipment Russia sent was actually usable once it arrived (the ventilators had voltage issues, for example), and the Russian government subsequently billed the United States $660,000 for the "aid." See https://abcnews.go.com/Politics/russia-bills-us-660k-aid-included-gas-masks/story?id=70451912, accessed October 7, 2020.

26. Note that Jonathan Grix argues that the Sochi Olympics were in fact successful as domestic soft power and should be seen as an element of both Russian internal and external policy. See Jonathan Grix, "The Sochi Winter Olympics and Russia's Unique Soft Power Strategy," *Sport in Society* 20, no. 4 (2017): 461–475.

27. Rutland and Kazantsev, "The Limits of Russia's 'Soft Power,'" 403.

28. Dimitrova et al., "The Elements of Russia's Soft Power," 8.

29. See Russia Today's official website at https://www.rt.com/about-us, accessed July 4, 2020.

30. All of the statistics and quotations come from RT-America's website, and are available at https://www.rt.com/about-us, accessed May 4, 2020. It is difficult to substantiate independently any of the viewership statistics.

31. Jim Rutenberg, "RT, Sputnik and Russia's New Theory of War: How the Kremlin Built One of the Most Powerful Information Weapons of the 21st Century—and Why It May Be Impossible to Stop," *New York Times Magazine*, September 13, 2017, available at: https://www.nytimes.com/2017/09/13/magazine/rt-sputnik-and-russias-new-theory-of-war.html, accessed May 1, 2020.

32. See Neil MacFarquhar, "Playing on Kansas City Radio: Russian Propaganda," *New York Times*, February 13, 2020, https://www.nytimes.com/2020/02/13/us/russian-propaganda-radio.html, accessed February 14, 2020.

33. This is the description on RT's website for the show "On Contact" with Chris Hedges, available at: https://www.rt.com/shows/on-contact, accessed May 4, 2020.

34. Valentina Feklyunina, "Russia's Soft Power beyond the Post-Soviet Space," in *Assessing Russia's Power: A Report*, ed. Valentina Feklyunina et al. (London: King's College, and New Castle University e-prints, 2017), 35–36, available at: https://eprint.ncl.ac.uk/file_store/production/231713/A8E19C50-A49A-4703-84CB-EE81B4D02428.pdf, accessed May 4, 2020.

35. Anna Matveeva, "Russia's Power Projection after the Ukraine Crisis," *Europe Asia Studies* 70, no. 5 (July 2018): 719–720.

36. Feklyunina, "Russia's Soft Power beyond the Post-Soviet Space," 35–36.

37. Thomas Boghardt, "Operation INFEKTION: Soviet Bloc Intelligence and Its AIDS Disinformation Campaign," *Studies in Intelligence* 53, no. 4 (December 2009): 2.

38. There is a large literature on the Soviet use of information to undermine the West, but see, for example, Herbert Romerstein, "Disinformation as a KGB Weapon in the Cold War," *Journal of Intelligence History* 1, no. 1 (2001): 54–67; David V. Gioe, Michael S. Goodman, and David S. Frey, "Unforgiven: Russian Intelligence Vengeance as Political Theater and Strategic Messaging," *Intelligence and National Security* 34, no. 4 (2019): 561–575; and Clint Watts, *Messing with the Enemy* (New York: Harper, 2018). Note that the Soviet Union was not alone in using information this way during the Cold War. See David Gioe, Richard Lovering, and Tyler Pachesny, "The Soviet Legacy of Russian Active Measures: New Vodka from Old Stills?" *International Journal of Intelligence and Counter Intelligence* 33, no. 3 (2020): 514–539.

39. Boghardt, "Operation INFEKTION," 7.

40. Ibid., 8.

41. Ibid., 14.

42. Ibid., 16.

43. Salvador Hernandez, "Russian Trolls Spread Baseless Theories like Pizzagate and QAnon after the Election," *Buzzfeed News*, available at: https://www.buzzfeednews.com/article/salvadorhernandez/russian-trolls-spread-baseless-conspiracy-theories-like, accessed May 7, 2020; and Amanda Robb, "Anatomy of a Fake News Scandal," *Rolling Stone*, November 16, 2017, available at: https://www.rollingstone.com/politics/politics-news/anatomy-of-a-fake-news-scandal-125877.

44. Renée Diresta and Shelby Grossman, "Potemkin Pages and Personas: Assessing GRU Online Operations, 2014–2019" (Stanford Internet Observatory, 2019).

45. Keir Giles, *Russia's New Tools for Confronting the West: Continuity and Innovation in Moscow's Exercise of Power* (London: Chatham House, 2016), 34.

46. Quentin E. Hobson, Logan Ma, Krystyna Marcinek, Karen Schwindt, "Fighting Shadows in the Dark: Understanding and Fighting Coercion in Cyberspace, (Santa Monica: RAND Corporation, 2019), 11–12.

47. Special Counsel Robert S. Mueller III, *Report on the Investigation into Russian Interference in the 2016 Presidential Election*, Vol. I (Washington, DC: US Department of Justice, March 2019), 38–48.

48. For a fascinating analysis of the Macron operation, see Jean-Baptiste Jeangene Vilmer, "The 'Macron Leaks' Operation: A Post-Mortem," The Atlantic Council, June 2019, available at: https://www.atlanticcouncil.org/wp-content/uploads/2019/06/The_Macron_Leaks_Operation-A_Post-Mortem.pdf, accessed May 8, 2020.

49. "Who Is Dmitri Badin, the GRU Hacker Indicted by Germany Over the Bundestag Hacks?" Available at https://www.newsbreak.com/news/1560058389049/who-is-dmitry-badin-the-gru-hacker-indicted-by-germany-over-the-bundestag-hacks, accessed May 8, 2020.

50. Mueller Report, 4–5 and 38–48.

51. For a very thorough analysis of how Russian operatives used cyber platforms to steer the narrative toward Donald Trump and against Hillary Clinton during the 2016 US presidential campaign, see Michael McFaul et al., "Securing American Elections: Prescriptions for Enhancing the Integrity and Independence of the US Presidential Elections and Beyond" (Stanford, CA: Cyber Policy Center, Freeman Spogli Institute, June 2019), available at: https://fsi-live.s3.us-west-1.amazonaws.com/s3fs-public/stanford_cyber_policy_center-securing_american_elections.pdf.

52. Mueller Report, 50–51.

53. Daniel Bagge, *Unmasking Maskirovka*, (New York: Defense Press, 2019); Jackob Hedenskog and Gudrun Persson, "Russian Security Policy," in Fredrik Westerlund and Susanne Oxenstierna, eds., *Russian Military Capability in a Ten-Year Perspective – 2019* (Stockholm, FOI: December 2019), 85; and Timothy Thomas, "Russia's Expanding Cyber Activities: Exerting Civilian Control While Enhancing Military Reform," in Stephen Blank, ed., *The Russian Military in Contemporary Perspective*, (Carlisle, PA: US Army War College Press, 2019), 491–574.

54. See Richard Weitz, "Moscow's Gray Zone Toolkit," in Nicole Peterson, ed., "Russian Strategic Intentsions: A Strategic Multilayer Assessment (SMA) White Paper,"" (United States Department of Defense, 2019), ch. 4, 21–26.

55. See Ofer Fridman, "On the Gerasimov Doctrine: Why the West Fails to Beat Russia to the Punch," *Prism* 8, no. 2 (2019): 106; see also Giles, *Russia's New Tools for Confronting the West*, 6.

56. Giles, *Russia's New Tools for Confronting the West*, 9.

57. "The Military Doctrine of the Russian Federation," February 5, 2010, available at: https://carnegieendowment.org/files/2010russia_military_doctrine.pdf, accessed April 30, 2020.

58. Timothy Thomas, "Russia's Expanding Cyber Activities: Exerting Civilian Control While Enhancing Military Reform," in *The Russian Military in Contemporary Perspective*, Steven Blank, ed. (Carlisle, PA: Strategic Studies Institute and the US Army War College, 2019), 530–531.

59. See, for example, *The National Security Strategy of the Russian Federation*, 2015, ch. 2, point 12, in the Russian-language version, *Strategiia Natsionalnaia Bezopasnosti Rossiskoi Federatsii*, 2015, available at: http://static.kremlin.ru/media/events/files/ru/l8iXkR8XLAtxeilX7JK3XXy6Y0AsHD5v.pdf, accessed April 30, 2020. See also Bagge, *Unmasking Maskirovka*,52.

60. "The National Security Strategy of the Russian Federation, 2015," ch. 4, paragraph 36.
61. Bagge, *Unmasking Maskirovka*, ch. 9; quote is from Anna Lukianova Fink, "The Evolving Concept of Strategic Deterrence: Risks and Responses," Arms Control Association, 2017, available at: https://www.armscontrol.org/act/2017-07/features/evolving-russian-concept-strategic-deterrence-risks-responses, accessed April 30, 2020.

Chapter 8

1. Vladimir Putin, March 10, 2020, speech at the State Duma plenary session, available at: https://en.kremlin.ru/events/president/news/62964.
2. James Scherr, "Ukraine and the Black Sea Region: The Russian Military Perspective," in *The Russian Military in Contemporary Perspective*, ed. Stephen Blank (Carlisle, PA: Strategic Studies Institute and United States War College Press, 2019), 783.
3. For more on patronalism in the former Soviet Union, see Henry Hale's excellent book, *Patronal Politics: Eurasian Regime Transitions in Comparative Perspective* (New York: Cambridge University Press, 2014).
4. Russia's membership in the OECD was postponed following the annexation of Crimea in March, 2014. See http://www.oecd.org/russia/oecd-and-the-russian-federation, accessed June 19, 2020.
5. See John Mearsheimer, "Why the Ukraine Crisis Is the West's Fault: The Liberal Delusion that Provoked Putin," *Foreign Affairs* 93, no. 5 (2014): 77–89; and Stephan Walt, *The Hell of Good Intentions: America's Foreign Policy Elite and the Decline of US Supremacy* (New York: Farrar, Straus & Giroux, 2018), 32.
6. Walt, *The Hell of Good Intentions*, 32.
7. Mearsheimer, "Why the Ukraine Crisis Is the West's Fault," 81.
8. Ibid.
9. Walt, *The Hell of Good Intentions*, 8.
10. See, for example, Bobo Lo, *Russia and the New World Disorder* (Washington, DC: Brookings Institution Press, 2015), 17.
11. Ibid., 18.
12. Stephen Kotkin, "Russia's Perpetual Geopolitics," *Foreign Affairs*, May/June 2016, 5–6.
13. Dmitri Trenin, *Should We Fear Russia?* (Malden, MA: Polity Press, 2016).
14. Mearsheimer, "Why the Ukraine Crisis Is the West's Fault," 80. Lo and Kotkin also emphasizes the importance of Russian history in its security concerns and also the conception of Russian "exceptionalism" in being both European and Asian, and thus that many contemporary Russian foreign policy elites view it as "special." Lo, *Russia and the New World Disorder*, 17–18, and Kotkin, "Russia's Perpetual Geopolitics," 3–4.
15. Sergei Karaganov, "Europe: A Defeat at the Hands of Victory," *Russia in Global Affairs*, March 19, 2015, available at: http://eng.globalaffairs.ru/number/Europe-A-Defeat-at-the-Hands-of-Victory-17361, accessed July 31, 2015.
16. Alexei Arbatov, "Collapse of the World Order?: The Emergence of a Polycentric World and Its Challenges," *Russia in Global Affairs*, September 23, 2014, available at: http://eng.globalaffairs.ru/number/Collapse-of-the-World-Order-16987, accessed August 12, 2015.
17. Vladimir Putin, address to the Federation Council, Duma, March 18, 2014, transcript available at: http://en.kremlin.ru/events/president/news/20603, accessed June 19, 2020.
18. Ibid.
19. For a quick chronology, see Robin Emmott, "After Long Wait, US to Unveil European Missile Shield," Reuters, May 11, 2016, available at: https://www.reuters.com/article/us-nato-shield-timeline/after-long-wait-u-s-to-unveil-european-missile-shield-idUSKCN0Y217P, accessed June 20, 2020, and for more on Romania, see Alison Mutler, "NATO Shows Off Missile Base in Romania, Calling It Purely Defensive," RFE/RL, November 25, 2019, available at: https://www.rferl.org/a/nato-shows-off-missile-base-in-romania-calling-it-purely-defensive-/30291193.html, accessed June 19, 2020.
20. Vladimir Putin, Munich Speech, February 10, 2007, transcript available at: http://en.kremlin.ru/events/president/transcripts/24034, accessed June 18, 2020; also Putin, address to the Federation Council, Duma, March 18, 2014. See also chapter 1.

21. Putin, address to the Federation Council, Duma, March 18, 2014.
22. Ibid.
23. Mearsheimer, "Why the Ukraine Crisis Is the West's Fault," 2014.
24. Putin, address to the Federation Council, Duma, March 18, 2014.
25. See Michael McFaul, "Faulty Powers: Who Started the Ukraine Crisis?" response to John Mearsheimer, *Foreign Affairs*, November/December 2014, available at: https://www. foreignaffairs.com/articles/eastern-europe-caucasus/2014-10-17/faulty-powers, accessed June 19, 2020.
26. Obama White House Archives, "US-Russia Relations: 'Reset' Fact Sheet," June 24, 2010, available at: https://obamawhitehouse.archives.gov/the-press-office/us-russia-relations-reset-fact-sheet, accessed June 17, 2020.
27. Obama White House Archives, "What the 'Reset' Achieved."
28. "Remarks by President Obama and President Medvedev after Bilateral Meeting in Seoul, South Korea," *Obama White House Archives*, March 26, 2012. Transcript available at: https:// obamawhitehouse.archives.gov/the-press-office/2012/03/26/remarks-president-obama-and-president-medvedev-russia-after-bilateral-me, accessed July 19, 2020.
29. Henry Foy and Ed Crooks, "ExxonMobil Abandons Joint Ventures with Russia's Rosneft," *Financial Times*, March 1, 2018, available at: https://www.ft.com/content/7e6a3212-1d1c-11e8-956a-43db76e69936, accessed June 19, 2020.
30. See also Trenin, *Should We Fear Russia?*
31. See "Fact Sheet: Very High Readiness Joint Task Force," NATO Allied Command Operations, available at: https://web.archive.org/web/20150414014221/http://www.aco.nato.int/page349011837.aspx, accessed June 19, 2020.
32. Rebecca Kheel, "Top US Commander: Russia Wants to Rewrite International Order," *The Hill*, February 25, 2016, available at: https://thehill.com/policy/defense/270796-top-us-commander-russia-wants-to-rewrite-international-order, accessed June 19, 2020. Cf. footnote 26.
33. Walter Russell Mead, "The Return of Geopolitics: The Revenge of the Revisionist Powers," *Foreign Affairs*, May/June 2014, available at: https://www-foreignaffairs-com.stanford.idm. oclc.org/print/node/1113233, accessed June 15, 2020.
34. Mead, "The Return of Geopolitics," 4.
35. See, for example, Graham Allison, "The New Spheres of Influence: Sharing the Globe with Other Great Powers," *Foreign Affairs*, March/April 2020, available at: https://www. foreignaffairs.com/articles/united-states/2020-02-10/new-spheres-influence, accessed June 15, 2020; and Kotkin, "Russia's Perpetual Geopolitics."
36. Lo, *Russia and the New World Disorder*, 23–26.
37. Robert Legvold, *Return to Cold War* (Malden, MA: Polity Press, 2016), 20.
38. As noted in chapter 1, there is disagreement on the extent to which ideology influence Soviet foreign policy—especially as the regime matured. See Alexander Dallin, "The Domestic Sources of Soviet Foreign Policy," in *The Domestic Context of Soviet Foreign Policy*, ed. S. Bialer (Boulder, CO: Westview Press, 1981), 335–408.
39. M. Steven Fish, "What Has Russia Become?" *Comparative Politics* 50, no. 3 (April 2018): 343.
40. Steven Levitsky and Lucan Way, *Competitive Authoritarianism: Hybrid Regimes after the Cold War* (New York: Cambridge University Press, 2010); Fish, "What Has Russia Become?"; Karen Dawisha, *Putin's Kleptocracy: Who Owns Russia?* (New York: Simon & Schuster, 2014); Samuel Greene and Graeme Robertson, *Putin v. The People* (New Haven: Yale University Press, 2019); Mikhail Zygar, *All the Kremlin's Men: Inside the Court of Vladimir Putin* (New York: Public Affairs, 2016); Andrei Tsygankov, "Managed Democracy," ch. 10 in *The Strong State in Russia: Development and Crisis* (New York: Oxford University Press, 2014); Brian Taylor, *The Code of Putinism* (New York: Oxford University Press, 2018); and Anders Åslund's excellent 2019 book, *Russia's Crony Capitalism: The Path from Market Economy to Kleptocracy* (New Haven: Yale University Press, 2019).
41. Taylor, *The Code of Putinism*, and Gleb Pavlovsky, "Russian Politics Under Putin: The System Will Outlast the Master," *Foreign Affairs* 95, no. 3 (May/June 2016): 15.
42. Henry Hale, *Patronal Politics: Eurasian Regime Transitions in Comparative Perspective* (New York: Cambridge University Press, 2014), 20.

43. Ibid., 10.

44. Greene and Robertson, *Putin v. The People.*

45. Juliet Kaarbo, "A Foreign Policy Analysis Perspective on the Domestic Politics Turn in IR Theory," *International Studies Review* 17, no. 2 (2015): 197–199; Joe Hagan, "Does Decision Making Matter? Systemic Assumptions vs. Historical Reality in International Relations Theory", *International Studies Review* vol. 3, no. 2:5–6; Joe Hagan and Margaret Hermann, *Leaders, Groups and Coalitions,* (Hoboken, N.J.: Blackwell, 2002); Shibley Telhami, "Arab Public Opinion and the Gulf War", *Political Science Quarterly,* vol. 108, vol. 3, 1993, 437–452 are examples. On Putin and opinion polls see Greene and Robertson, *Putin v. The People,* 13.

46. For more on this, see Sara Wengle and Michael Rasell, "The Monetisation of L'Goty: Changing Patterns of Welfare Provision in Russia," *Europe Asia Studies* 60, no. 5 (July 2008): 739–756.

47. Seymour Martin Lipset, "Some Social Requisites of Democracy: Economic Development and Political Legitimacy," *American Political Science Review* 53, no. 1 (March 1959): 69–105.

48. Fish, "What Has Russia Become?," makes a similar point at 331.

49. Constitution of the Russian Federation, Chapter 4, "President of the Russian Federation" and Chapter 5: "Federal Assembly of the Russian Federation."

50. See for example, Natalia Forrat, "Shock Resistant Authritarianism: School Teachers and Infrastructural State Capacity in Putin's Russia," *Comparative Politics* , vol. 50, no. 3, April 2013, 417–434.

51. Zygar, *All the Kremlin's Men,* claims this took place over a BBQ, but Taylor indicates that there is some doubt as to whether the message was delivered at a BBQ or at the second meeting in the Kremlin.

52. See Åslund, *Russia's Crony Capitalism,* chapter 1.

53. For useful insights into how Putin's regime uses the Russian legal system to disarm opponents, see Maria Popova, "Putin-Style 'Rule of Law' and Prospects for Change," *Daedalus* 146, no. 2 (Spring 2017): 64–75.

54. See fn. 55, below, but also Natalia Gevorkian, Natalia Timakova, and Andrei Kolesnikov, *From the First Person* (New York: Public Affairs, 2000).

55. See, for example, Dawisha, *Putin's Kleptocracy*; Fiona Hill and Cliff Gaddy, *Mr. Putin: Operative in the Kremlin* (Washington, DC: Brookings Institution, 2015); Steven Lee Meyer, *The New Tsar: The Rise and Reign of Vladimir Putin* (New York: Knopf, 2015); and Masha Gessen, *Man without a Face: The Unlikely Rise of Vladimir Putin* (New York: Riverhead Books, 2012).

56. Taylor, *The Code of Putinism,* 100.

57. Dawisha, *Putin's Kleptocracy*; Gessen, *Man without a Face*; Pavlovsky, "Russian Politics under Putin"; Hill and Gaddy, *Mr. Putin*; and Zygar, *All the Kremlin's Men* are but a few of many sources on Putin's networks and their influence on the system. See also Åslund, *Russia's Crony Capitalism.* For information on finances and the Panama Papers, see also Luke Harding, "Sergei Roldugin: The Cellist Who Holds the Key to Tracing Putin's Hidden Fortune," *The Guardian,* April 3, 2016, available at https://www.theguardian.com/news/2016/apr/03/sergei-roldugin-the-cellist-who-holds-the-key-to-tracing-putins-hidden-fortune, accessed June 22, 2020.

58. Dawisha, *Putin's Kleptocracy,* 8.

59. Ibid., 3.

60. Ibid., 4–5.

61. See Alena V. Ledeneva, *Can Russia Modernise? Sistema, Power Networks and Informal Governance* (New York: Cambridge University Press, 2013); Åslund, *Russia's Crony Capitalism*; Catherine Belton, *Putin's People: How the KGB Took Back Russia and Then Took on the West* (New York: Farrar, Straus & Giroux, 2020); and Taylor, *The Code of Putinism.*

62. Dawisha, *Putin's Kleptocracy,* 37.

63. Credit Suisse Bank, "The Global Wealth Report, 2019," October, 2019, 13, available at: https://www.google.com/search?q=credit+suisse+global+wealth+databook+2019&oq=Credit+Suisse+global+&aqs=chrome.6.0j69i57j0l6.7527j0j4&sourceid=chrome&ie=UTF-8, accessed June 22, 2020. For comparison, the top 1% in the United States owned about 35% of wealth.

64. Ibid., 47.

65. Ibid., 12 and 47. Putin himself was estimated by one political analyst, Stanislav Belkovskiy, as having holdings in the energy trading company Gunvor, Gazprom, and Surgutneftegaz totaling somewhere between $40 and $70 billion.

While these numbers are difficult to understand or assess, there is little doubt that people long connected with Putin are inexplicably wealthy—many of whom also retain high state office.

66. Timothy Frye, Scott Gelbach, Kyle L. Marquardt, and Ora John Reuter, "Is Putin's Popularity Real?" *Post-Soviet Affairs* 33, no. 1 (2017): 1–15.

67. Pavlovsky, "Russian Politics under Putin," 10–17.

68. "'No Putin, No Russia,' Says Kremlin Deputy Chief of Staff," *Moscow Times*, October 23, 2014, available at: https://www.themoscowtimes.com/2014/10/23/no-putin-no-russia-says-kremlin-deputy-chief-of-staff-a40702, accessed June 15, 2020.

69. Greene and Robertson, *Putin v. The People*, note this too.

70. Michael Enright, "Sleeping Next to a Very Cranky Elephant: The History of Canada-US Tensions," CBC Radio, June 17, 2018, available at: https://www.cbc.ca/radio/thesundayedition/the-sunday-edition-june-17-2018-1.4692469/sleeping-with-a-very-cranky-elephant-the-history-of-canada-u-s-tensions-1.4699017, accessed June 23, 2020.

71. Daniel Treisman, "Crimea: Anatomy of a Decision," in *The New Autocracy: Information, Politics and Policy in Putin's Russia*, ed. Daniel Treisman (Washington, DC: Brookings Institution Press, 2018); Michael A. McFaul, *From Cold War to Hot Peace: An American Ambassador in Putin's Russia* (New York: Houghton Mifflin Harcourt, 2018).

72. Agnia Grigas, *Beyond Crimea: The New Russian Empire* (New Haven: Yale University Press, 2016).

73. Greene and Robertson, *Putin v. The People*, 64–65.

74. Treisman, "Crimea: Anatomy of a Decision," 281–282.

75. For a clear indication of the impromptu nature of the intervention, See ibid., 279.

76. Steve Gutterman and Amy Ferris-Rotman, "Thousands of Russians Protest against Putin," *Reuters*, December 10, 2011, available at: https://www.reuters.com/article/us-russia-protests/thousands-of-russians-protest-against-putin-idUSTRE7B907W20111210, accessed June 9, 2020.

77. See, for example, Michael Crowley and Julia Ioffe, "Why Putin Hates Clinton," *Politico*, July 25, 2016, available at: https://www.politico.com/story/2016/07/clinton-putin-226153, accessed June 9, 2020.

78. Greene and Robertson, *Putin v. The People*, 25.

79. Gulnaz Sharafutdinova, "The Pussy Riot Affair and Putin's Demarche from Sovereign Democracy to Sovereign Morality," *Nationalities Papers* 42, no. 4 (2014): 615–621.

80. Greene and Robertson, *Putin v. The People*, 35. See also Regina Smyth and Irina Soboleva, "Looking beyond the Economy: Pussy Riot and the Kremlin's Voting Coalition," *Post-Soviet Affairs* 30, no. 4 (2014): 257–275.

81. Greene and Robertson, *Putin v. The People*, 37. See also Katie Riley, "Russia's Anti-Gay Law in Line with Public's View of Homosexuality," *Pew Research Center*, August 5, 2013, available at: https://www.pewresearch.org/fact-tank/2013/08/05/russias-anti-gay-laws-in-line-with-publics-views-on-homosexuality, accessed June 29, 2020, and Valerie Sperling, *Sex, Politics and Putin: Political Legitimacy in Russia* (New York: Oxford University Press, 2014).

82. See Greene and Robertson, *Putin v. The People*, 33–39.

83. For more on this, see ibid., 78.

84. Levada Center, http://www.levada.ru/eng/, accessed September 7, 2015. See also chapter 1, Figure 1.2.

85. For more on this, see McFaul, *From Cold War to Hot Peace*, 252–256.

86. See Joshua Yaffa, "Putin's Shadow Cabinet and the Bridge to Crimea," *New Yorker*, May 29, 2017; Kathrin Hille and Max Seddon, "Bridge to Crimea: Putin Strives to Complete a Historic Mission," *Financial Times*, September 23, 2016.

87. Taylor, *The Code of Putinism*, 85–95.

88. For the reader who wants to learn more about the preferred access of friends of Putin to state contracts and the intermingling of business and government in Russia more generally, see Dawisha, *Putin's Kleptocracy*; Zygar, *All the Kremlin's Men*; Åslund, *Russia's Crony Capitalism*;

and Catherine Belton, *Putin's People: How the KGB Took Back Russia and Then Took on the West* (New York: Farrar, Straus & Giroux, 2020), among other excellent studies.

89. Natalia Lamberova and Konstantin Sonin, "The Role of Business in Shaping Economic Policy," in Daniel Treisman ed., 140. See fn. 4 regarding the Forbes study.

90. Henry Hale, "How Crimea Pays: Media, Rallying 'Round the Flag and Authoritarian Support," *Comparative Politics* 50, no. 3 (April 2018).

91. *Prezident* is available in Russian at: https://russia.tv/video/show/brand_id/59329/episode_id/1193264/video_id/1165983/, accessed June 29, 2020, and on Amazon Prime in English as *President*.

92. See Maria Lipman, Anna Kachkaeva, and Michael Poyker, "Media in Russia," in *The New Autocracy: Information, Politics and Policy in Putin's Russia*, ed. Daniel Treisman (Washington, DC: Brookings Institution Press, 2018), 171–172.

93. For an interesting overview of how the Russian media has been used for "agit-ainment" (political agitation and entertainment fused), see Vera Tolz and Yuri Teper, "Broadcasting Agitainment: A New Media Strategy of Putin's Third Presidency," *Post-Soviet Affairs* 34, no. 4 (2018): 213–227.

94. Sergei Shoigu is quoted in "Russia Says Its Airstrikes Have Killed 35,000 Rebels," Reuters, December 22, 2016, available at: https://www.reuters.com/article/us-mideast-crisis-syria-russia-shoigu-idUSKBN14B1AC, accessed June 29, 2020.

95. Sharafutdinova, "The Pussy Riot Affair and Putin's Demarche from Sovereign Democracy to Sovereign Morality," 616.

96. Fish, "What Has Russia Become?," 332, and also Riley, "Russia's Anti-gay Law in Line With Public's View on Homosexuality", 2013.

97. Although Russia has come a long way, it could have come much farther without Putin's autocratic leadership. This argument is as true today as it was when Michael McFaul and I first made it in "The Myth of the Authoritarian Model: How Putin's Crackdown Holds Russia Back," *Foreign Affairs*, 87, no. 1, January 2008, 68–84.

INDEX